# KAUFMAN
# FIELD GUIDE
## TO
# NATURE
## OF THE
# MIDWEST

## KENN KAUFMAN,
## JEFF SAYRE,
### AND
## KIMBERLY KAUFMAN

with the collab
ERIC R. EA
T. TRAVIS BR
and
THOMAS D. B

Illustrated with
more than 2,000 images
based on photos
by the authors and
other top photographers

HOUGHTON MIFFLIN HARCOURT
BOSTON   NEW YORK

LAND AND SKY

HABITATS

WILDFLOWERS

GRASSES, RUSHES, AND SEDGES

TREES AND LARGE SHRUBS

SMALL SHRUBS AND VINES

PRIMITIVE PLANTS AND FUNGI

MAMMALS

BIRDS

REPTILES AND AMPHIBIANS

FISHES

BUTTERFLIES AND MOTHS

OTHER INSECTS

OTHER INVERTEBRATES

CONSERVATION

D0915848

For information about permission to reproduce selections from this book, write to
trade.permissions@hmhco.com or to Permissions, Houghton Mifflin Harcourt
Publishing Company, 3 Park Avenue, 19th Floor, New York, New York 10016.

www.hmhco.com

*Library of Congress Cataloging-in-Publication Data is available.*
ISBN 978-0-618-45694-9

Typefaces: Minion, Univers Condensed

Printed in China

SCP  12  11  10  9  8

4500804878

# CONTENTS

The main sections of this guide are marked with color tabs along the edges of the pages for quicker access.

# DEDICATION

To April, love of my life,
partner in adventure, and
my favorite animal in the universe.
— Jeff Sayre

To my parents, Reggie and Darlene,
who taught me the basic principles of
working hard and being kind to people.
— Kimberly Kaufman

To my grandparents,
proud midwesterners
who loved nature:
Pearl and Kenneth C. Kaufman,
Sara and J.R. Bader.
— Kenn Kaufman

# THE NATURAL MIDWEST
## A Note from Kenn Kaufman

People from either coast sometimes dismiss the Midwest as "flyover country," as a nebulous region of cornfields best viewed from 30,000 feet while flying to someplace more interesting. Those of us who have lived here know better. In particular, those of us who pay attention to nature regard the Midwest as a spectacular place.

From a natural perspective, this is a land of greatness. Even the names say so: we're bounded on the north by the Great Lakes, on the west by the Great Plains, both earning capital letters. The vast boreal forest of the north meets the hardwood forest of the east, and America's mightiest river has its headwaters here. For anyone interested in camping, hiking, fishing, boating, birding, botanizing, or just appreciating the diversity of nature, the Midwest offers endless rewards.

Born in the upper Midwest, I moved away at the age of nine, and didn't move back here until 2005. Soon after arriving I found myself caught up in the massive spectacle of bird migration on the shores of Lake Erie. That migration was the *raison d'être* of the Black Swamp Bird Observatory, and before long I was also married to Kimberly, the observatory's director. Together we have focused on the birds of northwest Ohio, but we've also traveled throughout all the states of the region, trying to look at everything in nature. Whether we're in the forests of Minnesota or in our own rural Ohio yard, every hour outdoors is golden, filled with discovery.

Kimberly is a gifted educator who loves to get new people excited about nature. We decided early in our relationship that we should write a field guide to the natural history of this region. To ensure our success, we enlisted my longtime friend Jeff Sayre as a coauthor. He and I share the same birthplace (South Bend, Indiana) and the same love of good science and bad puns. Jeff is a brilliant polymath who spends much of his time focused on things like the future of the Internet, but he's also a remarkable naturalist, with a particular focus on plants and birds. For someone so accustomed to original thinking, it was a concession on his part to contribute to an ongoing field guide series with an established format; but Jeff adapted gracefully, providing almost all the botanical material and improving the rest of the book as well. Along with his wife, prizewinning children's author April Pulley Sayre, he made multiple trips throughout the seven states of the region to gather photos for the book — followed by countless hours at the computer, writing text and producing maps.

So this project has been a team effort. But who is the most important person involved with this book? You. You're the one who can make this field guide worthwhile, by taking it outdoors on your own adventures. We hope it will help you to discover, as we have, that the Midwest is a land of endless natural wonders.

# HOW TO USE THIS BOOK

If you are already familiar with other books in the Kaufman Field Guides series, such as our guides to North American birds, butterflies, mammals, or insects, you should find it easy to pick up this volume and use it. But if you are new to the series or to field guides in general, a few words of introduction may be useful.

**The plan of the book.** It should be apparent that the guide is divided into sections, with each major section keyed to a different color tab along the edge of the pages, and this should make it easy to narrow down your choices when you're trying to identify something. If you see a rabbit, for example, you can turn immediately to the "Mammals" section. In some cases the boundaries between sections are vague, and we had to make arbitrary decisions — for example, is that a small shrub or a large wildflower? — so if in doubt, you may have to check more than one section. But most of the time, it should be easy to wind up in the right place.

Within each section, species are grouped by similarity. We arranged the wildflowers by color, but color is a poor way to classify most things. If you see a brown bird, for example, the color is not as important as noticing whether it's a duck, an owl, a hawk, a sparrow, or something else. So it's good to get in the habit of noticing shapes and markings of things, not just their colors. The introductory pages for many of the sections in this book include additional notes for ID of that particular group.

**Range maps.** For many groups of living things, we include range maps showing where each species is likely to be seen. It's always a good idea to glance at these to see what's expected in a given area. If you're in southern Illinois, for example, you're unlikely to see a flower that's mapped as occurring only in northern Michigan and Minnesota.

 Regular map: darker shades of green indicate where the species is more common

 Bird map: red for summer, blue for winter, purple for all seasons

Because many birds are migratory and may be common at some seasons and absent at others, the color scheme for the birds' range maps is more complicated. It is explained in some detail on p. 208.

In the text, we often refer to the range of a species with a comment like "more common to the south" or "scarcer toward the west." In these cases, we are referring strictly to the occurrence in the Midwest, although the point may also apply to the overall range of the species. In the interest of saving space, sometimes we say that a particular animal or plant is found "here," and that should be understood to mean "here in the Midwest."

**Scope of coverage.** The number of species of living things in the Midwest runs into the tens of thousands, and obviously we cannot begin to treat all of this variety in a compact field guide. Our intent has been to cover those things that people are most likely to notice, so we have exercised a bias toward the most conspicuous plants and animals. Of course, if you spend a lot of time exploring outdoors, you will find some things that are not in this guide. But this book should give you a good idea of what you are seeing the vast majority of the time.

We know many people who are strongly interested in a few aspects of nature but are at least mildly interested in everything else, and we hope that this guide will be useful for such people in a particular way — as a quick reference on those peripheral interests. If you are an expert botanist, for example, our treatment of plants may not tell you anything you don't already know, but the guide will still be handy for looking up turtles or bats or fish. If you are a keen birder, this guide may not have enough detail on birds to satisfy you, but you can carry it as a supplement to your favorite bird guide and use it to look up everything else.

**Sizes.** The size of a plant or animal is often a clue to its identity, but it's also a tricky thing to convey. This guide covers everything from trees and bears to tiny insects, and we try to give a general sense of the sizes of most things. For some small creatures, such as insects, we include a small silhouette of the actual size of one species on the page, an approach first used in our *Kaufman Field Guide to Butterflies* in 2003. For larger things, we generally give a measurement, either in the text or on the color plate.

Size is much more variable in some groups than in others. Considering trees, for example, the tallest specimens may be much larger than the average height. Fish may keep growing slowly throughout their lives, and anglers may occasionally pull up a fish that is much larger than average, even a record-sized individual. We have tried to convey the more typical or average sizes for most species, as a general guide to recognition, but you may run across individuals that are considerably larger or smaller than the measurements given in this book.

**Names.** Unless you've already studied some branch of natural history, you might be surprised to learn that not all species of living things have standardized or "official" names. Where standardized names do exist — for example, bird names recommended by the American Ornithologists' Union, or names on the official list of the Society for the Study of Amphibians and Reptiles — we have followed those authorities. In other cases, we've simply tried to use the names in most common usage. We follow most recent authorities in capitalizing the proper names of species. This helps provide clarity. For example, several kinds of turtles may live in the woods, but if we write Wood Turtle, we are referring to just one species. Many kinds of warblers are at least partly yellow, but if we write Yellow Warbler, it's the name of a particular species.

**"The sliver of land and sky where water flows and wind blows"** — a view from the International Space Station, looking west across the Great Lakes

*Geology section contributed by Thomas D. Bain*

Diverse living things thrive only within the sliver of land and sky where water flows and wind blows. This vital zone merges two essential formative cycles, the water cycle and the rock cycle. This dynamic union produced the rock formations, landforms, and soils around us and supports all life as we know it. Living things, through time, have greatly modified the makeup of oceans, atmosphere, and rock formations. The biosphere is firmly rooted in geology.

Geologically, the Midwest is both very old and very young. Everywhere, the foundations of landscapes are formed of deep interconnected bedrock formations that preserve clues to the geological history of one of the oldest landscapes on earth. At the surface, much of the Midwest is very young landscape, resurfaced by at least four continental ice sheets during the Pleistocene Epoch, ending just 10,000 years ago.

We are toddlers when we pick up our first colorful pebble; this is a nearly universal early experience in nature. In the glaciated Midwest, a curious toddler's first pebble is often a glittering igneous rock discovered along a rain-washed plow furrow or under rippling water along a shallow gravelly streambed. That pebble's journey — from its origin long ago, deep in the roots of a rising young mountain chain far away, to the surface of a modern Midwestern farm field or small streambed — followed an amazing path through the water cycle and the rock cycle.

## THE WATER CYCLE

Sunshine powers continuous exchange of moisture between oceans and atmosphere, and sunshine powers turbulence and currents in oceans and atmosphere that bring moist air and abundant precipitation over landscapes. The Coriolis effect, caused by the spin of the Earth, deflects large-scale currents, spinning off regular weather systems that bring rainfall and snowfall to landscapes, storm after storm, season after season, cycling water from oceans to atmosphere to landscapes and back to oceans along streams and rivers. Precipitation supports abundant terrestrial living things. Together, water and wind, with living things, slowly break down bedrock, chemically and mechanically. The breakdown of bedrock near Earth's surface is called weathering. Weathering reduces rock to small particles and ions easily eroded and carried as sediments in streams and rivers and by wind. Weathering and erosion slowly reduce landscapes and carry the sediments to ocean basins where deep accumulations of sediments eventually form sedimentary rocks. In geological time, weathering and erosion reduce mountains to foothills and foothills to plains.

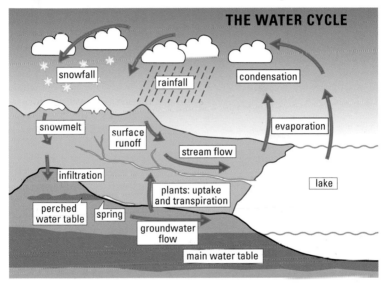

## PLATE TECTONICS

Plate tectonics, the grand unifying theory of Earth's geology, is the force that powers the rock cycle. Earth is made up of 99 percent hot core and mantle, 1 percent cool thin crust. Immense heat deep in Earth's interior circulates in plumes of softened mantle rock rising beneath rocky crust. Eons of rising and spreading currents of sticky mantle rock have torn Earth's brittle crust into huge mobile plates, pulling and pushing the plates into colossal collisions at plate

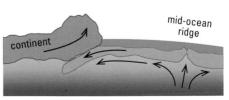

**A simple view of plate tectonics**

boundaries. The tears in Earth's crust are called spreading centers. Slowly colliding plates, moving just inches in a year, crumple, deform, melt, and elevate deep rock materials. Entire mountain chains, deep ocean trenches, and arcs of volcanoes form along plate collision zones. Sudden motions in Earth's crust release building tensions between plates, sending waves of earthquake energy rippling across continents.

## THE ROCK CYCLE

Earth systems recycle rock materials. All rock materials found near the surface of Earth formed initially by cooling from molten rock and most of these have remelted and cooled into renewed solid forms many times since formation of the Earth and Solar System a little more than 4.5 billion years ago. The journey of renewal through the rock cycle can be circuitous and often includes transformations of rock materials among basic kinds of rocks: igneous, metamorphic, and sedimentary. Rock materials are pushed through the rock cycle by the great forces of plate tectonics that slowly move entire continents into collisions.

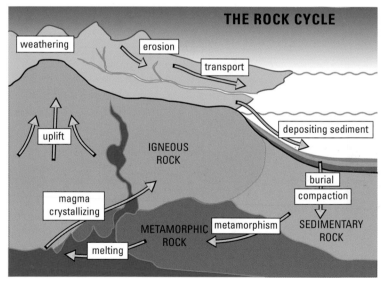

## ROCKS AND MINERALS

Rocks are composed of interlocking or cemented grains of solid matter, typically mineral matter. Coal is an important exception. Coal is a biogenic mixture of carbon compounds unlike typical rocks, but many geologists consider coal and similar organic solids to be rocks. Minerals are naturally occurring inorganic solids formed of single elements or of compounds of multiple elements. Minerals crystallize, forming unique internal lattice-works of bonded elements in repeating patterns. The internal structure and composition of a grain of quartz sand is nearly identical to the internal structure and composition of a large quartz crystal on display in a museum mineral collection. Minerals exhibit unique physical and chemical properties imparted by their composition and internal structure. Mineral properties such as hardness, luster, breakage patterns called cleavage, and crystal form are helpful for identifications.

**Large crystals of quartz**

**Igneous rocks** form by cooling of molten rock. *Intrusive* igneous rocks cool slowly from magma, molten rock deep inside the Earth. **Granite** is a common intrusive igneous rock. Granite and other coarse-grained intrusive igneous rocks are composed of easily visible interlocking crystals of constituent minerals. *Extrusive* igneous rocks cool rapidly from lava, molten rock flowing or exploding from vents at Earth's surface. **Basalt** is a common extrusive igneous rock formed as lava flows cool. Basalt is formed of very small interlocking crystals that cannot be seen without magnification.

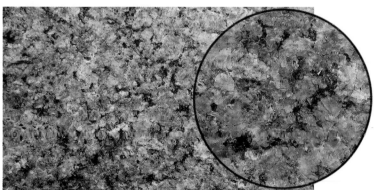

**Two views of granite, with an extreme closeup on the right**

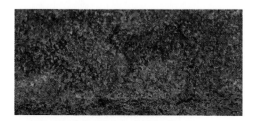

**A closeup of basalt, to show the very fine texture of interlocking crystals**

**Metamorphic rocks** form by alteration of existing rock formations deep in Earth's crust under conditions of great heat and pressure. Igneous and sedimentary rocks are squeezed and heated until deformed and recrystallized, without melting. Metamorphic rocks typically form platy, wavy, and banded rock textures. A low-grade metamorphic rock, **slate,** easily splits into thin plates. Large quantities of slate were split and trimmed for manufacture of roofing shingles and shipped from quarries in the East for use in the construction of older midwestern homes. Mid-grade metamorphism results in formation of platy and wavy (foliaceous) rocks called **schist,**

Slate (closeup view)

very uncommon in the Midwest. Schist tends to disintegrate when transported long distances by water and ice. High-grade metamorphic rocks form banded rocks called **gneiss.** Gneiss is very common throughout the Midwest. Gneiss occurs only as loose boulders and smaller rocks commonly found on the surface of midwestern farm fields and excavated when digging foundations. Gneiss boulders are popular driveway monuments throughout the Midwest. Metamorphic and igneous rocks found in fields and in excavations in the southern Midwest were rafted south from the Canadian Shield by Pleistocene ice sheets.

Schist (closeup view)

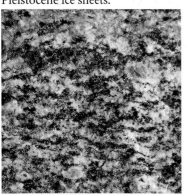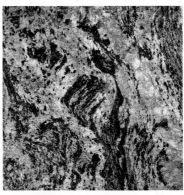

Gneiss (two examples)

**Sedimentary rocks** are composed of mineral and rock grains or chemical precipitates accumulated layer upon layer in oceans and inland seas. Deeply buried layers of sediment are compacted and cemented or bonded into rock layers. Sandstone, conglomerate, shale, and limestone are common sedimentary rocks that underlie most of the Midwest. **Sandstone** is formed of gritty sand grains. **Conglomerate** is formed of a poorly sorted mix of gravel and sand. Sandstone and conglomerate resist erosion more than other common sedimentary rocks. Many beautiful terrain features, monumental cliffs, and steep-walled gorges are formed of sandstone and conglomerate. **Shale** is a soft platy rock that forms slumping piles of chips as steep exposures weather. Shale is formed of tiny grains that are too small to feel gritty when rubbed between fingers. Shale forms steep walls along midwestern stream gorges that were recently eroded by modified drainage patterns during glacial advances and by glacial meltwater drainage as ice sheets receded. **Limestone**

**Honeycomb pattern of weathering in a sandstone outcrop**

**A typical conglomerate**

is a unique sedimentary rock that can be formed entirely of chemically precipitated calcium carbonate. More often, limestone is biogenic: that is, formed of tiny grains, shell fragments, or large fossils formed by living things. Most midwestern limestone formations are formed of accumulations of carbonate hard parts left by living organisms from long ago.

**Ohio shale formation**

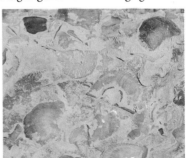

**Fossiliferous limestone**

## A BRIEF GEOLOGICAL HISTORY OF THE MIDWEST

Midwestern bedrock geology is aptly described as pancake geology. Thick sedimentary rock formations rest layer upon layer, like stacked pancakes, on a foundation of crystalline basement rock. Basement rock is composed of an ancient mosaic of igneous and metamorphic formations associated with long past mountain-building events and volcanic rift zones that were active earlier in Earth's geological history. These are the building blocks of the North American craton, the ancient core of the North American continent. Basement rock is covered by thick accumulations of sedimentary layers throughout the central and southern Midwest. We can glimpse the basement rock at the surface in the northern Midwest where Pleistocene ice sheets have uncovered it for us. Sedimentary layers thin northward along the Great Lakes and have been entirely removed from parts of northern Michigan, northern Wisconsin, and central and northern Minnesota. From the Great Lakes north through Hudson's Bay, most sedimentary formations have been stripped away, rafted southward into the Midwest by repeated ice sheet advances. The vast region of exposed ancient crystalline rocks is known as the Canadian Shield.

The Midwest is geologically stable today. Long ago it was an active tectonic zone fissured by large-scale rifts and compressed by continental collisions that forced early mountain building in the Appalachian Mountain belt. The earliest region scale tectonic structure that continues to influence surface geology across the Midwest formed about 1.1 billion years ago. A rift zone began to split the North American craton into separate continents. The Mid-continent Rift System spans four northern states, mostly deeply buried under Paleozoic rock formations. The rift system trends from Nebraska northeastward through Iowa, Minnesota, and Wisconsin, along the floor of Lake Superior, then southeastward through central Michigan. Lake Superior is pooled in part of the ancient rift valley formed by this system. Basalts found along Michigan's Keweenaw Peninsula and elsewhere formed as enormous quantities of lava flowed from vents opened by rifting. Rifting halted at least one billion years ago, possibly owing to a new phase of mountain building known as the Grenville Orogeny that raised mountains in eastern Canada and New England. Today, rift system deposits are an important source of economic ores. Rock hounds search lakeshores and glacial deposits south of Lake Superior for Superior agate, red-banded quartz that formed in voids left by large gas bubbles preserved in cooling lava over a billion years ago.

**Superior agate: a treasure from a billion years ago**

Mountain-building episodes have rejuvenated mountains along the axis of today's Appalachian region multiple times. Throughout the Paleozoic Era, the old life era, sediments eroded from Appalachian highlands have settled in basins across the Midwest. Thousands of feet of sedimentary layers accumulated. Very thick accumulations of sediments termed clastic wedges accumulate in deep ocean basins because of isostatic equilibrium: loading a sedimentary basin pushes the Earth's crust downward into the mantle to adjust for weight loading. When erosion removes and transports weight from mountains, the crust rises in proportion.

Most midwestern bedrock formations exposed at the surface were deposited during the Paleozoic Era. The bedrock exposures we see along roadways and the natural bedrock outcrops along river and stream gorges open windows to past life. Marine fossils are abundant in many limestone bedrock exposures. Many fossiliferous limestone formations are predominately composed of the carbonate remains of living things; corals, crinoids, brachiopods, and bryozoans are found in abundance.

**Limestone containing fossils of crinoids and other organisms**

Paleozoic bedrock formations have supported oil and gas development throughout large areas of the Midwest. Coal, oil, and natural gas are the organic remains of immense quantities of plant life and tiny animal life. When you break a fresh slab of oil shale, you can smell the organic echo of ancient sea life energized by sunshine hundreds of millions of years ago. This is the smell of fossil sunshine preserved in organic carbon compounds. Late in the Paleozoic, very large coal deposits formed in the East and Midwest from accumulations of large swamp plants. Economic quantities of coal have been produced in most midwestern states.

No record of bedrock deposition throughout most of the Midwest is younger than Permian, the final period of the Paleozoic Era ending more than 250 million years ago. Weathering and erosion have dissected midwestern landscapes for much of that time. Large river systems produced deeply dissected terrain that undoubtedly supported evolving assemblages of diverse terrestrial plant and animal communities.

Climate change dramatically altered midwestern geography and life beginning 2.6 million years ago, the commencement of the Pleistocene Epoch. At least four ice sheets advanced deep into the Midwest during the Pleistocene. Ice sheet erosion and deposition processes altered the landscape profoundly with each advance. Hilltops were reduced by prolonged abrasion; ravines and major valleys were filled with glacial deposits. The mass of snow and ice accumulating at spreading centers over the Canadian

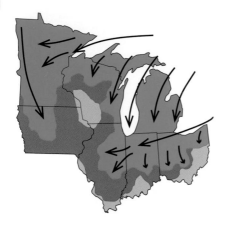

Extent of most recent glacial maximum, about 22,000 years ago

Main directions of movement of major ice sheets and smaller lobes in most recent glaciation

Maximum extent of ice cover in earlier glacial advances

These areas were not covered by ice sheets: i.e., unglaciated

Shield spread in all directions under its own weight. Southward-advancing ice scraped and plucked rock materials from bedrock underneath, entrained the materials in sediment-laden ice near the bottom of the ice sheet, and rafted the materials south through the Midwest. Bedrock erosion and material transport by ice rafting continued for many thousands of years during each major ice advance until each ice sheet stopped accumulating ice and rapidly shrank, dropping its load where it melted. With each ice sheet advance, the region was nearly leveled under a blanket of glacial till made up of unsorted mud, silt, sand, and rocks, released by melting ice. Large numbers of boulders called glacial erratics, many the size of major appliances, a few the size of a two-car garage, were rafted from the Canadian Shield to points south and dropped throughout glaciated areas of the Midwest where igneous and metamorphic rocks do not occur otherwise.

Ice sheets altered major drainage patterns. Northern-draining river systems, blocked by ice, were forced to reverse directions. The Ohio River was formed. The Great Lakes basins were excavated by moving ice laden with rocky sediments. Huge ice-front lakes formed, expanded, and con-

Glacial grooves carved in ancient bedrock on Kelleys Island in Lake Erie

**Glacial till texture with a rounded gneiss stone**

tracted with surging and retreating ice sheets. The weight of nearly two miles of accumulated ice depressed the Earth's crust below sea level near Hudson's Bay. Slow rebound continues, even today. Voluminous melt water drained southward from ice sheets, filling stream valleys with sand and gravel terraces extending far south of the maximum extent of ice. Leveled landscapes called till plains have been converted to vast farmlands today. Moraines, low hills of mounded till accumulated along the undulating margins of ice lobes, marked terminal positions and recessional positions where for prolonged periods, the rate of ice flow nearly equaled the rate of ice melting at the snout of the glacier.

Today, glaciated midwestern landscapes produce mainly cereal grains and livestock. Many special places do not support efficient agricultural production, but these special places preserve biological diversity.

**Mountain Spleenwort, a fern with limited distribution in the Midwest, growing in a crevice in a conglomerate rock formation in Ohio**

Nature explorers can find diverse living things thriving in unique geological terrains. Limestone solution caves and sandstone rock shelters commonly harbor unique organisms, some specially adapted for twilight, others adapted for total darkness. Less commonly known habitats are found in natural stream gorges and lakeshore cliffs. Steep ravine walls and natural cliffs preserve vertical habitats, offering sunny surfaces and shady crevices for uniquely adapted organisms. Northern White-cedars growing on limestone cliff ledges near the Great Lakes commonly live for hundreds of years, a few for over one thousand years. Unique habitats called alvars form on limestone surfaces leveled by ice sheets and scraped nearly bare. Alvars support populations of the rarest plants in the Midwest. Explore the Midwest and dig into the geology of your local terrain, and consider the importance of conserving unique natural rocky habitats.

# WEATHER AND CLIMATE

These terms are related but different. "Weather" refers to atmospheric conditions of the moment: things like temperature, humidity, wind speed and direction, cloud cover, and precipitation. Weather can change by the moment (and often does!). "Climate" represents the long-term average of weather conditions at all seasons at a particular location. Climate can change, too, but this usually happens very gradually, over long periods. To make the most of experiences with nature in the Midwest, it helps if we have an awareness of both climate and weather.

**Climate** of a local area has a major impact on what plants and animals can live there.

As a part of climate, temperature can be measured in various ways, including normal maximum and minimum temperatures, average temperature by month or season, and average number of frost-free days per year. In general, during the winter, temperatures in the Midwest are colder toward the north and west, warmer toward the southeast. In summer, temperatures are cooler toward the north, hotter toward the south and west. These maps show *average* temperatures for January and July for the 30-year period from 1981 to 2010. On any given day, of course, the pattern can be extremely different from what is shown here.

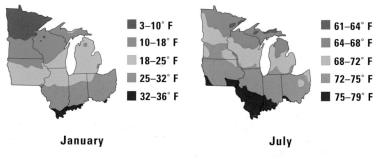

| January | | July |
|---|---|---|
| ■ 3–10° F | | ■ 61–64° F |
| ■ 10–18° F | | ■ 64–68° F |
| □ 18–25° F | | □ 68–72° F |
| ■ 25–32° F | | ■ 72–75° F |
| ■ 32–36° F | | ■ 75–79° F |

Precipitation also varies with geography. In a general way, within our region, the climate is wetter toward the east and drier toward the west. This map shows annual average precipitation for the period from 1981 to 2010.

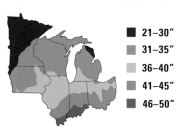

■ 21–30"
■ 31–35"
□ 36–40"
■ 41–45"
■ 46–50"

**average annual precipitation, 1981 to 2010**

It might seem odd that Minnesota, with its 10,000 lakes, should show up as the area with the least amount of precipitation. Remember that snow is measured differently than rainfall: 10 inches of snow melts down to only about one inch of water. Also, rates of evaporation tend to be lower in the cooler northern parts of our region, so these climates can remain relatively moist even with less actual precipitation.

**The Great Lakes** have impacts on nearby weather. The water in the lakes gradually absorbs heat during summer, so that in late fall and early winter, temperatures tend to be warmer near the lakes than elsewhere. The reverse happens in spring, as the lakes heat up more slowly than the land, making for cooler conditions near the lakes in spring and early summer.

Lake-effect snow can be significant in places like the south shore of Lake Superior, east shore of Lake Michigan, and southeast shore of Lake Erie (ne. Ohio). Especially in late fall and early winter, when the lakes are unfrozen and the water is warmer than the land, storms moving in from the northwest will pick up moisture from the lakes. Moving inland, these storms then dump that moisture on the land in the form of snow. Affected areas may get more than twice as much snowfall as other nearby regions.

**Weather** has an impact on everything we do outdoors. The science of weather prediction has continued to improve, despite the vast number of variables involved. In addition, technology has continued to give us more ways to receive weather forecasts. It's sensible to take advantage of this, and check the forecast before we head outside.

It may be helpful to think of the atmosphere as a whole system. It is constantly in motion, like a giant, fluid machine of great complexity. The sun provides the energy for the machine. As air is heated by the sun in equatorial regions, it rises and begins flowing toward the poles; in polar regions the air cools, sinks, and begins flowing back toward the tropics. The rotation of the earth puts a spin on these simple loops of air, turning them into prevailing westerly or easterly winds, depending on latitude. The water cycle — evaporation, condensation, precipitation — adds to the complexity. Warm air can hold more moisture than cold air, so water vapor will rise with warm air and then condense into clouds as it cools, eventually falling again as rain or snow.

At the latitude of the Midwest, major weather patterns generally move from west to east. Most significant changes in weather take place along fronts, which are boundaries between masses of warm air and masses of cold air. Because cold air is denser than warm air, the cold fronts tend to arrive with more force, sweeping in rapidly from the northwest. Warm fronts may move in more gently from the southwest. Passage of a front is almost always marked by changes in wind direction.

Areas of high pressure and low pressure form along the boundaries between air masses, and these highs and lows bring their own distinctive weather. A high-pressure system is usually marked by fair weather, while a low may bring clouds and stormy weather. In the Northern Hemisphere, winds move in a clockwise direction around a high, counterclockwise around a low (as viewed from above). By looking at detailed weather maps in newspapers or online, and then observing conditions outdoors, you can see the relationship between high- and low-pressure areas and local wind directions, and the relationship between warm fronts, cold fronts, and changes in local temperature.

**Clouds** are highly visible reflections of what is going on in the atmosphere.

When moist air rises, it cools off, causing molecules of water to condense into droplets or ice crystals. Masses of these droplets or crystals come together to form clouds. Different types of clouds form at different altitudes and under different conditions, and they can tell us a lot about what is happening, or what is going to happen, with the weather.

Low-level clouds form below about 6,500 feet. The two main types are stratus clouds, which form as horizontal layers, and cumulus clouds, which build up vertically. Stratus clouds tend to be dull, flat layers, and they may produce light drizzle or may just dominate a gray day. If they develop into dense nimbostratus layers, they may produce snow or steady rain. Cumu-

**cumulus clouds**

lus clouds are the puffy white clouds floating in the sky on hot summer days. With enough heat and moisture, they may grow rapidly into towering cumulus and then into massive cumulonimbus clouds, the type that can produce severe thunderstorms. At that point they are no longer low-level clouds, as their tops may extend up to 20,000 feet or higher.

Mid-level clouds, with their bases between about 6,500 and 20,000 feet, are given the prefix alto-, as in altocumulus and altostratus clouds. They seldom produce much precipitation, although they can signal the approach of a warm front or cold front and thus a change in the weather.

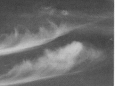
**cirrus clouds**

High-level clouds, above 20,000 feet, are given the prefix cirro-, as in cirrostratus clouds. Light, wispy clouds at the highest elevations, composed entirely of ice crystals, are called cirrus clouds. When these thicken from the west in winter, they may signal the approach of snow.

**Tornadoes** are more frequent in central regions of the U.S. than anywhere else in the world. A tornado is a rotating column of air extending down from the base of a cloud, typically in the form of a funnel, and touching the ground. These twisters vary in size and strength, with the weakest being designated F0 and the strongest F5. The most powerful ones, with winds in excess of 200 miles per hour, can obliterate practically everything in their path. Even relatively weak tornadoes can be deadly and can cause significant damage. Forecasters can issue warnings as a tornado is forming, but often with only minutes' worth of advance notice. Always listen for updates or storm sirens during severe thunderstorm outbreaks.

# WONDERS OF THE NIGHT SKY

Most of this field guide is focused on small wonders near at hand, so it might seem out of place to include a section on immense objects in the vastness of outer space. But campouts or night hikes become more fascinating if we learn to recognize some of the stars, planets, and other features of the night sky, and if we know something about them.

For best viewing of the night sky, try to get away from cities and other bright light sources on a clear night with low humidity. You'll be able to see more stars if the moon is not too bright, but ironically, it may be easier to begin learning about stars on the nights when you can't see quite so many: if the faint ones are out of sight, it can be a simpler task to pick out patterns among the fewer, brighter stars that are still visible.

**Constellations.** These patterns of stars in the sky have been recognized by many cultures back to ancient times. Constellations are not "real" — these apparent groupings are not necessarily close to each other in space. For example, the brightest star in Lyra is 30 times closer to Earth than it is to some other stars in the same constellation. The stars just look close together when viewed from our vantage point. Still, these star patterns have their own beauty and importance. Small birds migrating at night use them for navigation, and for centuries human travelers did the same. Even if we don't often need them to find our way today, knowing constellations can add to our enjoyment of the night sky as it changes with the seasons.

**Learning to recognize constellations.** On pp. 24–31 we present a series of sky charts showing the relative positions of major constellations late in the evening — after dark but before midnight — in the middle of each season. As the Earth rotates, stars appear to rise in the east and set in the west throughout the night. So if you stay out very late at night, you'll see constellations shown on the charts for other seasons.

A small, flat chart in a book can hardly represent the immense dome of the night sky. Our diagrams are mere caricatures of the real constellations, and it may take some practice to be able to make the translation from these little drawings to the patterns that you see in the sky. We suggest you start with some really distinctive constellations, such as Orion, Scorpius, or the Big Dipper, to see how their reality compares with the diagrams. Then work your way out to more obscure ones, using their locations relative to the ones that you already know.

**Names of constellations and stars.** Ancient civilizations looked at patterns of stars in the night sky, connected groups of stars with imaginary lines, and gave names and mythological meaning to the figures created in that way. Many of the names still in use today originated millennia ago in the Mediterranean world, which is why we still have constellations honoring Greek and Roman mythological characters. Today the names are standardized by the International Astronomical Union and are used to designate particular regions of the sky, not just the star groups themselves.

A few dozen bright stars have common names, such as Antares (in Scorpius) and Betelgeuse (in Orion), based on their ancient Greek or Arabic names. We label and discuss a few of these on pp. 32–37. In addition, however, thousands of stars are named in more formalized systems using either numbers or Greek letters and some version of the constellation names.

**Brightness of stars.** Some stars in the night sky look obviously brighter than others. This apparent brightness — caused by a combination of the star's actual properties and its distance from Earth — is referred to as the magnitude of the star. Over 2,000 years ago, the Greek astronomer Hipparchus classified stars into six groups, with the brightest in the first group and the faintest visible ones in the sixth. Modern instruments make it possible to measure magnitude with great precision. For example, Arcturus is magnitude –0.04, while Polaris (the North Star) is magnitude 2.0. The higher the number, the fainter the star. On our diagrams, we use larger spots for the brighter stars to give a general idea of how things look.

**Stars vs. planets.** Ancient stargazers, watching the heavens night after night, noticed that stars stayed in the same positions relative to each other but planets roamed across the sky, moving from one constellation to another over periods of months. If you look at the night sky only occasionally, it's harder to pick out the differences. We discuss all the visible planets on pp. 38–39, but for a rule of thumb, stars twinkle and planets don't! That sounds unscientific, but the reflected light from planets within our own solar system is less prone to being shifted by Earth's atmosphere than the points of light emanating from stars that are vastly farther away.

**The Milky Way.** On a clear night, with a good view of the sky and no distracting artificial light or moonlight, we can see a hazy, irregular band of brightness stretching all the way across the sky. This is our own galaxy, seen edge-on, from our position within it. Our galaxy is thought to be in the shape of a wide, flat spiral, containing a few hundred billion stars, and our sun is thought to be closer to the outer edge of the galaxy than to its center. Looking through the galaxy over the immense distances of space, these billions of stars seem to blend into a bright haze. We show the position of the Milky Way on the sky charts on the following pages, even though it won't be visible when viewing conditions are less than ideal.

**Observing the night sky.** A good astronomical telescope for viewing deep-space objects may have an astronomical price, but almost everything that we discuss in this field guide can be seen with the unaided eye on a clear night. Good binoculars will reveal even more, such as details on the surface of our moon, or the positions of the moons of Jupiter (see p. 39). A spotting scope purchased for birding or observing other wildlife can also be very useful for seeing details in the night sky. So don't assume that you need a giant telescope to make worthwhile observations.

**Meteors and meteor showers.** When an object in space gets close enough to be pulled in by our gravity, and begins to fall toward Earth, friction against our atmosphere will heat it up to glow white-hot before it burns up completely and disappears. We see this as a spot of white streaking across the sky — a "falling star." Technically, it's a meteor (the rare one that reaches Earth's surface is called a meteorite). Most meteors are tiny fragments of asteroids or comets. When Earth passes through the trail of debris left by a comet, meteors streak across our sky at a rate of several per minute. These meteor showers occur at predictable seasons. Two notable ones are the Perseids in August and the Geminids in December. During these, the meteors fall from a particular part of the sky and seem to radiate from the constellations Perseus and Gemini, respectively, hence the names.

**The Aurora Borealis** (Northern Lights). These shimmering, dancing bands of colored light in the night sky have fascinated humans for millennia. Like meteor showers, they are caused by something from space interacting with our upper atmosphere.

The input for the aurora comes from gusts of highly charged particles thrown out by the sun. These massive bursts of electrons and protons are largely deflected by Earth's magnetic field, except near the north and south magnetic poles. There, miles above the Earth, they collide with atoms of oxygen and nitrogen. As they recover from their reaction to these collisions, the atoms give off particles of light, or photons.

Green, the most common auroral color, is emitted by oxygen atoms up to 150 miles above the surface. At the highest elevations, up to 200 miles above the ground, oxygen atoms give off red light. Blue and purple light comes from nitrogen atoms. The shapes of the aurora — shifting curtains, ribbons, spirals — reflect elements in the magnetic field.

Caused by sunspot activity, the aurora may occur at any time of year, but may be easiest to see on long, clear winter nights. The best viewing is from the northernmost reaches of our region; spectacular displays are sometimes visible from northern Michigan, Wisconsin, and Minnesota. Because of the link to sunspot activity, good displays often can be predicted many hours in advance. Websites such as earthsky.org, spaceweather.com, and swpc.noaa.gov are worth checking regularly for predictions.

**A display of the Aurora Borealis over northern Michigan**

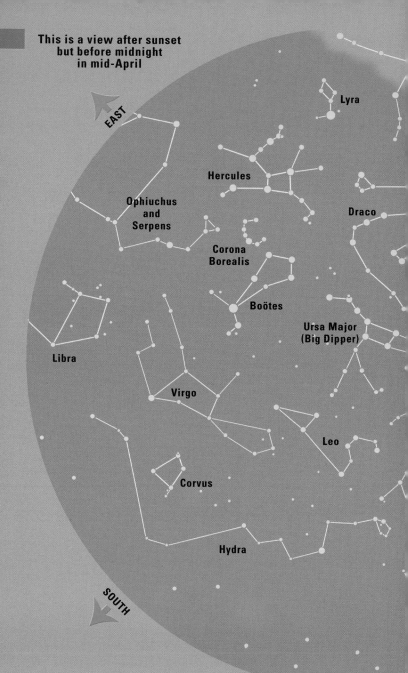

This is a view after sunset but before midnight in mid-April

EAST

Lyra

Hercules

Ophiuchus and Serpens

Draco

Corona Borealis

Boötes

Ursa Major (Big Dipper)

Libra

Virgo

Leo

Corvus

Hydra

SOUTH

# SPRING CONSTELLATIONS

## As seen over the upper Midwest

NORTH

Lyra

Cygnus

Cepheus

Cassiopeia

Draco

Polaris (the North Star)

Ursa Minor (Little Dipper)

Camelopardalis

Perseus

Ursa Major (Big Dipper)

Lynx

Auriga

Leo

Cancer

Gemini

Taurus

Canis Minor

Hydra

Orion

WEST

Monoceros

The pale band across the sky is the Milky Way

25

This is a view after sunset but before midnight in mid-July

EAST

Andromeda

Pegasus

Pisces

Cassiopeia

Cepheus

Aquarius

Delphinus

Cygnus

Draco

Aquila

Capricornus

Lyra

Hercules

Corona
Borealis

Ophiuchus
and
Serpens

Sagittarius

SOUTH

Scorpius

Libra

# SUMMER CONSTELLATIONS

As seen over
the upper Midwest

NORTH

Andromeda

Perseus

Cassiopeia

Camelopardalis

Cepheus

Lynx

Polaris
(the North
Star)

Ursa Minor
(Little Dipper)

Draco

Ursa Major
(Big Dipper)

Hercules

Boötes

Corona
Borealis

Leo

Libra

Virgo

WEST

The pale band across the sky
is the Milky Way

27

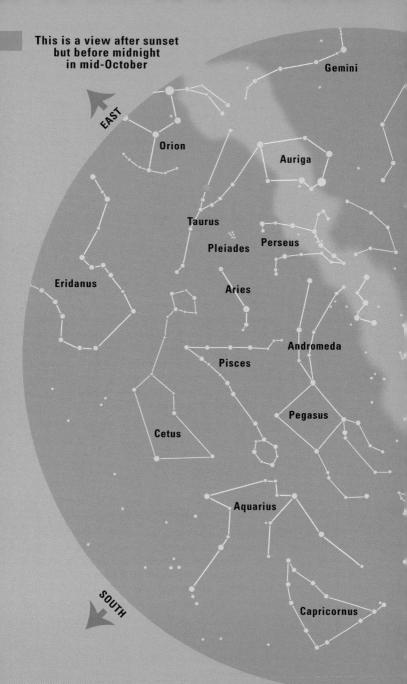

This is a view after sunset
but before midnight
in mid-October

EAST

Gemini

Orion

Auriga

Taurus

Pleiades    Perseus

Eridanus

Aries

Andromeda

Pisces

Pegasus

Cetus

Aquarius

SOUTH

Capricornus

# FALL CONSTELLATIONS

### As seen over the upper Midwest

NORTH

Lynx

Ursa Major
(Big Dipper)

Polaris
(the North
Star)

Camelopardalis

Ursa Minor
(Little Dipper)

Boötes

Cassiopeia

Cepheus

Draco

Corona
Borealis

Cygnus

Lyra

Hercules

Delphinus

Aquila

Ophiuchus
and
Serpens

WEST

Capricornus

The pale band across the sky
is the Milky Way

This is a view after sunset
but before midnight
in mid-January

EAST

Leo

Ursa Major
(Big Dipper)

Cancer

Hydra

Lynx

Canis
Minor

Gemini

Auriga

Monoceros

Orion

Canis
Major

Taurus

Lepus

Columba

Eridanus

SOUTH

# WINTER CONSTELLATIONS

### As seen over the upper Midwest

Boötes

NORTH

Ursa Major
(Big Dipper)

Draco

Ursa Minor
(Little Dipper)

Polaris
(the North
Star)

Cepheus

Cygnus

Camelopardalis

Cassiopeia

Auriga

Perseus

Andromeda

Pleiades

Taurus

Aries

Pegasus

Pisces

Cetus

WEST

The pale band across the sky
is the Milky Way

# CONSTELLATIONS OF THE ZODIAC

The orbit of the moon around the Earth, and the orbits of the Earth and the other major planets around the sun, all lie on about the same plane. From our perspective on Earth, that means the sun, moon, and visible planets all seem to follow approximately the same path across the sky. More than 2,000 years ago, stargazers divided this path into 12 sections and named the major constellation in each, designating these as the signs of the zodiac. Periods of the year were identified by the position of the sun within the zodiac. For example, the sun was in Aquarius from about January 20 to February 18 (of course, Aquarius itself was not visible during that period, since it was in the sky during the daytime). Because of shifts in the Earth's position in space, the sun now enters Aquarius almost a month later, but most astrological charts ignore the reality of the sky.

In ages past, astronomy (study of stars and other objects in space) and astrology (predicting the future based on stars) shared much of the same knowledge. Today astrology is a holdover of superstition from an earlier time. But the constellations of the zodiac are still worth recognizing.

**Capricornus** (the goat) contains no bright stars and is not conspicuous. Low in the south in summer and fall, it is most easily found by reference to other, more distinctive constellations. The same is true of **Aquarius** (the water bearer). **Pisces** (the fish) is visible during the first part of the night mainly in fall and winter. It may be found most readily by the oval of stars at the "head" of the fish and by its proximity to the "square" of the constellation Pegasus. **Aries** (the ram) is made up mainly of four stars, none very bright. **Taurus** (the bull), conspicuous during the early part of the night in fall and winter, is easily recognized by its sideways V anchored by the bright star Aldebaran. This star is so bright that its orange-red color can be seen. Associated with Taurus is the star cluster of the Pleiades, sometimes called the "seven sisters," although only six stars are visible to the naked eye; many more can be seen through binoculars or a telescope. **Gemini** (the twins), rising late at night in fall and easily located near Orion in winter and early spring, features the twin bright stars of Castor and Pollux. **Cancer** (the crab) is an inconspicuous group of relatively faint stars, most easily located by its position between Gemini and Leo. **Leo** (the lion), noticeable in spring and early summer, is known by its bright stars forming patterns of a sickle and a narrow triangle; at the base of the sickle is the bright star Regulus. **Virgo** (the virgin) extends over a large area of the sky, but most of its stars are fairly faint; its one bright star, Spica, seems isolated in the sky. Virgo is most easily located by its position below the diamond shape of Boötes in spring and summer. **Libra** (the scales) is another constellation without bright stars or a strong pattern, easiest to find in summer by its proximity to Scorpius. **Scorpius** (the scorpion), a dominant feature of the southern sky in summer, has a well-defined pattern — it almost suggests a scorpion! — and bright stars, featuring the reddish orange Antares. **Sagittarius** (the archer) is a sprawling constellation of summer, most easily located by its position near Scorpius. See the star charts on preceding pages for help in finding all of these constellations.

# CONSTELLATIONS OF THE ZODIAC

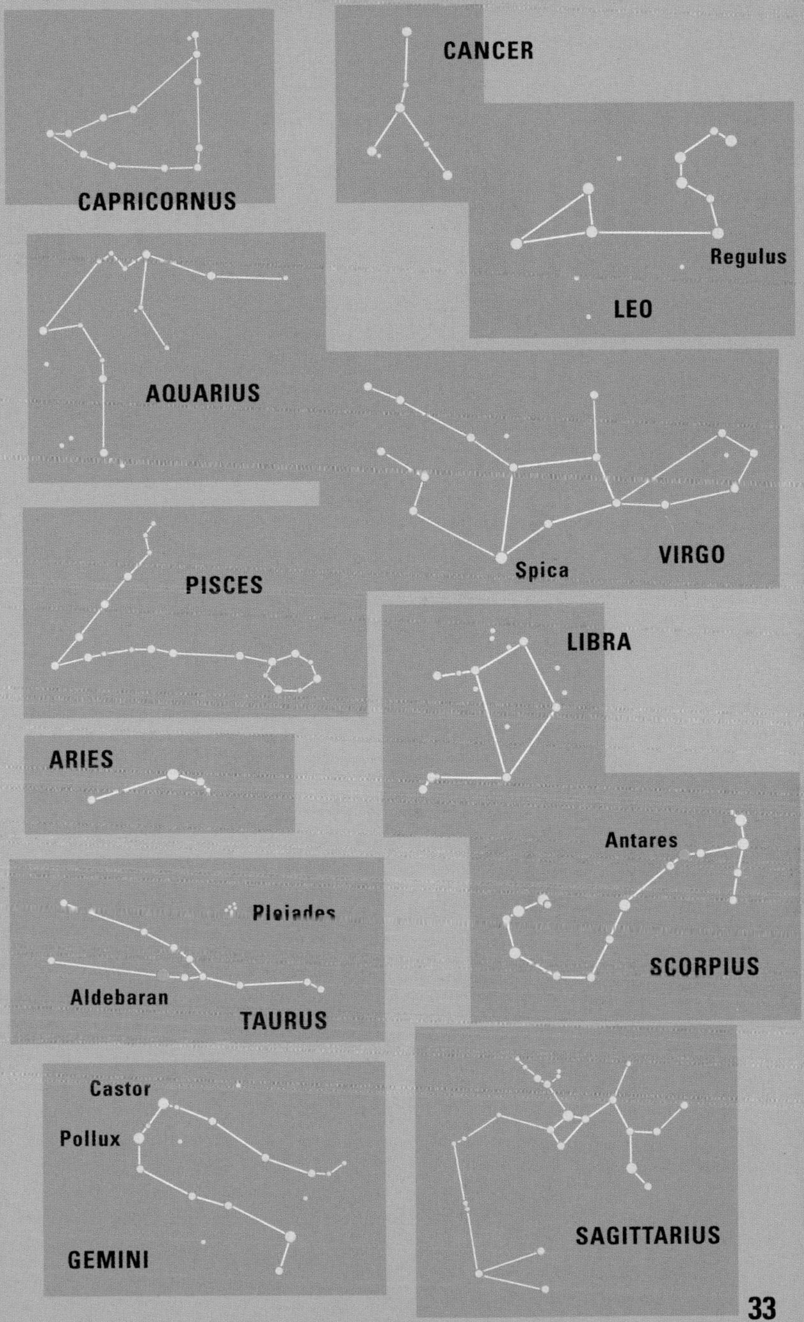

CAPRICORNUS

CANCER

LEO

Regulus

AQUARIUS

VIRGO

Spica

PISCES

LIBRA

ARIES

Pleiades

Aldebaran

TAURUS

Antares

SCORPIUS

Castor

Pollux

GEMINI

SAGITTARIUS

The Earth's axis points almost directly at Polaris, the North Star. If you were standing at the North Pole and looking up, Polaris would be straight overhead. Because of this, as the Earth spins on its axis, Polaris appears to stay in one place in the northern sky and all the other stars and constellations appear to rotate around it. From the latitude of most of the Midwest, Polaris is always fairly high in the northern sky. Constellations close to it are visible on clear nights at all times of year, although their positions change during the course of each night and each season. So you can practice finding and recognizing these constellations all year.

Once you've learned a few constellations, you can find others by reference to them. Even though the constellations appear to move around the sky, their positions relative to each other remain the same. Study the star charts on pp. 24–31 to see relative positions. The Big Dipper is a good place to start, because it's easily recognized and because it has pointers to other prominent stars.

The **Big Dipper** is only part of Ursa Major, but it's better known than the constellation as a whole. If you take the two outer stars of the "dipper" portion and extend an imaginary line outward, this line will lead you almost directly to Polaris. By extending an imaginary line somewhat farther from the tip of the "handle," you'll come to Arcturus, the bright star at the base of Boötes (p. 36), a prominent constellation of spring and summer.

**Ursa Major** is the official name of the constellation that includes the Big Dipper. The name means "great bear," and apparently several different cultures in ancient times saw a bear in this star pattern, though seemingly a rather funky, long-tailed bear. The middle star of the "tail" (or "handle") appears to have a faint companion, another star that is really much farther away from us in space, visible only with sharp eyes (or optical help). **Ursa Minor** (the little bear) is better known as the Little Dipper. Two moderately bright stars form the outer edge of the "dipper," but the rest of the constellation is less noticeable, except for the "handle's" end at Polaris.

**Cassiopeia** (the queen) circles the North Star on roughly the opposite side from Ursa Major and Ursa Minor. Shaped like a distorted M or W, depending on position, it is easily recognized. Cassiopeia also lies in a relatively bright part of the Milky Way (see p. 22). **Cepheus** (the king) has a less distinctive pattern and is most easily picked out by its position between Cassiopeia and Draco (see the seasonal sky charts).

The long, straggling **Draco** (the dragon) starts off between Ursa Major and Ursa Minor, wraps around Ursa Minor, and then loops away from the North Star, with the "head" of the dragon out near Cygnus (see sky charts and p. 36). **Perseus** (the hero) circles the North Star opposite Ursa Minor and a little farther out than Cassiopeia. The Perseid meteor shower in August (see p. 23) appears to radiate from this constellation. **Auriga** (the charioteer), as usually depicted, includes one star that is shared by Taurus (p. 32). Auriga can be recognized by its proximity to Taurus and Perseus, and by its inclusion of Capella, the sixth-brightest star in the sky. Both Perseus and Auriga lie along the Milky Way.

# CONSTELLATIONS NEAR POLARIS

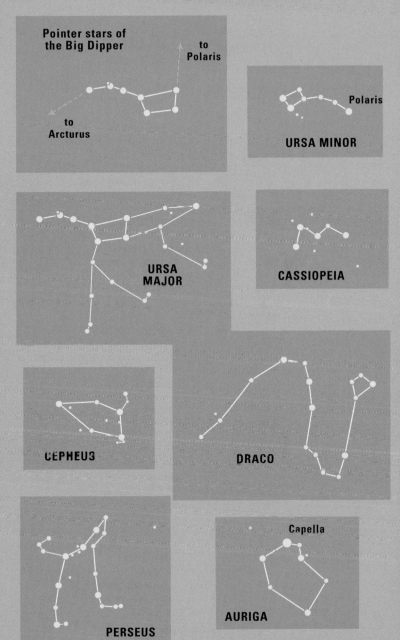

Pointer stars of
the Big Dipper

to
Polaris

to
Arcturus

Polaris

URSA MINOR

URSA MAJOR

CASSIOPEIA

CEPHEUS

DRACO

Capella

AURIGA

PERSEUS

Here are a few other major or notable constellations. They're arranged here by the times of year at which they are at their most obvious in the late evening sky — after sunset but before midnight. Everything appears to move across the sky as the night progresses, and before dawn you'll see constellations that would seem typical of other seasons.

Late in the evening in spring and summer, follow the stars of the "handle" of the Big Dipper and then continue out in the same direction — the next very bright star you come to will be Arcturus. The fourth-brightest star in the entire sky, and with a distinctly yellowish cast, Arcturus is at the base of the narrow kite shape of the constellation **Boötes** (the herdsman), pronounced boh-oh-teez. Prominent high overhead in the summer sky, Boötes is a good reference point for finding other constellations. See the sky charts on pp. 24–31 to see how these line up in the sky. Just to the left of the kite shape of Boötes is a half-circle of stars marking **Corona Borealis** (the northern crown), and just to the left of that is the more widely spaced constellation of **Hercules.** The name of this star group, like those of many others, comes from the mythology of the Greeks, Romans, and other early civilizations. Although we can't go into details on this aspect of the stars in this field guide, astronomy can be a fine entry point to learning about ancient mythology.

**Lyra** (the lyre), a small constellation with an easily recognized shape, includes the fifth-brightest star in the sky, Vega. Near Hercules and near the "head" of Draco (see p. 34), Lyra is visible at various times of the night for much of the year, but it is high overhead in summer. So is **Cygnus** (the swan), which is unusual in actually having a shape suggesting what it's named for! Its brightest star, Deneb, is at the "tail" of the swan. Cygnus is located in a bright part of the Milky Way (see p. 22). Also in the Milky Way, not far from Cygnus, is **Aquila** (the eagle). This group is most easily picked out by three stars close together in a straight line with the center one, Altair, being very bright.

**Pegasus** (the winged horse) is most prominent high in the sky in fall, farther from the North Star than Cygnus or Cassiopeia. It is most easily recognized by the arrangement of stars known as the Great Square of Pegasus, although it isn't exactly a square and one of the four corners is now usually considered a part of the adjacent constellation of **Andromeda.**

Dominating the winter sky is **Orion** (the hunter), probably the most recognizable of all constellations. Two very bright stars in Orion are Betelgeuse (pronounced "bettle-jooz," not "beetle juice") at one "shoulder" of the figure and Rigel at one "foot." Below the straight line of stars of Orion's "belt" is an area known as the "sword," and with binoculars you can make out a blurry area here, a cloud of gas and dust called the Orion Nebula. Not far to the east of Orion is **Canis Minor** (the little dog), a small constellation most notable for its bright star Procyon. This is about the eighth-brightest star, but it is upstaged by Sirius, the single brightest star in the sky, nearby in **Canis Major** (the great dog). In mythology, naturally, Canis Major and Canis Minor were regarded as Orion's hunting dogs.

# OTHER MAJOR CONSTELLATIONS

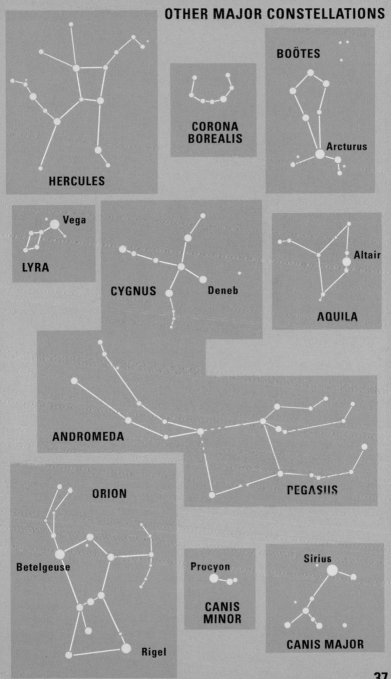

HERCULES

CORONA BOREALIS

BOÖTES

Arcturus

Vega

LYRA

CYGNUS

Deneb

Altair

AQUILA

ANDROMEDA

PEGASUS

ORION

Betelgeuse

Rigel

Procyon

CANIS MINOR

Sirius

CANIS MAJOR

# MOON, PLANETS, AND COMETS

The preceding pages were devoted to stars and other objects in deep space. Here we treat objects inside our own solar system: the planets and other objects that revolve around our sun.

**The moon.** Our closest neighbor in space, averaging only about 239,000 miles from Earth. The period of time between successive full moons (about 29.5 days) is the basis for the system of months on our calendars, and the moon's gravity is a major cause of our oceanic tides.

**Phases of the moon.** As the moon orbits the Earth, the same side of it always faces toward us. It appears to wax and wane depending on where it is situated, relative to us and to the sun. When the moon is opposite the sun, it rises as a full moon as the sun sets. Each night after that, the moon rises about 45 minutes later. By a week after the full moon, the moon is rising in the middle of the night and has waned to the phase called last quarter. The new moon is another week later, when the moon is between us and the sun and the side in shadow is toward us. After about another week, the moon is high in the southern sky at sunset and appears half full; this phase is called the first quarter. In about another week, the moon rises at sunset again and is full again, and the cycle repeats.

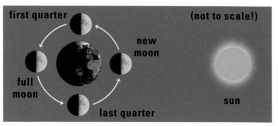

**Eclipses.** A partial or total eclipse of the moon (lunar eclipse) occurs at least twice per year, always during the full moon, when the moon is directly on the opposite side of the Earth from the sun. The eclipse results when the moon passes partly or completely into the Earth's shadow.

Eclipses of the sun (solar eclipses) occur about as often as lunar eclipses but are seen far less often from any one place. They are caused when the moon comes between the sun and the Earth; but because the moon is so small and so close, relatively speaking, its shadow falls on only a small area of our planet. The area affected by a total eclipse follows a path only about 160 miles wide. By contrast, a lunar eclipse can be seen from anyplace where the moon is visible, as it is caused by a shadow falling on the moon itself.

**The planets.** Eight or nine planets orbit the sun, and five are close enough to us to be noticeable at times. All travel across the sky in the path of the zodiac, gradually changing position relative to the constellations. Some newspapers have astronomy columns that tell the current positions of the planets, or you can find their current positions by looking online.

**Mercury** is closest to the sun, so it is never visible except at twilight, close to the horizon just after sunset or just before sunrise. When it's visible it can be close to the magnitude of some of the brightest stars. It can't compare to Venus, however.

**Venus** is the "morning star" or "evening star," but its reflected light is brighter than that of any actual star. The second planet out from the sun, Venus is usually visible low in the sky for only a few hours either after sunset or before sunrise. It has a very dense atmosphere, which makes the surface of the planet extremely hot (owing to the greenhouse effect) and also contributes to its very bright reflection of the sun's light. Because Venus is between Earth and the sun, it shows phases, from full to crescent, similar to those of the moon, and these can be seen through binoculars.

The orbit of **Mars** is the next one out beyond Earth, about one and a half times as far from the sun as we are. Mars takes almost two of our years to make a complete orbit around the sun. It looks brightest when it is closest to us, that is, when the Earth is between the sun and Mars. At such times the reddish color of Mars is quite obvious. Because Mars and the remaining planets are farther from the sun than Earth is, the side facing us is always illuminated, so they always appear to be in "full" phase.

Between the orbits of Jupiter and Mars are hundreds (at least) of small objects called asteroids. Even the largest ones are almost never visible to the unaided eye, but debris from this zone may wind up here as meteors.

The orbit of **Jupiter** is about five times as far from the sun as Earth's. This is a huge planet, about 11 times the diameter of Earth. It has at least 16 moons, and four of these are large enough that they can be seen through binoculars — in fact, this is a good way to check the identity of a planet suspected to be Jupiter. With a small telescope we often can see horizontal bands of color or darker spots in Jupiter's dense atmosphere.

**Saturn's** orbit is more than nine times as far from the sun as ours, and this planet is more than nine times the size of Earth. Famous for its rings, which can be seen with a small telescope, Saturn also has at least 18 moons, but none of these is visible without serious magnification.

**Comets.** These mysterious objects are masses of rock and frozen gases with varied orbits around the sun. Most that we see have elliptical orbits, looping past the sun and then traveling far outside the solar system, to return years, decades, or even centuries later. The most famous comet, Halley's, comes past the sun once every 76 years and is expected back in 2061. A few new comets are discovered every year, but most are too faint to be seen with the unaided eye.

The "tail" of a comet streams out directly away from the sun and consists of gases and dust melting from the comet and being pushed away by the sun's force. Only a few comets are bright enough to be visible to the unaided eye. In binoculars, a comet looks like a fuzzy star, with or without a "tail" pointing away from the sun.

**Halley's Comet in 1986**

The Midwest has no ocean and no high mountains, but the habitats here are still exceptionally varied. Within the limits of this region we go from Great Lakes to Great Plains, from northern forest to southern swamps. For anyone interested in nature, there is endless ground for exploration.

**Clark Lake Bog in Michigan's Upper Peninsula**

Every type of plant and animal has its characteristic habitat, or home. This isn't just a matter of geographic location; other aspects of the surroundings are more important. For example, we might see a meadowlark in Minnesota or Illinois or Ohio, but we're unlikely to see it in a swamp or a dense forest, because meadowlark habitat consists of open fields. Habitat associations are predictable: an experienced naturalist can look at an area and predict many of the plants and animals likely to live there. And the key to finding a rare species usually is to find exactly the habitat that it requires.

On land, a habitat is defined mostly by the plants there, and that in turn is influenced by factors such as soil type, temperature, precipitation, and local drainage. Types of plants that grow together make up a plant community. Certain kinds of animals are found in a particular plant community. There are incredible numbers of interactions within any natural habitat, from the insect that pollinates a flower to the tree that provides a nesting site for a bird, from the ants that disperse seeds to the fungi that provide benefits to the roots of many plants. Because of this vast web of interactions, habitats are often referred to by a more sweeping term, ecosystems.

## THE EVER-CHANGING LANDSCAPE

The habitats in the region have changed and shifted over the millennia. Past periods of slow but massive change have been caused by the advance and retreat of glaciers. The most recent period of change, exerting its impacts at a much more rapid pace, was caused by the arrival of European settlers. The reshaping of the region's landscape and biological communities by human activity continues today.

Was North America an untouched wilderness before the arrival of European settlers? Not at all. Native American cultures had thrived here for millennia, with profound impacts on their surroundings. All over the Mississippi Valley, starting before Egypt's pyramids were built, ancient cultures created impressive earthen mounds. (These were sometimes in the shape of effigies, such as Ohio's Great Serpent Mound, shaped like a snake and a quarter mile long.) Three centuries before Columbus sailed, a city near present-day Cahokia, Illinois, may have had a population of 40,000, complete with great plazas and at least 120 raised structures, the largest one as tall as a ten-story building. Even away from these population centers, native cultures farmed the land, hunted and fished, and often did controlled burns to maintain savanna or open grassland.

Of course, European settlers brought many more changes to the landscape. Much of the Midwest is now occupied by farms, cities, towns, and suburbs. But many plants and animals live in these human-altered habitats, and many more natural habitats are still to be found all over the region.

**Succession.** The idea of plant succession or ecological succession is a helpful one to understand. After a major disturbance — such as a big fire, or clearing of land — there is a predictable sequence to the kinds of plants that will grow up in an area. After the land is cleared, the first to colonize the bare soil will be hardy grasses and other low plants that can tolerate harsh conditions. Then other plants begin to establish themselves. Gradually, the land may transition from grassland to open shrubland, and then eventually grow up into forest. The species composition will change over time, as early colonizers are shaded out and more shade-tolerant plants take their place in the understory.

In theory, any tract of land will eventually reach a climax plant community — such as an old-growth forest — at which point the process of succession is complete and the habitat will remain stable. In practice, there may not always be such a stable final state. But the changes during the early stages of succession may be obvious, and they're worth noticing.

**Carrying capacity.** Any given patch of habitat can support a certain number of species and individuals. This will vary by season, of course. Plants may grow up and spread during the summer and die back in late fall. Insect numbers may peak in late summer, and bird variety will be highest during the peak of migration. But over the long term, the habitat will support only so many individuals of a given kind. So if a forest is cut down or a marsh is drained, the animals that live there can't simply move to another habitat — in poor habitats they won't survive, and the good habitats will be occupied already.

**Habitat fragmentation.** A small patch of habitat will support fewer individuals than a large one. That may be obvious; but a less obvious point is that it will also support fewer species. This is an aspect of island biogeography, a discipline first developed in the 1960s. Although it was applied first to actual islands, the same principles hold for "islands" of habitat. A large, unbroken forest will support more species of forest life than a small, isolated woodlot. The smaller the woodlot, and the farther it is from similar habitat, the fewer true forest species will live there.

This is cause for concern as natural habitats become more fragmented by development. Although any small preserve may have value for certain species, conservationists are now working to protect larger blocks of habitat and to provide habitat corridors between established sanctuaries so that more species can survive.

Here's a brief overview of habitats in the Midwest. The number of different habitat types in this region could be listed in the hundreds, depending on how narrowly they were defined, but we have broken them down into just a few broad categories. Remember that there are variations in all of these, and that one habitat often merges gradually into another.

## THE AIR COLUMN

Although it's often overlooked in discussions of habitat, the sky is essential habitat for many kinds of flying creatures. For some highly aerial species — dragonflies such as the Wandering Glider, birds such as Purple Martin and Red-tailed Hawk, or many kinds of bats — it doesn't seem to matter what habitat predominates on the ground below; they forage over all kinds of terrain. Migratory birds, bats, and insects fly over every square mile of the Midwest during certain seasons.

**Red-tailed Hawk**

## CITIES, TOWNS, AND SUBURBS

To start learning about nature, you don't have to travel to the wilderness, or even to a habitat that looks "natural." Some plants and animals manage to survive even in the most urban settings.

Many of the plants growing wild in cities are native to Europe and Asia, brought here accidentally in the past and now firmly established. In a way, these plants had a head start in adapting to urban life, having lived around cities in the Old World for many centuries. They may outcompete many of our native plants. But natives can be found in cities and towns as well.

Some birds are more prevalent in cities than elsewhere. This includes nonnatives like House Sparrows, but also natives with specialized nesting habits. Almost all Chimney Swifts now place their nests in chimneys in towns, not in hollow trees in the forest. Common Nighthawks nest on flat gravel roofs, and Peregrine Falcons nest on ledges of tall buildings. Beyond these, however, a wide variety of native birds, other animals, and plants can be found in any suburban backyard or city park. So it's possible to make nature discoveries practically anywhere.

## FARMLAND

The Midwest is one of the most important agricultural regions in the world. All seven states in the region have a significant amount of land devoted to farming, ranging from about 10 million acres in Michigan to about 30 million acres in Iowa, the latter accounting for more than 85 percent of the state's land area. So farmland can't be overlooked as one of the major habitats of the region.

Farmlands vary in their capacity to support native life. Some intensively farmed areas, heavily treated with pesticides and other chemicals, support the crop and almost nothing else. Other areas are not such stark monocultures. Farms that maintain some woodlots and undeveloped edges may support a good diversity of wildlife.

## GRASSLANDS

At one time, beautiful tall-grass prairie dominated much of the western part of our region, with a narrow extension eastward as far as Ohio, often called the "prairie peninsula." (Farther west, in areas with less annual precipitation, tall-grass prairies gave way to habitat called mid-grass prairie, and then to short-grass prairie near the base of the Rocky Mountains.) Original, native prairie, never broken by the plow, is now rather rare, although some fine parcels are protected in refuges or preserves. Such places are worth seeking out and visiting; they may host rare natives like Regal Fritillary or Greater Prairie-Chicken. But any grassland, original or regrown, will support a rich variety of plants and animals.

**Approximate extent of tall-grass prairie just before arrival of European settlers**

While grasslands all look similar at first glance, there are many variations caused by soil type, rainfall patterns, drainage, and local terrain. A dry, rocky prairie will have different plants from a low-lying wet meadow. Many of the latter areas are actually dominated by sedges, not grasses. (At the extreme, there may be no obvious dividing line between a wet meadow and a marsh, a habitat discussed later.) But all of these variations make grasslands even more worthwhile to explore.

In most of the Midwest, an area of grass left undisturbed will grow up to shrubs and then trees, in the process of succession described on p. 41. Scientists have debated why prairie was so prevalent in the era before European settlers arrived. The best current explanation is that a period of very dry climate, several thousand years ago, was unfavorable for forest and allowed the prairies to flourish. With the return to wetter conditions, areas of prairie were maintained mostly by frequent fires.

## SAVANNA

Although definitions vary, savanna is generally considered to be a mix of open grassland and scattered trees. Some classifications range from as little as one tree per acre to as much as an 80 percent tree cover, but a more typical savanna would have trees covering 10 to 50 percent of the area.

True savanna is another habitat that now exists mainly as small remnants. Areas of savanna, sometimes referred to as oak openings, often have a mix of native prairie grasses and stands of Bur Oak and some other fire-resistant trees. As with prairie, these open savannas often are maintained in that state by frequent fires.

## SCRUBLANDS

Scrublands, or scrub-shrub habitats, may look unimpressive, but they often teem with diversity. These scrublands may occur as an intermediate stage in plant succession, or they may persist for years in areas of poor soil or frequent fire. From a distance, they may look like extensive dense thickets, roughly 5 to 15 feet tall. Often they are dominated by dogwoods, wild plum, prickly-ash, or scrubby oaks. These are favored nesting habitats for some birds, such as Yellow-breasted Chat and Blue-winged Warbler.

## FORESTS

The Midwest is a meeting ground for the great coniferous (evergreen) forests of the north and the deciduous (hardwood) forests of the east. Within each of these broad categories, there are multiple forest types, defined by dominant tree species and soils. Forests may be composed of only conifers, deciduous trees, or a mixture of both. The region is also a place of transition between forest and grassland habitats.

The Midwest has several distinct forest types, with the exact number depending on just how narrowly they are defined. For most people exploring the outdoors, it should be enough to recognize common forest types such as those listed below.

**Aspen–birch forests** are dominated by Quaking Aspen, Bigtooth Aspen, and Paper Birch. These tend to be fast growing and short lived. Along with these species, Balsam Fir, Red Maple, and White Spruce are often found. These shade-tolerant species may eventually replace the aspens and birch.
**Beech–maple forests** represent a later-stage successional forest called a climax community. Towering Sugar Maples and American Beech trees create a dense canopy. Without a disturbance to the canopy layer that lets light into the understory, the dominant tree community remains intact, resulting in lower tree diversity than in some other hardwood forest types. Understory trees include Ironwood, Black Cherry, Sassafras, and Northern Red Oak. In early spring, wildflowers carpet the forest floor before the canopy leafs out. In northern areas of the region, Eastern Hemlock can take the place of American Beech, creating Sugar Maple–Hemlock forests.

**Black spruce forests** tend to occur in wet, peaty, poorly drained soils such as near bogs and muskegs. Sometimes intermixed with the dominant Black Spruce are Northern White Cedar, White Spruce, and Tamarack. Black Spruce are also associated with boreal forests farther north.

**Elm–ash–cottonwood–soft maple forests** primarily occur in riparian floodplains. The predominant species are American Elm, Green Ash, Eastern Cottonwood, and Silver and Red Maples. Black Ash and Black Willow can also be common. Some secondary tree species include Sycamore, Swamp White Oak, Quaking Aspen, and Yellow Birch.

**Pine forest** types represent the common pines. This is not a single forest type, but represents three specific pines. White Pines, Red Pines, and fire-adapted Jack Pines are each dominant in specific areas, but all of these pine forests include a mix of other trees as well.

**Northern hardwood forests** are represented by an impressive diversity of trees. The species composition may vary by location and soils. Some of the more prevalent trees include Sugar Maple, American Beech, Yellow Birch, Basswood, and Red Maple. Other hardwoods include Black Cherry, Paper Birches, Northern Red Oak, White Ash, and Quaking Aspen. Along with these deciduous trees, Eastern Hemlock and Balsam Fir can be found.

**Northern White-cedar forests** are located in the northern part of the Midwest, in rich, groundwater-fed organic soils. They are also called rich conifer swamps. The predominant tree species is Northern White-cedar. Other tree species include Red Maple, Balsam Fir, Black Spruce, Paper and Yellow Birches, Eastern Hemlock, and Quaking Aspen.

**Oak–hickory forests** are often dominated by oaks: Northern Red Oak, Eastern Black Oak, and Eastern White Oak, along with Shagbark Hickory and Pignut Hickory. Other hardwood species include Black Cherry, Basswood, Bigtooth Aspen, Red Maple, Bur Oak, Pin Oak, Black Walnut, and Sassafras.

**Spruce–fir forests** occur in the northernmost reaches of our region on cool, mesic to wet soils. They are sometimes considered a relic of boreal forest in our region, a biome more commonly found farther north. White Spruce and Balsam Fir are the dominant trees, but Red Maple, Eastern Hemlock, Quaking Aspen, Yellow and Paper Birches can also be found.

## STREAMS AND RIVERS

Flowing water is a central habitat for a great many species, both above and below the water's surface. Streamside or riverside areas, also known as riparian areas, often support a rich variety of life, but these areas may consist of forests, scrublands, or various other habitats. However, the flowing waters themselves serve as habitat for many aquatic species. Some fishes, such as Rainbow Darter and Banded Darter, live only in flowing streams and not in the still waters of ponds or lakes. Various aquatic insects, such as the larvae of certain caddisflies, mayflies, and dragonflies, are also adapted to the moving waters of streams and rivers. A great many other species can live in either flowing or standing water, as long as certain other requirements are met.

Many streams and rivers have been fouled by pollution or damaged by channelization. A channelized ditch is a much poorer habitat than a natural stream, with its meanders and deeper pools. But even a roadside ditch or irrigation canal may support a few interesting aquatic creatures.

## MARSHES

The Midwest is blessed with rich marshlands, especially around the edges of the Great Lakes and in interior regions of Michigan, Wisconsin, and Minnesota. A marsh is a habitat where the soil is consistently saturated or covered with shallow water, and with a dense stand of low vegetation but generally with no trees and relatively few shrubs. It may be located in the still waters along the edge of a lake or pond, or sometimes in slow-moving waters along a river with very shallow banks. Typical marsh plants include certain grasses, cattails, rushes, sedges, water-lilies, and various unique wildflowers. Among the many birds nesting in marshes are rails, bitterns, grebes, Red-winged Blackbirds, Marsh Wrens, and a wide variety of ducks. Common Muskrats and various frogs and snakes also favor these wetlands.

Only fragments remain of the vast western Lake Erie Marshes, which once blended evenly into the equally vast Great Black Swamp in northwestern Ohio, and the Kankakee River marshes, which may have occupied as much as one million acres in northern Indiana and Illinois.

## SPECIALIZED HABITATS: SWAMPS, BOGS, FENS, VERNAL POOLS

**Swamps.** Unlike a marsh, a swamp is a wetland with extensive cover of trees and/or shrubs. Only a few tree and shrub species in our region can thrive in standing water, so swamps can be characterized by their dominant plants. Red Maple swamps and Buttonbush swamps are fairly widespread. In extreme southern Illinois and southwestern Indiana, backwaters along rivers host swamps of Bald Cypress and other trees.

**Bogs.** These occur in cool northern climates. They are wetlands fed only by precipitation, not by flowing streams. Where water collects and plants such as sphagnum moss accumulate, organic matter decomposes very slowly, resulting in acidic, nutrient-poor conditions. Over time, a thick layer of sodden peat develops, perpetuating the bog conditions. Typically a bog in this region has an open pond at the center and a ring of trees such as Black Spruce and Tamarack. Pitcher-plants, sundews, cranberries, and other plants adapted to the acidic conditions may thrive in the understory.

**Fens** can be superficially similar to bogs, but are fed by flowing streams. The water in a fen is not so stagnant so it often is not so acidic, and can be quite alkaline, depending on conditions in the watershed that feeds it. An acidic fen may have many of the same plants as a typical bog, while a more alkaline fen is likely to have more variety of plant life, including trees such as Northern White-cedar and such local specialties as Showy Lady's-slipper.

**Showy Lady's-slipper**

**Vernal pools.** These small, ephemeral wetlands are filled with water for only part of the year. In the Midwest, these pools occur in forest or savanna; typically they are filled by rainfall or snowmelt in fall, winter, or spring, drying up by sometime in summer. Some amphibians, such as Wood Frog and Spotted Salamander, lay their eggs in these temporary pools, and the young develop before the ponds go dry. The larval stages of many aquatic insects develop there as well. Some rare and localized snails, fairy shrimp, and other invertebrates also live in vernal pools, their eggs surviving the dry season and then hatching out when the pool fills again.

## OPEN WATER

Natural ponds and lakes of all sizes abound in the northern part of our region. Farther south are fewer natural water bodies but many artificial ones, from farm ponds to major reservoirs. These sources of water become centers of activity for many animals from surrounding habitats, and also host their own distinctive aquatic life. Migratory water birds, aquatic insects, frogs, toads, turtles, snakes, and a wide variety of aquatic plants inhabit these lakes, ponds, and reservoirs. History plays a major role in determining which species will be found where — especially in the case of fishes, which can't get to an isolated body of water on their own. Past flooding events, connections to rivers, or intentional stocking may put fish in even small ponds, however.

American Beavers create their own ponds by building dams, and these beaver ponds are important habitat elements for some other species.

## THE GREAT LAKES

Four of the five Great Lakes touch the Midwest, helping to define our region and adding to the natural diversity here. These lakes are all interconnected in a living, flowing system. Water flows north out of Lake Michigan and east out of Lake Superior into Lake Huron, and then south via the St. Clair River and the Detroit River into Lake Erie. East of our region, water from Lake Erie enters the Niagara River, pours over Niagara Falls, and flows into Lake Ontario. From the northeast corner of Lake Ontario, water enters the St. Lawrence River, flowing 750 miles east-northeast to empty into the Atlantic Ocean via the Gulf of St. Lawrence in Quebec.

These huge freshwater seas have a profound impact on their surroundings, influencing weather patterns and local climate, and hosting a huge diversity of life. Many birds that are otherwise rare in the interior of the continent, including sea ducks such as scoters, occur in major flocks here. Scores of species of native fishes also live in the Great Lakes. At one time the region had major commercial fisheries for Lake Whitefish, Lake Sturgeon, and others. These were mostly depleted by overfishing before good management practices were understood. Today fishing is well regulated, and threats to local species come more from invasive exotics such as Sea Lamprey and Zebra Mussel, and from the effects of pollution.

# WILDFLOWERS

With their beauty and variety, wildflowers are among the major delights of the midwestern landscape. Beginning with woodland and prairie flowers in late winter to early spring, continuing through the flower-filled grasslands and wetlands of summer, and finishing with the last asters and goldenrods of autumn, they provide an ever-changing palette of colors and textures.

**The changing garden.** The modern botanical landscape is a dramatically different place than it was 300 million years ago. Back then, the dominant plants were spore-producing plants. Today the dominant plants are seed-producing, and an estimated 75 percent or more of those are flowering plants (angiosperms). Not all flowering plants are wildflowers. We cover additional flowering plants in the other sections of this guide.

**Diverse and plentiful.** Approximately 19,000 species of plants occur in the wild in the lower 48 states. The Midwest has a more modest representation of the total, with roughly 4,500 species encountered in the wild so far. Many of these are natives, but some are introduced species that have become established in the wild. In the botanical sections that follow, we're able to cover about 420 of the Midwest's most noticeable or important plant species. We also cover about 30 of the Midwest's fungi and kin.

**What is a wildflower?** There is no universally accepted definition. But for the purposes of this guide, we define a wildflower as an herbaceous (non-woody) flowering plant that is not a grass, rush, sedge, tree, shrub, or vine. Another term for wildflower, well known to grassland ecologists and often used in popular books, is forb. Out of about 4,500 plant species in the Midwest, roughly 2,800 of them are wildflowers (forbs).

But what one person might consider a wildflower, others might consider a weed. Goldenrods on a roadside, violets and dandelions in a lawn, milkweeds blooming in a field — all may be scorned as weeds but are in fact types of wildflowers.

**How this section is arranged.** In a standard botany text, all the plants are presented in taxonomic sequence, arranged by order, family, and genus, with related species close together. This isn't the most helpful approach for nonbotanists since unrelated plants may look superficially similar, and related plants may look quite different from each other. In this book we follow a simplified approach, grouping flowers by similarity, starting with their color.

Even within these color categories we had to make arbitrary choices; some flowers are on the borderline between white and yellow, and there's almost a smooth continuum from pink to pale purple to blue. Still, this breakdown should get you to the right area most of the time. In a couple of places, we broke with this simple categorization in favor of grouping similar species. For example, we have an entire spread on milkweeds and dogbanes (pp. 78–79) and another just on orchids (pp. 90–91).

**Parts of a flower.** We avoid technical terms as much as possible in this guide. When we do introduce a new technical term, we try to briefly describe it parenthetically. However, the fact is that some flowers are almost impossible to describe without using a few technical terms. For example, in some cases the flower itself is very small or petals are lacking, and what looks like showy petals may be sepals instead. In other cases, long stamens may be a notable feature of the flower or a flower's bracts may be an important clue to identification. The very simplified diagram below shows some basic flower parts.

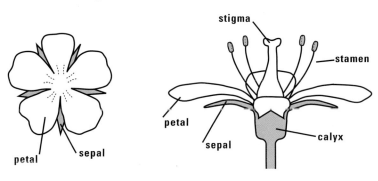

**Tools of the trade — observing plants in the field.** All naturalists have their preferred tools of the trade. Just as good binoculars are essential to a birder, a hand lens is an indispensable tool to someone studying plants. Unlike birds and other animals that often shy away from close approach, plants lend themselves to closer observation. Seeing certain details of a plant up close may prove useful to identification. Hand lenses, also called jeweler's loupes, are useful for studying other natural-history objects as well, such as rocks and minerals, insects, fungi, and more.

**Collecting.** Do not pick or collect any species unless you have permission. Even then, carefully consider if you truly need to collect a specimen. For many species, photos and detailed notes should suffice for making an ID. Some species do require more detailed investigation, such as close inspection under a microscope. In those cases, collecting is often necessary. If you are unsure whether to collect or not, in general it is considerate to leave plants (and fungi, insects, and other objects) as you found them so that others can enjoy them. Besides, you don't want to accidentally collect a rare species!

# WHITE WOODLAND FLOWERS

Some of the first wildflowers of spring are found in woodlands. Most of these put on a show before the trees have fully leafed out, while sunlight still bathes the forest floor. Referred to as spring ephemerals, these plants emerge in spring and quickly complete their growth and reproductive cycles. In summer they often die back to the ground, awaiting the next spring. Seeds of some woodland wildflowers are dispersed by ants. They have fleshy appendages (elaiosomes) that appeal to the ants.

### BLOODROOT  *Sanguinaria canadensis*

From rich deciduous woodlands to shaded bluffs, this spring ephemeral emerges with its single basal leaf initially wrapped around the stalk of its single flower. Poppy family (Papaveraceae). ▶ Gray-green leaf with scalloped edges and 3–9 major lobes. White flower up to 3" across with *yellow anthers*. Roots, leaf, and flower stem exude *reddish orange sap* if snapped.

### TWINLEAF  *Jeffersonia diphylla*

An uncommon wildflower of rich deciduous woods, slopes, and floodplains. Barberry family (Berberidaceae). ▶ Leaves divided vertically into 2 distinct leaflets. White flowers with 8 petals. Fruit an unusual seedpod with lid.

### MAYAPPLE  *Podophyllum peltatum*

A common wildflower of deciduous forests and woodland edges. Barberry family. ▶ Pairs of *large*, deeply lobed, umbrella-like leaves are joined to the main stem. A nodding flower positioned at the joint between the two petioles (leaf stalks) is later replaced with a large yellow-green fruit.

### WHITE BANEBERRY  *Actaea pachypoda*

Rich deciduous forests and occasionally coniferous forests. Buttercup family (Ranunculaceae). ▶ Sharply toothed compound leaves. White flower stalk produces *white berries* with *black spots* (like "doll's eyes") on thickened red stalks. Very similar **Red Baneberry** *(A. rubra)* develops *red* fruits.

### SQUIRREL CORN  *Dicentra canadensis*

Rich deciduous woods. Poppy family (Papaveraceae). ▶ Leaves *very finely divided.* Clusters of dangling, *heart-shaped* flowers. Yellow basal bulblets (actually corms) suggest corn kernels.

### DUTCHMAN'S-BREECHES  *Dicentra cucullaria*

Rich deciduous woodlands and occasionally wet forests. Poppy family. ▶ Leaves *finely divided.* Clusters of *dangling flowers* suggest pantaloons hanging on a clothesline. Pink basal bulblets.

### CUTLEAF TOOTHWORT  *Cardamine concatenata*

Blooms in spring in rich, moist to wet deciduous forests. Mustard family (Brassicaceae). ▶ Whorl of 3 leaves partway up stem; each leaf has 3 *deeply divided, coarsely toothed leaflets.* Cluster of long-stalked, 4-petaled flowers.

# WHITE WOODLAND FLOWERS

Bloodroot

Twinleaf

Mayapple

White Baneberry

Squirrel Corn

Dutchman's-breeches

Cutleaf Toothwort

51

A few more woodland flowers, blooming in spring or summer.

### WILD LEEK  *Allium tricoccum*

Usually found in high-quality, moist to wet deciduous forests. A summer-blooming woodland wildflower unique for the fact that the foliage dies back to the ground often before its flower stalk has emerged. Amaryllis family (Amaryllidaceae). ▶ Broad, glossy, flat green leaves with reddish leaf stalks. Blooms in midsummer with an umbel of creamy white flowers on long stalks.

### DWARF GINSENG  *Panax trifolium*

A petite spring wildflower of rich, moist deciduous and hemlock forests. Aralia family (Araliaceae). ▶ A whorl of small compound leaves partway up stem, each with 3–5 toothed leaflets. A single flower stalk produces an umbel of *tiny* white flowers.

### CANADA MAYFLOWER  *Maianthemum canadense*

A small flower of deciduous and coniferous forests, sometimes bogs and dunes. Blooms late spring to early summer. Asparagus family (Asparagaceae). ▶ Two (sometimes 3) alternate leaves with heart-shaped bases on a zigzagging stem. Cluster of tiny, 4-parted white flowers. Red-splotched, whitish green berries.

### FALSE SOLOMON'S-SEAL  *Maianthemum racemosum*

A taller woodland wildflower of dry to moist deciduous forests and wooded dunes; occasionally in floodplains. Blooms early summer. Asparagus family. ▶ Large, wide oval leaves with pointed tips alternate on an arching stem. A branching, *terminal cluster* of creamy white flowers produces bright red berries.

### SPRING BEAUTY  *Claytonia virginica*

An early blooming spring wildflower of rich deciduous woodlands. Montia family (Montiaceae). ▶ A pair of opposite, narrow leaves partway up stem. Clusters of 5-petaled white to pale pink flowers with thin, often vibrant, *pink veins.*

### BUNCHBERRY  *Cornus canadensis*

An herbaceous shrub (technically a subshrub) of moist woodlands. Stems arise from a woody, creeping rhizome at, or just below, ground level. Blooms midsummer. Dogwood family (Cornaceae). ▶ Leaves in 2–3 opposite pairs create a whorl-like appearance. Tiny greenish flowers are surrounded by 4 white, petal-like bracts. Cluster (bunch) of red fruits in late summer.

### SPOTTED WINTERGREEN  *Chimaphila maculata*

An evergreen subshrub of dry deciduous forests with sandy soil. Blooms midsummer. Heath family (Ericaceae). ▶ A whorl-like arrangement of alternating, lance-shaped, coarsely toothed, dark green leaves with noticeable *pale central stripe and venation.* Nodding 5-petaled white flowers.

# WHITE WOODLAND FLOWERS

Wild Leek

Dwarf Ginseng

Canada Mayflower

False Solomon's-seal

Spring Beauty

Spotted Wintergreen

Bunchberry

As mentioned on p. 50, the seeds of some woodland wildflower species are dispersed by ants. Trilliums participate in this mutually beneficial ant-plant interaction. Seed dispersal by ants is called myrmecochory. The ants are attracted to the seeds' elaiosomes — fleshy appendages rich in nutrients. The ants bring the seeds back to their nests, and the elaiosomes are either eaten by the adults or fed to their larvae. The seeds are then discarded ("planted") in the ants' nutrient-rich waste piles. Formerly placed in the lily family (Liliaceae), trilliums are now placed in the bunchflower family **(Melanthiaceae)**. All trilliums bloom in spring, producing a single three-petaled flower with three green sepals.

### WHITE TRILLIUM  *Trillium grandiflorum*

Found in dry to moist deciduous forests, in particular rich beech-maple forests; occasionally in mixed conifer-hardwood forests. ▶ Whorl of 3 large, oval leaves with pointed tips. Large (2–3") flower with 3 white petals rises above whorl. The flowers turn pink after pollination, which may be a visual cue to pollinators to pass on by.

### NODDING TRILLIUM  *Trillium cernuum*

Primarily on acidic soils in moist woodlands. ▶ White flower on a curved, short stalk hangs *below* the leaf whorl, often hidden. Has 6 *reddish anthers*. Petals and sepals strongly curved back.

### DROOPING TRILLIUM  *Trillium flexipes*

Rich deciduous forests, shaded riparian corridors. ▶ Long, drooping flower stalk positions flower usually *just above* leaf whorl. White flowers similar to above species but anthers often *cream colored.* In parts of range, flowers can be maroon.

### SNOW TRILLIUM  *Trillium nivale* (not shown)

A small trillium of rich woods and shaded slopes. Often blooms while snow still covers part of ground. ▶ *Small* oval leaves with *rounded tips.* Small white flower held above whorl on short stalk.

### PRAIRIE TRILLIUM  *Trillium recurvatum*

Deciduous woods and savannas. ▶ Light green to reddish stem holds whorl of oval leaves with distinctive *mottling.* Sessile (without stalk) reddish maroon flower with 3 petals strongly curving upward and 3 green sepals hanging below whorl.

### TOADSHADE  *Trillium sessile*

Found in rich, moist deciduous forests, especially shaded floodplains. ▶ Wide, oval, blunt-tipped leaves, often on reddish stem. Sessile reddish maroon flower with sepals pressed against top surface of leaf whorl.

### RED TRILLIUM  *Trillium erectum*

A large, often tall trillium of moist deciduous forests, especially beech-maple forests, occasionally wooded swamps. ▶ Reddish maroon flower held on a *long stalk,* sometimes drooping.

# TRILLIUMS

White Trillium

Nodding Trillium

Drooping Trillium

Prairie Trillium

Toadshade

Red Trillium

### BONESET    *Eupatorium perfoliatum*

A common, widespread plant of wetlands including marshes, wet prairies, roadside ditches. Aster family (Asteraceae). ▶ Leaves opposite, lance-shaped, finely toothed and *fused to each other at the base,* surrounding the hairy central stem. Flat-topped clusters of white (rarely pink tinged) flower heads of disk florets only.

### DAISY FLEABANE    *Erigeron annuus*

A native, often considered weedy, of disturbed fields and edges. Annual or biennial. Aster family. ▶ Leaves wedge-shaped with a few teeth along edge. Numerous, small composite flower heads with *narrow* white ray flowers surrounding a yellow central disk.

### YARROW    *Achillea millefolium*

Introduced from Eurasia; colonizes disturbed fields and edges. Aster family. ▶ Leaves *fernlike,* finely dissected. Flat-topped clusters of creamy white flower heads. All parts of plant aromatic.

### WHITE FALSE INDIGO    *Baptisia lactea*

Mostly uncommon on dry prairies and savannas. Grows to 6'. Pea family (Fabaceae). ▶ Leaves compound with 3 leaflets (trifoliate), bluish to grayish green. Sturdy, smooth central stem. Spike of white, pea-shaped flowers; *black* seedpods.

### ILLINOIS BUNDLEFLOWER    *Desmanthus illinoensis*

A localized wildflower of sandy to loamy prairies. Most common in the Illinois R. watershed. Pea family. ▶ Leaves alternate, doubly compound, fernlike. Small white flower heads produce a cluster of brown, flattened, curvy seedpods.

### ROUND-HEADED BUSH CLOVER    *Lespedeza capitata*

A common legume of prairies and savannas, sometimes on dry roadsides, dunes. Grows to 5'. Pea family. ▶ Sturdy main stem covered with white hairs. Trifoliate leaves. Hairy flower heads, with small white flowers, on short stalks at top of stem.

### CANADIAN MILKVETCH    *Astragalus canadensis*

Dry to moist prairies, savannas, forest edges. Pea family. ▶ Alternate compound leaves with up to 31 smooth-edged leaflets. Spikes of creamy white, 5-petaled flowers whorl around stalk.

### WHITE TURTLEHEAD    *Chelone glabra*

A wetland plant of barely acidic to alkaline soils. Plantain family (Plantaginaceae). ▶ Pairs of toothed leaves on stem, at right angles to adjacent pairs. Spike of *odd-shaped,* creamy white flowers.

### AMERICAN POKEWEED    *Phytolacca americana*

Large, bushy native of edges and disturbed soils. Pokeweed family (Phytolaccaceae). ▶ Large leaves. Clusters (often dangling) of small, 5-parted white to pinkish flowers on long greenish to magenta stalks. Mature berries *purplish black.*

# WHITE TO CREAM FLOWERS

Daisy Fleabane

Yarrow

Boneset

seedpods

Illinois Bundleflower

Canadian Milkvetch

White False Indigo

Round-headed Bush Clover

White Turtlehead

American Pokeweed

57

### WILD QUININE    *Parthenium integrifolium*
Primarily in somewhat dry to moist prairies and savannas. Aster family (Asteraceae). ► Leaves coarsely toothed, with a rough, sandpapery feel. A sturdy flower stalk arises out of a basal rosette of leaves, topped with a flat cluster of small white flower heads.

### SWEET EVERLASTING    *Pseudognaphalium obtusifolium*
An annual or biennial of disturbed, dry sites, including sandy savannas, fields, roadsides. Aster family. ► Leaves yellow-green on top, hairy and whitish below. Stem hairy and whitish. Clusters of small, creamy white flower heads, each surrounded by layers of whitish bracts. Rubbed foliage may have balsamlike odor.

### PALE INDIAN PLANTAIN    *Arnoglossum atriplicifolium*
Dry prairies, savannas, and sand dunes. This tall (3–9') native is hard to mistake for anything else. Aster family. ► Leaves palmately veined, medium green on top, whitish below. Sturdy flower stalk arises out of a basal rosette of leaves. Flat-topped clusters of whitish to greenish cylindrical flower heads.

### PRAIRIE INDIAN PLANTAIN    *Arnoglossum plantagineum*
An uncommon plant of fens, moist meadows and savannas, wet dolomite prairies. Aster family. ► Large, thick, rubbery, oval leaves with noticeable parallel veining. Flower heads similar to those of Pale Indian Plantain but often more whitish.

### SWEET-SCENTED INDIAN PLANTAIN    *Hasteola suaveolens*
Another uncommon plant of wet soils, primarily sedge meadows and marshes. Aster family. ► Leaves alternate, arrowhead-shaped with wide lower lobes, forward-pointing teeth, and winged stems. Flower heads similar to above species.

### CULVER'S ROOT    *Veronicastrum virginicum*
Moist soils of prairies, savannas, woodland and riparian edges. Plantain family (Plantaginaceae). ► Central stem smooth, unbranched. Leaves grouped in whorls of 3–7. *Long flower spike* of tiny white flowers, surrounded by a few shorter spikes.

### TALL THIMBLEWEED    *Anemone virginiana*
Prairies, savannas, other open woods. Buttercup family (Ranunculaceae). ► Whorl of 2–3 compound leaves with long petioles. Five-petaled white flowers on long stalks produce thimble-shaped fruit; cottony mature seedheads. **Thimbleweed** (*A. cylindrica*) similar but has longer fruit, whorl of 5–9 leaves.

### CANADA ANEMONE    *Anemone canadensis*
Moist soils of wet prairies, marshes, riparian corridors, floodplain forests, ditches near roads. Buttercup family. ► Flower stalk with *deeply divided*, opposite, *sessile (without stalk)* leaves that clasp stalk. Large white flower.

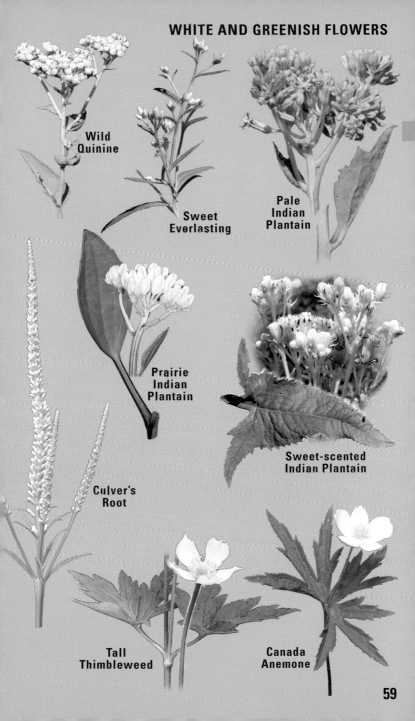

Wild Quinine

Sweet Everlasting

Pale Indian Plantain

Prairie Indian Plantain

Sweet-scented Indian Plantain

Culver's Root

Tall Thimbleweed

Canada Anemone

# FLOWERS IN THE CARROT FAMILY

Plants of the carrot, or parsley, family (**Apiaceae**) usually have hollow stems. Flower heads are often (but not always) a flat-topped to slightly convex umbel (with stalks radiating from the same point), and the foliage may be aromatic. While some species are used in culinary creations as seasonings or vegetables, care should be taken around plants of this family. The sap of some can cause severe contact dermatitis, with the impact of a few species being exacerbated by sunlight (phototoxicity). Others are deadly poisonous if even small quantities are ingested.

### GOLDEN ALEXANDERS    *Zizia aurea*

Moist prairies, savannas, fens, open woodlands, streambanks. Not known to cause contact dermatitis. ▶ Compound leaves with 3–5 toothed leaflets; bright yellow flower heads. Do not confuse with Wild Parsnip (p. 100), which can be phototoxic.

### RATTLESNAKE MASTER    *Eryngium yuccifolium*

Prairies and savannas. Flower heads look different from most in this family. Not known to cause contact dermatitis. ▶ Leaves yucca-like, alternate, with spiny teeth, bases clasping main flower stalk. Ball-like, whitish green flower heads on long stalks.

### ANISEROOT    *Osmorhiza longistylis*

Moist deciduous forests, wooded valleys. Not known to cause contact dermatitis. ▶ Compound leaves alternate, each with 3 compound leaflets. Umbel of white flowers; styles *longer* than petals. Foliage, roots have pleasant anise smell. **Sweet Cicely** (*O. claytonii*) similar but has hairy stems, styles shorter than petals.

### SPOTTED WATER-HEMLOCK    *Cicuta maculata*

A native plant of marshes, swamps, sedge meadows, wet woods. Considered the most deadly poisonous plant in North America. ▶ Stem green with *purple streaking*. Leaves alternate, compound with 3–7 toothed leaflets. White flower umbel.

### GREAT ANGELICA    *Angelica atropurpurea*

Wetlands and wet edges. Towering (up to 9'), majestic when in bloom. May cause contact dermatitis in sensitive people. ▶ Thick reddish purple flower stalks. Large, multiply-compound lower leaves with purplish sheaths at base. Large, spherical flower heads, each with many small whitish green flowers.

### COWBANE    *Oxypolis rigidior*

A toxic wetland wildflower. ▶ Alternate compound leaves with 5–9 narrow, *smooth* leaflets (sometimes a few teeth); leaf base sheathed. Slightly convex, white flower umbel. See next species.

### WATER PARSNIP    *Sium suave*

Blooms in summer and fall in swamps, muddy edges. *Not* related to the garden parsnip of culinary fame. ▶ Alternate compound leaves with 7–17 lance-shaped leaflets with tiny *teeth;* leaf base sheathed. Flat-topped white flower umbel.

# FLOWERS IN THE CARROT FAMILY

Golden Alexanders

Rattlesnake Master

Aniseroot

Spotted Water-hemlock

Great Angelica

Cowbane

Water Parsnip

61

# SUNFLOWERS

With over 23,000 species worldwide, the aster, or sunflower, family (**Asteraceae**) is one of the two largest families of flowering plants. The Midwest has over 500 aster family representatives. Species in this family have composite flowers: what may look like a single flower is actually composed of numerous small flowers, joined on a specialized part of the flower stalk called the receptacle. Composite flower heads can have both ray flowers (florets) and disk flowers (florets). Each ray floret looks like a petal in a non-composite flower, but it's actually a tiny, complete flower in its own right. Each disk floret is tubular. When present, ray florets ring the disk florets. Here are a few species in the genus *Helianthus,* sometimes called true sunflowers. All members of this genus have sterile ray florets.

### COMMON SUNFLOWER  *Helianthus annuus*

A conspicuous annual wildflower of disturbed soils, such as roadsides and fallow fields. Grows to 9'. The original native forms of this species were bred for cultivation by early Native Americans. Modern cultivars, like the Giant Sunflower and others, are important economic crops, producing such items as sunflower oil and birdseed. ▶ Wild sunflowers have smaller heads than agricultural varieties and numerous branching flower stalks.

### DOWNY SUNFLOWER  *Helianthus mollis*

Dry to moist prairies. Distinctive look. ▶ Stem and leaves covered with soft hairs. Sturdy, single stem has closely spaced pairs of opposite, greenish gray, smooth-edged leaves, often clasping the stem.

### WESTERN SUNFLOWER  *Helianthus occidentalis*

Dry, sandy prairies and savannas. Despite the common name, it's a Midwestern sunflower. ▶ A fragile-looking sunflower. From a basal rosette of leaves rises a single, practically leafless, green to reddish brown flower stalk with a few yellow flower heads.

### WOODLAND SUNFLOWERS  *Helianthus* sp.

A number of sunflower species live in open forests and woodland edges. Because of their tendency to hybridize, they can be difficult to identify.

### TALL SUNFLOWER  *Helianthus giganteus*

A wetland sunflower growing in fens, bogs, marshes, and wet prairies. ▶ *Hairy, red to purple stem.* Long lance-shaped, toothed leaves. The **Sawtooth Sunflower** (*H. grosseserratus*) is similar but has a smooth, not hairy, stem.

### FALSE SUNFLOWER  *Heliopsis helianthoides*

Often confused for a true sunflower of the genus *Helianthus*. Its species name, *helianthoides* (meaning helianthus-like), is a reference to this fact. ▶ Unlike the sterile ray florets of *Helianthus*, close inspection of the notched-tipped, yellow ray florets reveals they have styles and are capable of producing seed along with the disk florets. Leaves opposite, oval, toothed, on short stalks.

# SUNFLOWERS

Common Sunflower

Downy Sunflower

Western Sunflower

woodland sunflower sp.

Tall Sunflower

False Sunflower

63

More members of the aster family (see p. 62). These all bloom in summer and fall. Members of the genus *Silphium* are all stunning plants with sandpapery leaves and gorgeous flower displays. Unlike true sunflowers, silphiums have fertile ray florets and sterile disk florets.

### GRAY-HEADED CONEFLOWER    *Ratibida pinnata*

A common wildflower of prairies and savannas. ▶ Leaves with rough surface, 3–7 deep lobes. Long flower stalks hold flower heads with 13–15 yellow, drooping ray florets and a thimble-shaped, greenish gray to brown cone of disk florets.

### BLACK-EYED SUSAN    *Rudbeckia hirta*

A biennial or short-lived perennial of dry to moist prairies, savannas, roadsides, meadows, fens. ▶ Alternate, oblong, hairy leaves. Flower stems hairy. Flower heads of yellow ray florets and a compressed, *reddish brown* cone of disk florets.

### BROWN-EYED SUSAN    *Rudbeckia triloba*

Moist prairies, savannas, riparian edges, open woods. ▶ Leaves rough, usually *trident shaped*. Numerous small flower heads with glowing yellow ray florets and a dark brown cone of disk florets.

### CUTLEAF CONEFLOWER    *Rudbeckia laciniata*

Moist soils of riparian corridors, floodplains, open woods, marshes. ▶ Tall (to 10'). Large, often drooping, leaves with 3–7 deep, toothed lobes. Clusters of flower heads with 6–12 yellow, drooping ray florets and initially light green disk florets.

### COMPASS PLANT    *Silphium laciniatum*

A tall native of prairies and savannas. Named for the fact that the large basal leaves often orient north-south, minimizing exposure to the noontime sun. ▶ Grows to 12'. Large, deeply lobed leaves. *Thick, hairy* flower stalk with many *large* yellow flower heads.

### PRAIRIE DOCK    *Silphium terebinthinaceum*

Prairies, savannas, occasionally fens. ▶ Basal rosette of *very large* (up to 2' long), spade-shaped, coarsely toothed leaves. Slender, smooth, reddish flower stalk rises high (to 10') above leaves, holding a few yellow flower heads.

### ROSINWEED    *Silphium integrifolium*

Dry to moist prairies, open woods, rocky upland forests. ▶ Stems often *reddish*. Leaves sessile, stiff to raised, opposite, and clasping stem. Cluster of yellow flower heads on top.

### CUP PLANT    *Silphium perfoliatum*

Moist soils of prairies, floodplains, meadows, lake and riparian shores. ▶ Grows to 10'. Large, coarsely toothed, opposite leaf pairs wrapped around squarish stem form *deep, water-collecting cups*. Adjacent leaf pairs at 90 degrees, which helps maximize water catchment. Clusters of yellow flower heads on top.

# CONEFLOWERS AND SILPHIUMS

Gray-headed
Coneflower

Black-eyed
Susan

Brown-eyed Susan
typical leaf

Cutleaf
Coneflower

SILPHIUMS
(not shown at
same scale)

Compass
Plant

Prairie
Dock

Rosinweed

Cup
Plant

The first six species below are in the aster family (see p. 62), while the last two are in the pea family (**Fabaceae**).

### PRAIRIE COREOPSIS  *Coreopsis palmata*

Blooms in early summer, forming colonies in prairies, savannas, roadsides. ▶ Grows to 3'. Leaves deeply divided into usually 3 lobes (suggesting a bird's foot), and arranged in pairs. Usually only one flower head per stalk. Tips of ray florets mostly *notched.*

### SAND COREOPSIS  *Coreopsis lanceolata*

Blooms late spring to early summer on sandy, dry prairies; fields. ▶ Short (to 2'). Tufts of long, narrow, basal leaves. Long flower stalks with a few pairs of narrow leaves. Ray florets *notched* at tip.

### TALL COREOPSIS  *Coreopsis tripteris*

Blooms midsummer to early fall in prairies, savannas, open woods, and even wet meadows and marshes. ▶ Tall (to 8'). Sturdy, blue-green stem with pairs of compound leaves, each with 3–5 long leaflets. Tips of ray florets slightly notched to smooth.

### STIFF GOLDENROD  *Solidago rigida*

Goldenrods are diverse, with around 40 Midwestern species, most blooming in late summer and fall. Beneficial wildflowers, they provide nectar for many insects. These insect-pollinated plants are mistakenly maligned for causing hay fever; the real culprits are wind-pollinated plants, such as ragweeds (p. 88), which bloom at the same time. This species, Stiff Goldenrod, is an attractive wildflower of dry prairies, savannas, fields, and roadsides. ▶ *Domed to flat-topped cluster* of small flower heads. Alternating greenish gray leaves point upward, clasping hairy stem.

### ROUGH-STEMMED GOLDENROD  *Solidago rugosa*

Moist, sandy soils of prairies, open woodlands, swamps, roadsides. ▶ Alternate, toothed leaves appear wrinkled on top. Stems, leaves often hairy, but can be smooth in some populations.

### SHOWY GOLDENROD  *Solidago speciosa*

Spectacular in full bloom, this aptly named goldenrod is found mainly in dry, sandy prairies and savannas. ▶ Stems smooth, sometimes *reddish,* often grow in clumps. Tall *plumelike* flower spike.

### PARTRIDGE PEA  *Chamaecrista fasciculata*

An annual pea of dry prairies, savannas, roadsides. Grows to 2' tall. ▶ Yellow 5-petaled flowers with reddish bases. Alternate compound leaves with up to 18 pairs of tiny, oblong leaflets. Fruit a flat pod.

### WILD SENNA  *Senna hebecarpa*

An attractive, tall (to 6') perennial pea of wet meadows, riparian corridors. ▶ Compound leaves with 6–10 pairs of oblong leaflets.

# COREOPSIS, GOLDENRODS, AND PEAS
(not all shown at same scale)

Prairie
Coreopsis

Sand
Coreopsis

Tall
Coreopsis

Stiff
Goldenrod

Rough-stemmed
Goldenrod

Showy
Goldenrod

Wild
Senna

Partridge
Pea

### COMMON EVENING-PRIMROSE     *Oenothera biennis*

A native wildflower, usually biennial. Flowers often open late afternoon to evening and stay open all night, providing nectar for moths. Grows to 7', usually shorter. Evening-primrose family (Onagraceae). ▶ Spike of yellow, 4-petaled flowers that bloom from bottom up; petals heart-shaped. Long, narrow leaves crowd the stem. Fruits are tubular capsules filled with tiny black seeds.

### COMMON DANDELION     *Taraxacum officinale*

A European introduction that is now found almost everywhere in lawns and gardens. Aster family (Asteraceae). ▶ Yellow flower heads entirely of *ray florets* (no disk florets). Fluffy, spherical seedhead ("puffball"). Leaves and hollow stem exude *milky sap* when snapped. Jagged leaves. **Sow-thistles** (*Sonchus* sp.) taller, with branched flower stalks, large leaves with spiny edges.

### YELLOW GOAT'S-BEARD     *Tragopogon pratensis*

Another introduction. Biennial, sending up flower stalk in second year. Aster family. ▶ Long, grasslike leaves clasp a smooth stalk. Yellow flower head entirely of ray florets. Leaves and stem *exude milky sap*. Seedhead like a giant dandelion puffball.

### HAWKWEEDS     *Hieracium* sp.

In the Midwest, we have both native and introduced species of hawkweeds. The native species tend to grow as part of established habitats, while the introduced species tend to occur in disturbed areas. Aster family. ▶ Flower heads of only ray florets. Most species have yellow flower heads, but a few have orange.

### COMMON MULLEIN     *Verbascum thapsus*

Another Eurasian introduction. Although considered a weedy species by many, this biennial can be aesthetically pleasing when in bloom. Figwort family (Scrophulariaceae). ▶ First-year basal rosette of *large, soft, downy leaves*. In second year, flower stalk and leaves covered with dense, white hair. Five-petaled yellow flowers on *thick flower spike*, bloom from the bottom up.

### MOTH MULLEIN     *Verbascum blattaria*

Another biennial from Eurasia, fairly common on roadsides. Figwort family. ▶ Individuals have either all-yellow or all-white flowers. Stem leaves triangular to lance-shaped and toothed. Interesting pentagon-shaped flower buds mature to reveal 5-petaled flowers with purplish hairs surrounding the stamens.

### BUTTER-AND-EGGS     *Linaria vulgaris*

A Eurasian introduction, this small-statured wildflower (to 2') has become naturalized in many places. Plantain family (Plantaginaceae). ▶ Spike of pale yellow, tubular, snapdragon-like flowers with long spurs at the base. The lower lip of each flower has an area of "egg yolk" orange coloration.

# FLOWERS OF DISTURBED SOILS

Common Evening-primrose

Common Dandelion

Yellow Goat's-beard

hawkweeds sp.

Common Mullein

Moth Mullein

Butter-and-eggs

**69**

### COMMON SNEEZEWEED    *Helenium autumnale*

A wildflower of moist to wet soils. Named for the fact that its crushed flower heads were used to make snuff. Aster family (Asteraceae). ▶ Distinctive: *winged stem;* flower heads with *swept back, double notched,* ray florets and a ball-shaped center.

### PALE JEWELWEED    *Impatiens pallida*

Primarily shaded, moist habitats, such as open woods. Balsam family (Balsaminaceae). ▶ Funnel-shaped flowers hang from slender stalks. Fruit a bulging capsule that explodes at a touch, flinging seeds many feet. See Spotted Jewelweed, p. 72.

### WHORLED LOOSESTRIFE    *Lysimachia quadrifolia*

Dry to moist, sandy woodlands and savannas. Primrose family (Primulaceae). ▶ Whorl of 3–7 oval leaves. Small, long-stalked, star-shaped flowers emerge from leaf axils. **Prairie Loosestrife** (*L. quadriflora*) of wet prairies has narrow leaves, rounded petals.

### TUFTED LOOSESTRIFE    *Lysimachia thyrsiflora*

A wetland wildflower, distinctive when in bloom. Primrose family. ▶ Leaves opposite, often sessile (no leaf stalk) with pairs usually rotated at right angles to adjacent pairs. Dense, *ball-like flower clusters* on *long stalks* emerge from leaf axils.

### LARGE-FLOWERED BELLWORT    *Uvularia grandiflora*

A graceful, spring-blooming wildflower of moist, loamy to sandy soils of woodlands. Colchicum family (Colchicaceae). ▶ Leaves alternate, *perfoliate* (surround stem) at base. Long, drooping, 6-parted, slightly twisted flowers. One to a few flowers per stem.

### YELLOW TROUT-LILY    *Erythronium americanum*

A spring wildflower of rich, deciduous forests. Lily family (Liliaceae). ▶ One or 2 glossy, brown-splotched leaves. Nodding pale yellow flower, its petals curving back toward stem with age.

### CELANDINE POPPY    *Stylophorum diphyllum*

A spring flower of rich, deciduous woods. Poppy family (Papaveraceae). ▶ Leaves *deeply lobed.* Large 4-petaled flower. Fruit hairy, oval. Bright yellow sap. **Celandine** (*Chelidonium majus*) has smaller flowers, nonhairy seed capsules, orange-yellow sap.

### BUTTERCUPS/CROWFOOTS    *Ranunculus* sp.

The Midwest has almost 30 *Ranunculus* species (native and introduced). Buttercup family (Ranunculaceae). ▶ Flowers (usually yellow) with 5 petals. Varied leaves, often strongly dissected.

### AGRIMONY    *Agrimonia* sp.

Dry to moist deciduous and mixed forests, prairies, lake edges, marshes and swamps. Rose family (Rosaceae). ▶ Compound leaves with coarsely toothed leaflets. Small 5-petaled flowers. Fruit a seed covered with bristly hooks.

# FLOWERS OF WETLANDS AND WOODLANDS

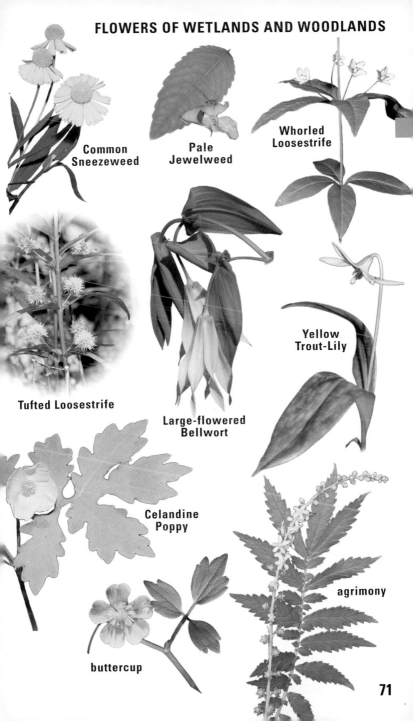

Common Sneezeweed

Pale Jewelweed

Whorled Loosestrife

Tufted Loosestrife

Large-flowered Bellwort

Yellow Trout-Lily

Celandine Poppy

agrimony

buttercup

# SOME NATIVE ORANGE AND RED FLOWERS

Many wildflowers are white, blue, or yellow, colors that attract the most pollinators. Orange and red flowers are more scarce. Bees and other insects do visit orange flowers, but are less likely to visit red ones. Bees can see red, but have a hard time picking it out from a green background; hummingbirds are the main pollinators of the last three species below.

### BUTTERFLY WEED    *Asclepias tuberosa*

Dry, often sandy places. Our only orange milkweed. Dogbane family (Apocynaceae). ▶ Cluster of small, 5-parted orange flowers. Unlike other milkweeds (p. 78), foliage *lacks* milky latex.

### SPOTTED JEWELWEED    *Impatiens capensis*

Edges of wet areas, blooming in late summer. Balsam family (Balsaminaceae). ▶ Funnel-shaped, dark-spotted pale orange flowers hang from slender stalks. See Pale Jewelweed (p. 70).

### MICHIGAN LILY    *Lilium michiganense*

Moist soils of prairies, swamps, open woods, fens. Lily family (Liliaceae). ▶ Whorls of 3–7 leaves. Orange, 6-parted flower with recurved petals. **Turk's Cap Lily** (*L. superbum*) similar but flower throat has greenish star pattern.

### WOOD LILY    *Lilium philadelphicum*

Dry woods, prairies, dunes; also fens. Lily family. ▶ Upright, 6-parted,  orange to red flowers with purplish spots at base. Stem leaves in whorls of 4–11.

### PRAIRIE SMOKE    *Geum triflorum*

Among the first spring-blooming prairie wildflowers. Although red flowered, pollinated by bumblebees. Rose family (Rosaceae). ▶ Basal rosette of hairy, divided leaves. Stalk with 3 nodding red flowers; upright once pollinated. Seeds with long, feathery plumes.

### COLUMBINE    *Aquilegia canadensis*

One of the first spring flowers used by migrating hummingbirds in our region. Buttercup family (Ranunculaceae). ▶ Nodding red flower with *long spurs, yellow centers*. Leaves lobed, 3-parted.

### CARDINAL FLOWER    *Lobelia cardinalis*

Grows in colorful patches on wet soils. Bellflower family (Campanulaceae).  ▶ Alternate, lance-shaped, toothed leaves. Long spikes of brilliant crimson, tubular flowers with lobed petals.

### FIRE PINK    *Silene virginica*

Uncommon in open woodlands. Pink, or carnation, family (Caryophyllaceae). ▶ Stems hairy. Oval basal leaves. Red 5-parted flowers with notched petal tips.

### ROYAL CATCHFLY    *Silene regia*
Rare, local wildflower of dry prairies, savannas; stunning in full bloom. Pink family. ▶ Stems, leaves hairy; leaves opposite. Brilliant, 5-petaled scarlet flowers; calyx of flowers covered with sticky hairs that trap insects.

Butterfly Weed

Spotted Jewelweed

seedpod

Michigan Lily

Wood Lily

seeds

Prairie Smoke

Columbine

Fire Pink

Royal Catchfly

Cardinal Flower

calyx with trapped insects

73

Most species in the mint family **(Lamiaceae)** have pairs of simple, oppo-site leaves that grow at right angles to adjacent pairs on the stem. A few have whorled leaves. In many species, all parts of the plant are aromatic, producing distinctive odors when foliage is rubbed or crushed. Many mints have a floral structure with numerous small flowers arranged on a terminal flower spike or rounded flower head. Stems are often square in cross section but not all members of this family have square stems, and some plants in other families have square stems but are not mints. All the species below are considered native.

### WILD BERGAMOT    *Monarda fistulosa*

Dry to moist prairies, savannas, and roadsides. A favorite of many pollinators, including hummingbird moths. ▶ Toothed leaves emit oregano-like scent when crushed. Rounded flower head of *lavender* flowers.

### SPOTTED BEEBALM    *Monarda punctata*

Dry, sandy soils of prairies, savannas, roadsides. ▶ Multiple whorls of purple spotted, creamy flowers; each whorl with large, showy *white to lavender bracts* underneath.

### SCARLET BEEBALM    *Monarda didyma*

Uncommon in the Midwest; mainly in moist woods, floodplains, and along riparian corridors in ne. Ohio. Leaves used to be used for tea by the Oswego Indians, hence the other common name, Oswego Tea. A hummingbird favorite. ▶ Leaves toothed, aro-matic. *Rounded* flower head of *red* flowers.

### OBEDIENT PLANT    *Physostegia virginiana*

Moist soils of prairies, open woods, floodplains, shores. Individ-ual flowers on floral spike remain for a time in whatever position they are moved. ▶ Leaves sessile (no leaf stalk), pointed, sharply toothed. Long flower spike of pink to lavender tubular flowers.

### HAIRY WOOD MINT    *Blephilia hirsuta*

Moist soils of deciduous forests, woodland edges, and flood-plains. ▶ Stem unbranched, very hairy. Leaves long stalked, oval, toothed, with pointed tips. Multiple whorls of white to lavender flowers with purple spots; whorls are covered with white hairs.

### GIANT YELLOW HYSSOP    *Agastache nepetoides*

Rich deciduous forests, open woods, and woodland borders. Of-ten in beech-maple forests. ▶ Large, egg-shaped, coarsely toothed leaves with long petioles. Tall spike of small, tubular, cream to pale yellow flowers.

### SELFHEAL or HEAL-ALL    *Prunella vulgaris*

Grows in many habitats, from dry to wet. Often found at the edges of mowed fields, trails, and parking lots. This mint is not aromatic. ▶ Thick spike of blue to violet flowers. Stem hairy. Smooth oval leaves with pointed tips, often edged with hair.

# MINT FAMILY FLOWERS

Wild
Bergamot

Spotted
Beebalm

Scarlet
Beebalm

Obedient
Plant

Hairy
Wood Mint

Giant
Yellow Hyssop

Selfheal

75

### NODDING ONION  *Allium cernuum*

Moist soils of prairie, savannas, wet meadows, and roadsides. Amaryllis family (Amaryllidaceae). ▶ Many slightly arching, narrow, light green basal leaves. Whitish to pinkish nodding umbel. All parts of plant emit an oniony odor when bruised.

### SPOTTED JOE-PYE-WEED  *Eutrochium maculatum*

Moist to wet soils of marshes, meadows, shores, blooming mid- to late summer. Aster family (Asteraceae). ▶ Stem *reddish* with long *purple streaks*. Whorls of 4–5 lance-shaped, toothed leaves. Large flat-topped flower head with clusters of pinkish flowers.

### WILD GERANIUM  *Geranium maculatum*

A spring wildflower often associated with moist deciduous forests. Cranesbill family (Geraniaceae). ▶ Long stalked basal leaves, each palmately divided. Clusters of pink to lavender, 5-petaled flowers. Fruit a long capsule (cranesbill) that, when dry, splits open and flings seeds.

### FIREWEED  *Chamerion angustifolium*

Dry fields, forests, roadsides, especially cleared edges. Colonizes burned areas. Evening-primrose family (Onagraceae). ▶ Long, lance-shaped, narrow leaves, often with a white central vein. Spike of rosy-pink to purple, 4-petaled flowers; behind each flower is a very long ovary, often mistaken for a flower stalk.

### PRAIRIE PHLOX  *Phlox pilosa*

Blooms late spring to early summer, primarily on dry prairie and savannas. Phlox family (Polemoniaceae). ▶ Hairy stem. Leaves opposite, narrow, often hairy, with no leaf stalk. Pink, tubular flowers, each with 5 flaring lobes. See Wild Blue Phlox (p. 80)

### PENNSYLVANIA SMARTWEED  *Persicaria pensylvanica*

Several smartweed species are common in the Midwest, mostly around wetlands and moist edges. Important as food for waterfowl. Buckwheat family (Polygonaceae). ▶ Stems often covered with small glandular hairs. Leaves with sheathed bases that ring the stem. Dense, erect spikes of small white to pinkish flowers.

### DEPTFORD PINK  *Dianthus armeria*

An introduced flower of dry, disturbed soils. Pink family (Caryophyllaceae). ▶ One to a few flowers at top of stalk; 5-petaled flowers, brilliant magenta with white dots and toothed petal tips.

### BOUNCING BET  *Saponaria officinalis*

An introduced perennial of disturbed soils, invasive in some areas. Also called Soapwort as its sap produces a soapy substance in water. Pink family. ▶ Leaves oval, opposite, with 3 obvious lateral veins; smaller leaves often grow at leaf pair axils. Cluster of tubular, white to pink flowers with 5 notched-tipped lobes.

Nodding
Onion

Spotted
Joe-Pye-weed

Fireweed

Wild Geranium

Pennsylvania
Smartweed

Prairie
Phlox

Deptford
Pink

Bouncing
Bet

# MILKWEEDS AND DOGBANES

This family (**Apocynaceae**) is mostly tropical, but the Midwest has about 20 native milkweed and 2 native dogbane species. Most milkweeds (genus *Asclepias*) have a milky latex sap, and all contain cardiac glycosides, toxic substances that confer some protection to insects that feed on the foliage and flowers. Predators consuming an insect that has fed on milkweed often get violently ill and learn not to eat that species again. Monarch butterflies (p. 336) are among those that benefit from this phenomenon. Flowers are small, usually five-parted floral structures fused into tubes. The showy flower heads are often flat-topped to rounded umbels. Fruit is a pod that contains wind-dispersed seeds.

### COMMON MILKWEED  *Asclepias syriaca*

Common and widespread in fields, woodland edges, disturbed soils. ► Long, wide leaves with a white to pink mid vein. Large, round clusters of light to dark pink, fragrant flowers emerge from upper leaf axils. Smooth to bumpy, long and wide green pods.

### SWAMP MILKWEED  *Asclepias incarnata*

This is our only milkweed found in wetland areas, often in saturated soils. ► Long, narrow, lance-shaped leaves. Umbel of *bright pink* flowers at top of stalk. Seedpods long and narrow.

### PURPLE MILKWEED  *Asclepias purpurascens*

Uncommon. Dry prairie edges, savannas. ► Similar to Common Milkweed but flower clusters *only at top*. Flowers vibrant, deep *purplish red*. Seedpods always *smooth*.

### CLASPING MILKWEED  *Asclepias amplexicaulis*

Uncommon. Dry, sandy soils of prairies, savannas, open woods. ► Leaves like those of Common Milkweed but with *noticeably wavy margins,* often clasping stem. Usually a single flower cluster.

### WHORLED MILKWEED  *Asclepias verticillata*

A short-statured milkweed of dry prairies, savannas, disturbed soils. ► Numerous whorls of 3–6 *very narrow* leaves. A few clusters of small umbels with white to greenish white flowers.

### GREEN MILKWEED  *Asclepias viridiflora*

Uncommon. Dry, sandy soils of dunes, prairies, fields. ► Stem can be erect or drooping. Leaves quite variable, depending on soil moisture. Dense, round umbels of *pale greenish* flowers.

### SPREADING DOGBANE  *Apocynum androsaemifolium*

Dry woodland edges, savannas, dunes, prairies. Colonizes burned areas. ► A few 5-parted, pinkish, bell-shaped flowers. Like most milkweeds, has toxic white sap. Narrow, long, reddish seedpods.

### HEMP DOGBANE  *Apocynum cannabinum*

Habitats like those of Spreading Dogbane, but also in wet soils. ► Clusters of small, white, bell-shaped flowers. Toxic white latex sap oozes out when foliage is bruised. Narrow reddish seedpods.

# MILKWEEDS AND DOGBANES

Swamp Milkweed

Purple Milkweed

Common Milkweed

Whorled Milkweed

Clasping Milkweed

Green Milkweed

Hemp Dogbane

Spreading Dogbane

## BLUE AND LAVENDER WOODLAND FLOWERS

All the species presented below are natives, except for a few introduced species among the many violets found in the Midwest.

### VIRGINIA BLUEBELLS  *Mertensia virginica*

An attractive spring-blooming ephemeral of rich, moist woods and shaded floodplains. The bloom period lasts less than a month. Borage, or forget-me-not, family (Boraginaceae). ▶ Leaves light green, oval, and droopy. *Hanging clusters* of *pinkish* flower buds and fully opened, trumpet-shaped *blue* flowers.

### VIRGINIA WATERLEAF  *Hydrophyllum virginianum*

Blooms in late spring to early summer in moist deciduous woods, savannas. Borage family. ▶ Leaves deeply divided (3–7 lobes) with coarse teeth. Upper surfaces of some leaves have whitish "stained" marks. Round, very hairy flower cluster. White to lavender flowers with noticeably protruding stamens.

### GREAT WATERLEAF  *Hydrophyllum appendiculatum*

Moist woodland habitats, ravines. Blooms late spring to early summer. Borage family. ▶ Very hairy stem. Leaves large, with 5–7 lobes, but not deeply divided; may suggest maple leaves. Flowers larger than those of Virginia Waterleaf but not as hairy.

### TALL BELLFLOWER  *Campanula americana*

A tall (to 6'), stunning wildflower of dry to moist deciduous forests; often on the edges of trails and fields. Blooms midsummer to early fall. Bellflower family (Campanulaceae). ▶ Toothed, oval leaves with long tips. Long spike of flowers at top of stalk with shorter secondary spikes often developing from leaf axils below. Flowers velvety blue, 5-lobed, with white ring at centers and a protruding, curving style.

### WILD BLUE PHLOX  *Phlox divaricata*

Very fragrant; a forest area filled with this wildflower in full bloom can offer quite an experience! Phlox family (Polemoniaceae). ▶ Flowers 5-parted, tubular, blue to violet. Petal tips may be notched or smoothly rounded. See Prairie Phlox (p. 76).

### HEPATICAS  *Hepatica sp.*

Early spring wildflowers of rich deciduous forests. Two species, sometimes lumped into one. Buttercup family (Ranunculaceae). ▶ Three-lobed basal leaves often overwinter. Hairy flower stalks hold a single flower each; flowers may be white, pink, or lavender. **Sharp-lobed Hepatica** (*H. acutiloba*) has very pointy leaf lobes; **Round-lobed Hepatica** (*H. americana*) has rounded leaf lobes.

### VIOLETS  *Viola sp.*

More than 30 species of violets (most native, a few introduced) occur in the Midwest. All are small and spring blooming; most are blue to purple, some are yellow or white. Violet family (Violaceae). ▶ Many have heart-shaped, toothed to scalloped leaves. Most have similar-looking flowers.

**80** WILDFLOWERS

Virginia
Bluebells

Virginia
Waterleaf

Great
Waterleaf

Tall
Bellflower

Wild
Blue
Phlox

hepatica sp.

violets
sp.

81

### PURPLE CONEFLOWER  *Echinacea purpurea*

A showy wildflower of prairies and savannas. Actually uncommon in the wild in most of the Midwest, but very popular in the nursery trade. Varietal forms sometimes "escape" from gardens or are planted along roadsides. Aster, or sunflower, family (Asteraceae). ▶ Wide lance-shaped leaves with evenly spaced teeth. Single flower head on a sturdy stalk. Light to bright pink ray florets with a center cone of brownish orange disk florets.

### PALE PURPLE CONEFLOWER  *Echinacea pallida*

More common than Purple Coneflower, especially in the southeastern part of our region, and blooms a few weeks earlier. Aster family. ▶ Similar to Purple Coneflower but with narrow, drooping ray flowers and narrow, hairy, smooth-edged leaves.

### CHICORY  *Cichorium intybus*

Introduced from Eurasia. Widespread and common in disturbed soils, such as roadsides, fields, prairie restorations. Not a problem species, as it is outcompeted by natives as a restored ecosystem starts to establish. Aster family. ▶ Flowering stalk of bright, light blue flower heads; each ray floret with a 4-notched tip.

### OHIO SPIDERWORT  *Tradescantia ohiensis*

Prairies, savannas, roadsides. Spiderwort family (Commelinaceae). ▶ Long, grasslike leaves wrap around stem. Cluster of 3-petaled lavender to violet flowers; stamens with yellow anthers.

### WILD LUPINE  *Lupinus perennis*

Stunning in full bloom. Exclusive larval food plant of endangered Karner Blue Butterfly (p. 330). Pea family (Fabaceae). ▶ Hairy-edged, palmate leaves with 7–11 leaflets. Spike of pea flowers in shades of white, blue, and purple.

### PURPLE PRAIRIE CLOVER  *Dalea purpurea*

Dry, sandy and rocky soils. Pea family. ▶ Compound leaves with 3–7 tiny leaflets. Long, thimble-shaped flower stalk densely packed with small, 5-petaled purple flowers; long stamens with orange anthers.

### GREAT BLUE LOBELIA  *Lobelia siphilitica*

Swamps, fens, wet meadows, floodplains. Bellflower family (Campanulaceae). ▶ Sessile (no leaf stalk) alternate leaves. Long spike of odd-shaped, tubular, light blue to violet flowers with an upper and lower lip.

### FRINGED GENTIANS  *Gentianopsis sp.*

Uncommon. Two species: **Fringed Gentian** *(G. crinita)* and **Lesser Fringed Gentian** *(G. virgata)*, both mainly found in calcareous soils. Gentian family (Gentianaceae). ▶ Upright flower at tip of stalk, blue to deep violet, tubular, with fringed lobes.

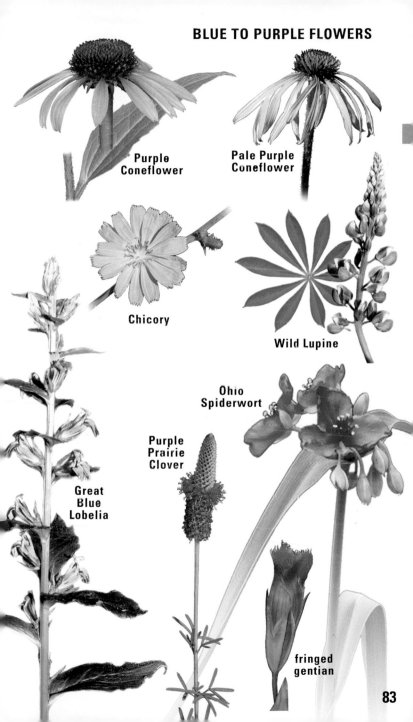

# BLUE TO PURPLE FLOWERS

Purple
Coneflower

Pale Purple
Coneflower

Chicory

Wild Lupine

Ohio
Spiderwort

Purple
Prairie
Clover

Great
Blue
Lobelia

fringed
gentian

### HOARY VERVAIN   *Verbena stricta*

Dry, sandy prairies, savannas, fields, disturbed edges. Verbena family (Verbenaceae). ► Square, hairy stems. Leaves opposite, wide, oval, coarsely toothed, hairy, and greenish gray. Long, thick flower spikes with large, 5-parted purple flowers.

### BLUE VERVAIN   *Verbena hastata*

Wet to saturated soils of meadows, prairies, floodplains, riparian corridors, and lake edges. The wetland counterpart to Hoary Vervain. Verbena family. ► Grows to 5'. Square green to reddish stems. Leaves opposite, lance-shaped, coarsely toothed. Small, 5-parted violet flowers on thin, branching spikes.

### SHOOTING STAR   *Dodecatheon meadia*

A late-spring-blooming wildflower primarily of dry to moist prairies and savannas. Primrose family (Primulaceae). ► Basal rosette of leaves (can be impressive on older plants), with one or more flower stalks emerging from center. Each stalk has a cluster of dangling, 5-parted flowers with petals swept back. Flower color ranges from white to pink to lavender.

### WILD FOUR-O'CLOCK   *Mirabilis nyctaginea*

Edges and disturbed soils. Likely native in western third of our region; considered introduced in Ohio, Michigan. Four-o'clock family (Nyctaginaceae). ► Leaves opposite, heart-shaped, with short leaf stalks. Cluster of magenta, 5-parted flowers.

### GLAUCOUS WHITE LETTUCE   *Prenanthes racemosa*

A unique-looking wildflower of calcareous fens, wet prairies, shores. Aster family (Asteraceae). ► Very hairy stems with nodding, hairy flower buds. Leaves clasping. Flowers (ray florets only) white to pale lavender, erect when open.

### JIMSONWEED   *Datura stramonium*

An introduced large, annual, bushy wildflower of disturbed soils. **Note:** this plant is toxic, causing potentially deadly, severe hallucinations. Nightshade family (Solanaceae). ► Thick, reddish stems. Large triangular to egg-shaped, lobed leaves with a few coarse teeth. Very showy, long, funnel-shaped, fluted, tubular flowers, varying from white to lavender. Inner surface often with purple center. Spiny seed capsule.

### CLOVERS   *Trifolium* sp.

Although the Midwest has a couple of rare native clovers of the genus *Trifolium,* we focus here on 2 (of the dozen or so) introduced legumes of lawns, fields, and disturbed ground. Pea family (Fabaceae). ► **White Clover** (*T. repens):* rounded, white flower heads. **Red Clover** (*T. pratense):* rounded, rosy flower heads. Both have compound leaves with (usually) 3 leaflets. These are the species famous for producing the occasional 4-leaf clover.

Hoary
Vervain

Blue
Vervain

Shooting
Star

Wild Four-o'clock

Glaucous
White Lettuce

Jimsonweed

White
Clover

Red
Clover

## ASTERS, BLAZING-STARS, AND IRONWEEDS

All in the aster, or sunflower, family **(Asteraceae)**. As described on p. 62, their flower heads can have ray florets, disk florets, or both. The first four below have both types of florets, while the last four have only disk florets.

### BIG-LEAVED ASTER    *Eurybia macrophylla*

An impressive woodland aster, blooming in late summer and fall. ▶ *Large, heart-shaped,* coarsely toothed basal leaves with long petioles (leaf stalks). Flower heads of violet ray florets and yellow disk florets (turn brownish red with age).

### FROST ASTER    *Symphyotrichum pilosum*

A common, weedy aster of fields, prairies, roadsides, and disturbed edges. ▶ Sturdy, many-branched stems often covered in fine, white hairs. Flower heads with 16–35 white ray florets, yellow centers (turn brownish red with age).

### NEW ENGLAND ASTER    *Symphyotrichum novae-angliae*

Moist, open areas of prairies, swamps, roadsides. Stunning in full bloom in late summer and fall. ▶ Stem often reddish and hairy. Leaves alternate, lance-shaped, clasping stem. Flower heads with over 40 narrow, pink-purple ray florets and yellow disk florets.

### SWAMP ASTER    *Symphyotrichum puniceum*

A gorgeous wetland aster, blooming mainly in fall in marshes, swamps, fens, sedge meadows, stream corridors. ▶ Bright red to purplish, hairy stems. Leaves alternate, lance-shaped, toothed, clasp stem. Large flower heads of 30–60 narrow, lavender to violet ray florets and yellow centers (turn reddish purple with age).

### ROUGH BLAZING-STAR    *Liatris aspera*

Dry, sandy prairies, savannas, roadsides. ▶ Leaves mainly basal, narrow, alternate, sometimes whorled. Tall (to 5') spikelike cluster of many purplish, short-stalked to stalkless flower heads with *rounded, spreading phyllaries* (bracts around floral receptacle).

### CYLINDRICAL BLAZING-STAR    *Liatris cylindracea*

A short-statured (to 2'), uncommon *Liatris* of dry, sandy prairies, savannas, dunes, fields. ▶ Many narrow, alternate leaves. Spikelike cluster of often only a few (up to 25) pink to purple, *long-stalked* flower heads with *sharp-tipped* phyllaries.

### PRAIRIE BLAZING-STAR    *Liatris pycnostachya*

Moist prairies, meadows, fields. ▶ Many narrow, alternate leaves. Single, tall (up to 5') spikelike cluster of small, densely packed, stalkless, purplish flower heads with reddish pink phyllaries.

### IRONWEEDS    *Vernonia* sp.

Ironweeds (about 7 species in the Midwest) bloom in late summer and fall in open areas, marsh edges, roadsides. ▶ Roughly flat-topped clusters of *purplish red* flower heads. Leaves alternate; shape varies. Compare to Spotted Joe-Pye-weed (p. 76).

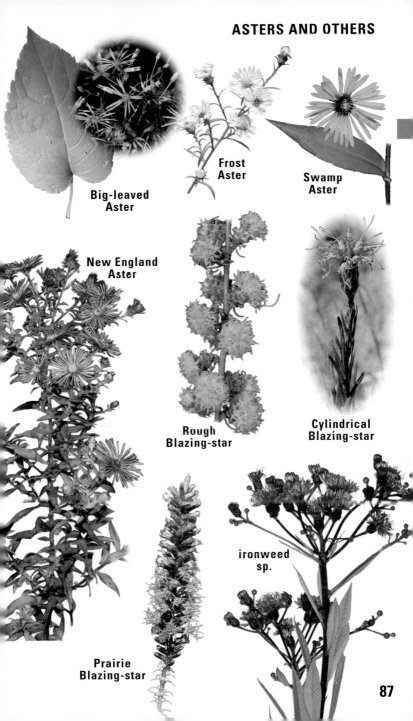

# ASTERS AND OTHERS

Big-leaved
Aster

Frost
Aster

Swamp
Aster

New England
Aster

Rough
Blazing-star

Cylindrical
Blazing-star

Prairie
Blazing-star

ironweed
sp.

### SKUNK CABBAGE   *Symplocarpus foetidus*

This native of wooded wetlands and forested streamsides is unique. Its odd flower can emerge as early as February, melting snow with the heat it generates. Its flowers emit a foul odor that attracts its pollinators — flies. Arum family (Araceae), plants with interesting floral structures: a spathe (large bract) surrounding a spadix (flower spike). ► A *large* green spathe (often streaked red) envelops a yellow to reddish spadix. Basal rosette of huge leaves that emerge after flowering.

### JACK-IN-THE-PULPIT   *Arisaema triphyllum*

A native of rich, moist deciduous forest, blooming spring to early summer. Arum family. ► One or 2 compound leaves, each with 3 leaflets. Greenish to reddish spadix stands in a *hooded, tubular spathe,* which may be streaked with red. Varies in size and color.

### WILD GINGER   *Asarum canadense*

A native of rich, moist woods, often on sloping terrain. Colonial grower. Bruised roots and stems emit gingerlike aroma. Pipevine family (Aristolochiaceae). ► Pair of *heart-shaped* leaves, fuzzy on the bottom. Single 3-part maroon flower near ground level.

### LATE FIGWORT   *Scrophularia marilandica*

A native of moist woods, savannas, floodplains, woodland edge. Figwort family (Scrophulariaceae). ► *Stems often squarish.* Leaves opposite with long stalks, toothed edges. Long, branched flower cluster (panicle) of small, maroon-green flowers.

### STINGING NETTLE   *Urtica dioica*

A wide-ranging native of disturbed areas of woodlands, marshes, swamps. Stem with sharp, hollow, *stinging hairs* that cause a burning sensation. Urtica nettle family (Urticaceae). ► Leaves opposite, lance-shaped, sharply toothed. Compact panicles of small, white to greenish flowers.

### COMMON RAGWEED   *Ambrosia artemisiifolia*

Our 2 common native ragweeds, wind-pollinated, bloom in late summer and fall, contributing to the hay fever often blamed on goldenrods. Aster family (Asteraceae). ► Finely divided leaves, small greenish yellow flowers.

### GIANT RAGWEED   *Ambrosia trifida*

► Larger than Common Ragweed (to 15') with *trident-shaped* leaves.

### ENGLISH PLANTAIN   *Plantago lanceolata*

A handful of native *Plantago* species occur in the Midwest; more familiar are 2 Eurasian introductions commonly found in lawns, vacant lots, and disturbed sites. Plantain family (Plantaginaceae). ► Basal rosette of *narrow* leaves, each with 3–5 veins; white flowers on short spikes.

### COMMON PLANTAIN   *Plantago major*

► Basal rosette of *broad, oval,* veined leaves; white flowers on long spikes.

# MAROON AND GREENISH FLOWERS

**Skunk Cabbage**

**Jack-in-the-pulpit**

**Late Figwort**

**Wild Ginger**

**Stinging Nettle**

**Common Ragweed**

**Giant Ragweed**

**English Plantain**

**Common Plantain**

# ORCHIDS

With 22,000 to 26,000 species worldwide, the orchid family (**Orchidaceae**) is one of the two largest families of flowering plants. The Midwest has about 70 species, most uncommon to rare. During seed germination, orchids are dependent on certain fungi. Orchids have minute seeds with very little stored energy. They rely on their fungal symbionts to provide practically all their nutrition until the orchid starts photosynthesizing. Most orchids will not survive transplanting, and some have hairs that can cause severe skin reactions. It's best to enjoy them where they're found.

### PINK LADY'S-SLIPPER    *Cypripedium acaule*

Generally uncommon in acid soils of woods and swamps. ▶ The lady's-slipper orchids have distinctive *pouchlike* flowers, *pink* in this species. Two oblong, many veined, clasping, basal leaves.

### YELLOW LADY'S-SLIPPER    *Cypripedium parviflorum*

Perhaps the most numerous of our orchids, but still rather uncommon. ▶ Pouchlike *yellow* flower; 3–6 oblong, clasping leaves. Several natural varieties differ mainly in flower size, sepal color.

### SHOWY LADY'S-SLIPPER    *Cypripedium reginae*

A stunning orchid of wet woods, bogs, fens, coniferous swamps. Blooms in early summer. ▶ Pouchlike *white and pink* flowers; 4–12 oblong, many veined, clasping leaves.

### GRASS-PINK ORCHID    *Calopogon tuberosus*

Bogs, coniferous swamps, wet meadows, fens. ▶ Single grasslike leaf. Small cluster of stalked, bright pink to purple flowers with irregular shape. Upper lip of flower a modified petal, triangular in shape and held above other petals.

### NODDING LADIES'-TRESSES    *Spiranthes cernua*

Moist, open areas of bogs, prairies, wet meadows, dune swales. Blooms late summer to early fall. ▶ A few grasslike basal leaves. Single, spiraling spike of pure white flowers.

### GIANT RATTLESNAKE PLANTAIN    *Goodyera oblongifolia*

Rare, in northern woods. ▶ Basal rosette of *dark green* leaves with *central white stripe*. Flower stalk a gentle spiral with white flowers. Leaves of other species have many white cross veins.

### LESSER PURPLE FRINGED ORCHID    *Platanthera psycodes*

Blooms late summer in meadows, marshes, streambanks, forest edges. ▶ Lower leaves oval, upper leaves lance-shaped. Spikelike cluster of lavender to purple flowers; 3 lower lobes *deeply fringed*.

### BROAD-LEAVED HELLEBORINE    *Epipactis helleborine*

Woodlands. As most orchids are uncommon, it might be surprising to learn that the Midwest has an introduced orchid species. Originally from Europe, it has become a problem in a few areas, listed as an invasive in Wisconsin. ▶ Spikelike stalk with *greenish pink* flowers. Leaves similar to those of lady's-slippers.

# ORCHIDS

Pink Lady's-slipper

Showy Lady's-slipper

Yellow Lady's-slipper

Grass-pink Orchid

Lesser Purple Fringed Orchid

Giant Rattlesnake Plantain

Nodding Ladies'-tresses

Broad-leaved Helleborine

91

Forest and grassland are widespread here, but the Midwest also has some amazing and localized habitats. From sand dunes to alkaline fens and acidic bogs, there are jewels to be discovered in these seemingly desolate places. Here are some native plants of these rare habitats.

### HAIRY PUCCOON  *Lithospermum caroliniense*

Spectacular in full bloom, adding color to its sparse dune habitat; occasionally in sandy savannas. Borage, or forget-me-not, family (Boraginaceae). ▶ Stem often covered in fine white hairs. Leaves alternate, narrow, with no stalk. Flat-topped cluster of tubular, 5-parted, yellowish orange flowers.

### BEACH WORMWOOD  *Artemisia campestris*

A biennial or perennial primarily of dunes and sandy beaches, but also dry savannas, fields, and prairies. Also called Field Sagewort. Aster family (Asteraceae). ▶ Basal rosette first year, followed by reddish stems with numerous feathery leaves. Branched flower cluster, often reddish, with many small greenish white flowers.

### SAND DUNE THISTLE  *Cirsium pitcheri*

A stunning thistle, federally listed as threatened, restricted to Great Lakes dune habitat. Aster family. ▶ Basal rosette of deeply divided, narrow, grayish green leaves, often spine-tipped. Rosette lasts 2–8 years, sending up a flower stalk in its final year with numerous creamy to light pinkish flower heads.

### SWAMP THISTLE  *Cirsium muticum*

A beautiful wetland thistle found mainly in fens, also swamps, sometimes bogs. Aster family. ▶ Stem with *rather few spines* for a thistle. Flower heads brilliant pinkish purple; greenish black phyllaries (bracts around floral receptacle) with whitish hair.

### GRASS-OF-PARNASSUS  *Parnassia glauca*

A short-statured wetland plant, primarily found in fens, but also meadows, bogs, and sandy shores. Bittersweet family (Celastraceae). ▶ Egg-shaped basal leaves. White, 5-petaled flower with intricate, undulating, green veining; 1 flower per stalk.

### NORTHERN PITCHER-PLANT  *Sarracenia purpurea*

A plant of acidic habitats such as bogs, tamarack swamps, peaty fens. Carnivorous, the plant lures insects and then traps them in its water-filled, pitcherlike leaves. Pitcher-plant family (Sarraceniaceae). ▶ Basal rosette of highly specialized leaves: tubular, the inside surface near the top lined with downward-pointing hairs. A single, nodding, reddish purple flower.

### SUNDEWS  *Drosera* sp.

Another carnivorous plant. Four species live in bogs or fens of the Midwest. Sundew family (Droseraceae). ▶ Small and inconspicuous. Glandular hairs on leaves secrete a sticky substance that traps insects. Uncurling flower stem with tiny white flowers.

# FLOWERS OF UNIQUE HABITATS

Hairy Puccoon

Sand Dune Thistle

Grass-of-Parnassus

Swamp Thistle

Beach Wormwood

sundew

Northern Pitcher-plant

93

# AQUATIC WILDFLOWERS

All of these native plants can be found in waters up to two feet deep. The first three are obligate aquatic plants, meaning their roots need to be submerged. The last five are found in aquatic conditions but also can be found in emergent conditions with shallow to subsurface water.

### AMERICAN WHITE WATER-LILY    *Nymphaea odorata*

Calm waters of lakes, ponds, protected inlets of rivers. Water-lily family (Nymphaeaceae). ▶ Floating, circular leaves with cleft on one side; leaf edges may turn up, revealing purplish undersides. Single, large (to 6" across), fragrant white flower, closing at night.

### YELLOW POND-LILY    *Nuphar lutea*

Lakes, ponds, streamsides. Water-lily family. ▶ Long, oval leaves with a cleft base; may lie flat on water's surface or stick up. *Spherical* yellow flower partly open by day, closes up at night.

### AMERICAN LOTUS    *Nelumbo lutea*

Uncommon, but can form large stands in ponds, marshes, and slow-moving waterways. Lotus family (Nelumbonaceae). Formerly placed in water-lily family, now known not to be a close relative. ▶ Large, round, concave leaves with stalk attached to leaf center. Large white to pale yellow flowers (to 9"), with a *raised yellow disk* at center, are held above water's surface.

### PICKERELWEED    *Pontederia cordata*

Shallow waters of ponds, swamps, marshes, riparian edges. Can form extensive patches. Water-hyacinth family (Pontederiaceae). ▶ *Arrowhead-shaped*, glossy leaves on long stalks. Flower spike with many brilliant, *bluish purple* flowers.

### COMMON ARROWHEAD    *Sagittaria latifolia*

Shallow waters of ponds, swamps, marshes, stream edges, flooded ditches. Water-plantain family (Alismataceae). ▶ Rosette of large leaves, with *arrowhead shape* even more pronounced than those of Pickerelweed. Stalk with whorls of 3-petaled white flowers.

### GIANT BUR-REED    *Sparganium eurycarpum*

Edges of lakes, swamps, open bogs, marshes, streamsides. Cattail family (Typhaceae). ▶ Tall bladelike leaves like those of cattails, spherical flowers. Fruit a macelike ball with many beaked nutlets.

### HALBERD-LEAVED ROSE MALLOW    *Hibiscus laevis*

In marshes, ponds, streamsides, this perennial is eye-catching in late summer. Mallow family (Malvaceae). ▶ Grows to 6' tall. *Showy flowers* (to 6" across), white to pink, with *column of yellow stamens* and often with red center. Distinctive *leaf shape*.

### SWAMP ROSE MALLOW    *Hibiscus moscheutos*

Another conspicuous perennial of submerged to wet soils in marshes and streamsides. Mallow family. ▶ Grows to 6'. Flowers like those of the preceding species. Large, *unlobed, oval* leaves.

# AQUATIC WILDFLOWERS

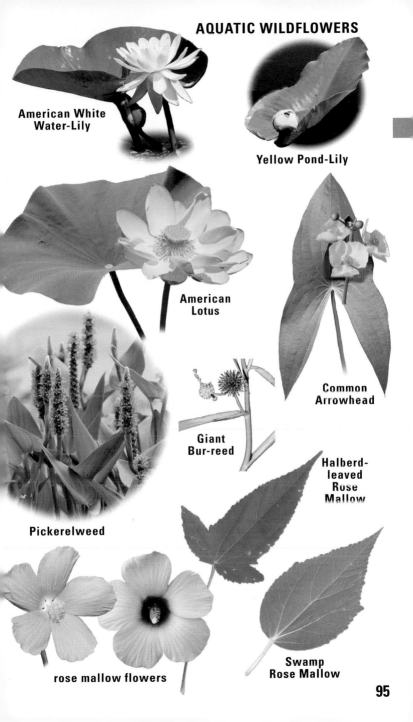

American White
Water-Lily

Yellow Pond-Lily

American
Lotus

Common
Arrowhead

Giant
Bur-reed

Halberd-
leaved
Rose
Mallow

Pickerelweed

rose mallow flowers

Swamp
Rose Mallow

95

These natives grow in very wet soil or shallow water.

### YELLOW MARSH MARIGOLD  *Caltha palustris*

A gorgeous spring wildflower of swamps, wooded stream channels, shorelines, and seeps. Buttercup family (Ranunculaceae). ▶ Leaves round to kidney-shaped; mainly basal. Bright yellow flowers with 5–9 petal-like sepals with distinct veining. Fruit a 5-parted curved capsule.

### LIZARD'S TAIL  *Saururus cernuus*

Stream and pond edges, swamps, floodplains, and seeps. A colonial spreader. Lizard's-tail family (Saururaceae). ▶ Alternate heart-shaped leaves with palmate venation (veins radiate from a central point at petiole base). Flower spike with whorls of small, white flowers. Flower stalk often white, bends at tip.

### MONKEY FLOWER  *Mimulus ringens*

Wet soils of open (sunny) swamps, marshes, ponds, swales, and ditches. Lopseed family (Phrymaceae). ▶ Square stem with pairs of opposite, clasping, toothed leaves. Irregular-shaped, tubular, violet to purple flowers, with 2 upper and 3 lower lips, on a long stalk; flower throat has white to yellowish patches.

### SOUTHERN BLUE FLAG IRIS  *Iris virginica*

Widespread and common in wetlands of the Midwest. Iris family (Iridaceae). ▶ Long, broad, arching basal leaves. Blue to violet flowers with 3 rising petals, 3 drooping sepals. Fruit an oblong, 3-parted capsule. Similar **Northern Blue Flag Iris** (*I. versicolor*) mainly in northern Midwest and ne. Ohio.

### SWAMP LOOSESTRIFE  *Decodon verticillatus*

Swamps, marshes, pond and lake edges, bogs. A woody perennial that may seem shrublike during the growing season. Loosestrife family (Lythraceae). ▶ Leaves opposite or in whorls of 3; arching stems with floating tips that root when they hit water. Whorls of magenta flowers with 4–7 frilly petals emerge from leaf axils.

### AMERICAN WATER-WILLOW  *Justicia americana*

Muddy soils of pond and stream edges, marshes, swamps. Can be an aggressive colonial spreader. Acanthus family (Acanthaceae). ▶ Long, narrow, opposite leaves. Long flower stalks emerge from leaf axils, holding clusters of a few irregular, short, tubular white flowers streaked with purple.

### CATTAILS  *Typha* sp.

These familiar plants form extensive stands in marshes, ponds, flooded ditches. Cattail family (Typhaceae). ▶ Tall bladelike leaves; stem with brown "sausage" of pistillate flowers. **Broad-leaved Cattail** (*T. latifolia):* native; wider (up to 1") bluish green leaves. **Narrow-leaved Cattail** (*T. angustifolia):* introduced; narrow (½" or less) green leaves. Hybrids also occur.

# EMERGENT WETLAND WILDFLOWERS

Yellow Marsh Marigold

Lizard's Tail

Southorn Blue Flag Iris

Monkey Flower

Swamp Loosestrife

American Water-willow

cattail

97

Roughly 4,500 species of plants live in the wilds of the Midwest. A little more than a quarter of them are nonnative, introduced here from other regions or other continents. But being nonnative is not necessarily an issue. Only when an introduced species starts spreading aggressively and outcompeting the natives is it termed invasive. Each of these species is officially listed as invasive in one or more midwestern states.

### PURPLE LOOSESTRIFE    *Lythrum salicaria*
Lake and riparian shorelines, marshes, wet ditches. Stunning when it carpets a marsh in full bloom, but this plant has become a major problem, outcompeting native species. Loosestrife family (Lythraceae). ▶ Square, hairy stem. Leaves lance-shaped, smooth edged, and in opposite pairs or whorls of 3–4. Dense flower spike of magenta to purple flowers.

### SPOTTED KNAPWEED    *Centaurea stoebe*
Dry fields, roadsides, disturbed sites. Sometimes called Michigan Star Thistle, but not native to this continent. Aster family (Asteraceae). ▶ Pink to purple thistle-like flower heads with *brown to black-tipped bracts*.

### CANADA THISTLE    *Cirsium arvense*
Edges, fields, roadsides. An aggressive colonial spreader. Despite the name, native to Europe. Aster family. ▶ Leaves wavy margined, lobed, spine-tipped. *Many small* pink to lavender flower heads with spineless bracts.

### BULL THISTLE    *Cirsium vulgare*
Dry fields, disturbed edges. Aster family. ▶ Spiny stem and leaves. Leaves hairy with 3 or more narrow lobes. *Large* magenta to purple flower heads with sharp, spiny bracts.

### TEASELS    *Dipsacus* sp.
Common in disturbed soils, sometimes taking over entire fields. Honeysuckle family (Caprifoliaceae). ▶ Paired leaves clasp or surround stem. Thistle-like, soft spiny heads with numerous small flowers. **Cut-leaf Teasel** (*D. laciniatus*) has white flowers. **Fuller's Teasel** (*D. fullonum*) has lavender flowers. Brown, dried flower heads persist through winter.

### SWEET CLOVER    *Melilotus officinalis*
Fields, roadsides. Flowers may be yellow or white; some authorities recognize 2 species: **Yellow Sweet Clover** (*M. officinalis*) and **White Sweet Clover** (*M. albus*). Pea family (Fabaceae). ▶ Leaves with 3 leaflets. Pealike flowers on narrow spikes. Yellow form blooms earlier than white.

### BIRD'S-FOOT TREFOIL    *Lotus corniculatus*
Forms patches in roadsides, fields. Originally introduced from Eurasia as a forage crop; escaped into the wild. Pea family. ▶ *Small.* Cloverlike leaves and clusters of bright yellow, pealike flowers.

### GARLIC MUSTARD    *Alliaria petiolata*
An aggressive spreader in woodlands, shaded edges; may monopolize large areas. Mustard family (Brassicaceae). ▶ Triangular to rounded, toothed leaves. Small 4-petaled flowers in round cluster at top of stalk; *thin* seedpods.

# INVASIVE WILDFLOWERS

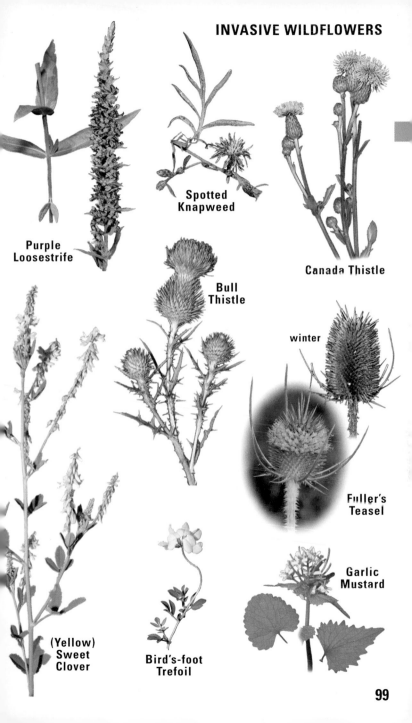

Purple Loosestrife

Spotted Knapweed

Canada Thistle

Bull Thistle

winter

Fuller's Teasel

(Yellow) Sweet Clover

Bird's-foot Trefoil

Garlic Mustard

A few more nonnatives that have become problems in some areas.

### QUEEN ANNE'S LACE  *Daucus carota*

Often abundant in dry fields, roadsides, vacant lots, disturbed soils. The edible garden-variety carrot originally was bred from this inedible wild species, hence its other common name, Wild Carrot. Carrot, or parsley, family (Apiaceae). ▶ Lacelike compound leaves. Flat-topped umbel of tiny white flowers; central umbel often with a *single dark purple flower.* Very showy bracts at base of umbel.

### WILD PARSNIP  *Pastinaca sativa*

Dry to moist fields, roadsides, open forests. The wild form of the cultivated root vegetable. Although not poisonous, it is inedible, and parts of plant can cause phototoxicity in some people. Carrot family. ▶ Compound leaves with 3–15 oval, cleft, coarsely toothed leaflets. Flat-topped umbel of *tiny yellow flowers.*

### POISON HEMLOCK  *Conium maculatum*

A tall (to 8') biennial of disturbed sites. Avoid bruising foliage as juices are deadly poisonous if ingested. Carrot family. ▶ Light green stem with *purple splotches.* Large (about a foot), triangular, multiply-compound leaves (2 to 3 times compound). Many flat-topped umbels of tiny white flowers.

### DAME'S ROCKET  *Hesperis matronalis*

Common in moist fields, roadsides, forest openings. Mustard family (Brassicaceae). ▶ Sharp-tipped, alternate, toothed leaves. Panicle (branched flower cluster) of 4-petaled, white to purple flowers with yellow stamens.

### MOTHERWORT  *Leonurus cardiaca*

Dry to moist roadsides, forest edges, open floodplains, and open woods. Mint family (Lamiaceae). ▶ Square stem. Leaves *trident-shaped,* opposite. Whorls of whitish lavender flowers emerge from the leaf axils.

### YELLOW IRIS  *Iris pseudacorus*

Pond edges, marshes, streamsides. A beautiful wildflower that is causing issues in some habitats. Iris family (Iridaceae). ▶ Leaves sword-shaped, often rising above flower stalk. Large (to 4" across) bright yellow flowers.

### JAPANESE KNOTWEED  *Fallopia japonica*

Roadsides, open woods, streamsides. This escapee from cultivation is quickly becoming a major problem. Sometimes marketed as Japanese or Mexican Bamboo, but it is an herbaceous perennial, while bamboo is a grass. Buckwheat family (Polygonaceae). ▶ Fast-growing, *bamboolike,* reddish brown stems. Alternate, egg-shaped, smooth-margined leaves. Panicle of small, creamy white to greenish flowers.

### ORANGE DAYLILY  *Hemerocallis fulva*

Roadsides and woodland edges. Quickly spreads by rhizomes, forming dense colonies. Aloe family (Xanthorrhoeaceae). ▶ Long, swordlike leaves. Panicle of 3–9 *brilliant orange, upright, lilylike flowers* on a sturdy, long stalk; each flower lasts a single day.

# INVASIVE WILDFLOWERS

Queen Anne's Lace

Wild Parsnip

Poison Hemlock

Dame's Rocket

Motherwort

Yellow Iris

Japanese Knotweed

Orange Daylily

101

# GRASSES, RUSHES, AND SEDGES

The Midwest has an amazing diversity of ecosystem types. What sets this region apart from many of the other regions in the country is its once diverse and extensive grassland ecosystem. In this section, we focus on a few families in the **order Poales,** specifically the grasses, rushes, and sedges. Before delving into the specifics of these grass and grasslike families, let's look at the treasure that once was the tall-grass prairie.

**Taming of the prairie.** In its prime, the tall-grass prairie biome was the most biodiverse ecosystem in the Midwest. It may also have been North America's largest contiguous ecosystem. It occurred in parts of 21 states and 2 Canadian provinces. Ranging from south-central Manitoba to southeastern Texas, and from central Indiana to eastern Nebraska, it conservatively covered 170 million acres — although some estimates place the total closer to 240 million acres.

A finger of tall-grass prairie poked up into southwestern Michigan, tenuously reaching into the Lake Erie peninsular region of Ontario. Small pockets of tall-grass prairie — remnants from an earlier post-glacial time — even punctuated the landscape in Ohio, Kentucky, Tennessee, Arkansas, Louisiana, Mississippi, and Alabama.

The arrival of nonnative peoples with their plows, saws, cattle, and desire to tame the land had an immense and seemingly sudden impact on the region's landscape and ecosystems. In fewer than 80 years (starting in the late 1830s), what had taken thousands of years to evolve and develop was literally plowed under and converted to agriculture and pasture. The vast, rich, and highly diverse tall-grass prairie was reduced to about 2 percent of its original acreage.

In the Midwest, the statistics are more shocking. The tall-grass prairie once covered almost 30 percent of this region. Today, less than one-tenth of one percent of the tall-grass prairie remains in the Midwest. The few prairie and savanna remnants that still exist provide critical habitat for some of this region's rarest plants and animals.

**Those amber waves of nonnative grain.** One might think that the expansive grasslands of the Midwest are gone, plowed out of existence long ago. Grasslands still exist — but whereas they used to be a vibrant, diverse community of myriad native species, they are now represented by just a few introduced species of grass: corn, wheat, barley, oats, and other grains. Almost all of the Midwest's native grasslands have been replaced by monotypic stands of nonnative grasses, in either agricultural fields or lawns.

## MEET THE GRASSES

**Grasses (family Poaceae)** are represented by about 12,000 species worldwide, making this the fifth largest of all plant families. As this family includes corn, rice, wheat, barley, oats, and other grains, it is the most economically important plant family as well. In the Midwest, there are about 400 species representing the family.

Grasses have nodes (swollen joints) on their stems (culms). Their stems are hollow and usually round. The part of the leaf (blade) that attaches to the stem and wraps around it is called the sheath. In most grass species, the sheath is partly open, meaning it is not joined or closed at the edge.

**General categories of grasses.** Grasses are often categorized by two different growth habits. The first is whether they are cool-season or warm-season grasses. The second is whether they are primarily sod-forming or clump-forming grasses.

Cool-season grasses tend to grow in spring and fall when the soil temperatures are relatively cool. Their growth slows in mid- to late summer as soil temperatures increase, and they may go dormant when conditions get too hot and dry. Warm-season grasses break dormancy in late spring as soil temperatures increase. They are most productive during the summer months.

Sod-forming species can form dense monotypic stands, spreading by lateral stems that run on top of the soil (stolons) or beneath the surface (rhizomes). The thick-rooted mats of grass roots and soil were used by early prairie homesteaders to construct sod houses. Clump-forming grasses, called bunchgrasses, tend to spread via seed and punctuate the landscape with clumps of growth. This latter growth form allows for a greater diversity of plants in a community as other species can colonize the areas in between the clumps. Some species can exhibit either the sod-forming or the clump-forming growth pattern, depending on local growing conditions.

## MEET THE RUSHES AND SEDGES

**Rushes (family Juncaceae)** are represented by about 400 species worldwide, with 50 members in the Midwest. **Sedges (family Cyperaceae)** are represented by about 5,500 species worldwide, with about 360 members in the Midwest.

Unlike grasses, both rushes and sedges lack nodes and their stems are solid. Also, their leaf sheaths tend to be closed. Rushes typically have round stems, while sedges have triangular stems. Whereas some grass species have showy flowers, many of the rushes and sedges have inconspicuous flowers. Like the grasses, though, their seed heads are often very obvious and interesting.

Identifying the true sedges (genus *Carex*) down to the species level can be fraught with challenges, often requiring a hand lens or even a stereo microscope. As a result, this group of plants is often overlooked — on purpose — by naturalists and even some botanists. Sedges are to botanists what flycatchers are to birders. With a little work, determination, and observation, many of the difficulties of identification can be overcome and a new world of wonder and enjoyment discovered.

# GRASSES OF PRAIRIE AND SAVANNA

These are all warm-season perennials, blooming in midsummer to early fall. The first four are sometimes referred to as the "Big Four" native grasses. They provided the foundation to the tall-grass prairie ecosystem that once covered vast stretches of the Central Plains and Midwest. The last four species are more drought tolerant than the first three.

### BIG BLUESTEM GRASS    *Andropogon gerardii*

Historically the predominant grass of the tall-grass prairie region, now primarily relegated to prairie and savanna remnants, railroad rights-of-way, roadsides. This deep-rooted grass can reach heights of 4–10' (rarely 12'). Often considered a bunchgrass, it's actually a sod-forming species that sometimes can form dense stands. ▶ Also called turkeyfoot for its 3-spiked (sometimes 4 or 5) inflorescence, looking somewhat like a bird's foot.

### INDIAN GRASS    *Sorghastrum nutans*

A historically dominant grass of tall-grass prairie, also mainly relegated to remnant patches. Reaches heights of 3–7'. Although referred to as a bunchgrass, it's a sod-forming species, in dense colonies in ideal conditions. ▶ In bloom its upright clumps with distinctive, golden brown inflorescence make it easy to identify.

### SWITCH GRASS    *Panicum virgatum*

Another characteristic grass of tall-grass prairie. Adapted to a variety of soils; reaches heights of 3–8'. Primarily a sod-forming grass, it can form dense stands. ▶ It produces an upright, multi-branched, open and airy inflorescence of up to 2' in height.

### LITTLE BLUESTEM GRASS    *Schizachyrium scoparium*

Adapted to a variety of soils in moist to dry habitats, this bunchgrass reaches heights of 2–3' (rarely 5'). ▶ Pairs of reddish brown to purplish bronze florets occur on alternate sides of each spikelet, maturing into fuzzy, white-haired seed heads.

### SIDE-OATS GRAMA    *Bouteloua curtipendula*

In full sun and sandy, drier soils, this sod-forming grass reaches heights of 1½–2' (sometimes 3'). It can tolerate light shade. ▶ Distinctive oatlike spikelets tend to hang from one side.

### PRAIRIE DROPSEED    *Sporobolus heterolepis*

An impressive clump-forming grass. Mature dense hummocks have numerous long, narrow leaves. Reaches heights of 3–4' in bloom. ▶ Wispy, numerous flower heads produce an interesting odor (suggesting cilantro) and round, black seeds.

### PURPLETOP    *Tridens flavus*

A bunchgrass most likely to be found in partly shaded to open, disturbed areas. Reaches heights of 3–5' (rarely 6'). ▶ Similar to Switch Grass but deep red to maroon color and densely packed spikelets make it hard to mistake.

# GRASSES OF PRAIRIE AND SAVANNA

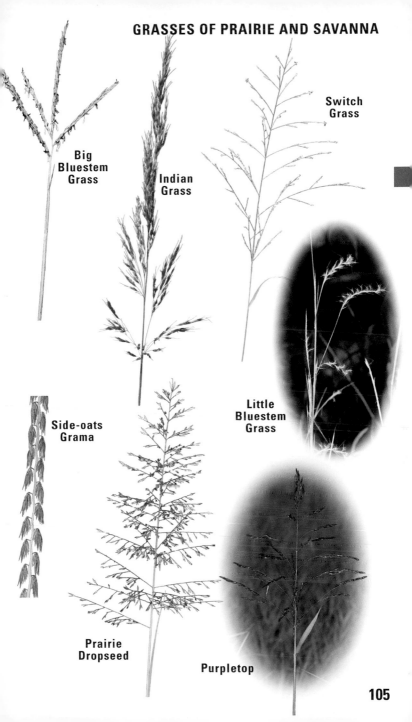

Big Bluestem Grass

Indian Grass

Switch Grass

Little Bluestem Grass

Side-oats Grama

Prairie Dropseed

Purpletop

# GRASSES OF PRAIRIE, SAVANNA, AND BEACH

The first two species are sod-forming grasses. As grasses that colonize sand dunes, they have exceptional drought tolerance — a required trait in such a desiccating environment. All the species below, except for Sand Reed, are cool-season perennials.

### AMERICAN BEACHGRASS    *Ammophila breviligulata*

Normally associated with the beaches of the Atlantic coast, this species is also found on dunes in our region; reaches heights of 2–4'. As one of the first species to colonize dunal areas, it is arguably the most important plant that slows down blowing sand and stabilizes shifting dunes. ▶ Its long, plumelike flower head and its thin, upright leaves make it easy to identify.

### SAND REED    *Calamovilfa longifolia*

Unlike other species on this page, Sand Reed is a warm-season perennial grass. It reaches heights of 2–6'. It's found on sand dunes and beaches, and occasionally farther inland — from the dry soils of sand and hill prairies, to savannas, and even Jack Pine forests. ▶ Stem with 3–12 alternating, thin, greenish gray leaves and an airy flower head.

### JUNE GRASS    *Koeleria pyramidata*

A bunchgrass more likely to be found in high-quality habitats, June Grass reaches heights of 1–2'. It forms a dense, compact tuft of grayish green vegetation with the overall diameter of the mound rarely exceeding 6". ▶ Spikelike flower heads, 2–6" long, turn tannish brown when mature, opening up to reveal a more plumelike, fluffy seed head.

### BOTTLEBRUSH GRASS    *Elymus hystrix*

A bunchgrass that grows 2½–4'. This is a grass of dry to moist soils that can tolerate full sun but prefers partial to full shade. Widespread and rather common in sandy, loamy, or rocky savannas, woodlands, riverbanks, and even deciduous and mixed forests. ▶ Its attractive, distinct, bottlebrush-like seed head is hard to mistake.

### CANADA WILD RYE    *Elymus canadensis*

A bunchgrass growing in full sun to partially shaded habitats; reaches heights of 3–6'. It is quick to establish but individual plants are not typically long lived. ▶ In early summer produces a wheatlike, drooping flower spike that is 4–8" in length with long, wispy awns that curve outward.

### PORCUPINE GRASS    *Hesperostipa spartea*  (not shown)

Found in dry to mesic, sandy to gravelly prairies and savannas, this bunchgrass reaches heights of 2–4'. The stems are erect, gradually arching as they grow taller and produce distinctive flower heads. ▶ The awns (hairlike or bristlelike extensions of the flower head) are amazingly long (4–8"), razor-sharp and barb-tipped.

# GRASSES OF PRAIRIE, SAVANNA, AND BEACH

American
Beachgrass

Sand
Reed

June
Grass

Bottlebrush
Grass

Canada
Wild Rye

# GRASSES OF WETLANDS AND WOODLANDS

With the exception of the two species of wild rice, which are annuals, all the species below are perennials. The first three species are cool-season bunchgrasses and the next two are sod-forming grasses.

### AMERICAN BEAK GRASS    *Diarrhena americana*

Found in moist, loamy soils in shaded woodlands, floodplains, wooded slopes; reaches heights of 2–3'. In optimal conditions, can form dense colonies. ▶ Flowering stem has alternating medium-wide, shiny leaves up to 2' long. Initially erect, the stem *bends* under the weight of the *large, swollen seed heads*. The similar *D. obovata* occurs in central and northern parts of region.

### WOODOATS    *Chasmanthium latifolium*

Growing in alluvial plains, wet meadows, stream and river-banks, and forest floodplains, this grass is primarily distributed throughout the southern portion of the Midwest. Most likely to be found in partial to full shade; reaches 2–4' in height. ▶ Clusters of *flattened, oatlike spikelets* form on arching stems and dangle gracefully from slender stalks.

### FOWL MANNA GRASS    *Glyceria striata*

Common throughout river, lake, and pond shores, as well as in fens, swales, and wet woodlands, this 2–3½' tall grass thrives in saturated, loamy soil in full to partial sun. ▶ Each erect stem has five or six 12" long, alternating, greenish blue leaves. Flowering stems produce a drooping, foot-long flower head with numerous small spikelets.

### BLUE JOINT GRASS    *Calamagrostis canadensis*

A cool-season grass of full to partial sun, reaching heights of 2–5'. Adapted to a wide range of soil types, it prefers moist to wet conditions. Habitats include wet prairies, sedge meadows, fens, bogs, and wet depressions on railroad rights-of-way. ▶ Swollen olive to bluish colored stem nodes. Flower heads purplish, upright, turn tan and droop when mature.

### PRAIRIE CORD GRASS    *Spartina pectinata*

A warm-season grass, dominant in wet zones of the tall-grass prairie. Reaches heights of 4–8'. Can be found in wet prairies, meadows, pond edges, and ditches. ▶ Widely spaced, coarse, comblike flower spikes held high above leaves on rigid stems.

### WILD RICE    *Zizania aquatica* and *Z. palustris*

Grains of these emergent aquatic grasses are considered a delicacy by people, and eaten by other animals as well. They reach heights of 5–10' and grow in slow-moving bodies of water (rivers, ponds, and marshes) with silty or mucky substrates. Bloom in mid- to late summer. ▶ Flower head up to 2' tall and a foot across. Stiff, upright leaves 3–5' long and 2" wide. Mature seeds are linear, up to an inch long, and wrapped by a husk with a long awn.

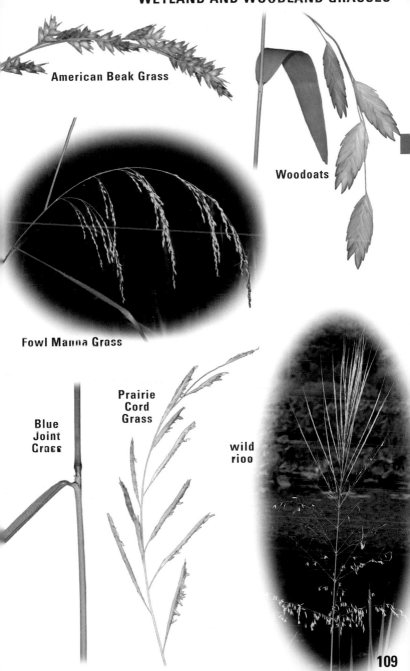

American Beak Grass

Woodoats

Fowl Manna Grass

Blue
Joint
Grass

Prairie
Cord
Grass

wild
rioo

## SEDGES AND RUSHES

Two often-overlooked plant families are the sedges (Cyperaceae) and rushes (Juncaceae). While they might look like grasses, they are not the same; differences among these families are covered on pp. 102–103. The first six below are in the sedge family, while the last is a rush.

### TRUE SEDGES    *Carex* sp.

The genus *Carex* contains the true sedges. There are over 230 species in the Midwest, all of them perennial. **Brown Fox Sedge** (*Carex vulpinoidea*) is one of the most widespread and abundant in the region. Sedges grow in a wide variety of habitats, from dry soils to year-round inundated soils. Some need only full sun, others full shade. ▶ The majority of sedges have obvious *triangular stems*, a feature best seen in cross section.

### SPIKE RUSHES    *Eleocharis* sp.

Members of the sedge family, but not true sedges, these wetland annuals reach heights of 1–2' (rarely taller). Preferring full sun, they grow in a variety of wetland types. ▶ Produce a distinct egg-shaped, scaly flower head reminiscent of a tiny pine cone.

### COTTON GRASSES    *Eriophorum* sp.

Despite the common name, these are not grasses. Growing 1–3' in height, cotton grass is restricted to acidic habitats (bogs, conifer swamps) and calcareous habitats (fens). More common at northern latitudes, becoming very common in tundra regions of the Arctic. ▶ Slender leaves and *fluffy, cottonlike seed heads*.

### HARD-STEMMED BULRUSH    *Schoenoplectus acutus*

An erect, emergent wetland plant. Despite common name, members of this genus are not rushes. Grows in waters up to 3' deep, reaching heights of 3–8' (sometimes 10'). ▶ *Round*, firm-feeling, olive-green stems. Long-stalked, oval to oblong clusters of grayish brown spikelets emerge near top of stem.

### CHAIRMAKER'S RUSH    *Schoenoplectus pungens*

This bulrush grows in muddy to sandy wetland soils in up to 3' of water. It can be 2–5' tall. ▶ Bluish green, firm-edged, *triangular* stems with a tight spikelet cluster emerging near top.

### WOOL GRASS    *Scirpus cyperinus*

Reaching heights of 3–5' (rarely 6'), this clump-forming perennial grows in saturated to moist soils. ▶ Numerous spikelets emerge at top of round, sometimes bluntly triangular, rigid stems. They droop on thin stalks, turning fuzzy and reddish brown.

### TORREY'S RUSH    *Juncus torreyi*

Although a few species above have "rush" in their common name, true rushes are in the genus *Juncus*. Growing in moist to wet soils in full to part sun, it reaches heights of 1–3'. ▶ Dense, spherical, spiky seed heads emerge at the tip of the stem.

# SEDGES AND RUSHES

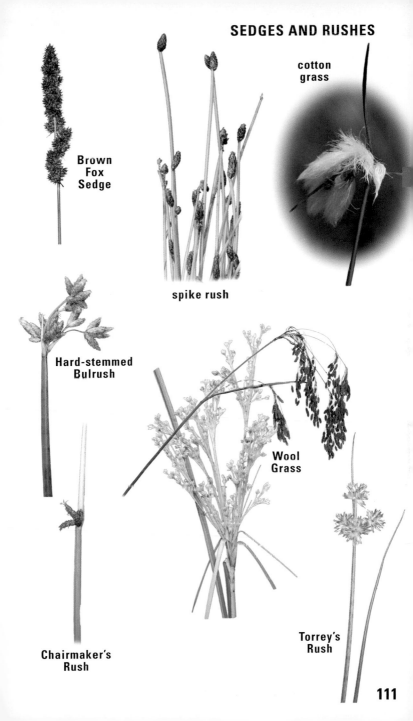

Brown Fox Sedge

cotton grass

spike rush

Hard-stemmed Bulrush

Wool Grass

Chairmaker's Rush

Torrey's Rush

# NONNATIVE, INVASIVE GRASSES

This final spread deals with introduced grasses that have become problematic or invasive. The first two are not as aggressive or disruptive as the last two. As grasses are foundational organisms in many ecosystems, when an invasive grass becomes established, it can have a negative impact on a whole community of native plants and animals. Each of these species is officially listed as invasive in one or more Midwestern states.

### GIANT FOXTAIL    *Setaria faberi*

In disturbed soils of meadows, agricultural fields, railroad rights-of-way, recently burned prairies, open woodlands, and even banks of lakes, ponds, rivers, and streams, this warm-season annual reaches heights of 2–4' (sometimes 6'). Introduced in the 1920s from China, it has become well established on the East Coast and in the Midwest, and is spreading westward. ▶ Distinctive, arching, bristly but soft seed head up to 7" long.

### TIMOTHY    *Phleum pratense*

A short-lived, perennial, cool-season bunchgrass with shallow roots, it reaches heights of 2–3½'. Introduced from Eurasia in the early 1700s, it's planted in some states for hay, forage, or silage. Grows in full to part sun in rich, moist soils. More likely to occur in disturbed areas, but it can spread via seed into natural communities. ▶ Dense, narrow, cylindrical flower heads and a bulbous stem base.

### REED CANARY GRASS    *Phalaris arundinacea*

A cool-season, sod-forming perennial, this highly aggressive invasive grass reaches heights of 2–5'. Historically native to North America and Eurasia, but nonnative strains (genotypes) were introduced into North America in the mid-1800s. These strains crossed with our native strains, eventually producing a hybrid strain that has become a pernicious invader of wetlands, stream and lake banks, and wet prairies. For this reason, we list it as a nonnative grass. ▶ Dense cluster of greenish purple flowers; when seeds mature, seed head opens up and turns tan.

### COMMON REED    *Phragmites australis*

Growing in marshes, stream and lake banks, wet ditches, wet prairies, and along roadsides, this invasive reaches heights of more than 15'. As with the previous species, there are native and nonnative subspecies. Although native populations remain, they are being replaced by their more aggressive nonnative cousins. Spreading primarily via vegetative growth, the invasive strain quickly takes over, forming dense, almost impenetrable, monotypic stands. In some areas, managing wetlands for wildlife has turned into a constant fight against *Phragmites*. ▶ Long, wide (2½"), bluish green leaves, tan stems, and a plumelike, reddish purple flower head up to 18" long.

Giant Foxtail

Timothy

Reed
Canary
Grass

Common
Reed

# TREES AND LARGE SHRUBS

Although grasslands are a defining characteristic of the Midwest, the forests here are rich and diverse as well. The eastern and central parts of the region have their oak-hickory and beech-maple forests. The middle and upper latitudes of Michigan, Wisconsin, and Minnesota have their jack pine, white pine, aspen-birch, and mesic northern hardwood forests. The region's uppermost latitudes have upland boreal conifer and lowland conifer swamp forests. In the western parts of the region, oak savannas — a unique grassland-hardwood mix — are dominant. Finally, in extreme southwestern Indiana and southern Illinois, the northernmost edge of the cypress-tupelo and cypress-cottonwood swamps can be found. In this section, we look at some of the trees and large shrubs that add to the diversity of plant life in the Midwest.

**What is a tree? What is a shrub? What is a vine?** Trees and shrubs are woody, perennial plants. Vines can be woody or herbaceous (die back to the ground each fall). In general, shrubs are multistemmed plants, whereas trees often have a single trunk. Shrubs usually grow no taller than 25 feet but trees can grow much taller. There are exceptions. Some shrubs have single stems; some trees have multiple trunks or do not grow much taller than 20 feet. In this guide, we've arbitrarily considered shrubs growing no taller than 8 feet as small shrubs (see Small Shrubs and Vines, pp. 154–165).

**Identifying trees** is a valuable exercise for anyone interested in nature. Habitat types are often defined by their dominant trees.

**Leaf size, shape, and type** are important, but be sure that you're looking at the whole leaf! Some trees have compound leaves, with multiple leaflets attached to a central stalk. If you're not sure whether you're looking at a whole leaf or at one leaflet of a compound leaf, check its base. Where a leaf stalk attaches to a twig, typically there's a small bud and a small structure called a stipule. Where a leaflet attaches to a central stalk, there's no bud or stipule. With a little practice, it's easy to tell the difference.

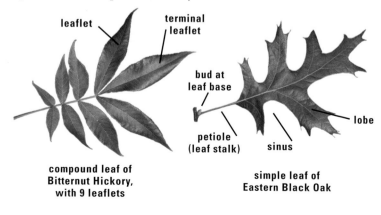

leaflet

terminal leaflet

bud at leaf base

lobe

petiole (leaf stalk)

sinus

compound leaf of Bitternut Hickory, with 9 leaflets

simple leaf of Eastern Black Oak

There is often a lot of variation in leaf shape. For instance, oaks (pp. 120–123) are known for leaf shape variability — between individuals of the same species and even on the same individual tree. The leaves that experience more sunlight (near the crown or branch tips) often have more pronounced lobes and deeper sinuses. Therefore checking more than one leaf, and choosing leaves from different parts of the tree, is often necessary.

On coniferous trees, the leaves are modified into needles or scales. It's still important to note their shape, their length, their number, and how they're attached to the twigs.

**Bark features** can be useful in determining a species. The bark pattern of some species is so unique, it can be enough to identify a species. Sycamore (p. 134) and birches (p. 124) have very distinctive bark patterns.

Some species have lenticels, specialized plant tissues in the surface of the bark that function as pores. They appear as cutlike marks, or scars, on the bark's surface and vary from round to elliptical in shape depending on species. They often change with the age and size of a plant.

**Flowers and fruit** can be very useful for identifying trees and shrubs. Most species have inconspicuous, short-lived flowers, but some have large and showy ones. What a botanist calls a fruit is the seed-bearing structure of the plant — think of berries, cones, nuts, kernels, grains, and more.

**Influence of geography.** Growth habit and height are often affected by habitat and local climate. The sizes of trees and shrubs can be much different in the central parts of their range than at the extreme ends of their range. As an example, Bur Oak (p. 122) tends to be noticeably shorter toward its eastern, northern, and western limits. But since the range of the species extends beyond the Midwest in all directions, our whole region could be considered to lie within the central part of its range.

**Pollination.** Unlike the spore-producing plants (pp. 166–175), plants that produce seeds do not require the direct assistance of water in fertilization. But there are differences in how they get pollinated. In the conifers and other gymnosperms (pp. 116–119), pollination is assisted by the wind. In the angiosperms, pollination may be wind assisted, or may be aided by insects, birds, or other animals. Some plant species are dioecious, meaning an individual bears only male (staminate) flowers or female (pistillate) flowers, not both: there are separate male and female plants. Only the female plants produce fruit. Some plants are monoecious, meaning an individual bears both male and female flowers.

**Diversity and hybridization.** Sometimes identification is challenging because species within a genus are similar. This issue is compounded as the diversity within a genus increases. As an additional challenge, within some genera of trees, there are regularly occurring hybrids. Oaks are notorious for hybridization, but other groups of trees hybridize too.

**115**

# PINES AND SPRUCES

Gymnosperms and angiosperms (flowering plants) are the two groups of seed-producing plants. Pages 116–119 introduce the gymnosperms, notably the conifers. Conifers are wind-pollinated seed plants that bear cones. This page covers the pine family (**Pinaceae**), focusing on a few true pines (genus *Pinus*) and spruces (genus *Picea*). True pines often have long needles (leaves) that are joined at the base into bundles of two to five depending on species. Spruces have single needles directly attached to the branch in a spiral pattern. Their needles are short, blunt-tipped, and roughly four-sided. All species on this page are evergreens.

### EASTERN WHITE PINE    *Pinus strobus*

Once the primary tree of the timber industry in the upper Great Lakes, this long-lived, fast-growing conifer grows in a variety of soils. Normally reaches 70–120'; historically some trees were much taller. ▶ Branches emerge almost at *right angles* to trunk, in a whorl-like arrangement. Long (2–5") pale blue-green, flexible needles, 5 to a cluster. Cones at least twice as long as wide.

### RED PINE    *Pinus resinosa*

Another historically important timber tree in the Great Lakes region. ▶ Grows 60–100'. Long (4–6") stiff needles, 2 to a cluster, rather *brittle* and may snap if bent. Bark reddish brown.

### JACK PINE    *Pinus banksiana*

A fairly small pine of dry soils. Fire-adapted, some cones open only under intense heat. Young Jack Pine forests host the endangered Kirtland's Warbler (p. 264). ▶ Grows to 60'. Short (up to 1½") yellow-green needles, 2 to a cluster. Cones often *curved*.

### PITCH PINE    *Pinus rigida*

A small to medium height pine of dry, sandy to rocky soils. After fire, dormant buds in trunk may sprout. ▶ Grows to 60'. Long (3–5"), stout, *twisted yellow-green needles*, usually 3 to a cluster.

### SCRUB PINE (VIRGINIA PINE)    *Pinus virginiana*

A relatively small-statured pine of dry uplands. ▶ Grows to 40'. Short (up to 2½") twisted needles, 2 to a cluster. Cone egg-shaped, somewhat prickly.

### WHITE SPRUCE    *Picea glauca*

A medium to tall spruce of mesic to wet soils, such as bogs and lake borders, but can occur in upland sites too. ▶ Grows to 50–80' tall. Oblong cones longer and more narrow than those of Black Spruce. Needles have *unpleasant odor* when crushed.

### BLACK SPRUCE    *Picea mariana*

A small to medium-sized spruce almost exclusive to wet soils, particularly bogs and muskegs. ▶ Grows to 50'. Very narrow growth form, resembling a pipe cleaner from a distance. Small, round cones have slightly scalloped scale margins.

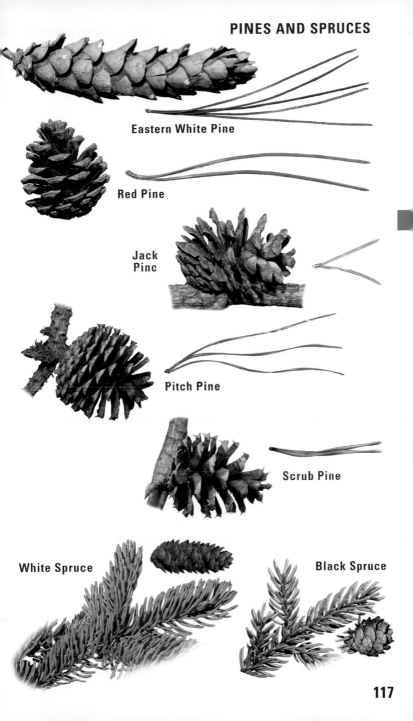

Eastern White Pine

Red Pine

Jack
Pinc

Pitch Pine

Scrub Pine

White Spruce

Black Spruce

# OTHER CONIFERS

The first three species below are in the pine family, introduced on p. 116; the other four are in the cypress family (Cupressaceae). Not all conifers are evergreen. The first and last species on this spread are deciduous conifers, losing all their needles in late fall to early winter.

### TAMARACK    *Larix laricina*

A medium to tall conifer found in wet soils such as bogs, swamps, and lakesides. In bog habitats often grows out onto sphagnum mats and is associated with Black Spruce (p. 116). ▶ Grows 40–75'. Needles, arranged in *fanlike clusters*, turn golden yellow in fall before being shed. Very small cones (½").

### EASTERN HEMLOCK    *Tsuga canadensis*

A long-lived, slow-growing tree of moist, shaded habitats such as the edges of conifer swamps, wooded dunes, and rocky ravines; can be found in drier areas prone to fire. ▶ Grows to 80', infrequently 100'. Short, flattened, dark yellow-green needles, the undersides with a *whitish line* on each side of midrib. Small cones.

### BALSAM FIR    *Abies balsamea*

A northern tree with aromatic foliage. ▶ Differs from spruces (p. 116) in having *flatter*, blunt needles, curved upward on the twigs. Short cones stand *upright* on the upper branches.

### EASTERN REDCEDAR    *Juniperus virginiana*

Common in dry soils of fields, open woodlands, dunes, gravelly slopes, roadsides. ▶ Columnar or pyramidal form. Short, pointed leaves on young shoots; overlapping, compressed, scalelike leaves on older stems. Small, bluish, berrylike seed cones with a waxy whitish bloom. Reddish brown bark shreds into thin strips.

### COMMON JUNIPER    *Juniperus communis* (not shown)

A widespread juniper; can grow as a small tree or a sprawling shrub (varies by subspecies and soils). ▶ Leaves in whorls of 3, with a white band on the surface. Berrylike seed cones similar to those of Eastern Redcedar but larger and bluish black.

### NORTHERN WHITE-CEDAR    *Thuja occidentalis*

A small to medium conifer found in neutral to alkaline wet soils of swamps, riparian borders, and lakesides. Also in drier habitats such as upland areas with limestone bedrock. ▶ Grows 30–60'. Aromatic, flattened, yellow-green, fanlike foliage. Shredding brown to grayish red bark. Small upright cones with few scales.

### BALDCYPRESS    *Taxodium distichum*

Uncommon as a wild native in the Midwest except in swampy wetlands of extreme sw. Indiana and s. Illinois. Planted as an ornamental elsewhere throughout the region. ▶ Light green feathery leaves turn golden to bronze yellow in autumn before falling off. Older trees have buttressed trunks and may produce "knees" (vertical projections rising above water).

# OTHER CONIFERS

Tamarack

Eastern Hemlock

Balsam Fir

Eastern Redcedar

Baldcypress

Northern
White-cedar

119

# RED OAK GROUP

The next two spreads cover the oaks (genus *Quercus*), members of the beech family **(Fagaceae)**. In the Midwest there are 48 types of oaks — 21 distinct native species, 1 introduced, and 26 naturally occurring hybrids — and we cover 14 of them. Oaks are wind-pollinated plants that produce acorns, an important food source to many animals. Some oaks are dominant plants in the varied communities that comprise the temperate deciduous forest, temperate savanna, and riparian biomes of our region. Identifying oaks can be challenging as oak species regularly interbreed, and because leaf shape and size can vary considerably on a given individual or between individuals of the same species. The first five oaks below are tall trees, regularly reaching heights of 80 feet or more.

### NORTHERN RED OAK    *Quercus rubra*

Common and widespread on moist rich to dry, sandy soils of forests, sunny slopes, and plains. ▶ Large dull leaves, often with red petioles (leaf stems); sinuses (separations between lobes) not as deep compared to similar species. Reddish twigs and hairless red buds. Large (1"), shallow-cupped acorns with white kernels.

### PIN OAK    *Quercus palustris*

Normally in moist, poorly drained soils in bottomlands, riparian corridors, and forest or swamp edges. ▶ Smaller, deeply lobed leaves with wide, round sinuses; underleaf lighter green; slender reddish brown twigs sometimes more crooked than on other oaks; buds small, pointed, hairless. Small, shallow-cupped acorns.

### SCARLET OAK    *Quercus coccinea*

Found on dry, sandy uplands and slopes. Fall foliage can be more vibrant red than on other oaks. ▶ Smaller leaves, deeply lobed with narrower sinuses; underleaf lighter green. Twigs not crooked; buds small, hairy, grayish. Deep acorn cups without fringe.

### EASTERN BLACK OAK    *Quercus velutina*

Common in dry, sandy forest and savanna soils; also slopes with well-drained mesic soils. ▶ Large glossy, deep-lobed leaves; underleaf has fine brownish orange hairs. Buds large, hairy, grayish. Deep acorn cups with hairy fringe cover 1/3 to 2/3 of nut; kernel yellowish orange.

### SHUMARD'S OAK    *Quercus shumardii*

A medium to tall tree of bottomlands, swamps, and riparian corridors, rarely on dry uplands. ▶ Large, broad, shiny leaves with many deep-lobed, narrow sinuses. Buds on twigs grayish brown, hairless. Large (up to 1"), shallow-cupped acorns.

### SHINGLE OAK    *Quercus imbricaria*

A distinctive-looking, slow-growing, medium-sized oak of upland, swamp, and savanna edges; intolerant of shade. ▶ Oblong, smooth-edged, unlobed leaves with bristle tips. Leaves shiny on top, hairy on bottom, feel leathery. Acorn cups rather deep.

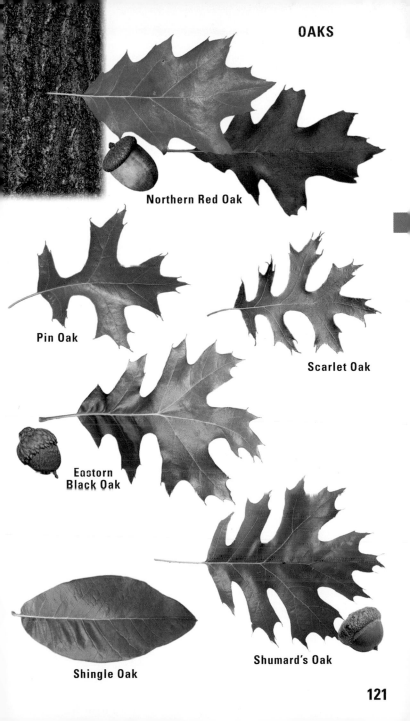

# OAKS

Northern Red Oak

Pin Oak

Scarlet Oak

Eastern
Black Oak

Shingle Oak

Shumard's Oak

**121**

# WHITE OAK GROUP

We have two primary oak groups. Red oak leaves generally have pointed lobes and bristly tips. Their acorns take two to three years to mature, are high in tannins, and have caps with flat scales. White oak leaves have rounded lobes and lack bristly tips. Their acorns mature in one year, are lower in tannins, and have caps with more pronounced, bumpy scales.

### EASTERN WHITE OAK  *Quercus alba*

A common and widespread tree, reaching heights of 80–100' or more. ▶ Large, greenish gray leaves with deep, round lobes. Trunk a *light ash gray*; mature trees have long, vertical strips of bark that separate from trunk. Acorns with *shallow* cups.

### BUR OAK  *Quercus macrocarpa*

North America's northernmost native oak. A widespread tree of bottomlands, riparian corridors, and dry, sandy uplands — the archetypal savanna tree. Reaches 80' or more. ▶ Large leaves wider near top; deep-cut central sinuses give leaf a waisted appearance. *Large* acorns (up to 2") have deep cups with burry fringe.

### OVERCUP OAK  *Quercus lyrata*

A flood-tolerant tree of bottomlands, swamp edges, and riparian corridors. Usually less than 50' tall; often has short, twisted or crooked trunk. ▶ Leaves have pointed lobes, upper pair often at *right angles*. Large acorn; cap encloses ¾ to almost entire nut.

### SWAMP WHITE OAK  *Quercus bicolor*

A tall tree of moist to wet soil, reaching 70–100'. ▶ Leaves with shallow, pointed to rounded lobes, dark green on top, whitish below; often with wavy edges. Acorns with *long stalks,* deep cups.

### CHESTNUT OAK  *Quercus montana*

Growing in dry, poor rocky soils, it reaches heights of 70–100'. ▶ Leaves of this and next 2 species suggest those of American Chestnut (p. 124); leaves with rounded, wavy lobes; dark green on top, pale green below. Narrow, long acorn with deep cup.

### CHINKAPIN OAK  *Quercus muehlenbergii*

Uncommon tree mainly found on rocky, calcareous soils; grows 50–70' tall. ▶ Small, variable leaves, many with coarse-toothed lobes. Small acorns with *deep* cups covering up to half of nut.

### DWARF CHINKAPIN OAK  *Quercus prinoides*

A colonial shrub (rarely short tree) of dry hill prairies, rocky slopes, woodland edges. Begins producing acorns at a very early age, making it important in habitat succession. ▶ Leaves like previous species but lobes fewer and rounded.

### POST OAK  *Quercus stellata*

Common on dry or rocky soils of savannas, ridges, slopes, and barrens. ▶ Leaves variably shaped, dark green, rough; some crosslike; lobes more rounded than in Overcup Oak.

# OAKS

Eastern White Oak

underside of leaf

Bur Oak

Overcup Oak

Swamp White Oak

Chestnut Oak

Chinkapin Oak

Dwarf Chinkapin Oak

Post Oak

123

# BEECHES AND BIRCHES

The first two species are in the beech family **(Fagaceae)**. The last six are in the birch family **(Betulaceae)** with 21 representatives in our region. Members of the birch family have seeds dispersed primarily by wind. Their leaves are mostly oval to oblong, simple, alternate, and toothed.

### AMERICAN BEECH    *Fagus grandifolia*

A majestic tree of flat to rolling terrain with moist, well-drained soil; grows 60–90' tall. Co-dominant with Sugar Maples (p. 132) in some forest types. ▶ Usually smooth, silver-gray trunks with thin, easy-to-scar bark. Elliptical leaves with coarse teeth, parallel veins, short petioles. Very *long,* pointed, reddish brown buds on zigzagging twigs. Spiny 4-part husk with triangular nuts.

### AMERICAN CHESTNUT    *Castanea dentata*

A once grand, massive tree, regularly reaching 100–120' tall; arguably one of the most important trees in the temperate deciduous forest. Virtually entire population wiped out over a few decades by a fungal disease introduced in early 1900s. A few, rare mature trees remain. In places, offshoots still sprout from old stumps; these eventually succumb to the disease.

### YELLOW BIRCH    *Betula alleghaniensis*

Tallest birch in range (60–90'); prefers moist, rich soils. ▶ Leaves alternate on branches, often paired on short, lateral twigs. Bark peels in small strips, like curled wood shavings. *Bronze-yellow bark* on mature trees. Bruised tissue emits wintergreen odor.

### RIVER BIRCH    *Betula nigra*

A birch of riparian corridors, edges of flooded bottomlands; can survive as a semi-aquatic tree (under 70' tall). ▶ Leaves triangular; reddish brown to pink exfoliating bark.

### PAPER BIRCH    *Betula papyrifera*

A stunning tree, often 50–70' tall. ▶ Creamy white bark peels off in strips or large papery sections. Oval leaves; alternate on branches but often grouped by threes on short, lateral twigs.

### GRAY BIRCH    *Betula populifolia*

Rare in Midwest; under 30' tall. ▶ Long, pointed triangular leaves. Smooth splotched bark doesn't peel. Dark chevrons under bases of branches.

### AMERICAN HORNBEAM    *Carpinus caroliniana*

An understory tree (20–40' tall), fairly common in bottomlands, particularly beech-maple forests. ▶ Clusters of dangling pairs of nutlets, each surrounded by 3-lobed leafy bract. Smooth, blue-gray bark on ropy, corrugated trunk (called "musclewood").

### EASTERN HOPHORNBEAM    *Ostrya virginiana*

An understory tree of mesic to dry deciduous forests, rocky ridges; grows 25–45' tall. ▶ Leaves like Yellow Birch but veins branching at the margin. Clusters of overlapping inflated sacs contain nutlets; mature trees with shaggy brownish bark.

# BEECHES AND BIRCHES

long buds

bark

American
Beech

American Chestnut

Yellow
Birch

River
Birch

Paper
Birch

Gray
Birch

American Hornbeam

Eastern
Hophornbeam

# HICKORIES AND WALNUTS

The next three spreads (pp. 126–131) cover trees and large shrubs with compound leaves. This page features the walnut family (**Juglandaceae**) with 17 representatives in our region. This family has large, alternately arranged, compound leaves that are finely to sharply toothed. They are wind pollinated, producing an important wildlife and commercial food source — edible nuts. Botanically their seeds are not true nuts, but we'll use this more colloquial term. The hard-shelled nuts, surrounded by a husk, vary in size, shape, and taste by species. Hickories (genus *Carya*) have a showy spring leaf emergence with large, leafy, greenish red bracts unfolding to reveal groups of young chartreuse leaves.

### SHAGBARK HICKORY    *Carya ovata*

A common forest tree of dry to well-drained, rich uplands; grows 70–100' tall. ▶ Peeling bark gives trunk a distinctively *shaggy* look; large leaf with 5 to 7 leaflets (often 5); large fruit with thick husk; sweet-tasting, 4-ribbed nut.

### SHELLBARK HICKORY    *Carya laciniosa*

The forested wetland counterpart to Shagbark Hickory; grows 70–90' tall. ▶ Similar to Shagbark Hickory, with *shaggy bark*; leaf often with 7 leaflets (can have 5–9); largest nut of any hickory (to 2"); very thick husk; flattened, 4–6 ribbed, sweet-tasting nut.

### BITTERNUT HICKORY    *Carya cordiformis*

Medium to tall tree (50–80') of moist hardwood forests, lower upland slopes. ▶ Large leaf with 7 to 11 lance-shaped leaflets; 4-part husk splits halfway to base; bitter-tasting nut avoided by humans and often other animals; *buds bright yellow*.

### PIGNUT HICKORY    *Carya glabra*

Dry to slightly moist upland forests; grows 50–70' tall. ▶ Leaf with 5 to 7 leaflets (often 5); thin 4-part husk slightly splits open; thick-shelled, pear-shaped nut.

### NATIVE PECAN    *Carya illinoinensis*

A tree primarily of rich, moist riparian corridors, among the largest native hickories (70-110' tall); prized for its sweet-tasting nut. ▶ Long leaf with 9 to 17 (usually 11) recurved leaflets; narrow 4-part husk, winged on seam; nut thin-shelled, pointed, oblong.

### BLACK WALNUT    *Juglans nigra*

Prized for its wood. Rich, moist soils of bottomlands and open riparian corridors; grows 70–100' tall. ▶ *Long* leaf (1–2') with 13 to 23 finely toothed leaflets; terminal leaflet often *missing*. Leaf scar without fuzz; smooth husked fruit (to 2") with roundish nut.

### BUTTERNUT    *Juglans cinerea*

Uncommon, becoming rare; rich, moist bottomlands to dry limestone soils; grows 40–60' tall. ▶ Long leaf (12–18") with 11 to 17 finely toothed leaflets. Leaf scar fuzzy on top; fruit sticky, fuzzy, oblong (to 3"); nut oblong, pointed, furrowed

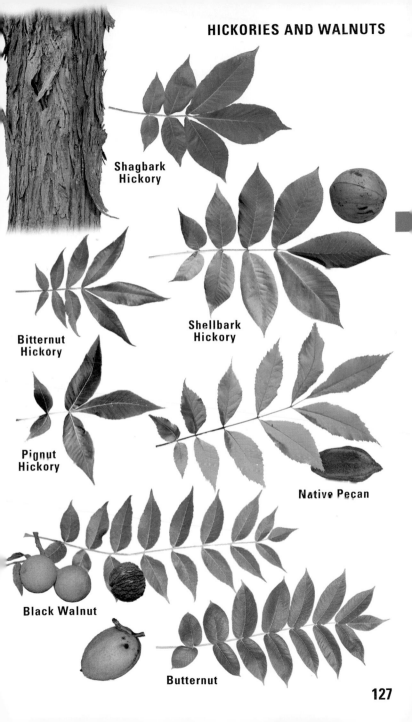

# HICKORIES AND WALNUTS

Shagbark
Hickory

Shellbark
Hickory

Bitternut
Hickory

Pignut
Hickory

Native Pecan

Black Walnut

Butternut

# SUMACS AND OTHERS

The first four species below are in the cashew family (**Anacardiaceae**). They have brilliant reddish orange to crimson-purple fall foliage. Those in the genus *Rhus* can spread via offshoots from shallow roots, creating thickets. The next two species are in the rue, or citrus, family (**Rutaceae**), while the last species is in the bladdernut family (**Staphyleaceae**).

### STAGHORN SUMAC  *Rhus typhina*

Usually grows as a single-stemmed small to medium-tall tree (to 35'), but can grow as a many-stemmed shrub. Found in open, disturbed areas with mesic to dry soils. Can hybridize with Smooth Sumac. ▶ Compound leaves (to 2' long) with many toothed leaflets. Stems and twigs brown with upper stems *densely hairy;* leaf less hairy. Erect clusters of reddish, hairy fruit eaten by birds in winter when more desirable wild fruits become scarce.

### SMOOTH SUMAC  *Rhus glabra*  (not shown)

A many-stemmed shrub or small single-stemmed tree. ▶ Grows to 20'. Similar to Staghorn Sumac except twigs and leaves hairless (smooth). Twigs can be green or red often with a whitish bloom. Fruit cluster is not as dense and droops as winter progresses.

### WINGED SUMAC  *Rhus copallina*

A common shrub of dry, sandy or rocky roadsides, woods, prairies, and savannas. ▶ Leaf stalk of leaves noticeably *winged* and leaflets smooth-edged. Upper leaflet surface green and very shiny (hence alternate name of Shining Sumac).

### POISON SUMAC  *Toxicodendron vernix*

A shrub exclusive to wetlands, primarily bogs, fens, and swamps. Most people have a severe allergic reaction from touching any part of plant; see Eastern Poison Ivy (p. 160). ▶ Leaves often have *bright red petioles and stalks;* leaflets *shiny,* smooth-edged, and oblong. Clusters of dangling white fruit a favorite of birds.

### NORTHERN PRICKLY-ASH  *Zanthoxylum americanum*

A multistemmed shrub of swamp and riparian edges, moist forests, sometimes drier habitats. ▶ Grows to 25'. Pairs of stiff, short prickles scattered along stems. Leaves with up to 11 lance-shaped to oblong leaflets; leaflets may have prickles. Small red fruits turn black when mature. All parts of plant emit a lemony fragrance.

### COMMON HOPTREE  *Ptelea trifoliata*

A shrub of dry to mesic habitats including savannas, bluffs, open woodlands, and dunes. ▶ Grows to 20'. Leaves with 3 smooth-edged leaflets. Fruits are *thin-winged, flattened disks.*

### BLADDERNUT  *Staphylea trifolia*

A large shrub to small tree of deciduous woodlands. ▶ Grows to 15'. Leaves with 3 leaflets, finely toothed. Attractive 5-petaled, drooping white flowers produce *bladderlike, papery fruits.*

# SUMACS AND OTHERS

Staghorn Sumac

old fruits

flowers

Winged Sumac

fruits

Poison Sumac

Northern Prickly-ash

Common Hoptree

Bladdernut

129

# TREES WITH COMPOUND LEAVES

These six trees represent three different families. Mountain-ashes are in the rose family (**Rosaceae**), while true ashes are in the olive family (**Oleaceae**). The last two are in the legume, or pea, family (**Fabaceae**). The last four species on this page are dioecious, meaning that they have separate male and female individuals.

### AMERICAN MOUNTAIN-ASH    *Sorbus americana*

A small tree (15–30'), beautiful when in bloom and in fruit; edges of swamps, streams, bogs, and rocky hillsides. ▶ Leaves alternate, compound with 9–17 narrow, lance-shaped, toothed leaflets. Flat-topped white flower clusters produce orange-red berries prized by birds. Prominent horizontal lenticels on trunk at all ages; lenticels on younger trees tan-orange with protruding edges.

### EUROPEAN MOUNTAIN-ASH    *Sorbus aucuparia*

Widely planted, often becomes invasive in natural habitats. ▶ Similar to American Mountain-ash but has shorter, more blunt-tipped leaflets.

### WHITE ASH    *Fraxinus americana*

Uplands with rich, well-drained soils. Like all ashes, threatened by Emerald Ash Borer (p. 372). ▶ Grows 50–90' tall. Leaves opposite, compound with 7–9 leaflets, often smooth-edged; petioles grooved. Younger twigs never hairy. Elongated papery wing extends just to top of swollen seed cavity. Mature trunk ashy to brownish gray with deep, diamond-shaped furrows.

### GREEN ASH    *Fraxinus pennsylvanica*

Historically a common tree of floodplains, swamp edges, riparian corridors. Now threatened by Emerald Ash Borer. ▶ Grows 40–60' tall. Leaves with 7–9 smooth to finely toothed leaflets. Leaf petioles and younger twigs may be slightly hairy. Elongated papery wing extends halfway down slender seed cavity. Mature trunk brownish gray with shallow, diamond-shaped furrows.

### HONEY LOCUST    *Gleditsia triacanthos*

Adapted to various habitats from moist bottomlands to upland wood edges and rocky limestone glades. Menacing thorns may once have been a deterrent to megaherbivores of the Pleistocene. ▶ Zigzagging stems with short to long thorns. Clusters of very long (up to 14"), multibranched thorns on trunk are diagnostic. Narrow, twisted, long bean pods (6–10" or more).

### KENTUCKY COFFEE TREE    *Gymnocladus dioicus*

Found in rich bottomland woods, open riparian corridors. Does not naturally spread by seed anymore, possibly owing to absence of suitable seed dispersers — Pleistocene megaherbivores. ▶ Very large, alternate, doubly compound leaves (up to 3' long by 2' wide). Tough, woody seedpods reddish brown, wide (to 2") and long (3–8"). Sweet, mucilaginous pulp surrounds extremely hard seeds; seeds toxic when raw.

# TREES WITH COMPOUND LEAVES

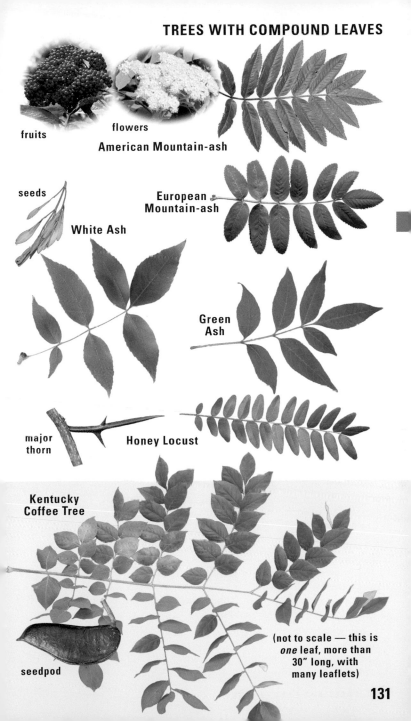

fruits

flowers

**American Mountain-ash**

seeds

**European Mountain-ash**

**White Ash**

**Green Ash**

major thorn

**Honey Locust**

**Kentucky Coffee Tree**

seedpod

(not to scale — this is *one* leaf, more than 30" long, with many leaflets)

# MAPLES AND BUCKEYES

These are in the soapberry family (**Sapindaceae**). Maples (genus *Acer*) have opposite leaves, with most species having palmately lobed leaves. As a group, the maples are among the most colorful of trees in autumn. Maples have a distinctive winged fruit (usually paired) called samaras. Each samara encases a single seed. The papery wing helps distribute the seed a distance from the parent tree. The last two species are in the genus *Aesculus,* the buckeyes and horsechestnuts.

### SUGAR MAPLE  *Acer saccharum*

A widespread medium to large tree of well-drained, sandy to loamy soils; grows to 90'. Co-dominant with American Beech (p. 124) in beech-maple forest types. ▶ Leaves often 5-lobed with short basal lobes. May be confused with Norway Maple (p. 150).

### RED MAPLE  *Acer rubrum*

A medium-tall tree of moist to wet soils. Farther north, occurs in drier habitats as well. With Silver Maple, among the first trees to bloom in spring. ▶ Grows 40–70' tall. Leaves often 3-lobed; petiole (leafstalk), twigs, flowers, fruit, and even leaves *red*.

### SILVER MAPLE  *Acer saccharinum*

A widespread medium to large tree, usually growing in moist soils, also widely planted in towns. ▶ Grows to 80'. Toothed leaves with 5 *deep* lobes. Undersides of leaves *silvery gray* (hence the common name). Broken twigs may emit unpleasant odor.

### STRIPED MAPLE  *Acer pensylvanicum*

A typical understory tree of cool, rich deciduous forests, bluffs, and conifer-hardwood forests. Grows to 30' as a tall shrub or short tree. ▶ *Large,* finely toothed leaves with 3 lobes; bark on younger trees *green with white stripes*. Drooping clusters of bell-shaped yellow flowers.

### BOXELDER  *Acer negundo*

A common small to medium-tall tree of shaded swamps, floodplains, fields, and disturbed sites. ▶ Grows to 60'. Among the maples presented here, the only one without palmately lobed leaves. Instead, leaves are pinnately compound with 3–7 (usually 5) toothed leaflets.

### OHIO BUCKEYE  *Aesculus glabra*

A large shrub or medium tree of rich deciduous woodlands and riparian valleys. ▶ Grows to 60'. Palmately compound leaves with 5 finely toothed leaflets. Terminal clusters of chartreuse to light yellow flowers; stamens noticeably *extend out of flower*. Fruit a *spiny* husk containing 1 to 2 seeds (buckeyes).

### YELLOW BUCKEYE  *Aesculus flava* (not shown)

A medium to large tree of rich mixed deciduous woodlands; grows to 80'. ▶ Similar to Ohio Buckeye but often taller. Stamens do *not* extend out of flower; fruit has *smooth* husk.

# MAPLES AND BUCKEYES

bark

fruit

**Sugar Maple**

fall color

fall color

**Red Maple**

fruit

underside of leaf

bark

**Silver Maple**

flower

**Striped Maple**

bark

**Boxelder**

fruit

**Ohio Buckeye**

flower

133

# TREES WITH DISTINCTIVE LEAVES

These trees represent five distinct families.

### EASTERN SYCAMORE   *Platanus occidentalis*

A large, stout tree of mesic to wet forests, riparian and lake borders, and floodplains. A preferred nesting tree for Yellow-throated Warbler (p. 264). Often planted for its ornamental appeal. Plane-tree family (Platanaceae). ▶ Grows to 120'. *Large,* coarse-toothed leaves with 3–5 palmate lobes. *Blotchy appearance* of trunk, as exfoliating grayish brown bark reveals a tannish white inner bark. Single ball-shaped brownish fruits hang from long stalks. European and Oriental Sycamores, often planted in parks, have 2 or more fruits per stalk.

### AMERICAN BASSWOOD   *Tilia americana*

A fast-growing medium to tall tree of mesic upland deciduous forests, wooded ravines, and stabilized sand dunes. The flowers produce a significant amount of nectar, making them an important food source for bees. Basswoods and lindens were formerly considered a separate family but are now placed in the mallow family (Malvaceae). ▶ Grows to 90'. Leaves egg-shaped to heart-shaped with distinctly *uneven base.* (Compare to Northern Catalpa, p. 136.) Fragrant creamy to chartreuse flowers hanging beneath a *thin, winglike structure* mature into ball-shaped fruits (nutlets) that are small, hard, and brown.

### SWEETGUM   *Liquidambar styraciflua*

A medium to tall tree of mesic to wet floodplains, riparian corridors, and swamp edges. Often planted for its ornamental appeal. Sweetgum family (Altingiaceae). ▶ Grows to 80'. Finely toothed *star-shaped* leaves with 5 (rarely 7) palmate lobes. Fruit a *spiky ball* on long stalks. Purple-red foliage in autumn.

### SASSAFRAS   *Sassafras albidum*

A small to medium-sized tree of dry, sandy habitats such as savannas, woodland edges, and open fields. Twigs and leaves have a light spicy aroma when rubbed. Roots are very aromatic, and used to be used for soaps, tea, and to flavor root beer until the oil (safrole) was discovered to be carcinogenic. Laurel family (Lauraceae). ▶ Grows to 60'. Leaves *variable,* with 3 different shapes often on the same branch (oval, mitten-shaped, 3-lobed). Fruits dark bluish black, held up on bright red stalks with red cups. Yellow to fiery reddish orange fall foliage.

### RED MULBERRY   *Morus rubra*

Once common, now uncommon. A small to medium native tree of rich woods and floodplains. Mulberry, or fig, family (Moraceae). ▶ Grows to 60'. Leaves *quite variable* in shape (0 to 5 lobes), with coarse teeth. Leaves have *sandpapery* upper surface; leaf tips always pointed. Mature fruits are red to black. Easily confused with White Mulberry (p. 150), an invasive nonnative.

# TREES WITH DISTINCTIVE LEAVES

trunk
bark

Eastern
Sycamore

American
Basswood

Sweetgum

Sassafras
(3 examples)

Red Mulberry

135

These distinctive trees are in five separate families.

### PAWPAW  *Asimina triloba*

A small to medium understory tree of floodplains, wet forests, riparian corridors, and wooded slopes. Can spread by roots. In the custard apple family (Annonaceae), a family of primarily tropical species. ► Grows to 40'. Smooth-edged, oblong leaves that are very long and often shiny. Showy, deep maroon flowers (pollinated by flies) produce a smell ranging from fresh bread dough to rotting meat. The taste of its large, edible fruit with large, brown seeds is often compared to that of banana and has the consistency of custard.

### TULIPTREE  *Liriodendron tulipifera*

A large tree of sandy mesic soils in rich deciduous forests. It's among the tallest of hardwood species, regularly reaching 100' or more. Magnolia family (Magnoliaceae). ► Distinct 4-lobed, squarish leaves. *Large yellow-green flowers* reminiscent of tulips (hence common name) with orange bases. Pollinated flowers produce a conelike fruit composed of a dense cluster of one-seeded samaras. Leaves turn golden yellow in autumn.

### NORTHERN CATALPA  *Catalpa speciosa*

A medium to large tree of mesic to wet soils along lakes and riparian corridors. Native but uncommon in the wild, it is often planted for its ornamental appeal. Although it has an impressive beanlike seedpod, it is not a legume. Bignonia family (Bignoniaceae), a family primarily of woody tropical species. ► Grows to 90'. Very *large, heart-shaped, long-tipped leaves.* Upright clusters of large, spectacular, tubular white flowers with flared frilly edges (look orchidlike); flowers often have purple and yellow streaks. Very *long* (over 12"), thin seedpods.

### EASTERN REDBUD  *Cercis canadensis*

A small understory tree of edge habitats along riparian corridors and forests. Flowers and fruits produced directly on the main trunk and branches (termed cauliflory), a strategy primarily seen in some tropical trees and vines. Legume, or pea, family (Fabaceae). ► Grows to 30'. Leaves *heart-shaped.* In spring, numerous clusters of lavender to light pink flowers emerge on the trunk and branches before the leaves. Flattened bean pods.

### WITCH HAZEL  *Hamamelis virginiana*

A large, multitrunked shrub of sandy forests, savannas, dunes, and riparian slopes. Flowers in mid- to late autumn, often after leaves fall. Witch-hazel family (Hamamelidaceae). ► Grows to 25'. Asymmetrically shaped leaves with rounded teeth. Clusters of fragrant yellow flowers in fall, each with 4 ribbonlike petals. Hard, 4-segmented, brown seed capsules.

# TREES WITH SHOWY LEAVES AND FLOWERS

Pawpaw

Tuliptree

Northern Catalpa

Eastern Redbud

Witch Hazel

137

# CHERRIES AND OTHERS

These all belong to the rose family **(Rosaceae),** which includes around 300 species in our region. Most rose family members are deciduous and have showy, five-petaled flowers. Roses span the spectrum from small wildflowers to tall trees, so we treat other species in two other sections.

### DOWNY SERVICEBERRY     *Amelanchier arborea*

A common large shrub to small tree of dry to mesic soils; found in the understory of deciduous forests, riparian corridors, swamps, and sandy mixed woods and savannas. Its white flowers emerge in early spring, around the same time as Eastern Redbud (p. 136). ▶ Grows to 30'. Alternate, fine-toothed, oval leaves; soft, hairy undersides on younger leaves. Leaves of the similar **Smooth Serviceberry** *(A. laevis)* are reddish when they emerge.

### HAWTHORNS     *Crataegus* sp.

There are over 60 species of hawthorn in the Midwest, although the exact number is still up for study and debate. Accurately identifying species of hawthorns can be a challenging task, even to botanists. ▶ Long, unbranched thorns that can be curved or straight. Clusters of white flowers. Mature fruit are small, reddish to yellow, and reminiscent of tiny apples.

### WILD BLACK CHERRY     *Prunus serotina*

A common and widespread tree of deciduous forests, savannas, and fields. ▶ Grows to 80'. Oblong, fine-toothed leaves, often with a *long tip*. Bark of younger trees reddish to silvery brown with light-colored horizontal lenticels. Profuse hanging clusters of white flowers in spring; fruit bluish black with a large pit.

### CHOKE CHERRY     *Prunus virginiana*

Widespread but not abundant, this large shrub to small tree is found in open and edge habitats. ▶ Grows to 25'. Similar to Wild Black Cherry, but leaves wider and without a long tip, and berries reddish purple.

### SAND CHERRY     *Prunus pumila* (not shown)

A small shrub of dry, sandy or gravelly habitats such as shores, foredunes, sand prairies, and inland dunes. ▶ Grows to 6'. Leaf shape varies. Small clusters of white flowers attached to leaf axil. Berries larger than those of Wild Black and Choke Cherries.

### PURPLE-FRUITED CHOKEBERRY     *Aronia prunifolia*

A medium-sized shrub, considered a hybrid between Black Chokeberry *(A. melanocarpa)* and Red Chokeberry *(A. arbutifolia).* ▶ Grows to 12' tall. Fruits of chokeberries have several small seeds whereas cherries have a single large pit.

### NINEBARK     *Physocarpus opulifolius*

A shrub of riparian corridors, sandy seeps, rocky banks. ▶ Grows to 9' tall. Round white flower clusters. Arching branches have layers of exfoliating bark.

# FRUITING SHRUBS AND TREES

Downy Serviceberry

hawthorns

Wild Black Cherry

Choke Cherry

Purple-fruited Chokeberry

Ninebark

# HACKBERRIES, ELMS, COTTONWOODS, & ASPENS

These represent three separate families. Hackberries are in the hemp family **(Cannabaceae)**, although they used to be classified in the same family as the elms **(Ulmaceae)**. The last three species, from the willow family **(Salicaceae)**, are in the genus *Populus,* which includes 13 species in the Midwest. They are wind pollinated and dioecious (separate male and female plants). The cottonwoods and aspens below have long, laterally compressed petioles (leafstalks) that make the leaves flutter in even a light breeze. Woodpeckers often excavate cavities in the trunks and limbs, and these later become homes for other cavity-nesters.

### NORTHERN HACKBERRY    *Celtis occidentalis*

A medium to tall tree of moist to wet habitats. ▶ Leaves coarse-toothed with long-pointed tips, usually lopsided bases, and often darker on top. Inconspicuous green spring flowers produce small, dull reddish brown fruits that tend to shrivel on stem. Trunks with corky, winglike ridges.

### AMERICAN ELM    *Ulmus americana*

Once a canopy tree of riparian corridors, swamps, rich woodlands. Owing to introduced Dutch elm disease, now usually an understory tree. Historically grew to 90'. ▶ Large coarse-toothed leaves with a short stalk and often uneven base. Upper leaf surface may be rough but lower surface smooth. Clusters of *long-stalked* flowers. Flat papery fruit with *long stalk* and *deep notch*.

### SLIPPERY ELM    *Ulmus rubra*

Fairly common in a variety of habitats. ▶ Similar to American Elm but leaves have a sandpapery upper *and* lower surface. Flowers and fruits have *short* stalks; fruits *lack* deep notch.

### SIBERIAN ELM    *Ulmus pumila* (not shown)
Introduced, widely cultivated; resistant to Dutch elm disease. ▶ Similar to Slippery Elm but with noticeably smaller leaves.

### EASTERN COTTONWOOD    *Populus deltoides*

Common and conspicuous in riparian corridors, lake edges, and other open habitats with moist soils; often a massive tree, growing to 110'. ▶ Triangular leaves with coarse teeth. Hanging clusters of fruit capsules release small seeds attached to cottonlike filaments, which float on the breeze in early summer.

### QUAKING ASPEN    *Populus tremuloides*

A common tree of northern forests, riparian and lake edges, and sandy open sites. ▶ Grows to 60'. Rounded, finely toothed leaves with petiole (leafstalk) usually longer than main leaf blade. Pale whitish gray trunk; sometimes mistaken for Paper Birch (p. 124).

### BIGTOOTH ASPEN    *Populus grandidentata*

A common, but not numerous, medium to tall tree of sandy, dry sites such as savannas, mixed forests, and recently burned areas. ▶ Grows to 70'. Round to oval, blunt-toothed leaves.

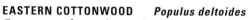

# HACKBERRIES, ELMS, ASPENS

**Northern Hackberry**

upperside and underside of leaf

**American Elm**

**Slippery Elm**

**Eastern Cottonwood**

**Bigtooth Aspen**

**Quaking Aspen**

141

# WILLOW TREES AND SHRUBS

The willow family (**Salicaceae**) was introduced with the cottonwoods and aspens on p. 140. Below are typical willows in the genus *Salix,* represented by more than 40 species in the Midwest. Plants in this genus can be hard to identify, all the more so because certain species hybridize. Willows are fast-growing plants, intolerant of shade. Pollinated by both insects and wind, they are dioecious — an individual is either a female plant with pistillate catkins or a male plant with staminate catkins.

## WEEPING WILLOW    *Salix* sp.

What is commonly called Weeping Willow *(Salix babylonica)*, an introduced tree from China, is rare in the Midwest but is regularly planted as an ornamental in the southeastern states. As this species is not winter hardy, few individuals can survive in our region. Most trees with this general appearance in the Midwest are actually a variety of **European White Willow** *(S. alba* var. *tristis)* or various hybrids between *S. babylonica* and *S. alba.* ▶ All have a strongly "weeping" shape, with branches and leaves drooping toward the ground.

## BLACK WILLOW    *Salix nigra*

Our largest native willow, growing to 65'. A medium-sized tree of moist to wet soils such as riparian corridors, lake and swamp edges. ▶ Long, narrow, lance-shaped leaves with fine-toothed edges; leaves dark green on top, light green below. Bark of mature trees very dark, deeply fissured with long, vertical, flat ridges.

## PUSSY WILLOW    *Salix discolor*

A medium to large native shrub primarily of mesic to wet soils. ▶ Grows to 20'. Leaves are wider than most willows with barely scalloped to almost smooth edges. Large flower buds split open in early spring, revealing their soft, furry catkins. Males of the species in full bloom are among the showiest in the genus.

## PRAIRIE WILLOW    *Salix humilis*

A short to medium shrub of dry to mesic sandy habitats, such as prairies, savannas, and mixed forests. Compared to most willows, this species is drought tolerant. ▶ Grows to 12'. Leaves grayish to bluish green with a smooth to slightly scalloped edging.

## SANDBAR WILLOW    *Salix interior*

A common shrub of mesic to wet sandy habitats, such as shorelines, streambanks, gravel and sandbars, prairie swales, and ditches. ▶ Grows to 20'. Long, narrow, lance-shaped leaves with widely spaced, distinct teeth.

## SAND DUNE WILLOW    *Salix cordata* (not shown)

An uncommon shrub restricted to shores and dunal ecosystems of the Great Lakes. ▶ Leaves finely toothed, elliptical to oval, with a rounded or heart-shaped base; both sides of leaf very hairy.

# WILLOWS

weeping
willow
sp.

opening
buds

Black Willow

full
bloom

Pussy
Willow

Prairie
Willow

Sandbar Willow

143

The six species below represent five separate families.

## BUTTONBUSH  *Cephalanthus occidentalis*

A common, multistemmed shrub of moist to wet soils, some-times in standing water. Found in wooded swamps, lake and pond edges, floodplains, riparian corridors, black soil prairie seeps, bogs, and wet thickets. Mature shrubs are large, often with impressively twisted trunks. Can form dense thickets at the edge of water. Madder family (Rubiaceae). ▶ Grows to 12'. Leaves smooth-edged and opposite or in whorls of 3; upper surface glossy. White-blooming, fragrant, *spherical flower balls* attract bees and butterflies.

## SPICEBUSH  *Lindera benzoin*

A medium to large understory shrub of moist to wet soils. Dioecious (separate male and female plants). Crushed leaves, scraped twigs, and bruised fruit are very aromatic, releasing a pleasant fruity to peppery smell. This and Sassafras (p. 134) are the region's only members of the laurel family (Lauraceae). ▶ Grows to 15'. Leaves glossy and smooth edged. Clusters of yellow flowers emerge in spring before leaves; more showy on staminate (male) plants. Fruit fleshy, bright red, one-seeded.

## AMERICAN HOLLY  *Ilex opaca*

An understory evergreen tree of acidic moist soils, mainly south-eastern. Dioecious (separate male and female plants). Grows to 40' farther south but usually much shorter in the Midwest. This and the next are 2 of the region's 5 species in the holly family (Aquifoliaceae). ▶ In good conditions, pyramidal growth form. Evergreen leaves somewhat shiny, leathery, and with *spiny tips* along the edge. Bitter-tasting red fruits last well into winter, eaten by birds only when more desirable wild fruits become scarce.

## WINTERBERRY  *Ilex verticillata*

A deciduous, shrubby holly of moist soils in wooded swamps, riparian and lake edges, bogs, and wet thickets. ▶ Grows to 12'. Leaves finely toothed and elliptical to oval. Inconspicuous white flowers. Fruits similar to those of American Holly.

## SHRUBBY ST. JOHNSWORT  *Hypericum prolificum*

A shrub of moist soils in prairies, lake and swamp edges, and rocky bluffs. One of 27 species of the St. Johnswort family (Hypericaceae) in the region. ▶ Clusters of bright yellow flowers, with *numerous long stamens,* cover the shrub in midsummer. Fruit a dry capsule that splits to release many small seeds.

## HIGHBUSH BLUEBERRY  *Vaccinium corymbosum*

A shrub of moist to wet peaty or sandy habitats. Heath family (Ericaceae). ▶ Grows to 12'. Compared to Early Low Blueberry (p. 154), it's much larger, with larger leaves (up to 3" long).

**Buttonbush**

**Spicebush**

**American Holly**

**Winterberry**

**Shrubby St. Johnswort**

**Highbush Blueberry**

# DOGWOODS AND BLACK GUM

These are all in the dogwood family **(Cornaceae),** with the first five representing the typical dogwood genus *Cornus.* The veins of their smooth-edged leaves curve toward the margins. A useful test to see if a tree is a member of this genus is to carefully pull the top and bottom of a leaf apart. The presence of obvious, silky threads between the veins will confirm that the plant is a dogwood of the genus *Cornus.* The last species represents the tupelos, formerly considered a separate family.

### FLOWERING DOGWOOD  *Cornus florida*

A large shrub to small tree of the understory or edges in a variety of dry to moist habitats. ► Grows to 30'. Leaves smooth-edged to wavy-edged. Twigs brown to reddish gray, sometimes even light purple. Four *very showy, large, white petal-like bracts* with *notched tips* surround the actual flowers in the center (small and greenish). Clusters of shiny, red berries. Burgundy fall foliage.

### GRAY DOGWOOD  *Cornus racemosa*

A common shrub of riparian and lake edges, swamps, and moist prairie edges; can form dense thickets. ► Grows to 12'. *Dome-shaped* clusters of many small, 4-petaled, white flowers produce white berries on reddish stalks. Young stems are pale green to reddish brown; older stems are ashy gray.

### ROUGH-LEAVED DOGWOOD  *Cornus drummondii*

A large shrub to small tree of riparian edges, savannas, and fence rows. ► Grows to 16'. Top surface of leaves *rough.* Flowers similar to those of Gray Dogwood except clusters are flat-topped. In fall, white berries on reddish stalks.

### RED-OSIER DOGWOOD  *Cornus sericea*

A shrub of varying moist habitats. ► Grows to 10'. Stems and twigs a *showy red,* more so in winter. Flowers and berries similar to those of Rough-leaved Dogwood; berry stalks may be green.

### ALTERNATE-LEAF DOGWOOD  *Cornus alternifolia*

A common large shrub to small tree growing as an understory or edge plant of moist to wet habitats . ► Grows to 30'. The only dogwood species on this page with *alternate leaves,* the others having opposite leaves. Distinctive-looking layered growth form due to its horizontal branches. Flowers, but not berries, similar to those of Rough-leaved Dogwood. Berries are dark bluish black on dull to bright red stalks.

### BLACK GUM  *Nyssa sylvatica*

A tree of varying habitats, from drier wooded slopes and sandy plains to lake and riparian edges. Also called Black Tupelo. Often dioecious (separate male and female plants). ► Grows to 80'. Glossy, smooth-edged, elliptical leaves. Lower branches droop toward base and are crooked. Bluish black fruits hang from long stalks in groups of 2 to 5. Brilliant fiery orange autumn foliage.

Flowering
Dogwood

Rough-leaved
Dogwood

Gray
Dogwood

Red-osier
Dogwood

Alternate-leaf
Dogwood

Black Gum

# VIBURNUMS AND ELDERBERRIES

Formerly placed in the honeysuckle family, these large shrubs or small trees are now classified in the moschatel family **(Adoxaceae)**. Members of this family have opposite, often toothed leaves, and flat-topped to dome-shaped flower clusters. Their fruits are readily consumed by birds and other animals.

### MAPLE-LEAVED VIBURNUM    *Viburnum acerifolium*

A short understory shrub of deciduous woods and forested dunes; often on slopes. ► Leaves 3-lobed, reminiscent of the shape of a maple leaf. Round clusters of small, white flowers; fruit black and shiny.

### NANNYBERRY    *Viburnum lentago*

A large shrub to small tree of riparian, lake, and swamp borders as well as fens, sedge meadows, and wet woods. One of our tallest viburnums. ► Grows to 25'. Glossy, finely toothed, oval leaves (2–4" long) with long pointed tips. Clusters of small, white, flat-topped flowers; fruit bluish black on red stalks. Flower stamens protrude halfway or more out of the corolla.

### BLACKHAW    *Viburnum prunifolium*

An understory to edge shrub of riparian, swamp, sedge meadow, wet thicket, and even rich deciduous upland forests. ► Grows to 15'. Leaves, flowers, and fruit similar to those of Nannyberry, but Blackhaw's leaves tend to be smaller and lack the longer tips. Also, flower stamens do not protrude out of the corolla nearly as far as they do in Nannyberry.

### ARROWWOOD VIBURNUMS    *Viburnum* sp.

Large shrubs of streambanks, swamps, moist forests. May be classified as multiple species or as one variable species. ► Unlobed leaves with coarsely pointed teeth along the margin. Flower clusters similar to those of Nannyberry, but with an *unpleasant odor.* Fruit blue to black initially on greenish brown stalks.

### COMMON ELDERBERRY    *Sambucus canadensis*

A common shrub of moist soils, often in open woodlands or at the edges of swamps, floodplains, ditches, meadows, and roadsides. ► Grows to 10'. Compound leaves with 5–9 finely toothed leaflets (often 7). *Flat-topped* clusters of white flowers, wider than they are tall, produce numerous *purplish black* berries.

### RED ELDERBERRY    *Sambucus racemosa* (not shown)

A shrub mainly of shaded habitats, such as beech-maple forests, mixed forests, wooded bogs, and swamps. ► Grows to 18'. Leaves like those of Common Elderberry, but often with only 5 leaflets. Flower clusters *dome-shaped to conical,* taller than they are wide; *red* berries.

# VIBURNUMS AND ELDERBERRIES

Maple-leaved
Viburnum

Nannyberry

Blackhaw

arrowwood viburnum sp.

Common
Elderberry

149

The first three species below are native to the U.S., with the first two being native in parts of our region. However, sometimes even our own native plants can become aggressive when habitats are significantly altered or when they are introduced into new areas outside of their normal range. The last three are aggressive, introduced, exotic species, trees that were never native to our region or country. In addition to these trees, see European Mountain-ash (p. 130).

## BLACK LOCUST  *Robinia pseudoacacia*

Native to about the southern one-third of our region. Introduced elsewhere as a landscape tree for its stunning spring bloom. Has become established and has spread, proving difficult to control. Pea family (Fabaceae). ▶ Alternate compound leaves with oval leaflets. Twigs often with *pairs of thorns* at each node. Hanging clusters of aromatic white flowers in spring.

## FALSE INDIGO  *Amorpha fruticosa*

A shrub of lake, river, and marsh edges. Native throughout much of region but can be aggressive outside of range, crowding out other natives. Pea family (Fabaceae). ▶ Grows to 15'. Alternate compound leaves with oblong leaflets, each leaflet usually with a *minute spiny tip*. Spikelike clusters of purplish flowers with protruding yellow stamens.

## OSAGE ORANGE  *Maclura pomifera*

Native to Oklahoma, Arkansas, and e. Texas, this tree has been widely planted in the Midwest as a living hedge fence. Sprouts from roots can be difficult to control. Mulberry, or fig, family (Moraceae). ▶ Leaves dark green, glossy, with a slightly wavy edge and long tips; exude *white latex sap* when picked. Twigs with single thorn at each leaf node. *Large*, bumpy, spherical fruit ("hedge apples") to 5" in diameter.

## WHITE MULBERRY  *Morus alba*

Introduced from Asia for a failed silkworm industry in colonial times. Has spread, impacting our native Red Mulberry (p. 134) via hybridization and competition. Fig family (Moraceae). ▶ Similar to Red Mulberry but upper surface of leaves *smooth*. Leaves with 0–7 lobes; tips of lobes often round, not pointed. Leaves and fruit smaller; fruit usually whitish to red (sometimes black), while Red Mulberry's mature fruits are red to black.

## NORWAY MAPLE  *Acer platanoides*

Originally introduced as a landscape tree, it has become a problem in some wild habitats. Soapberry family (Sapindaceae). ▶ Similar to Sugar Maple (p. 132) but its petioles exude *milky sap* when removed from stem and its samaras (fruits) have widely diverging wings.

## TREE-OF-HEAVEN (AILANTHUS)  *Ailanthus altissima*

Introduced from Asia for the colonial silkworm industry, later planted on roadsides for its pollution resistance, it has become a problematic species. Quassia family (Simaroubaceae). ▶ *Very long* compound leaves (to 3') with up to 41 smooth-edged leaflets, each with one or more *coarse basal teeth*. Inconspicuous greenish flowers produce clusters of dry, hanging fruit.

# INVASIVE EXOTICS AND AGGRESSIVE NATIVES

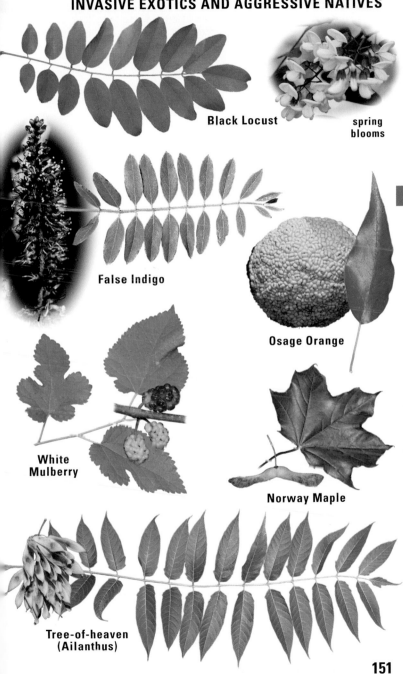

**Black Locust**

spring blooms

**False Indigo**

**Osage Orange**

**White Mulberry**

**Norway Maple**

**Tree-of-heaven (Ailanthus)**

Not all introduced species become problematic; some have little to no impact within our varied habitats. Others turn out to be well adapted to our local conditions. If they then lack many or all of the limiting factors that normally kept them in check back in their original ranges, they may aggressively spread, outcompeting our natives. Such species are called invasive. On this page we cover a few of the most insidious exotic shrubs that are outcompeting our natives in many habitats. These all produce fruit, and their seeds are dispersed over long distances by birds.

### AMUR HONEYSUCKLE    *Lonicera maackii*
Several exotic bush honeysuckles, invasive in the Midwest, can be difficult to identify to species. Honeysuckle family (Caprifoliaceae). ▶ Densely branched. Leaves oval to lance-shaped. Very fragrant, white, tubular flowers are either on *very short* pedicels (flower stalks) or sessile (attached directly to stem); flowers turn yellow with age. Dark red berries. **Morrow's Honeysuckle** (*L. morrowii*) is similar but flowers have long, often hairy pedicels. **Tatarian Honeysuckle** (*L. tatarica)* has leaves with a slightly heart-shaped base; white to pink flowers that do not turn yellow as they age.

### EUROPEAN HIGHBUSH CRANBERRY    *Viburnum opulus*
An invasive shrub of streambanks, forest edges, roadsides. Moschatel family (Adoxaceae). The true cranberries in the genus *Vaccinium* (p. 154) are unrelated. ▶ Leaves 3-lobed, maple-like, with a few teeth; have bristly stipules (leaflike growth at base of leaf). Clusters of white, flat-topped flowers produce hanging reddish orange berries. **American Highbush Cranberry** (*V. trilobum)*, an uncommon native, is similar, but leaves have longer central lobe and fewer to no teeth, and often lack stipules.

### GLOSSY BUCKTHORN    *Rhamnus frangula*
An invasive shrub of wetlands, also moist prairies and rich woodland edges. Buckthorn family (Rhamnaceae). ▶ Oval leaves with smooth edges, glossy on the upper surface. Fruits black. **European Buckthorn** (*R. cathartica)* has finely toothed leaves and tends to invade drier upland soils.

### AUTUMN OLIVE    *Elaeagnus umbellata*
Introduced from Asia as an ornamental. Now a major problem. Oleaster family (Elaeagnaceae). ▶ Twigs and green leaves have silvery and brownish scales; overall silvery green, shiny appearance. Small clusters of strongly fragrant, white, 4-lobed, tubular flowers; juicy red fruits. **Russian Olive** (*E. angustifolia)*, also invasive, has silvery gray upper leaf surfaces, yellowish flowers, dry yellowish brown fruits.

### JAPANESE BARBERRY    *Berberis thunbergii*
Barberry family (Berberidaceae). ▶ Leaves smooth-edged, unlobed. Spines at leaf nodes. Clusters of small, creamy flowers produce bright red fruit.

### WINGED EUONYMUS    *Euonymus alatus*
Bittersweet family (Celastraceae). ▶ Pairs of finely toothed, opposite leaves. Stems distinctly *winged*. Small, 4-petaled chartreuse flowers. Purplish fruit capsules curl back when ripe, exposing red arils (fleshy seed covering).

# EXOTIC INVASIVE SHRUBS

Amur
Honeysuckle

Glossy Buckthorn

European
Highbush
Cranberry

Autumn Olive

Japanese Barberry

Winged
Euonymus

153

# SMALL SHRUBS OF BOGS AND ACIDIC SOILS

The species below all belong to the heath family (**Ericaceae**), which includes 36 species in the Midwest. All require, or do best in, moist, acidic soils. Most of the small shrubs below are found in very specific habitats — bogs, poor fens, and other nutrient-poor acidic environments.

## BOG ROSEMARY *Andromeda polifolia*

An evergreen shrub, often standing out from other vegetation; grows to 18". ▶ Leathery, blue-green, alternating lance-shaped leaves held erect; *leaf edges rolled down;* undersurface usually *white.* Small white to pink urn-shaped flowers hang in clusters.

## BOG LAUREL *Kalmia polifolia*

An evergreen shrub of bogs, poor fens, sphagnum hummocks of dune swales. ▶ Grows to 2'. Opposite leaves leathery, linear, blunt to pointed, edges turn down but not obviously rolled; often white below. Light to dark pink flowers are large, showy, open, saucer-shaped, *not* bell or urn shaped.

## EASTERN TEABERRY *Gaultheria procumbens*

A low-stature, creeping evergreen shrub of moist, sandy, acidic forest soils; can tolerate dry soils and fire. ▶ Dark green, shiny, oval leaves turn reddish green with frost. Urn-shaped flowers small, usually white, sometimes tinged pink. Ripe fruit bright red. Bruised leaves and fruit emit *wintergreen odor.*

## BEARBERRY *Arctostaphylos uva-ursi*

Unlike others on this page, often found in habitats without acidic soils: oak openings, jack pine forests, dunes. Evergreen, and can form extensive carpets. ▶ Glossy, leathery, spoon-shaped leaves turn reddish brown with frost. Reddish bark, peeling in places. Small, white urn-shaped flowers tinged pink at tip.

## LEATHERLEAF *Chamaedaphne calyculata*

One of our most abundant evergreen shrubs of open bogs; forms large thickets. ▶ Grows to 3'. Leathery oval leaves, reducing in size as they approach tips of branches, green on top side, olive green below; turn purplish in winter. Branches covered in tiny, tan scales. Small, white bell-shaped flowers.

## EARLY LOW BLUEBERRY *Vaccinium angustifolium*

A common deciduous shrub of peatlands; also damp sandy soils of savannas, prairies, dunes, and woodlands. One of the economically important species of native, wild blueberry. ▶ Grows up to 2' tall. Small, glossy, finely toothed, elliptical leaves. Small, white bell-shaped flowers; edible ripe fruit light to dark bluish black.

## LARGE CRANBERRY *Vaccinium macrocarpon*

A trailing evergreen shrub; can form thick mats, especially near water in bogs. ▶ Grows to 8". Leaves tiny, oblong, leathery, glossy. Pinkish white flowers with 4 curved-back petals. Tart red oblong berries hang from slender twig; unripe berries white-tinged.

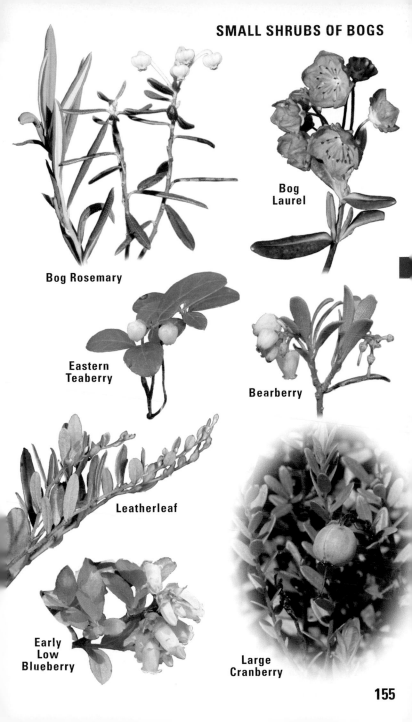

# SMALL SHRUBS OF BOGS

Bog Rosemary

Bog Laurel

Eastern Teaberry

Bearberry

Leatherleaf

Early Low Blueberry

Large Cranberry

155

# ROSES AND ROSELIKE SHRUBS

These are all in the rose family **(Rosaceae)**, which includes 314 species in our region. Most rose family members are deciduous and have showy, five-petaled flowers. They span the spectrum from small wildflowers to tall trees, so other species appear in other sections of this guide.

### PASTURE ROSE  *Rosa carolina*

A rose of dry to slightly moist oak savannas, rocky glades, disturbed areas, dunes, and sandy to black soil prairies. ▶ Leaves with 5–7 (sometimes fewer) coarse-toothed leaflets; straight, round prickles on stem, fewer to none on newer growth. Large, pale to bright pink showy, fragrant flowers; red berrylike fruit (rose hip). Grows 1–4' (rarely taller).

### SWAMP ROSE  *Rosa palustris*

A rose of wet, often acid soils such as marshes, riparian banks, seeps, and bogs. ▶ Leaves with 5–9 (usually 7) finely toothed leaflets; downward-curving prickles on stem. Grows to 8' tall.

### COMMON BLACKBERRY  *Rubus allegheniensis*

Definite ID of the next 2 might be challenging, as there are roughly 80 species of *Rubus* in the Midwest. This very common species is found in dry to moist fields, forest edges, and other partly to sunny disturbed areas. ▶ Compound leaves often have 3 oval leaflets but may have 5–7; edges sharply toothed; numerous small prickles on long petiole. Stems (canes) erect, greenish with straight prickles; older canes arching, reddish purple, hooked prickles. Terminal clusters of white flowers produce large black berries longer than wide. Grows 3–7' tall.

### BLACK RASPBERRY  *Rubus occidentalis*

Edges of woods, prairies, roadsides, other clearings. ▶ Grows to 6' tall. Compound leaves have 3 leaflets (rarely 5), with whitish underside. Slender prickly canes have white waxy covering; older canes purplish. Whitish berries turn red, then black when ripe; when picked berry has hollow center.

### MEADOWSWEET  *Spiraea alba*

Moist to wet prairies, riparian and marsh edges, bogs. ▶ Alternate leaves long, narrow, fine-toothed, sharp-tipped. Clusters of tiny white flowers arranged in a conical spike. Grows 2–5' tall.

### STEEPLEBUSH  *Spiraea tomentosa*

Moist to wet sandy or peaty soils. ▶ Alternate, elliptical, toothed leaves, often blunt-tipped; underleaf with whitish orange fuzz. Clusters of tiny pink flowers in conical spike. Grows 2–4' tall.

### SHRUBBY CINQUEFOIL  *Dasiphora fruticosa*

Uncommon on wet calcareous soils, tamarack swamps, rocky shores. ▶ Leaves with 3–7 lobes covered in *fine silver hairs*. New stems reddish brown and hairy; older stems grayish brown with shredding bark. Bright yellow flowers. Grows to 3' tall.

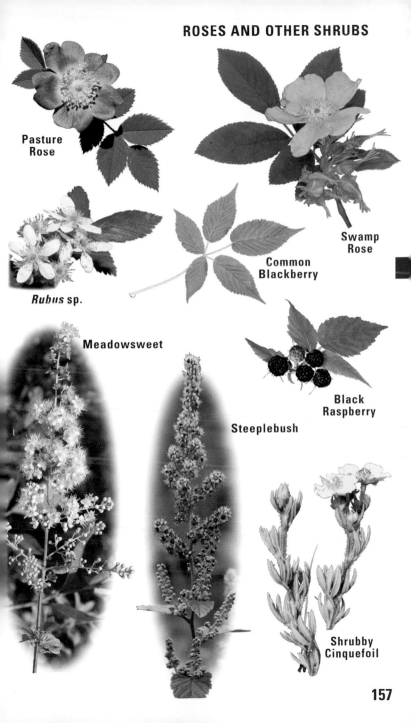

# ROSES AND OTHER SHRUBS

Pasture
Rose

Swamp
Rose

*Rubus* sp.

Common
Blackberry

Meadowsweet

Black
Raspberry

Steeplebush

Shrubby
Cinquefoil

### NORTHERN BUSH-HONEYSUCKLE    *Diervilla lonicera*

A shrub of shaded, dry woodlands, savannas, rocky slopes. A recommended native substitute for the highly invasive species of nonnative *Lonicera* (see Japanese Honeysuckle, p. 164). ▶ Grows to 4'. Wide, oval, finely toothed opposite leaves; terminal clusters of yellowish orange, five-part, tubular flowers on arching stems.

### LEAD PLANT    *Amorpha canescens*

A deep-rooted, hardy shrub of dry sand prairies and savannas. Pea family (Fabaceae). ▶ Grows to 3'. Compound leaves with tiny, bluish gray leaflets, covered with *whitish hairs*. Terminal flower spike a cluster of small purple flowers with orange anthers.

### NEW JERSEY TEA    *Ceanothus americanus*

A shrub of sunny to partially shaded prairies, savannas, and openings. ▶ Grows to 4'. Green elliptical, fine-toothed leaves, grayish and hairy below. Round clusters of fragrant, tiny, white flowers appear on the ends of long stalks. Young twigs *yellow*.

### WILD BLACK CURRANT    *Ribes americanum*

Moist to wet soils in partially shaded riparian corridors, lakes, wetlands, swamps, forests. ▶ Grows 3–5' tall. Toothed leaves with 3–5 lobes; surfaces of leaf have tiny yellow dots (glands); stems arching, older ones slightly winged; dangling bell-shaped, chartreuse flowers produce edible black berries.

### PRICKLY WILD GOOSEBERRY    *Ribes cynosbati*

Partially shaded woodland slopes and borders, in dry to moist, often rocky soils. ▶ Grows 2–4' tall. Scalloped-edged leaves with 3–5 lobes. Stem may or may not have prickles; stem nodes often with spines; edible (but prickly) berries purple when ripe.

### ALDER BUCKTHORN    *Rhamnus alnifolia*

An uncommon shrub of high-quality wetlands. ▶ Grows to 3'. Oval leaves with rounded teeth; small chartreuse flowers look like 5-pointed star, lack petals (have only sepals); fruit black. Compare to nonnative Glossy Buckthorn (p. 152).

### EASTERN PRICKLY PEAR    *Opuntia humifusa*

One of 3 native species of cactus (family **Cactaceae**) in the region. Dry, sandy prairies, savannas, rocky bluffs. ▶ Grows 8–12" tall. Paddle-shaped leaves (pads) may have obvious, long spines; buds on pads and fruit protected by hairlike spines (glochids) that easily enter skin and are hard to remove. Large, waxy yellow flowers may have orange centers. Produces a red, edible fruit.

### PLAINS PRICKLY PEAR; TWISTSPINE    *Opuntia macrorhiza*

(not shown) A native cactus of well-drained clay to sandy soils. ▶ Grows 6–18" tall. Similar to above species but areoles often with 2 or more spines, some pointing downward. Tuberous roots.

# OTHER LOW SHRUBS
(not all shown at same scale)

Northern
Bush-Honeysuckle

New
Jersey
Tea

Lead
Plant

Wild
Black
Currant

Prickly
Wild
Gooseberry

Alder
Buckthorn

Eastern
Prickly Pear

# WOODY VINES

Vines on this page are woody, meaning their stems do not die back to the ground each fall. The first six lack tendrils; they creep along the ground or climb by twining. The last two have tendrils that assist with climbing.

### RUNNING STRAWBERRY BUSH    *Euonymus obovatus*

In woodlands, growing as a shrub or creeping vine. ► Opposite, oval leaves. One to 4 small, coppery green, 5-petaled flowers attached to leaf axis on long stalk. Whitish, 3-part fruit capsule turns *pink or orange* when ripe; bright scarlet fruits enclosed.

### MOONSEED    *Menispermum canadense*

A dioecious vine (separate male and female plants) of shaded riparian corridors, thickets, deciduous woods. ► Leaves alternate, shallowly lobed, with smooth edges. Fruit (poisonous to humans) resembles a wild grape drupe; inside is a *crescent-shaped* seed.

### VIRGIN'S BOWER    *Clematis virginiana*

A twining vine of riparian corridors, moist woodlands, lake and wetland borders; very shade tolerant. ► Bright green compound leaf with three leaflets. Clusters of showy white flowers produce clumps of *fluffy, plumelike seeds.*

### RED HONEYSUCKLE    *Lonicera dioica*

A low-climbing vine of forests and wetland edges. ► Oblong, opposite leaves. Last pair of leaves *fused* to form cup from which a cluster of tubular flowers emerges; flower tubes often deep maroon with yellow to orange petals. Produces red berries.

### TRUMPET CREEPER    *Campsis radicans*

Common in lower Midwest, climbing by attachment of aerial rootlets. In full sun and rich soil, becomes aggressive. ► Long compound leaves; leaflets with jagged edges. Long (to 4") orange to scarlet, tubular flowers produce beanlike seed capsules.

### EASTERN POISON IVY    *Toxicodendron radicans*

Common as groundcover or climbing vine. Most people have allergic reaction from touching any part of plant. Cashew family (Anacardiaceae). ► Compound leaves with *3 pointy leaflets,* variable in shape, often shiny. Older stems thick, hairy (actually aerial rootlets); clusters of *white, waxy berries,* favored by birds.

### VIRGINIA CREEPER    *Parthenocissus quinquefolia*

A very common, widespread vine in the grape family (Vitaceae). Climbs with the help of tendrils. ► Distinct, compound leaves usually with 5 toothed leaflets; younger leaves may have only 3 leaflets, can be mistaken for Poison Ivy. Leaves bright red in fall.

### WILD GRAPES    *Vitis* sp.

The region has 7 grape species. Grape vines can quickly spread to cover large areas. ► Large, lobed leaves with big teeth; shape varies between and within species. Clusters of edible, purplish berries.

# WOODY VINES

ripe fruit

**Running Strawberry Bush**

**Moonseed**

**Virgin's Bower**

seeds

**Red Honeysuckle**

**Trumpet Creeper**

fall color

**Eastern Poison Ivy**

**Virginia Creeper**

**Wild Grape**

# NONWOODY (HERBACEOUS) VINES

All of these herbaceous vines die back to the ground each fall and lack woody stems. The first four lack tendrils and climb objects via twining. The last four have tendrils that assist with climbing up objects.

### WILD YAM    *Dioscorea villosa*

A twining vine of moist woodlands, sand prairies and savannas, wetland edges, riparian corridors. Dioecious (separate male and female plants). ▶ *Heart-shaped leaves* with strong venation. Male flowers tiny, white, branching clusters. Female flowers similar but with swollen base; produce 3-winged seed capsules.

### HEDGE BINDWEED    *Calystegia sepium*

A twining vine in the morning glory family (Convolvulaceae). ▶ Long triangular leaves with *squarish to rounded lobes* at base. Showy, white to pinkish funnel-shaped flowers up to 3" across.

### GROUND NUT    *Apios americana*

A common, low-climbing vine of moist woodland edges, wetlands, prairies, and rivers; has edible tubers, hence the common name. Pea family (Fabaceae). ▶ Compound leaf with 3–7 leaflets. Cluster of pink to red-brown flowers arises from leaf axis.

### UPRIGHT CARRION FLOWER    *Smilax ecirrhata*

### SMOOTH CARRION FLOWER    *Smilax herbacea*

Plants in the genus *Smilax* can be vines or small shrubs. Some species are herbaceous, some are woody. Some have thorns, others do not. Members of this genus with thorns are the woody Green Briers or Catbriers. Those that lack thorns or bristles are the herbaceous Carrion Flowers. Here are 2 herbaceous species — the second with tendrils, the first without.

### BEACH PEA    *Lathyrus japonicus*

A creeping vine of sandy or gravelly beach shorelines along the Great Lakes. Has tendrils, often climbs beach grasses. Pea family. ▶ Bluish green, waxy, compound leaves with up to 6 pairs of leaflets and a branching tendril at tip. Clusters of bluish pink to lavender pea flowers, often with white lower petals; produces flattened pea pods.

### DODDER    *Cuscuta* sp.

These odd vines, with 15 species in our region, lack chlorophyll (mostly) and parasitize other plants to obtain food. Morning glory family. ▶ *Leafless, orange or yellow twining stems* are obvious against green foliage of host; stem attaches to host via suckers (haustoria). Clusters of tiny flowers erupt along the stem.

### WILD CUCUMBER    *Echinocystis lobata*

A climbing vine of wet soils, including riparian corridors, swamp forest, wetlands. Gourd family (Cucurbitaceae). ▶ Leaves with 5 pointed lobes; smooth stems with branching tendrils. White flowers with 6 petals; seedpod *like a small, spiny watermelon.*

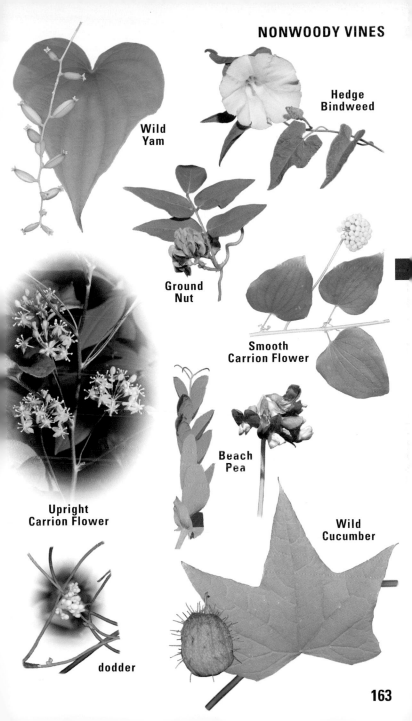

Wild Yam

Hedge Bindweed

Ground Nut

Smooth Carrion Flower

Upright Carrion Flower

Beach Pea

Wild Cucumber

dodder

163

# INVASIVE SMALL SHRUBS AND VINES

A few nonnative small shrubs and vines that have become problematic or invasive. Each is listed as invasive in one or more midwestern states, with a few recognized as major problems throughout their U.S. range.

### MULTIFLORA ROSE  *Rosa multiflora*

An aggressive woody rose introduced from Asia in the late 1880s; disturbed fields and woodlands, roadsides, fencerows. Can grow as a shrub (to 6') or climbing vine (to 12'). ▶ Compound leaves with 3–9 toothed leaflets; distinct, feathery stipules at the leaf base. Long, arching canes (stems) with thick, curved thorns. Profuse white, 5-petaled flowers yield berrylike fruits (rose hips).

### PERIWINKLE  *Vinca minor*

A small shrub (to 10") or trailing vine in sunny to partly shaded woodlands. Can invade native stands of woodland wildflowers, smothering them with dense carpet of vegetation. ▶ Leaves dark green glossy, oval, waxy; ooze milky liquid when broken. Lavender colored, 5-petaled flowers with blunt tips.

### BITTERSWEET NIGHTSHADE  *Solanum dulcamara*

A trailing or twining vine of moist soils in wetlands, forest edges, disturbed fields. ▶ Purplish brown stems with 3-lobed, spade-shaped leaves. Dangling clusters of purple flowers with five curved-back petals, their yellow anthers forming a protruding cone; bright red berries that can be toxic to humans.

### JAPANESE HONEYSUCKLE  *Lonicera japonica*

An aggressive, woody, twining vine of sunny to partially shaded areas; can cover large areas and climb other plants. ▶ Older stems with light reddish brown shredding bark. Opposite, oval leaves can be evergreen. White, fragrant, 2-lipped flowers turn dingy yellow with age; produce small, often paired, black berries.

### ORIENTAL BITTERSWEET  *Celastrus orbiculatus*

A climbing, woody vine that winds tightly around host; can kill trees by girdling. Invader of edge habits in forests, lakes, roads, fields. ▶ Oval, finely toothed, blunt-tipped leaves. Clusters of chartreuse flowers from leaf axils. Distinctive orange-yellow capsules that contrast with red fruit. Native **American Bittersweet** (*C. scandens*) has terminal cluster of flowers. Its capsules and fruit are all the same reddish orange, without contrast in color.

### ENGLISH IVY  *Hedera helix*

A woody, evergreen climbing vine. Aggressive, can invade natural areas. Attaches to trees and other surfaces with rootlike structures. ▶ Waxy, dark green, variably shaped leaves, often 3–5 lobed.

### KUDZU  *Pueraria montana*

A very aggressive, rapid-growing, climbing vine that can smother or girdle plants. Pea family (Fabaceae). ▶ Large, compound, 3-lobed leaves; upright clusters of fragrant, purple flowers.

Multiflora
Rose

Periwinkle

Bittersweet
Nightshade

Japanese
Honeysuckle

Oriental Bittersweet

English Ivy

Kudzu

165

As a group, these are living representatives of the oldest plants on Earth. A few are often referred to as living fossils, as surviving examples of their lineage, having first evolved hundreds of millions of years ago.

Primitive plants produce spores instead of seeds. It is primarily this trait, and not their evolutionary age, that gives them the label primitive. Primitive plants are dependent on water to assist with fertilization. This is why ferns, mosses, and other primitive plants for the most part are found in moist to wet places — although some ferns and mosses are known to live and thrive in periodically desiccating environments.

Although green algae are considered primitive plants by some, we cover them only briefly in introducing the fungi and kin (pp. 176–177).

**Origins and diversity.** Ferns first appeared near the end of the Devonian Period. Fossil records indicate that the start of their lineage (the monilophytes) was around 380 million years ago. Most of the modern families of ferns, those that are alive today, evolved in the middle of the Cretaceous Period, arriving on scene as the flowering plants were rising to dominance. There are now about 11,500 species of ferns worldwide, making them the second largest group of plants in terms of diversity, behind the flowering plants. In the Midwest, we are fortunate to have roughly 120 species.

**Ferns in detail.** Ferns are most evident in the growing season. Most species are herbaceous, dying back in the winter. But a few of our ferns are evergreen — their leaves remain green and visible throughout the year.

Fern leaves are called fronds. In many species, fronds emerge in spring, tightly coiled into so-called fiddleheads. As they grow, the fiddleheads uncoil, expanding and unfurling to become full-grown fronds. The fronds arise from the fern's rhizome. This horizontal (in many species) stem might be mistaken for the fern's roots. But the rhizome is actually the stem to which leaves attach. The true roots grow down from the stem on most species. The rhizome runs either just below or along the soil's surface. This trait often depends on the species and can be helpful in identification.

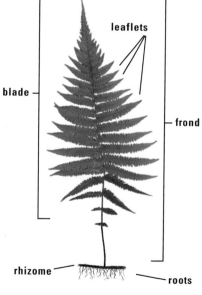

**Simplified diagram of the parts of a fern**

In this guide we avoid technical terms when possible, but it's useful to know a few botanical terms (see diagram to left). In the species accounts, we use the word *blade* for the leafy part of the frond, while *frond* applies to the entire leaf. In those species that have compound leaves (divided leaf blades), we use the term *leaflet* for the smaller sections of the blade. We refer to the central part of the frond as the *stalk*, but botanists divide the stalk into two parts: the lower part of the leaf, the area below the leafy part, is called the *stipe* (petiole or leafstalk); the upper part of the leaf, the leaf-bearing part, is called the *rachis.*

The majority of fern reproduction is probably asexual. Ferns often spread via vegetative growth, by clone formation off of their rhizomes. But ferns also reproduce sexually; most of the fern species, and other primitive plants, require liquid water to assist with fertilization.

Like all other primitive plants, ferns do not produce flowers or seeds. Instead, sexual reproduction is accomplished via spores. A fern's spores are microscopic and produced in tiny cases called sporangia. These sporangia are gathered into clusters called sori, which appear as brownish tan dots or sacs, often on the undersides of the leaflets. When the spores are mature, the sporangia open and the spores waft away in the wind.

The shape and type of a fern's spore-producing structures can be a useful identifying feature. In some species, sporangia occur on a modified portion of a normal frond and may occur on many or all of the fronds. In others, they are found on special, modified fronds that look entirely different from the normal, leafy fronds (see Cinnamon Fern, p. 168). Fronds that produce sporangia are termed fertile, whereas those that have no sporangia are termed sterile.

**Other primitive plants: mosses, clubmosses, and more.** Most of this section deals with ferns, but the final spread in this section (pp. 174–175) covers some non-fern primitive plants of the region. In particular, we look at a few of the bryophytes (true mosses, liverworts, and hornworts) and lycophytes (clubmosses, quillworts, spikemosses).

Modern bryophytes are representatives of the most primitive of all the land plants. Like their aquatic cousins the green algae, they lack vascular tissues. They are thought to have evolved before the first vascular plants. Lycophytes represent the most ancient of vascular plants, having evolved around 420 million years ago. Ferns, gymnosperms, and angiosperms make up the other groups of vascular plants. They branched off from an ancient relative of the modern-day lycophytes.

The coal deposits of the region are the compressed remains of the ancient bryophytes, lycophytes, and ferns that dominated the hot, moist tropical swamp forests of the Carboniferous Period. The next time you turn on your lights, think about the bryophytes!

Included on this page are representatives of the oldest living groups of ferns. Horsetails may not look like "typical" ferns, and until recently they were not treated as such. They were placed in the nebulous, artificial grouping of "fern allies." Recent molecular, fossil, and morphological studies now position horsetails within the fern lineage.

## HORSETAILS  *Equisetum* sp.

Found on edges of shady to sunny habitats in moist to wet soils. Perennial, most species herbaceous, a few evergreen. The genus *Equisetum* is the only remaining genus in its family, order, and class, making these living fossils of the primitive plant world. They are among the most ancient of the fern lineage, with fossils dating back 380 million years. Globally there are 20 species; in the Midwest, we have 10. ▶ Stems are cylindrical and segmented, with thickened nodes that superficially give them a bamboo appearance. Stems are hollow in some species, pith filled in others. A spore-producing, conelike structure (strobilus) appears at the tip of fertile stems, holding layers of spore cases (sporangia).

## CUT-LEAVED GRAPE FERN  *Sceptridium dissectum*

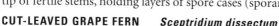

A short-stature, evergreen fern of moist, shaded woods. ▶ Grows up to 2' tall but often much shorter. Blades appear somewhat triangular; margin of blade varies between individuals, from deeply cut and lacy to smooth with few or no cuts. Fertile frond rises noticeably above rest of plant and has clusters of round sporangia. Green sterile fronds turn a bronze-green color after frost.

## CINNAMON FERN  *Osmundastrum cinnamomeum*

A fern of rich, wet, shaded to sunny habitats with sandy, acidic soils. ▶ Rosette of large, slightly arching fronds, 3–4' long or longer. *Upright fertile fronds* with *cinnamon-brown sporangia* rise from the center of the plant. Frond stem and leaflet bases have clumps of woolly brown hairs on the underside.

## INTERRUPTED FERN  *Osmunda claytoniana*

A fern of rich, sandy to rocky acidic soils, often found on sloping terrain. ▶ Grows to 5'. Doesn't have separate frond devoted to spore production. Instead, some fronds have spore-bearing structures (looking like withered, dried leaflets) that "interrupt" the blade in the middle. Frond stem and leaflet bases *lack* clumps of hair, a good distinction from Cinnamon Fern when there are no fertile structures.

## ROYAL FERN  *Osmunda regalis*

Another fern of rich, wet, shaded to sunny habitats with sandy, acidic soils. ▶ Grows 3–5' tall. Frond leaflets are themselves compound with their own large, oblong leaflets. No separate frond devoted to spore production; instead, spore-producing structures top some fronds.

# FERNS
(not all shown at same scale)

Cut-leaved
Grape Fern

horsetails

Cinnamon
Fern

Interrupted
Fern

Royal
Fern

# FERNS

The families on the next two spreads started appearing around 140 million years ago, with most evolving around the time flowering plants were rising to dominance. All of these ferns are members of the polypod fern order **(order Polypodiales).** With more than 9,300 species worldwide, ferns in this order account for about 80 percent of all living fern species. In the Midwest, we have around 70 species of polypod ferns.

### BRACKEN FERN    *Pteridium aquilinum*

A large, common fern that tolerates dry soils: woodland edges, disturbed areas. Often forms large colonies. Grows 3–4' tall (can be much taller). All parts of plant, from fiddleheads to spores, contain a potent carcinogen; levels can be reduced, but contrary to some culinary customs, it's best to avoid consuming these fiddleheads. ▶ Sturdy, erect petiole (stem) of frond can grow 3' high before unfurling its *3-part, triangular* compound blade.

### MAIDENHAIR FERN    *Adiantum pedatum*

A widespread, distinctive, delicate-looking fern of shaded, moist deciduous woods and slopes, ravines, rocky seeps. ▶ *Arc-shaped,* compound fronds often held horizontal to ground. Shiny black to deep reddish brown stalk, contrasting with greenish yellow, *fan-shaped to plume-shaped leaflets.*

### CHRISTMAS FERN    *Polystichum acrostichoides*

An evergreen fern of moist, shady woodlands, especially hillsides, riparian corridors, and rocky slopes. ▶ Grows to 18", rarely taller. Fronds emerge in circular clumps, arching, leathery, compound. Leaflets primarily alternate on stalk, each leaflet with conspicuous *basal lobe.* Stalk with whitish tan scaly appearance.

### COMMON POLYPODY    *Polypodium virginianum*

Grows in wooded and riparian areas on top of moist, mossy rocks and cliffs. ▶ Leathery evergreen leaves up to 12" long. Blades appear compound, but they're not: sinuses (separations between lobes) *deeply cut,* almost reaching stalk. Large sori appear in rows on underside of blade.

### LOWLAND FRAGILE FERN    *Cystopteris protrusa*

A common fern of moist, semi-shaded deciduous woodlands, riparian corridors. One of our spring ephemeral ferns: emerging in early spring, most fronds disappear by midsummer. Can carpet small areas. ▶ Fronds yellowish green, attractive, with finely cut compound leaflets. Stalk breaks easily, can be grooved, flattened, squarish. Stem (rhizome) extends past current year's fronds.

### COMMON OAK FERN    *Gymnocarpium dryopteris*

A fairly common, small, colonial fern of cool, moist, shady mixed forests, northern swamps. ▶ Broad triangular (3-part) blade with doubly compound leaflets held horizontally. Leaf stalk usually green, can be dark brown to black, especially near base.

# FERNS

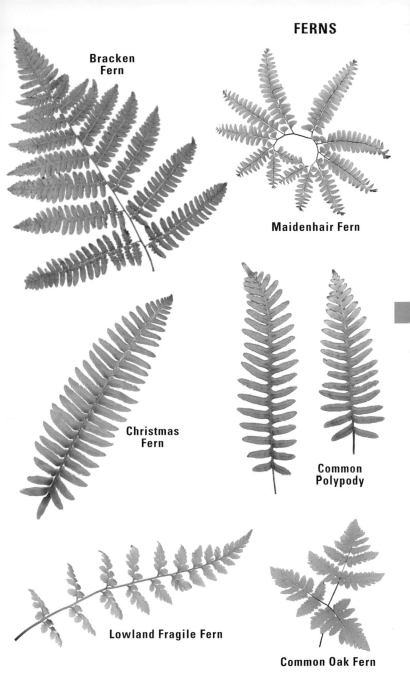

Bracken Fern

Maidenhair Fern

Christmas Fern

Common Polypody

Lowland Fragile Fern

Common Oak Fern

# FERNS

These are further examples of polypod ferns, introduced on p. 170. Each of the first three species below is in a separate family. The last two are the only members of the sensitive fern family (**Onocleaceae**).

### NORTHERN BEECH FERN *Phegopteris connectilis*

A fern primarily of coniferous and mixed forests, often on rocky slopes, streambanks, or moist hummocks; rarer in upland deciduous woodlands. ► Grows 1–2' tall. Compound blade longer than wide; bottom pair of leaflets usually point downward, sometimes at more than a 45-degree angle to leaflets above. *Winged extensions* join bases of leaflet pairs to stalk except on the bottom one or two pairs.

### LADY FERN *Athyrium filix-femina*

Widespread and common, growing in a variety of habitats with moist, rich soils. Loose circular clusters grow to 3'. ► Blades are doubly compound with finely toothed edges to leaflets. Blade *wider in the middle,* narrower toward the bottom, and tapering to a pointed tip. Slightly curved to hook-shaped sori on underside of some frond leaflets. Some individuals have red-tinted stalks.

### VIRGINIA CHAIN FERN *Woodwardia virginica*

A rare fern of the region found in moist, acidic sandy to peaty lake edges, forested swamps, and bogs. ► Leathery, doubly compound blades with deeply cut leaflets. Often linear (rather than clumping) growth results in formation of long colonies; fronds tend to orient in same direction. Common name comes from distinctive "chainlink" arrangement of oblong, immature sori along midvein of each subleaflet; double row of mature, orangish tan sori outline major veins of leaflet's underside.

### OSTRICH FERN *Matteuccia struthiopteris*

A large fern of moist swamp, stream, and wooded wetland edges and bottomland forests; can form large colonies. Fiddleheads of this species are a commonly collected wild edible. ► Grows in urnlike clusters 3–6' tall. Large, *plumelike* blade has deeply lobed leaflets; wider above the middle, quickly tapering to the tip. Erect fertile fronds up to 2', dark brown when mature.

### SENSITIVE FERN *Onoclea sensibilis*

Perhaps our most abundant fern. Found in a wide variety of moist to wet, shaded to sunny habitats; grows 1–3' tall (rarely taller). ► Sterile frond triangular in shape with central portion of stalk *winged* (compare to Northern Beech Fern above); fertile frond emerges from rhizome, forming branches of spore-containing, beadlike structures that turn dark brown when mature. Sterile frond dies back after a hard frost, hence the common name; dried fertile fronds persist through winter.

# FERNS

Northern Beech Fern

Lady Fern

detail: underside of leaflet

Virginia Chain Fern

Ostrich Fern

Sensitive Fern

173

# OTHER PRIMITIVE PLANTS

Like ferns, the first four species below are vascular plants. Lycophytes (clubmosses, quillworts, spikemosses) first evolved around 420 million years ago. These are living relatives of the most ancient of vascular plants. The last four species are bryophytes (true mosses, liverworts, and hornworts). They represent the most primitive of all land plants. Lacking vascular tissue, they do not have true leaves or roots.

### FAN CLUBMOSS    *Diphasiastrum digitatum*

May look like miniature cedar tree, but clubmosses are not conifers. In moist, sandy to rocky acidic soils; can form extensive colonies. ▶ Up to 8" tall. Small, scalelike leaves held closely to flattened fanlike horizontal branches; cylindrical strobili (conelike, spore-producing structures) held above plant on long stalks.

### BRISTLY CLUBMOSS    *Lycopodium annotinum*

Found in moist sandy soils, usually in coniferous or in mixed conifer-hardwood forests. ▶ Vertical stems with small, pointed leaves; noticeable constriction on stem indicates end of prior year's growth; strobili *stalkless,* attached directly to top of stem.

### GROUNDPINES    *Dendrolycopodium* sp.

Clubmosses of mixed conifer and hardwood forests; dry to moist, acidic sandy soils. Spread by underground stems (rhizomes) to form large colonies; named for treelike appearance.

### SPIKEMOSSES    *Selaginella* sp.

Four species in Midwest. Often mistaken for true mosses. Moist, acid to calcareous soils that are sandy to rocky. May form small colonies. ▶ Branching stems with small, scalelike leaves.

### HAIR CAP MOSSES    *Polytrichum* sp.
This and the next are true mosses. There are a handful of hair cap mosses in the Midwest, growing 2–16" tall. ▶ Erect, stemlike structures with leaflike whorls form a *starry look* when viewed from above.

### SPHAGNUM MOSS    *Sphagnum* sp.
Bogs, fens, conifer swamps, and other wet, acidic habitats. This genus represents a subclass of mosses called the peat mosses; there are more than 30 species in our region. Can hold up to 25 times its dry weight in water.

### GREAT SCENTED LIVERWORT    *Conocephalum conicum* (not shown)
Found on moist surfaces of forest and streamside soils. Can form large mats. ▶ Leathery, flat branching leaflike structures, dark green with scalelike polygons dividing top surface; resembles snake skin. Emits distinctive, musty cinnamon odor when bruised.

### COMMON LIVERWORT    *Marchantia polymorpha*
Common, widespread. Moist habitats, especially soils recently disturbed (such as by fire). ▶ Surface of leaflike structure similar to above, but polygons not as regular or scalelike; cuplike male reproductive structures; female structures like tiny umbrellas.

# OTHER PRIMITIVE PLANTS
## Lycophytes and Bryophytes

Fan Clubmoss

Bristly Clubmoss

groundpine

spikemoss

sphagnum moss

hair cap moss

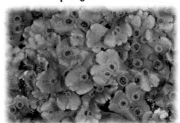

Common Liverwort

# FUNGI AND THEIR KIN

Historically fungi were classified as plants. Science now firmly places fungi into a separate kingdom. Nonetheless, mycology (the study of fungi) and botany share a deep tradition, so we cover this interesting group of organisms at the end of the botanical sections of this guide.

Fungi range from yeasts to molds to those that produce mushrooms. Unlike most plants, fungi cannot photosynthesize (use the sun's energy to convert carbon dioxide and water into nutrition). Instead, they are heterotrophs. They must get their food from other living (or formerly living) things.

Fungi employ one or more of the following methods to get nutrition. Some form a mutualistic relationship with plants (see Mycorrhizal associations). Others are saprophytes (they secrete enzymes to break down dead organic matter). Finally, some are parasites (they obtain their nutrition in a non-beneficial manner directly from a living host).

The next time you're at a restaurant and see mushrooms listed among the vegetable choices, feel free to educate the servers, chef, and restaurateur about the fact that mushrooms are not plants. But you might want to do this after your food has been served and you have paid the bill!

**The importance of fungi.** Organisms get nutrition from their ecosystem. Some, like plants, can manufacture much of their food via photosynthesis. These are called autotrophs. Others, like animals and fungi, obtain all their nutrients from their environment. These are the heterotrophs. They must obtain their food source by consuming parts of other organisms.

But when organisms die, the nutrients they produced or consumed — which were then converted into bodily structures — are trapped within their tissues. Without a mechanism to recycle these nutrients back into the ecosystem, they would remain locked into the tissues of the dead organism. This is where the decomposers fit into the web of life. Decomposers, the organisms that break down tissues of usually dead things, play a key role in nutrient recycling. It is thought that fungi are among the most important of the decomposers.

**Meet a fungus.** The bodies of all fungi, except the single-celled yeasts, are made up of a network of microscopic filaments (hyphae) that weave throughout their growth medium. These filaments come together to form a larger, sometimes visible, stringy growth form called a mycelium. In certain species, when conditions are optimum, groups of mycelium (mycelia) combine to form mushrooms.

Not all fungi produce visible fruiting structures (mushrooms). In the following pages, we show a few of the obvious mushroom-forming fungi.

**A word of warning!** When picking mushrooms for consumption, you *must* be absolutely *positive* about their identification. Many edible mushrooms have dangerous or deadly look-alikes, and this field guide cannot even begin to provide enough detail for you to safely identify them. Do not even think about eating wild mushrooms unless you are already an expert!

**What are mushrooms?** Many people use the terms *fungus* and *mushroom* interchangeably. But mushrooms are simply the visible part of a fungus, the aboveground fruiting structure of the organism that produces spores, facilitating its reproduction. Like an iceberg with only a small part of its bulk showing above the water's surface, a mushroom represents only a small fraction of the overall size of the fungus. The rest of the organism is buried within the substrate in which it grows.

**Mycorrhizal associations.** Some species of fungi have a close, unique, and mutually beneficial relationship with plants. Their microscopic hyphae intermingle with and connect to the microscopic root hairs of the partner plant. This is called a mycorrhizal (from the Greek for fungus and roots) association. The extensive network of fungal hyphae can significantly increase the plant's water absorption rates and efficiency. The fungus also provides micronutrients that might otherwise not be accessible. In return, the fungus obtains nutrition in the form of carbohydrates (sugars) produced by the plant.

The vast majority of all vascular plants are thought to engage in some form of mycorrhizal relationship with fungi. Such mutualistic associations between fungi and plants occur in forest, prairie, wetland, and many other habitat types.

**What are lichens?** On the last spread of this section (pp. 184–185), we introduce the lichens. Lichens are not single organisms. Instead each is a symbiotic partnership, usually mutualistic, between at least two different species of organisms. One organism is a fungus (referred to as the mycobiont) and the other is a photosynthetic partner (referred to as the photobiont). The photobiont can be a species of green algae, a cyanobacterium, or rarely both. This collective is thus formed from different species of organisms from at least two different kingdoms or rarely from three.

It is important to note that the various species of green algae that are known to associate with certain fungi to form lichen are related to, but different from, the lineage of green algae from which land plants evolved.

As discussed above, fungi are heterotrophic. That is, they must obtain their nutrition from an outside source. Through photosynthesis, the photobiont serves this role, providing simple sugars (carbohydrates) to its fungal partner. The fungus, in return, provides suitable conditions for the long-term survival of the photobiont. The lichen body (often referred to as the thallus) is manufactured by the fungus. This structure provides a protective enclosure for the photobiont, keeping it safe from desiccation and ultraviolet radiation.

This relationship is quite successful. Lichens colonize a wide range of habitats, some with extreme conditions. Although lichens are slow growing, they can be very long lived. The average growth rate of lichens is thought to be no more than 0.16 inches (4 mm) per year. Lichens that are several thousand years old have been discovered.

The species below are a sampling of some of the fungi that produce gilled mushrooms. The first six species grow out of the ground. The last two grow out of wood. Not only is the presence or absence of gills a useful field mark for identifying fungi when they fruit and form a mushroom, but noting the substrate on which they grow is useful as well.

### E. NORTH AMERICAN DESTROYING ANGEL    *Amanita bisporigera*

Most amanitas are mildly to severely poisonous if eaten. This one is deadly. A common fungus of mixed woods, often associated with oaks. Microscopic and chemical examination required to distinguish it from similar *Amanita* species. ▶ All-white mushroom with white gills and sac (volva) at base (volva may be buried, as in the illustrations here); thin skirt ringing upper stalk. Cap initially domed, flattening with age.

### THE BLUSHER    *Amanita rubescens*

Common in deciduous and coniferous woods; another oak associate. The common name comes from the fact that the mushroom turns red if bruised. ▶ Convex to flat brownish cap with toffee-colored raised patches; ring at top of stalk.

### YELLOW PATCHES    *Amanita flavoconia*

Perhaps our most common *Amanita*; grows in mixed woods. ▶ A yellow-orange cap with *yellow raised patches* that fall off easily if rubbed. Stalk white to yellowish; yellowish veil fragments often at base of stem. The **Fly Agaric** (*A. muscaria*) is similar but has white patches on yellow or red cap.

### RUSSULAS    *Russula* sp.

With colors ranging from white, to yellow, to rosy red, to brown and black, fruiting russulas add visual intrigue to forests in which they grow. ▶ Stalks often (not always) white; gills white; top of caps often convex.

### DEEP ROOT MUSHROOMS    *Xerula* sp.

Deciduous woods. ▶ Mushrooms in this genus have *slender, long stalks* that taper toward tannish brown cap with white gills. Stalk, which goes deep into ground, is confused by some for a root, hence the common name.

### WAXY CAP MUSHROOMS    *Hygrocybe* sp.

Grows in grasslands, forest edges, mossy and wet mixed woods. ▶ Often brightly colored: yellow, red, orange, or green, depending on species. Cap feels *waxy or slimy* when wet.

### ORANGE MYCENA    *Mycena leaiana*

Small mushrooms that grow in clusters on dead wood. ▶ Short-stalked and small-capped (to 1.5" across). Shiny bright orange cap that fades to dull yellow or tan with age; numerous orange-edged gills under cap.

### PINWHEEL MARASMIUS    *Marasmius rotula*

A small mushroom of decaying twigs and other wood. ▶ Wiry dark stalks hold up tiny, white, umbrella-shaped mushrooms that have widely spaced gills.

# GILLED FUNGI

**gilled fungi on the ground**

**Eastern North American Destroying Angel**

**The Blusher**

**Yellow Patches**

**russulas**

**deep root mushrooms**

**waxy cap mushroom**

**gilled fungi on wood**

**Orange Mycena**

**Pinwheel Marasmius**

# NON-GILLED FUNGI ON THE GROUND

These produce non-gilled mushrooms that grow out of the ground, not out of wood. You may need to dig around the base of the mushroom to see if it is actually emerging from soil, or from a buried piece of wood.

**BOLETES**   *Boletus* sp.

Common in woods. Instead of gills, undersides of caps have tiny pores through which spores are released. ► Sturdy thick stem, broad rounded cap with a spongy feel underneath. In some, flesh turns blue when bruised.

**CHANTERELLES**   *Cantharellus* sp.

Common in woodlands. Species range from golden to orangish yellow to red. All edible, some delectable. ► Fluted, vase-shaped cap; most have ridges (not true gills) running partway down stalk. Don't confuse with superficially similar, and poisonous, **Jack O'Lantern** *(Omphalotus illudens).*

**GIANT PUFFBALL**   *Calvatia gigantea*

Grassy clearings, forest and riparian edges. ► Grows to 8–24" in diameter. No other fungi produce such a large, irregularly spherical mushroom. White surface with firm white interior; no stalk.

**EARTHSTARS**   *Geastrum* sp.

Sandy soils of open woods, dunes. ► Grows to 2" wide. Grayish black skin unfurls into star-shaped pattern (rays), revealing whitish spore sac. Rays close on dry days, protecting the sac, and reopen on wet days.

**BLACK TRUMPET**   *Craterellus fallax*

In coniferous and deciduous forests in mossy to exposed soils. Color, shape, and size make it hard to see. ► Grows to 3". Brown to black, hollow, funnel-shaped with smooth surface; single or in small clumps.

**ELEGANT STINKHORN**   *Mutinus elegans*

Odd fungus of woods and lawns, commonly found on landscaping wood chips. ► Long, pink to orangish tapering mushroom; tip initially covered with slimy brown substance. Strong, foul-smelling odor attracts flies.

**JELLIED FALSE CORAL**   *Tremellodendron pallidum*

Common fungus of deciduous and mixed woods. ► Series of fused, flattened, whitish to buff-colored branches, resembling coral.

**YELLOW MORELS**   *Morchella* sp.

Common in deciduous forests, orchards; a prized wild edible. ► Spongelike cap with yellow ridges. Roughly 10 species of yellow morel occur in our region, challenging to separate. True morels have hollow interiors (stems and caps); don't confuse with poisonous **False Morels** *(Gyromitra* sp.).

**YELLOW EARTH TONGUE**   *Microglossum rufum*

Uncommon on moist, mossy forest floors. ► Yellow to orange flattened, somewhat translucent, spoon-shaped heads on scaly stalks. Grows to 2".

**SCARLET CUPS**   *Sarcoscypha* sp.

An early spring and summer mushroom of deciduous forests. ► Cups with bright red interiors and dull, pale exteriors.

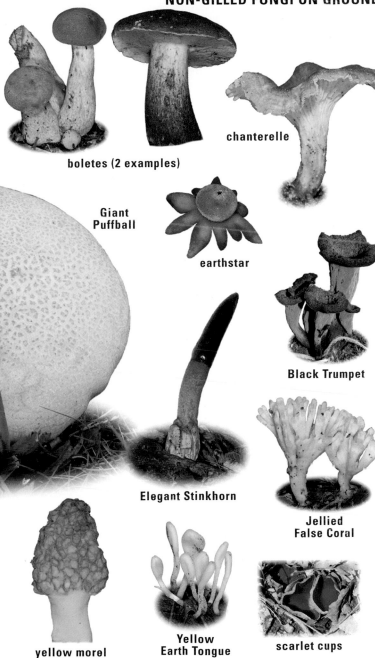

boletes (2 examples)

chanterelle

Giant
Puffball

earthstar

Black Trumpet

Elegant Stinkhorn

Jellied
False Coral

yellow morel

Yellow
Earth Tongue

scarlet cups

The first five entries below are non-gilled mushrooms that grow on wood. The last three are sometimes mistaken for fungi, but are unrelated.

## BLUE STAIN FUNGUS    *Chlorociboria* sp.

Two species in region; found in mixed woods. ▶ A bluish green discoloration of rotting wood is often the only evidence of these fungi. Their tiny, bright turquoise-colored, goblet-shaped fruiting bodies (mushrooms) emerge only after protracted periods of rain.

## BEECH BARK DISEASE    *Nectria* sp.

Fungal disease of American Beech (p. 124); caused by a combination of introduced Beech Scale insect *(Cryptococcus fagisuga)* and a fungus of the genus *Nectria*. Scale insect and fungus discovered in Michigan in 2001; confirmed in Ohio in 2003. ▶ Orange to red fruiting bodies emerge from underneath the cankered bark. Superficially similar to native, much less destructive Red Cushion Hypoxylon fungus *(Hypoxylon fragiforme)*.

## PHEASANT BACK    *Polyporus squamosus*

This and the next two are types of polypores. These fungi produce semi-circular, shelflike mushrooms on wood; some are soft textured, others are hard and leathery. They're often referred to as bracket fungi. ▶ Pheasant Back gets its name from the brownish red, featherlike pattern on its top surface; center of cap depressed.

## SULPHUR SHELF    *Laetiporus sulphureus*

A polypore of dead and living trees; brackets up to 12" across and 1" thick. ▶ Top surface is orange with thin to thick yellow edging; bright sulphur yellow underneath.

## TURKEY TAIL    *Trametes versicolor*

A common polypore often covering the surface of dead wood. ▶ Top fuzzy with concentric bands of contrasting, variable colors (browns, reds, greens, grays, whites); visible pore surface below.

## SLIME MOLDS

Although slime molds are often confused for fungi, they are not in the kingdom Fungi. Each slime mold is actually a collection of nuclei organized into a single, gelatinous mass of protoplasm called a plasmodium. This mass acts as a single organism, oozing around the surface of dead wood, engulfing its food. They reproduce via spores.

## GHOST PLANT    *Monotropa uniflora*

Often mistaken for a fungus. This wildflower lacks chlorophyll so it cannot photosynthesize to produce its own food. Instead it parasitizes fungi that are in a symbiotic relationship with trees. ▶ Nodding translucent white flower on white (sometimes pinkish) stalk; pollinated flowers erect.

## AMERICAN CANCER-ROOT    *Conopholis americana*

Sometimes mistaken for a fungus or pine cone, but it's a wildflower. Lives underground except when flowering; parasitizes oaks. ▶ Tiny, creamy white flowers emerge from tannish scales on pinecone-like inflorescence.

# FUNGI AND OTHERS

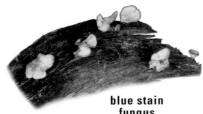

blue stain
fungus

beech bark disease

Pheasant
Back

Sulphur Shelf

Turkey
Tail

other things often mistaken for fungi

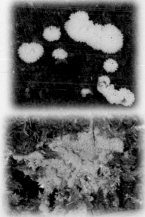

slime molds (2 examples)

Ghost
Plant

American
Cancer-root

# LICHENS

As discussed in the introduction (pp. 176–177), lichens are not single organisms. Each is a combination of a specific fungus (mycobiont) and a specific photosynthetic partner (photobiont) joined in a symbiotic relationship. Here are a few of the many types of lichens in our region.

### REINDEER LICHEN    *Cladonia rangiferina*

As caribou regularly eat them, a number of *Cladonia* species are called reindeer lichen. (Sometimes called reindeer moss, but lichens are not related to the true mosses, p. 174.) This fruticose (bushy and upright) lichen is widespread in northern portions of the region. Forms extensive mats in coniferous forests with sandy soils, bogs, exposed tundra. ▶ Grows to 4" tall. A tangle of coarse, grayish white, intricately branching tufts with a fine hairy surface. Similar species are greenish yellow.

### BRITISH SOLDIERS LICHEN    *Cladonia cristatella*

A common fruticose lichen of decaying wood; found at bases of trees, mossy logs, and sometimes soil, in open forests and partially shaded fields. ▶ Greenish gray branching stalks with bright red apothecia (rounded or disc-shaped spore-producing structures).

### PIXIE CUP LICHENS    *Cladonia* sp.

Also called goblet lichens for their cup-shaped fruiting bodies, which occur in a handful of the several species in our area. Found in mixed woods, bogs, and dunes on wet stumps and mossy places. ▶ Flaring, greenish gray to yellowish white cups with long tapering stalks, resembling golf tees.

### LIMP-TUFTED LICHEN    *Evernia mesomorpha*

Another fruticose lichen. Grows on twigs, branches, and trunks of trees, often where bark has fallen off; also on other pieces of exposed wood, such as fenceposts. ▶ Green to yellow-green limp, tuftlike fingers with a very granular surface.

### WRINKLED SHIELD LICHEN    *Flavoparmelia caperata*

A widespread and common foliose (flattened and leaflike) lichen; grows on tree trunks in areas with clean air, sometimes carpeting large areas of a trunk. ▶ Bright green when well hydrated, yellow-green when dry. Center of lichen wrinkled, with rounded, leaflike lobes on the perimeter.

### ROSETTE LICHEN    *Physcia* sp.

A common foliose lichen often found growing on branches and twigs of deciduous trees near roads and well-traveled paths. ▶ Primary lichen body grayish green with numerous lobes around the perimeter; large dark brown to black spore-producing disks (apothecia).

### ORANGE LICHEN    *Xanthoria* sp.

Another foliose lichen. Various species found on surfaces of exposed rock, roadside trees, and branches of deciduous trees. ▶ Bright orange when in full sun; some species more yellow-green when in a more shaded location; lobes can easily be peeled away from surface, unlike some orange crustose (surface hugging, crustlike) lichens that look superficially similar.

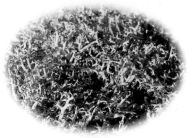

**Reindeer Lichen**

**British Soldiers Lichen**

**pixie cup lichen**

**Limp-tufted Lichen**

**Wrinkled Shield Lichen**

**orange lichen**

**rosette lichen**

The wild mammals of the Midwest make up a varied lot: everything from mice to moose, as well as bats that take to the air and moles and pocket gophers that live underground. All mammals in North America are warm-blooded creatures that give birth to live young.

This section includes most of the large and noticeable mammals of the Midwest. For more thorough information on the smaller or more elusive species, see the *Kaufman Field Guide to Mammals of North America.*

Some wild mammals are easy to observe: squirrels are frequent visitors to backyard bird feeders, White-tailed Deer are numerous in some areas, and Woodchucks and ground squirrels may be seen along roadsides in open country. But seeing most mammals requires some effort or luck.

To seek nocturnal mammals, try driving slowly on rural roads at night or walking quietly with a flashlight on a deserted road or trail. In either situation, you will spot many mammals first by their *eyeshine.* Many species that are active in the dark have an additional reflective layer, the *tapetum lucidum,* at the back of the retina. Light reflected from this layer may be seen at a great distance, but in order for you to see it, your own eyes must be lined up with the source of the light. This occurs more or less automatically when you are driving, as you will be looking along the beam of the headlights. With a flashlight, try holding it up next to your head at the level of your eyes, or use a headlamp. You may spot creatures at a surprising distance: not only mammals, but also night birds such as Whip-poor-wills, and even the eyeshine of spiders! Check to see if your local nature center offers night hikes, as these can be fine opportunities for learning.

**Signs of mammals** may be apparent even when we don't see the actual animals. Beaver lodges and dams are distinctive, and Muskrat lodges are often visible in shallow marshes. The alert naturalist often can see squirrel nests in trees, the ridges and mounds left by tunneling moles, and the burrow entrances of Woodchucks and other ground-nesting mammals. Signs of feeding behavior are sometimes noticeable: for example, the pointed stump left when an American Beaver has chewed down a tree, or the piles of clipped green grass left by voles. And of course, tracks (see next page) can tell us not only what kinds of mammals have been present, but a little about what they have been doing.

**Safety issues:** A few wild mammals are large enough to be potentially dangerous, although common sense will usually be sufficient to prevent problems. Mother bears with cubs or moose with calves should be avoided, of course, and male moose or even deer can be belligerent in mating season. It is generally a bad idea to feed animals such as bears or coyotes, as these may become dangerous once they learn to associate humans with food. A mammal such as a fox, skunk, or bat that is behaving strangely and approaching humans, or allowing close approach, might have rabies. Such animals should be avoided and reported to local law enforcement or wildlife authorities.

Tracks of some mammal species are more likely to be observed than the animals themselves. Freshly fallen snow or fresh mud around ponds and streams may reveal the recent history of creatures that have passed by unseen. Identifying animal tracks is a rewarding pursuit in itself, and for those who want to know more, we recommend *A Field Guide to Animal Tracks* in the Peterson series, or *Tracking and the Art of Seeing* by Paul Rezendes. A few sample tracks (not all to scale) are shown below.

**Eastern Cottontail:** hind feet (up to 3" long) land in front of the front feet. Furry feet make tracks look soft-edged.

**Virginia Opossum:** notice the splayed "thumb." Hind track can be more than 2" wide.

hind foot  front foot

**Northern Raccoon:** five long toes usually show on each track. Hind foot up to 3" long.

hind foot  front foot

**American Beaver:** huge, webbed hind foot can be up to 6" long.

hind foot  front foot

hind foot

**Black Bear:** hind track about 7" long.

front foot

**Bobcat:** front track about 2" long. Claws usually do not show in track.

**Red Fox:** front track about 2½" long. Dog tracks can be similar.

**Striped Skunk:** front track about 1½" long, with long claws.

**White-tailed Deer:** track about 2½" long.

**Moose:** track about 5" long.

# RABBITS, OPOSSUM, AND WOODCHUCK

Rabbits and hares (family **Leporidae**) are prolific vegetarians with big ears. The opossum is our only member of the family Didelphidae, while the Woodchuck is related to the squirrels, introduced on p. 190.

### SNOWSHOE HARE     *Lepus americanus*

Named for its huge hind feet, this hare of the north woods is well equipped for hopping and running across the surface of deep snow. It forages mostly at night, hiding in dense thickets by day. Noted for its population cycles, and may become very common for a few years before its numbers "crash" again. ▶ Mostly brown in summer, all-white in winter. In summer, separated from cottontail by its smaller tail, *much larger* hind feet.

### EASTERN COTTONTAIL     *Sylvilagus floridanus*

Though it seems a timid creature, the cottontail is tough and adaptable, managing to survive even in suburbs. Most common in open country, farmland, marshes, rare in regions of unbroken forest. Females in the Midwest may have 4 litters per year; baby cottontails are sheltered in a nest on the ground, lined with grass, leaves, and fur from the mother. ▶ Brown and gray, with orange tinge on legs, pale feet. Puffy tail is white below. Compare to next two species. In s. Illinois, **Swamp Rabbit** (*S. aquaticus,* not shown) is larger, with darker feet, smaller tail.

### WHITE-TAILED JACKRABBIT     *Lepus townsendii*

Mostly uncommon in the western part of our region, in open grassland, farmland. Active mainly at night. ▶ Larger and lankier than Snowshoe Hare, with *longer ears*. Molts to mostly white in winter. Tail is noticeably *white* above and below.

### VIRGINIA OPOSSUM     *Didelphis virginiana*

Fairly common in forests, farmland, streamsides, even in towns. This odd mammal is North America's only marsupial, a group in which the young are born tiny and complete their development in a pouch on the mother's body. Slow-moving omnivores, Opossums will feed on anything they can catch. A good climber, but does most of its feeding on the ground. If threatened, may play dead ("playing possum"). ▶ Vaguely ratlike but much larger, with *whitish face* and small, rounded ears. Long fur is usually gray; tail is naked and whitish for most of its length.

### WOODCHUCK     *Marmota monax*

Also called "groundhog," and briefly famous on February 2 for its supposed forecasting ability. This is the only eastern species of marmot, a group of very large ground squirrels (see p. 192). Woodchucks are common in open country, feeding on many low plants, digging long burrows with multiple entrances. Usually seen on the ground, they also climb trees at times. ▶ Distinctive shape with heavy body, short legs, and short, bushy tail.

# RABBITS, OPOSSUM, AND WOODCHUCK

winter

**Snowshoe Hare**
**L 18"**

**Eastern Cottontail**
**L 17"**

summer

**White-tailed**
**Jackrabbit**
**L 24"**

**Virginia**
**Opossum**
**L 26"**

**Woodchuck**
**L 22"**

# TREE SQUIRRELS AND FLYING SQUIRRELS

The squirrels and chipmunks (family **Sciuridae**) include some of our most familiar mammals, active by day (except for the flying squirrels) and often found in backyards and city parks. Most have varied diets, eating many seeds and nuts but also including leaves, berries, fungus, insects, birds' eggs, and other items. They are often quite vocal.

### EASTERN GRAY SQUIRREL    *Sciurus carolinensis*

Common almost throughout the region, from wilderness to city parks, wherever there are enough large trees. Spends most of its time in trees, building big, bulky nests of leaves and twigs among the branches or in hollows in the trunk. Eats nuts, berries, seeds, sometimes birds' eggs or insects, and often raids bird feeders. Active all year but may stay in its nest for days during harsh winter weather. ▶ Usually mostly gray with a brownish tinge. A blackish form is common in some areas, and the town of Olney, Illinois, is famous for its population of white squirrels.

### EASTERN FOX SQUIRREL    *Sciurus niger*

Often found with the preceding species but also ranges into more open areas with scattered trees. Not quite as agile a climber as the other squirrels on this page, and spends more time on the ground, although it seeks shelter in trees. ▶ Larger and bulkier than Eastern Gray Squirrel, with orange wash on belly and tail.

### RED SQUIRREL    *Tamiasciurus hudsonicus*

This noisy little squirrel is common in coniferous and mixed forest, scarcer toward the south. Although it has a varied diet like other squirrels, it feeds heavily on cones of evergreens, harvesting the unripe cones in late summer and hoarding them. ▶ Smaller and redder than other squirrels, with stronger white eye-ring. Blackish line along side is more apparent in summer.

### SOUTHERN FLYING SQUIRREL    *Glaucomys volans*

These wide-eyed gnomes are actually common and widespread, but usually overlooked. Living in deciduous forest and even in well-wooded suburbs, they hide in tree holes by day, coming out at night to glide (not fly) through the woods. The squirrel leaps from a high branch and spread-eagles itself in the air, spreading flaps of loose skin that stretch from the forelegs to the hindlegs. Using its tail as a rudder, it can steer among the trees, gliding as much as 200' before landing on another tree trunk. Sometimes comes to bird feeders at night. ▶ Small size, big eyes, loose skin along sides, flat tail. Compare to next species.

### NORTHERN FLYING SQUIRREL    *Glaucomys sabrinus*

The ranges of our two flying squirrels overlap across Minnesota, Wisconsin, and Michigan, but this species is usually in coniferous forest. ▶ Very similar to Southern Flying Squirrel but averages larger, with longer fur. Its tail tends to be darker toward the tip.

# SQUIRRELS

Eastern
Gray
Squirrel
L 19"

Eastern
Fox Squirrel
L 23"

Red
Squirrel
L 12"

Northern Flying Squirrel
L 12"
(Southern Flying Squirrel
is very similar)

# CHIPMUNKS AND GROUND SQUIRRELS

are related to tree squirrels, and some can climb well, but they spend most of their time on the ground. All dig extensive burrows underground, and use these shelters for hibernating, storing food, and raising their young. All have varied diets that include both plant and animal matter.

### EASTERN CHIPMUNK    *Tamias striatus*

A common and confiding animal of forests and well-wooded suburbs, seen sitting on logs or running with its tail held straight up. Often raids bird feeders, taking food to stash in its burrow. Its winter hibernation is fitful, and it may awaken in winter to eat stored food or even to venture outside. Makes a variety of chirping and clucking sounds. ▶ Small size and striped back are diagnostic in most areas. Compare next 2 species.

### LEAST CHIPMUNK    *Tamias minimus*

Fairly common in the northern stretches of our region, mainly in coniferous forest. Makes a variety of chirps, clucks, and trills, and flips its tail up and down while calling. ▶ Similar to Eastern Chipmunk but smaller, with less of a reddish tinge in the rump area, and *more sharply contrasting stripes on face.*

### THIRTEEN-LINED GROUND SQUIRREL
### *Spermophilus tridecemlineatus*

Originally native to short-grass prairies of the Great Plains, this ground squirrel has adapted to new habitats provided by humans who mow grass — parks, golf courses, cemeteries, roadsides — and has spread eastward in our region. This is the so-called gopher often seen sitting upright along roads. ▶ Strong pattern above, with series of *pale-spotted dark stripes* on back.

### FRANKLIN'S GROUND SQUIRREL    *Spermophilus franklinii*

This species lives in thicker growth than its relatives, including tall grass, brushy fields, and woodland edges, so it may be harder to see. Like other ground squirrels on this page, it has a very long hibernation period, lasting up to 7 months or more. ▶ Larger and grayer than other ground squirrels, with bushy tail. Eastern Gray Squirrel (p. 190) has larger ears and longer tail.

### RICHARDSON'S GROUND SQUIRREL
### *Spermophilus richardsonii*

This ground squirrel of short-grass prairie enters our area in w. Minnesota, where it often lives in agricultural fields or over-grazed pasture. May stand upright at entrance to its burrow and give a shrill whistle when alarmed. ▶ Pale and plain, without distinctive markings. Smaller, paler, and more buff-colored than Franklin's Ground Squirrel, with thinner tail.

# CHIPMUNKS AND GROUND SQUIRRELS

**Eastern Chipmunk**
**L 10"**

**Least Chipmunk**
**L 8"**

**Thirteen-lined Ground Squirrel**
**L 10"**

with cheek pouches full

**Franklin's Ground Squirrel**
**L 15"**

**Richardson's Ground Squirrel**
**L 11"**

These are similar in size but belong to six different families.

### NORTHERN RACCOON  *Procyon lotor*

The adaptable "masked bandit" lives almost anyplace it can find trees and water, even around suburbs and city parks. An omnivore, eating fruits, nuts, small creatures caught on land or in the water, and items scavenged from trash cans. Our only member of the family Procyonidae. ▶ Overall color varies from gray to brown. *Black face mask;* tail ringed dark and light.

### STRIPED SKUNK  *Mephitis mephitis*

Skunks (family Mephitidae) are famed for their smelly defenses. Glands near the tail can shoot a foul spray up to 15'. Active mostly at night, feeding on carrion, insects, small animals, fruits, refuse. Skunks behaving oddly might have rabies, and should be avoided for multiple reasons! ▶ Unmistakable, although pattern varies: stripes broad or narrow, tail with more or less white.

### EASTERN SPOTTED SKUNK  *Spilogale putorius*

Uncommon, declining, now apparently gone from Indiana and Illinois. Active at night in brushy country, farmland. ▶ Small, with striking pattern of *white spots and stripes* on black.

### AMERICAN BEAVER  *Castor canadensis*

The most impressive landscape architect among wild mammals, the beaver cuts down trees, builds lodges and dams, and creates ponds. Along rivers, beavers may nest in burrows in banks instead. Once wiped out over most of the Midwest but has made a good comeback. Family Castoridae. ▶ Large size, bulky head, and *wide flattened tail,* which it slaps against the water in alarm.

### COMMON MUSKRAT  *Ondatra zibethicus*

Although it belongs to the rat family (Muridae), the muskrat acts like the beaver's little brother, swimming and diving with ease. Common in marshes and ponds, building lodges out of cattails or digging burrows in banks. ▶ Much smaller than beaver with a *narrow, ratlike tail.* Swims higher in water, with back exposed.

### NORTH AMERICAN PORCUPINE  *Erethizon dorsatum*

This sluggish vegetarian (of the family Erethizontidae) can move with surprising speed if threatened, lashing out with its quill-covered tail. ▶ Unmistakable, our only animal with spiny armor.

### AMERICAN BADGER  *Taxidea taxus*

Powerful diggers of open country, badgers are widespread but not often seen. Active mostly at night, they dig up rodents and other small animals to eat. Signs of their presence include large oval holes, with dirt kicked out to the side. Weasel family (Mustelidae). ▶ Stout-bodied, short-tailed, and short-legged, with long claws on front feet. Strong *face stripes* and pointed snout.

# MEDIUM-SIZED MAMMALS

**Northern Raccoon**
**L 30"**

**Striped Skunk**
**L 27"**

**Eastern Spotted Skunk 18"**

**American Beaver**
**L 40"**

**beaver lodge**

**Common Muskrat**
**L 20"**

**North American Porcupine**
**L 27"**

**American Badger**
**L 28"**

19

# WEASELS LARGE AND SMALL

These are all members of the weasel family (**Mustelidae**), along with the American Badger (p. 194) and the Wolverine (formerly found in the Midwest). Members of this family are all active and agile predators.

### NORTHERN RIVER OTTER    *Lontra canadensis*

A powerful swimmer, diving deep to catch fish, frogs, and other prey. Often in family groups; lucky observers may get to watch them sliding down muddy or snowy banks into the water. Once wiped out over much of the Midwest, but has been reintroduced, now widely common. ▶ Large and *long-bodied,* with thick-based tail, short legs. Mostly dark brown, paler on face and throat.

### AMERICAN MINK    *Mustela vison*

Widespread and common around marshes, rivers, and lakes, but often unnoticed because it does much of its hunting at dusk and at night. Its den may be in a waterside burrow or in an old muskrat house. ▶ Mostly smooth dark brown. Larger and darker than Long-tailed Weasel, smaller and more slender than Fisher.

### FISHER    *Martes pennanti*

An uncommon forest animal. Misnamed, hunting not for fish but for small mammals and birds. One of the few predators able to take porcupines, flipping them upside down to reach the unprotected belly. ▶ A bulky, muscular weasel with furry tail and small head. Dark brown, often with darker legs and feet.

### AMERICAN MARTEN    *Martes americana*

An agile weasel of northern forest, hunting on the ground but also climbing trees. Feeds on many small animals, also berries, seeds, and carrion. ▶ Overall color varies, but legs and feet darker than body, throat and chest paler creamy to orange.

### LONG-TAILED WEASEL    *Mustela frenata*

Found throughout the Midwest, in many habitats but often near water. Usually uncommon and hard to see. May hunt by day or night, sometimes taking prey larger than itself. ▶ Slender, with tail almost as long as body. Brown above, creamy to brownish below. In northern half to two-thirds of our region, usually molts to white fur in winter. Tip of tail always black.

### ERMINE    *Mustela erminea* (Short-tailed Weasel)

Widespread but uncommon, and not often observed. Hunts by day or night at all seasons. ▶ Smaller than Long-tailed Weasel, with *much shorter tail.* Brown above and white below in summer, all-white in winter, always with extensive black tail tip.

### LEAST WEASEL    *Mustela nivalis*

This tiny carnivore is a hyperactive hunter; it must eat nearly half its body weight daily, or starve. ▶ Tiny and short-tailed, with no black tail tip. In northern areas, turns white in winter.

# WEASELS AND THEIR RELATIVES

Northern
River Otter
L 40″

American Mink
L 23″

Fisher
L 38″

American
Marten
L 24″

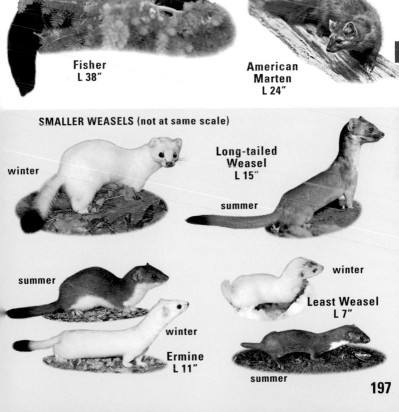

SMALLER WEASELS (not at same scale)

winter

Long-tailed
Weasel
L 15″

summer

summer

winter

Least Weasel
L 7″

summer

winter

Ermine
L 11″

Domestic dogs and housecats, allowed to run loose, do tremendous damage to wildlife. However, our native dogs (family **Canidae**) and cats (family **Felidae**) play essential roles in natural habitats.

### RED FOX    *Vulpes vulpes*

Common in farmland and semi-open country, even surviving around edges of cities. An adaptable hunter and scavenger. Den is usually in a burrow; litters, averaging 5 pups, are born in spring, cared for by female until fall. ▶ Usually reddish brown with white tail tip, black feet. Some variants show much black or gray.

### GRAY FOX    *Urocyon cinereoargenteus*

Fairly common in forest and brushy fields, avoiding open farmland. An omnivore, eating fruits and insects as well as rodents, birds, etc. Unlike most canines, regularly climbs trees. ▶ Mostly gray with rusty trim, white face, *black stripe and tip on tail.*

### COYOTE    *Canis latrans*

Widespread and common in many habitats, even in cities, but adept at staying out of sight. Coyotes communicate with yips and howls, often heard at night. ▶ Larger and longer-legged than foxes. Similar to some dogs, but when running, usually holds tail curled down, while dogs often run with tail raised.

### GRAY WOLF    *Canis lupus*

These magnificent animals are now uncommon and local in the north of our region. Maligned by some because of their fairy-tale image as bloodthirsty killers, wolves are actually intelligent, social animals that play an important part in natural ecosystems. Their howls are among the most stirring sounds of the American wilderness. ▶ Usually grizzled gray-brown, but color varies. Larger than Coyote, with broader snout and bigger feet. When running, bushy tail is usually held straight out behind.

### CANADIAN LYNX    *Lynx canadensis*

Almost a missing lynx in the Midwest, this mysterious cat is still found in forests of ne. Minnesota and sometimes wanders into n. Wisconsin and Michigan. Its large, furry feet allow it to run across the surface of snow in pursuit of Snowshoe Hares, one of its main prey species. ▶ Like Bobcat but usually a little larger, with *all-black tip* on very short tail, longer tufts on ears.

### BOBCAT    *Lynx rufus*

Formerly almost gone from the southern Midwest, this wily wildcat is making a comeback, expanding its range. Most common in woods with rocky ledges, where it may sleep in its den by day. Hunts rabbits and a variety of other small animals. ▶ Bigger than a housecat. *Short tail* is black-tipped on top, *white below.* Black stripes on legs and face ruff, large *white spot* on back of ears.

pups

Red
Fox
L 38"

Gray Fox
L 38"

Coyote running

Gray Wolf
L 53"

Coyote
L 45"

Bobcat
L 32"

Canadian Lynx
L 35"

# BEARS, DEER, AND BISON

In general, the advance of civilization has not been good for populations of large wild animals. Grizzly Bears are gone from the Midwest, leaving only one member of the bear family **(Ursidae)**. Only one member of the deer family **(Cervidae)** is still widespread here, and the bison (family **Bovidae)** is now limited to a few managed herds on sanctuaries.

### BLACK BEAR    *Ursus americanus*

Once more widespread, but still numerous in northern part of region, and may be expanding again; increasingly seen outside mapped range. An omnivore, feeding on fruits, nuts, roots, grubs, carrion, and small animals. Usually no threat to humans, but bears that are fed may become dangerous. ▶ Unmistakable. In this region, typically black with a tan muzzle.

### WHITE-TAILED DEER    *Odocoileus virginianus*

The most familiar large mammal in the Midwest today. In some areas, with most of their natural predators gone, deer are so abundant that they can damage forest by wiping out the understory. They are grazers and browsers, feeding on a wide variety of plant material, including garden plants at times. Males (bucks) grow antlers every year, starting in spring and growing through the summer. The soft velvet covering of the antlers is shed in fall. Fawns (usually 2) are born in spring and summer. ▶ Overall color more reddish brown in summer, grayer in winter. Elk averages larger, has darker neck and pale rump patch.

### MOOSE    *Alces alces*

This famous, impressive creature is a member of the deer family, but big as a horse. Uncommon in the northern Midwest, around forests, swamps, lakes. Moose are well adapted to cold, but to cope with hot weather they spend time in deep shade or in the water. ▶ Very large with *elongated head, shoulder hump,* short tail. Males are much larger than females; they shed their broad antlers in late winter and regrow them during spring and summer.

### ELK    *Cervus elaphus*

Once widespread in the Midwest, this regal deer was wiped out by the late 1800s. It has been reintroduced into parts of n. Michigan, Minnesota, and Wisconsin, and may become established elsewhere. ▶ Larger than White-tailed Deer, with contrastingly darker head and neck, large pale patch on rump. Antlers of males are longer when full-grown.

### AMERICAN BISON    *Bison bison*    (Buffalo)

Before Europeans arrived, herds of bison roamed almost throughout the Midwest, and the total North American population numbered at least 30 million. Uncontrolled slaughter drove this iconic animal almost to extinction. Today, managed herds can be seen at several large parks and refuges in the western part of our region. ▶ Almost unmistakable. Males larger than females, with stouter horns and longer hair on the front quarters.

# BEARS, DEER, AND BISON

female
with cubs

Black Bear
L 6'

White-tailed
Deer
L 6'

doe with fawn

Moose
L 9'

bull
moose

cow moose
with calf

male

Elk
L 7½'

male

American Bison
L 9'

## HOUSE MOUSE    *Mus musculus*
Native to the Old World and long associated with humans, this mouse now lives with us worldwide. In the Midwest, found everywhere except wilderness regions. ▶ Any mouse indoors in cities or suburbs is likely this species. Plainer than any native mouse, dusty gray without sharp contrasts.

## NORTH AMERICAN DEERMOUSE    *Peromyscus maniculatus*

Widespread in many habitats, foraging on ground or climbing trees. Active all year; feeds on seeds, berries, insects, fungi. Nests in burrows, hollow logs, other sheltered spots. ▶ Brown above, white below, with big ears, big eyes, long tail, whitish feet.

## WHITE-FOOTED DEERMOUSE    *Peromyscus leucopus*

Another very common mouse, widespread in forests and fields. Builds a domed nest, sometimes on top of old birds' nest. ▶ Very similar to previous species, tail more lightly furred.

## MEADOW VOLE    *Microtus pennsylvanicus*

An abundant little rodent of fields, marshes, woods. Makes runways through grass, leaves little piles of short grass clippings. The females can give birth to a new litter every 3 weeks. Many predators rely on voles as a staple in their diet. ▶ Compact, with *short tail, short snout,* small ears. Brown above, pale gray below.

## PRAIRIE VOLE    *Microtus ochrogaster*

Common in grassland and farmland, making runways through grass like Meadow Vole. ▶ Slightly shorter tail than Meadow Vole (not as short as S. Bog Lemming), often more buff on belly.

## SOUTHERN RED-BACKED VOLE    *Clethrionomys gapperi*

Fairly common in damp forest, bogs, edges of meadows, especially in areas with many fallen logs. May be more active by day in winter, at night in summer. ▶ Longer snout, bigger ears than Meadow Vole. Stripe down back *usually red,* sometimes gray.

## SOUTHERN BOG LEMMING    *Synaptomys cooperi*

Lives in forests and fields as well as bogs, feeding mainly on grasses and sedges. Usually nests underground. Active mostly at night. ▶ Big head, small ears, *very short tail;* dark brown all over.

## MEADOW JUMPING MOUSE    *Zapus hudsonius*

This mouse of fields or open woods may leap away when startled. Placed in a different family (Dipodidae) from all others on this page (Muridae); unlike them, it hibernates in winter. ▶ Jumping habits, *tricolored pattern* (white belly, buff sides, dark back).

## BROWN RAT (NORWAY RAT)    *Rattus norvegicus*
This introduced rat, native to the Old World, is now widespread in the Midwest, mainly around cities and farms. ▶ Large, with a naked, scaly tail, usually just a bit shorter than total head/body length.

**House Mouse**
L 6½"

**North American Deermouse**
L 7"

**White-footed Deermouse**
L 7"

**Meadow Vole**
L 6½"

**Prairie Vole**
L 6"

**Southern Red-backed Vole**
L 5½"

**Southern Bog Lemming**
L 5"

**Meadow Jumping Mouse**
L 8"

**Brown Rat**
L 15"

# GOPHERS, MOLES, AND SHREWS

Pocket gophers make up a family of rodents (**Geomyidae**) specially adapted for living underground. Moles and shrews may look like rodents, but they belong to a separate order, the Insectivora. Moles (family **Talpidae**) are the ultimate burrowers, with small eyes covered by a thin layer of skin, no external ear openings, and large, flat front feet. They dig rapidly through the soil, seeking the insects and earthworms that they eat. Shrews (family **Soricidae**) are frenetic little predators, constantly dashing about in search of small prey. They eat mostly insects, earthworms, and other invertebrates, but will also take amphibians, small fish, even mice. At least ten species occur in the Midwest, but most are rarely seen.

### PLAINS POCKET GOPHER   *Geomys bursarius*

In open grassland, this rodent tunnels along rapidly just below the surface of the soil, pushing up mounds of loose dirt every few feet. Its big incisors and front claws aid in digging, and its loose skin and soft fur allow it to turn around in its burrows; it can run just as fast backward as forward. ▶ Seldom seen on the surface, but recognized by large head, front teeth, and claws.

### EASTERN MOLE   *Scalopus aquaticus*

Fairly common but not often seen. Usually detected by ridges left by its burrowing near the surface. Digs deeper in cold weather, and to make nest for raising young. Eats insects, earthworms, and some plant matter. ▶ Broad feet, partly naked snout, dark fur.

### STAR-NOSED MOLE   *Condylura cristata*

A mole of very wet habitats, active at all seasons in marshes, swamps, pond edges, damp fields. Its tunnels may lead into the water, where it swims well. The 11 pairs of protuberances on the snout are very sensitive and may be able to detect prey underwater by electrical impulses. ▶ *Ring of short "tentacles" on snout.* Hairy tail, longer than that of Eastern Mole.

### MASKED SHREW (CINEREOUS SHREW)   *Sorex cinereus*

Common but not often seen. Especially active at night, running about under leaf litter in damp woods, fields. Feeds on a variety of small prey; may eat some plant material in winter. ▶ Small, very dark, with relatively long tail for a shrew.

### LEAST SHREW   *Cryptotis parva*

Common in brushy fields, marshes, woods. Most shrews are solitary but this species may be found in small groups. ▶ Small, with *very short tail*. Dull brown in summer, grayer in winter.

### NORTHERN SHORT-TAILED SHREW   *Blarina brevicauda*

Our largest shrew, and one of the most often seen. Active all year, may make shallow burrows under leaf litter or snow. Poisonous saliva may help it subdue small animals or paralyze invertebrates for later consumption. ▶ Bigger head and shorter snout than most shrews, short tail, silvery gray fur.

# GOPHERS, MOLES, AND SHREWS
### (shown at different scales)

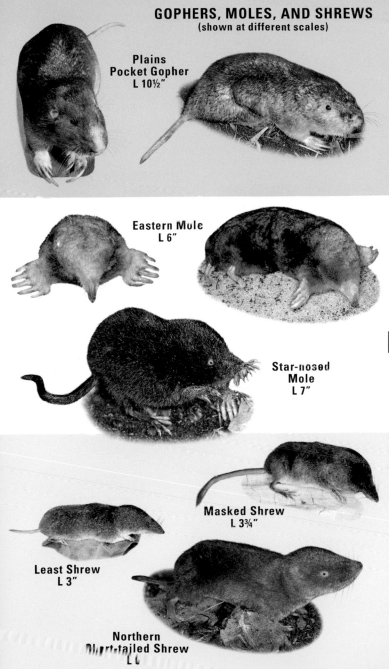

Plains
Pocket Gopher
L 10½"

Eastern Mole
L 6"

Star-nosed
Mole
L 7"

Masked Shrew
L 3¾"

Least Shrew
L 3"

Northern
Short-tailed Shrew
L 6

# BATS

(order **Chiroptera**) were once persecuted by superstitious humans, but they now have a more positive public image. The only mammals that can truly fly, bats have elongated bones of the fingers and outer arm, connected by a membrane of skin and tissue. Bats roost during the day by hanging upside down in caves, trees, buildings, or other shelters. Identifying bats in flight can be challenging. Size offers some clues. Sizes given here are total length of head, body, and tail; distance from wingtip to wingtip is much larger. Bats play important roles in natural ecosystems, and declining populations are cause for concern. Many bats have been killed in recent years by white-nose syndrome, a mysterious, fungus-based ailment that is spreading through the Midwest.

### EASTERN PIPISTRELLE    *Pipistrellus subflavus*

A tiny bat, seen in slow, fluttering flight at dusk. In summer, small colonies live in buildings, hollow trees. Large winter roosts in caves. ▶ *Very small*, buffy to gray-brown, with *pale* face and ears.

### BIG BROWN BAT    *Eptesicus fuscus*

Common and widespread in our region, roosting in barns and buildings, often with Little Brown Myotis. Forages at night over farmland, rivers, towns; catches many beetles in flight. ▶ Mostly brown, with rounded blackish ears and blackish face.

### LITTLE BROWN MYOTIS    *Myotis lucifugus*

The most commonly seen bat in the Midwest, foraging over towns, rivers, lakes, often roosting or raising young in barns, sheds. Winter roosts are often in caves. ▶ Very small, pale brown, with conspicuously *darker ears and face.*

### INDIANA MYOTIS    *Myotis sodalis* (not shown)

Considered endangered throughout its range. Roosts in summer under loose bark of trees, but almost the whole population hibernates in winter in just a few caves. ▶ Duller fur than Little Brown Myotis; toes with fewer and shorter hairs.

### EASTERN RED BAT    *Lasiurus borealis*

A bat of forested areas, roosting alone by day among foliage of trees. Migratory, and may leave northern parts of our region in winter. ▶ Male tinged pale orange-red, female more brown, frosted gray, with orange-red head. Looks golden red in flight.

### HOARY BAT    *Lasiurus cinereus*

Uncommon but widespread in summer, roosting alone in trees. ▶ Large, with *fast, direct flight.* White-tipped fur gives hoary or frosted look. *Yellow* face, *whitish spots* on folded wings.

### SILVER-HAIRED BAT    *Lasionycteris noctivagans*

Migratory, widespread in summer in forested areas. ▶ Medium-sized, with distinctly *slow flight*, often low over water. Blackish to dark brown fur with *silvery tips*, especially on younger bats.

# BATS

(Size given is length from nose to tail.
Wingspan is much larger.)

**Eastern
Pipistrelle
L 3¼"**

**Big Brown Bat
L 4¼"**

**Little Brown Myotis
L 3½"**

roosting
in tree

**Eastern
Red Bat
L 4½"**

**Hoary Bat
L 4¾"**

**Silver-
haired
Bat
L 4"**

207

# BIRDS

(class Aves) are the most noticeable wildlife in the Midwest, and the most popular. Millions of people feed birds; growing numbers of people travel for birding as well. Serious birders come from all over the continent to witness midwestern spectacles of migration, such as hawks at Duluth, Minnesota, warblers at Ohio's Magee Marsh, and various birds at Whitefish Point, Michigan. Festivals now celebrate Bald Eagles along the Mississippi River in winter and cranes in Wisconsin in fall.

This section treats the birds you are most likely to see, but if you get hooked on birding, you'll want a more comprehensive guide such as the *Kaufman Field Guide to Birds of North America*.

**Birdlife of the Midwest** changes with the seasons. Some species live here year-round, but more are seasonal visitors. Many, especially songbirds that feed on insects, arrive here in spring to spend the summer in this region, building nests and raising young before they leave in fall. They may spend the winter in the southern U.S. or in the tropics. Other birds arrive here in fall from much farther north and spend the winter with us. Still others nest farther north and spend the winter much farther south, migrating through the Midwest in spring and fall. The comings and goings of all these birds create much of the excitement of birding.

Because birds move so much, range maps for them have to convey more kinds of information than the other maps in this guide. We use colors on these maps to indicate different seasons and different levels of abundance, as shown on these examples.

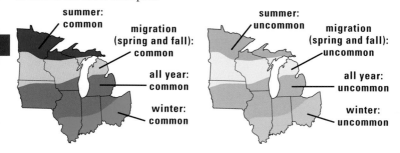

This might seem like a lot of colors, but there are really only three to remember: red (a hot color) for summer, blue (a cool color) for winter, and gray for migration. Red plus blue makes purple, for birds found all year. And for all colors, paler shades mean that the birds are less common.

**Binoculars** can make birds easier to identify and enjoy. It's good to try binoculars before buying them. Try to visit a nature center or wild bird supply store that carries several models. Check for a bright, sharp image, good close-focusing ability (we often want to look at birds that are fairly close), and comfortable fit for your hands and eyes. A magnification of 7× or 8× is ideal for birding. Good optics are expensive but well worth it.

**Finding birds** is a skill that you can develop with practice. A big part of it is simply being alert, watching and listening for bird activity. Visiting different habitats, and visiting them in different seasons, will help you to find more different kinds of birds. In spring and summer, birds can be much easier to find early in the morning when they are actively singing and foraging. In cold weather, time of day is less important.

**Feeding birds** is a rewarding way to bring them in close for observation. By placing feeders in strategic locations, visible from your windows, you can enjoy watching and learning about birds from the comfort of your home.

You can purchase or build a wide variety of bird feeders. No matter which types of feeders you select, it's important to keep them clean. Wild bird seed is now widely available, and, as you might expect, the best bird seed tends to be a little more expensive. Black oil sunflower seed, thistle (nyjer) seed, and white proso millet are the standard types for the best variety of native seed-eating birds. For insect-eaters, try commercially available suet cakes or homemade peanut-butter mixtures. In summer, humming-bird feeders add another dimension to backyard bird-attracting.

**Identifying birds** is rewarding but sometimes challenging. When you see an unfamiliar bird, try to see as much detail on it as possible before you reach for the field guide. To begin with, try to place the bird in the right general group. A bird's color is usually less important than its shape and behavior. Song Sparrow and Great Horned Owl are both mostly brown, but their shapes and behavior are very different! In particular, the shape of a bird's bill is often a good clue to its identity. Look at the bill shapes of birds in the illustrations on the following pages and you'll see what we mean: warblers have thin bills, hawks have hooked bills, and so on.

A bird's size is a good clue, although it can be hard to judge sizes accurately in the wild. In this field guide, sizes are given in inches, indicating the total length of the bird from the tip of its bill to the end of its tail. These are average figures for each species. It's most effective to compare an unknown bird to the size of a familiar one: for example, to say that a given bird was about the size of a robin, or a little smaller than a crow.

With practice, you'll learn to look for *field marks,* the "trademarks of nature." Does the bird's face have stripes or a pale eye-ring? Is the wing crossed by contrasting pale wing bars? Is the chest striped, spotted, or plain? Does it have contrasting white outer tail feathers? The more such details you can notice, the better your chances of identifying your bird.

# DABBLING DUCKS

With geese and swans, ducks make up the family **Anatidae**. Dabblers are familiar ducks of ponds and marshes, dipping their heads underwater or upending with tails in the air. Brightly patterned males are distinctive, but only females incubate the eggs and tend to the young.

### MALLARD     *Anas platyrhynchos*

Abundant in open marshes. Also lives in a semiwild state around farms, parks, cities. ▶ Male has dark green head, white neck ring, curly feathers above tail. Female mottled brown, with orange and black bill. **Voice:** thin whistles, loud quacks like barnyard ducks.

### AMERICAN BLACK DUCK     *Anas rubripes*

Mainly eastern, especially Lake Erie marshes. Declining, perhaps being replaced by Mallard. ▶ Like a *very dark* female Mallard, but male has *yellow bill,* grayer head. **Voice:** like Mallard's.

### GADWALL     *Anas strepera*

Common, especially toward the west, favoring marshes and lakes. ▶ Fairly plain. Male is mostly gray, with black hind end. Female brown with gray and orange bill. **Voice:** short *ghenk.*

### AMERICAN WIGEON     *Anas americana*

Very common in migration, local in summer and winter. Likes marshy ponds, flooded fields. ▶ Pinkish body, gray head. Male has green eye patch, *white crown.* **Voice:** shrill 3-noted whistle.

### NORTHERN PINTAIL     *Anas acuta*

A trim, swift-flying duck, common in marshes during migration. ▶ Slim with long neck and tail. Male has white neck stripe, brown head. Female brown with gray bill. **Voice:** whistles, quacks.

### NORTHERN SHOVELER     *Anas clypeata*

Swims with head low, bill half submerged, straining the muddy water for food. ▶ *Long, wide bill* is diagnostic. Male has green head, white chest, rusty belly. **Voice:** low *thook-thook.*

### BLUE-WINGED TEAL     *Anas discors*

A common nesting duck, and a very common migrant, around marshy ponds. Migrates earlier in fall and later in spring than most ducks. ▶ *Small.* Spring male has *white face crescent.* Females and many fall males brown, with paler face. Pale blue wing patch shows mostly in flight. **Voice:** high peeps, quacks.

### GREEN-WINGED TEAL     *Anas crecca*

Our smallest dabbler. Widespread on marshes, very common in migration. ▶ Male has dark head, gray body. Female brown with gray bill. Both have yellow "tail-light." **Voice:** squeaky *chyerk.*

### "PARK POND DUCKS"
Tame ducks around parks and farms may show almost endless variety of plumages. Most are descended from Mallard or Muscovy Duck.

# DABBLING DUCKS

female

Mallard
23"

male

male

American Black Duck
23"

female    Gadwall
20"

male

female

male

American Wigeon
19"

female

male

Northern Pintail
20"–26"

shoveler
in flight

female

male

Northern Shoveler
19

female

male

Blue-winged Teal
15"

male

female

Green-winged Teal
14"

"park pond
ducks"
(highly variable)

# WOOD DUCK AND DIVING DUCKS

Wood Duck has dabbling behavior like the ducks on p. 210. The others here forage mostly by diving and swimming underwater. Diving ducks are awkward on land and must patter across the water's surface to take flight. The divers are generally less vocal than the dabblers.

### WOOD DUCK *Aix sponsa*

Most numerous along wooded ponds and streams in summer, this beautiful duck nests in tree hollows or in nest boxes placed near water. Pairs may be seen perched high in trees. ► *Long tail,* crested head. Colorful male is unmistakable at most seasons. Female and young duller, with *white eye patch.* **Voice:** shrill whistled *oowheak!* given mainly in flight.

### LESSER SCAUP *Aythya affinis*

Sometimes in flocks of thousands on Great Lakes, and can be fairly common in migration and winter elsewhere. ► Male scaup are "black at both ends and white in the middle," with *blue bill.* Females are brown, with white face patch. See next species.

### GREATER SCAUP *Aythya marila*

Usually less common than Lesser Scaup, especially southward and inland. ► Very similar to Lesser Scaup but has more *rounded* head, heavier bill. Male may show greener head, whiter sides.

### RING-NECKED DUCK *Aythya collaris*

Occurs on lakes but also on small tree-lined ponds, unlike most divers. ► Neck ring is faint, but *bill ring* is obvious. Male has black back, white side mark. Female has bill ring, peaked crown.

### REDHEAD *Aythya americana*

Nests on prairies, may stop at shallow marshes and flooded fields in migration, unlike most divers. ► Male *gray* with *rounded, rusty head.* Female very plain and brown, with slight ring on bill.

### CANVASBACK *Aythya valisineria*

Another diver nesting on the northern prairies. Fairly common migrant through Midwest. Wary and swift in flight. ► Large, with *long, sloping head and bill.* Male has rusty head, black chest, white back. Female rather plain, best known by head shape.

### SURF SCOTER *Melanitta perspicillata*

Scoters are big diving ducks that nest in the far north and winter mostly along the coasts. All three species occur on the Great Lakes in migration and winter, but are very rare elsewhere in the region. ► Male has *white head patches,* ornate bill. Female has long bill, pale face patches.

### WHITE-WINGED SCOTER *Melanitta fusca*

► *White wing patch* visible mainly in flight. Male has white eye spot.

### BLACK SCOTER *Melanitta americana*

► Male black, with *orange bill knob.* Female dark, with bicolored head.

# WOOD DUCK AND DIVING DUCKS

female

**Wood Duck**
18"

male

female

**Lesser Scaup**
16½"

male

female

male

**Greater Scaup**
18"

female

male

**Ring-necked Duck**
17"

**Redhead**
19"

male

female

**Canvasback**
21"

female

male

female

**Surf Scoter**
20"

male

males

**Black Scoter**
19"

**White-winged Scoter**
21"

# DIVING DUCKS
All of these feed mostly by diving and swimming underwater.

### RED-BREASTED MERGANSER    *Mergus serrator*

Unlike most ducks, mergansers eat fish (mainly very small ones). This species can be abundant on the Great Lakes, especially in late fall and early spring; less common inland. ▶ Male has shaggy green head, *contrasting white collar,* red bill. Female has dull brown head fading to whitish throat, gray body, red bill.

### COMMON MERGANSER    *Mergus merganser*

Widespread on Great Lakes and inland waters. Nests in large hollow trees. Mergansers in flight look thin, horizontal, often fly low over water. ▶ Striking male *mostly white* with *dark green head, red bill.* Female has rusty head, *sharply contrasting* white throat.

### HOODED MERGANSER    *Lophodytes cucullatus*

Less numerous but more widespread than other mergansers, often on woodland ponds. Nests in tree cavities or in Wood Duck boxes. ▶ Male's black-rimmed white crest may be raised or flattened. Female dull, with shaggy brown crest.

### COMMON GOLDENEYE    *Bucephala clangula*

A winter duck in most areas, seen in flocks on deep water. Wings make a whistling sound in flight. ▶ Male has round white spot in front of eye on black head. Female mostly gray with puffy brown head, usually yellow tip on bill.

### BUFFLEHEAD    *Bucephala albeola*

Our tiniest diving duck, usually seen in small flocks. ▶ Male has large white "scarf" on black head; looks mostly white at a distance. Female mostly gray, with a white central face spot.

### RUDDY DUCK    *Oxyura jamaicensis*

An odd little diving duck, often gathering in tightly packed flocks on deep lakes during migration. Nests in marshes. ▶ Stiff tail feathers *often pointed up.* Compact, squat shape, with flat bill. Male has *white cheeks and dark cap;* blue bill and rusty body in summer. Female duller at all seasons, with dark face stripe.

### LONG-TAILED DUCK    *Clangula hyemalis*
Regular in winter on Great Lakes, more common toward the north, where large flocks may gather. Very rare visitor elsewhere in the region. ▶ Mostly pale in winter, male with striking pattern and long pointed tail. Female duller, with dark spot on pale face.    **Voice**: more vocal than most diving ducks, musical *yow-owdle-ow,* often heard from flocks.

### HARLEQUIN DUCK    *Histrionicus histrionicus*
A few occur every winter on the Great Lakes; very rare elsewhere in the region. ▶ Clown-patterned male is unmistakable. Female just looks small and dark overall, with white spots on face.

# DIVING DUCKS

female
**Red-breasted Merganser**
23"
male

female
**Common Merganser**
25"
male

female
**Hooded Merganser**
10"
male

female
**Common Goldeneye**
18½"
male

male
**Bufflehead**
13½"
female

**Ruddy Duck**
15"
female
male

female
**Long-tailed Duck**
16"–22"
male

female
**Harlequin Duck**
16½"
male

Among these birds, unlike their relatives the ducks, males and females look the same, and both parents take part in raising the young.

### CANADA GOOSE *Branta canadensis*

Historically, mostly a migrant over most of the Midwest. Introduced populations are now common all year in many areas, even in city parks, although migratory flocks still arrive in fall from the north. ▶ *Black* head and neck with *white chin strap,* pale chest, brown body. Size varies. **Voice:** deep, rich honking.

### CACKLING GOOSE *Branta hutchinsii*

Now recognized as a distinct species, this small goose migrates and winters mainly in western parts of our region. ▶ A bit smaller than the smallest Canada Geese: Mallard-sized, with small, blunt bill. **Voice:** high-pitched yelping or cackling cries.

### GREATER WHITE-FRONTED GOOSE *Anser albifrons*

A common migrant, mainly in western areas. Flocks feed in open fields, roost in marshes. ▶ Gray-brown with *pink bill, orange feet.* Adult has white face patch, *black bars on belly.* Some barnyard geese can be similar. **Voice:** high-pitched yelping.

### SNOW GOOSE *Chen caerulescens*

Very common in migration, often feeding in open fields with other geese, roosting in marshes. ▶ Two color morphs. White morph all-white with black wingtips, pinkish bill. Dark morph ("Blue Goose") dark with white head. Young either pale gray or very dark, with dark bill and feet. **Voice:** loud, nasal *owk-owk.*

### ROSS'S GOOSE *Chen rossii*

Uncommon, usually seen with Snow Geese. ▶ Like white morph Snow Goose but much smaller. Short bill lacks black "lips," has gray patch at base. **Voice:** higher-pitched than Snow Goose.

### TUNDRA SWAN *Cygnus columbianus*

Large flocks migrate through parts of the Midwest, with some remaining through winter. ▶ Huge, long-necked, white. Black bill usually has *yellow spot* at base. As with other swans, head and neck may be stained orange. **Voice:** musical yodeling.

### TRUMPETER SWAN *Cygnus buccinator*

Formerly a resident but wiped out long ago, this swan has been reintroduced in some areas. ▶ Like Tundra Swan but even larger, with heavier bill. Lacks yellow spot at base of bill. **Voice:** lower than voice of Tundra Swan, deep nasal bugling.

### MUTE SWAN *Cygnus olor*

Introduced from Europe, now locally common in parts of the Midwest. ▶ Huge and white. Bill mostly orange with black knob. May swim with wings arched. **Voice:** mostly silent.

# GEESE AND SWANS

**Cackling Goose**
23"

**Canada Goose**
34"–46"

**Greater
White-fronted
Goose**
28"

dark morph
("Blue Goose")

**Snow
Goose**
28"

white morph

**Ross's
Goose**
23"

swans (not shown
at same scale)

**Trumpeter Swan**
60"

**Tundra Swan**
53"

**Mute Swan**
60"

217

# VARIOUS WATERBIRDS

These represent five families. Cormorants (**Phalacrocoracidae**), loons (**Gaviidae**), coots and gallinules (**Rallidae**), and grebes (**Podicipedidae**) all swim well underwater, but pelicans (**Pelecanidae**) feed at the surface.

### AMERICAN COOT     *Fulica americana*

This odd bird flocks with ducks on marshes and lakes, grazes on grassy shores. ▶ Mostly slaty with blacker head, *thick white bill,* green feet. Nods its head as it swims. **Voice:** clucks, whines.

### COMMON GALLINULE     *Gallinula galeata*

Less common and less conspicuous than the coot, often hiding in marshes. ▶ Slaty with brown back, white side stripe, *thick colorful bill* (red and yellow, or all yellow). **Voice:** varied clucks, whines.

### PIED-BILLED GREBE     *Podilymbus podiceps*

Common on marshes, ponds. Grebes are highly aquatic, helpless on land; can swim with just the head above water. ▶ Compact and brown, with tailless look. In summer, thick bill is black and white ("pied"), throat is black. **Voice:** cooing, gobbling chatter.

### EARED GREBE     *Podiceps nigricollis*

Nests at prairie marshes, migrates mostly through western areas. ▶ Like Horned Grebe but smaller, with thinner bill, more peaked head. *Black neck* in summer; grayer overall in winter.

### HORNED GREBE     *Podiceps auritus*

Common migrant, mostly on deeper waters. ▶ Seen mainly in winter plumage, sharply black and white. Breeding plumage more colorful, with reddish neck, buff "horns."

### WESTERN GREBE     *Aechmophorus occidentalis*

Nests in Minnesota marshes, in noisy colonies. Migrates through western edge of region. ▶ Long neck, long yellow bill, striking black-and-white pattern. **Voice:** reedy *krrrik krrrikk.*

### COMMON LOON     *Gavia immer*

A classic bird of northern lakes in summer; widespread during migration. ▶ Striking in adult summer plumage. Fall and winter birds (and summering young birds) gray above, white below, with daggerlike bill. **Voice:** wild yodeling, often at night.

### AMERICAN WHITE PELICAN     *Pelecanus erythrorhynchos*

Nests in colonies at lakes, migrates mainly through western half of region. Flocks often seen soaring overhead, slowly turning in unison. ▶ *Huge.* White with *black in wings.* Long, heavy bill.

### DOUBLE-CRESTED CORMORANT     *Phalacrocorax auritus*

Abundant and increasing in summer and migration; rare in winter. Flocks fly low over water, swim and dive, perch on rocks and trees at water's edge. ▶ Snaky and gaunt, with long tail. Adult is black with orange throat; young bird paler and browner.

# VARIOUS WATERBIRDS

**American Coot**
15″

**Common Gallinule**
14″

winter

summer

**Pied-billed Grebe**
13″

winter

summer

**Eared Grebe**
12½″

winter

summer

**Horned Grebe**
13½″

summer

## LARGER BIRDS
(not at same scale as above)

winter

**Western Grebe**
25″

**Common Loon**
32″

summer

**Double-crested Cormorant**
32″

adult

**American White Pelican**
62″

young

# GULLS

are adaptable, omnivorous birds of the water's edge, but they also occur far from water, feeding in open fields and parking lots. Along with terns (p. 222), they make up the family **Laridae**. Gulls take two to four years to develop full adult plumage. Brown gulls are just young birds, not different species; compare sizes and shapes to help identify them. Most gulls can be quite noisy, but their varied voices are not described here.

### RING-BILLED GULL    *Larus delawarensis*

Our most widespread, numerous gull, although it withdraws from northernmost areas in winter. Nests in colonies on islands and lake shores, but nonbreeding birds occur far from colonies in summer. Often seen in parking lots in towns. ▶ Adult has *black ring on yellow bill, yellow-green legs*, white spots in black wingtips. Its white head develops brown marks in winter. Young birds have pinkish legs, more dark markings on body, wings, and tail.

### HERRING GULL    *Larus argentatus*

Very common, especially around Great Lakes and large rivers. Nests in colonies on islands and shores, often scavenges around landfills. ▶ Adult similar to Ring-billed Gull (gray back, white spots in black wingtips) but is larger and has heavier bill, variably marked with red and black. *Legs pink*. White head marked brown in winter. First-year birds are *mottled dark brown;* any all-brown gull in the Midwest is probably a young Herring Gull.

### GREAT BLACK-BACKED GULL    *Larus marinus*

Regular in winter around eastern Great Lakes. Wanderers appear elsewhere in the region. ▶ The *largest* gull (almost eagle-sized). Adult has black back, heavy yellow bill, dull pink legs. Young have checkered back pattern, black bill at first.

### LESSER BLACK-BACKED GULL    *Larus fuscus*

Formerly a rare stray from Europe, now increasing as a visitor, mostly in winter and in eastern part of our region. ▶ Like Herring Gull in size and shape, but with *dark gray* back. Smaller and paler than Great Black-backed, with *yellow legs*. Youngest birds very similar to youngest Herring Gulls.

### BONAPARTE'S GULL    *Chroicocephalus philadelphia*

This small, elegant gull is mostly a migrant and wintering bird here, although a few nonbreeders stay through summer. Flocks of thousands occur on Lake Erie and elsewhere. ▶ Adult known by *white triangle* on outer part of wing; black hood in spring and summer. Young has black wing outline, tail band, face spot.

### FRANKLIN'S GULL    *Leucophaeus pipixcan*

Nests at prairie marshes and migrates through western part of region, spending the winter in South America. ▶ Adult has wingtips *mostly white*, crossed by *ragged black bar;* black hood in spring and summer. Young has dark wings, half hood, dark tail band.

# GULLS

adult

young

**Ring-billed Gull**
19"

young

young

**Herring Gull**
25"

young

young

**Great
Black-backed Gull**
30"

**Lesser
Black-backed
Gull**
23"

**Franklin's
Gull**
15"

young

winter
adult

**Bonaparte's
Gull**
13"

spring
adult

spring
adult

young

# TERNS

are related to gulls, introduced on p. 220. On average, terns are smaller than gulls, with more sharply pointed bills and more graceful flight. They feed mostly by plunging into the water to catch tiny fish in their bills, so they require open water, and all leave the Midwest for the coldest part of the winter. They nest in scattered colonies on beaches or marshes.

### FORSTER'S TERN  *Sterna forsteri*

Away from the Great Lakes this is usually the most numerous of the terns, nesting in marshes and foraging over ponds, rivers, and lakes. ▶ Slender, with *long, forked tail.* Spring and summer adult mostly pale gray and white, with black cap. Fall adults and young have white head with pale nape and *black ear patch.* Compare to next species. **Voice:** harsh *kyaar,* other notes.

### COMMON TERN  *Sterna hirundo*

Locally common in summer in northern Midwest, nesting in colonies on beaches, islands, sandbars. Large flocks may gather in migration on Great Lakes. ▶ Very similar to Forster's Tern. In spring and summer, upperside of wingtips usually *darker gray;* base of bill more *red,* not so orange. Fall adult and young have *partial* black cap. **Voice:** long, harsh *keeaaaar,* other notes.

### CASPIAN TERN  *Hydroprogne caspia*

The largest of the terns, as big as a medium-sized gull. Seen in good numbers around the Great Lakes during the warmer months, nesting in a few scattered colonies, but mostly an uncommon migrant elsewhere. ▶ Known by *large size,* short crest, *thick red bill.* Shows dark underside of wingtip in flight. Juvenile has black marks on upperparts. **Voice:** rough, guttural *kahhrrrr.* Juvenile makes thin whistle while following its parents.

### BLACK TERN  *Chlidonias niger*

This beautiful, graceful tern is declining in numbers, and has disappeared from many marshes where it formerly nested. Still widespread as a migrant through the Midwest, and locally common in summer in some northern areas. ▶ Spring and summer adult has *black head and body,* silvery wings and tail. Young and fall adults mostly white below, but darker above than other terns. **Voice:** mostly quiet. Sharp *kik* and *kteek.*

### LEAST TERN  *Sternula antillarum*

This tiny tern formerly nested on sandbars along major rivers, but habitat changes caused by humans have made most of those habitats unsuitable. The inland population is now listed as endangered, and current nesting colonies are often on artificial sites. Away from nesting areas, wanderers may appear almost anywhere. ▶ Tiny size, *yellow bill* with black tip, sharply defined *white forehead.* **Voice:** high notes, *zzrreep* and *kvick.*

**222**  BIRDS

# TERNS

**Forster's Tern**
14½″ w 30″

w = wingspan

**Common Tern**
14″ w 30″

juvenile

adult

**Caspian Tern**
21″ w 50″

adult
Caspian
in flight

spring

**Least Tern**
8½″ w 20″

**Black Tern**
10″ w 24″

fall

# SOARING HAWKS

belong to the family **Accipitridae**. These birds hunt by day, relying mostly on keen eyesight to find prey. Shape and flight action are important for distinguishing among various groups of hawks. The first five below are buteos, with relatively short tails and broad wings, often seen soaring.

## RED-TAILED HAWK  *Buteo jamaicensis*

The most frequently seen hawk in the Midwest. Any large hawk seen in the open should be considered a Red-tail until proven otherwise. Often perches along roads, soars above open fields, woods, towns. ▶ Adult's tail is *reddish brown above,* whitish below, with color showing through in flight overhead. Juvenile's tail is brown with darker bars. At all ages, usually shows whitish chest, *dark "belly-band"* of streaks. **Voice:** squealing *keeeyahh.*

## RED-SHOULDERED HAWK  *Buteo lineatus*

A relatively noisy hawk of forested areas, often heard before it is seen. Now becoming more common in some suburbs and even urban parks with enough mature trees. ▶ Strong *narrow black and white barring* on wings and tail. Reddish on shoulders and chest. Flies with quick wingbeats followed by a glide. Juvenile brown, streaked below. At all ages, shows *pale crescent* near wing-tips in flight. **Voice:** repeated clear cries, *keeyar, keeyar.*

## BROAD-WINGED HAWK  *Buteo platypterus*

Fairly common in northern forests in summer, mostly migrating to the tropics in winter. ▶ Small and compact for a buteo. From below, wings whitish with narrow black outline. Adult has *broad black and white tail bands,* reddish chest. Juvenile has narrower tail bands, streaked chest. **Voice:** thin, high whistle, *eeh-eeeeeh.*

## ROUGH-LEGGED HAWK  *Buteo lagopus*

This cold-weather hawk arrives from the Arctic in late fall, hunts over open country, sometimes hovering on rapidly beating wings. ▶ Tail is *whitish at base,* with dark banding at tip. Wings show *dark wrist patch* in flight. Quite variable in body plumage, from very dark to very light; look for wing contrast in flight.

## SWAINSON'S HAWK  *Buteo swainsoni*

A western prairie hawk, uncommon in migration and local in summer in our region. Winters in South America. ▶ Slim shape, fairly long wings. Typical adult has *white wing-linings* and dark flight feathers; *brown chestband.* Some are much darker overall. Juvenile usually has heavy streaks below.

## NORTHERN HARRIER  *Circus cyaneus*

Longer-winged and longer-tailed than buteos; hunts by flying slowly and low over fields and marshes. Seldom seen perched in trees. Nests on the ground. ▶ In flight, notice *white rump,* long wings held above horizontal. Adult male mostly pearl gray, adult female brown, juvenile brown with orange-tinged chest.

# SOARING HAWKS

**Red-tailed Hawk**
19" w 50"

adult

young

adult

(w = wingspan:
distance from
wingtip to wingtip)

**Red-shouldered Hawk**
17" w 40"

adults

**Broad-winged Hawk**
16" w 34"

adults

young

**Rough-legged Hawk**
21" w 53"

light
morph

dark
morph

**Swainson's Hawk**
19" w 51"

young

adult

**Northern Harrier**
18" w 44"

females

adult
male

young

225

# LARGE BIRDS OF PREY

The Osprey is now placed in its own family, **Pandionidae,** while eagles are related to the hawks introduced on p. 224. American vultures (family **Cathartidae),** unrelated to similar birds found in the Old World, are scavengers with naked heads. Soaring over the landscape in search of dead animals, they could be considered part of nature's cleanup crew.

### OSPREY      *Pandion haliaetus*

This "fish hawk" is often seen hovering over the water on rapidly beating wings, or plunging feet-first to grab a fish in its talons. It was in serious trouble as recently as the 1970s; effects of DDT and other persistent pesticides kept pairs from raising young. Conservation efforts have succeeded, and Ospreys are now increasing and spreading as summer residents in the Midwest. ▶ *Black face stripe* on white head. In flight, the long wings are held *angled* at the wrist. **Voice:** very vocal, clear *keyew keyew keyew . . .*

### BALD EAGLE      *Haliaeetus leucocephalus*

Another conservation success story, with a great comeback since the low point in the 1970s. Now might be seen anywhere in the Midwest. A powerful predator, but also may feed as a scavenger on dead animals or fish. ▶ Adult almost unmistakable. Immatures take 5 years to reach full adult plumage. Youngest juveniles are all dark brown on head and body with some whitish mottling on wings and tail. Older immatures may have much white on body. **Voice:** harsh chatter, rather weak for size of bird.

### GOLDEN EAGLE      *Aquila chrysaetos*

Mostly a rare migrant through the Midwest, although seen regularly at established hawkwatch sites in early spring and late fall. A few stay through the winter in wilder, open habitats. ▶ Huge, mostly dark brown, with long, broad wings *held flat* while soaring. Immature has *white patches* in wings and tail. Adult resembles darkest young Bald Eagles (which are *much* more numerous in Midwest); Golden has longer tail, smaller head, golden plumes on nape, lacks white mottling on body and wing-linings.

### TURKEY VULTURE      *Cathartes aura*

Very common over much of the Midwest in summer, in warmer areas in winter. Usually seen soaring in slow, lazy flight, or gathered around roadkill or other carrion. Nest is well hidden in an abandoned building, hollow log, etc. ▶ Huge, with *long wings, long tail,* small head. Wings, held in *shallow V* while soaring, have two-toned look. Head red on adults, gray on young.

### BLACK VULTURE      *Coragyps atratus*

Locally common in southern part of our region. Spends less time soaring than previous species, except on hottest days. ▶ Different shape from Turkey Vulture: *short tail,* larger head, broad wings. Soars with wings held *flat. Whitish patch* near wingtips. Head gray (as on young Turkey Vulture).

# LARGE BIRDS OF PREY

**Osprey**
23" w 63"

(w = wingspan:
distance from
wingtip to wingtip)

**Bald Eagle**
31" w 80"

young

adult

adult

**Golden Eagle**
30" w 80"

young

**Turkey Vulture**
26" w 67"

**Black Vulture**
25" w 59"

# HAWKS, KITES, AND FALCONS

The first four species here belong to the hawk family, introduced on p. 224. Of these, the first three are Accipiters, bird-hunting hawks with long tails and short, rounded wings. Mississippi Kite is a graceful, gliding hawk that captures large insects in midair. The last three are members of the falcon family **(Falconidae),** fast-flying birds of prey with pointed wings and fairly long tails, unrelated to hawks.

### COOPER'S HAWK   *Accipiter cooperii*

Widespread and fairly common in forest, towns, farms. ▶ Very similar to Sharp-shinned Hawk but larger (especially female), with larger head. Tip of tail usually looks *rounded.* **Voice**: in alarm near nest, harsh *keh-keh-keh . . .*

### SHARP-SHINNED HAWK   *Accipiter striatus*

Fairly common, but not seen as often as Cooper's Hawk. Lurks in forest, may come out to nab small birds near feeders. ▶ Adult blue-gray above, reddish below; young is brown, streaked below. Female larger than male. Tip of tail usually looks *squared.*

### NORTHERN GOSHAWK   *Accipiter gentilis*

A powerful hunter of northern forests. Nests in northern edge of our region, migrates south in late fall. ▶ Adult mostly *gray,* with *white eyebrow* above *black face.* Young bigger than young Cooper's Hawk, with zigzag tail bands.

### MISSISSIPPI KITE   *Ictinia mississippiensis*

A summer bird of river groves and semi-open country at south edge of region, but may wander far north. ▶ Adult mostly gray with pale head, *white patch* on top of wing. Young browner, striped below. Best known by graceful, gliding flight.

### AMERICAN KESTREL   *Falco sparverius*

Our smallest falcon. Often perched on roadside wires, or hovering over fields on rapidly beating wings. Eats mostly grasshoppers, rodents. ▶ *Reddish brown tail* and back; male has blue-gray wings. **Voice**: shrill *killy-killy-killy.*

### MERLIN   *Falco columbarius*

Uncommon, mainly a migrant in most areas. ▶ Dashing flight. Compact shape, larger than kestrel, with *narrow white bars* across *shorter dark tail.* Adult male blue-gray above, female and young browner. **Voice**: chattering *ki-ki-ki-ki . . . ,* mostly near nest.

### PEREGRINE FALCON   *Falco peregrinus*

The world's fastest bird, able to reach 200 m.p.h. when power-diving on prey. Formerly endangered, making a good comeback; nests on buildings in many cities. Migrants may appear anywhere in the region, especially near water. ▶ Pointed, angular wings like other falcons, long tail, broad shoulders, *dark hooded effect.* Adult blue-gray above, narrowly barred below. Young brown, streaked below. **Voice**: near nest, harsh *kyah kyah . . .*

# HAWKS, KITES, AND FALCONS

adult

young

adults

Sharp-shinned Hawk
9"–13"

young

young

Cooper's Hawk
14"–19"

adult

Northern
Goshawk
18"–24"

Mississippi Kite
14"

female

male

American Kestrel
10"

female

Merlin
11"

male

adult

young

Peregrine Falcon
17"

# OWLS

Typical owls (family **Strigidae**) and barn owls (**Tytonidae**) often go unseen, although some species are fairly common. They can see well in daylight, but their eyes are especially adapted for seeing in dim light. Exceptional hearing allows some to locate and capture prey in complete darkness.

### EASTERN SCREECH-OWL  *Megascops asio*

Often overlooked, but common in forest, riverside groves, even suburbs. Nests in tree holes, nest boxes. ▶ *Small*. "Ear" tufts may be raised or flattened. Two color morphs, either gray or reddish brown. **Voice**: descending, wailing whinny, and long low trill.

### NORTHERN SAW-WHET OWL  *Aegolius acadicus*

A tiny northern gnome. Sometimes found roosting in evergreens in winter, may be absurdly tame. ▶ No "ear" tufts. Warm brown, with reddish streaks on chest. **Voice**: series of tooting notes.

### GREAT HORNED OWL  *Bubo virginiensis*

Common but easily overlooked, this big nocturnal hunter takes prey as large as rabbits, even skunks. Starts nesting as early as January, so may be very vocal in midwinter. ▶ Very large, with ear tufts ("horns"), white throat, fine *horizontal bars* on belly. **Voice**: low hoots, often in pattern of 5: *hoo huhoo, hooo, hoooh.*

### LONG-EARED OWL  *Asio otus*

Shy and uncommon, sometimes found roosting in evergreen groves. ▶ Smaller than Great Horned Owl, with *stripes* on belly, *black* around eyes. **Voice**: moaning hoots, not often heard.

### SHORT-EARED OWL  *Asio flammeus*

An owl of marshes and fields, sometimes active by day. Flies low, with floppy wingbeats. ▶ Buffy with streaked chest, black around eyes. *Contrasting wing patches* in flight. **Voice**: wheezy barks.

### BARRED OWL  *Strix varia*

Locally common in dense forest, swamps. ▶ Large with round head, *dark brown eyes,* barred chest, stripes on belly. **Voice**: rich hooting, *who cooks for you? who cooks for you-alll?*

### BARN OWL  *Tyto alba*

Now scarce and local. Nests in barns, hollow trees, nest boxes. Hunts at night over open fields, eating rats, mice. ▶ *Very pale* with *dark eyes,* heart-shaped face. **Voice**: rough hiss, harsh shrieks.

### SNOWY OWL  *Bubo scandiacus*

This Arctic owl is an uncommon winter visitor, mostly seen perching low in open country, lake shores. ▶ Big, with round head, *yellow eyes*. Amount of black spotting varies. Compare Barn Owl, white young of other owls.

### GREAT GRAY OWL  *Strix nebulosa*

A rare owl of northern bogs and woods, mainly in n. Minnesota and nw. Wisconsin. ▶ Huge, gray, with *dark face rings, yellow eyes, white neck spots.*

# SMALL AND LARGE OWLS
(at two different scales)

gray morph

red morph

**Eastern Screech-Owl**
8½"

**Northern Saw-whet Owl**
8"

**Great Horned Owl**
23"

**Long-eared Owl**
15"

**Short-eared Owl**
15"

**Barred Owl**
21"

**Great Gray Owl**
27"

**Barn Owl**
16"

**Snowy Owl**
24"

# CHICKENLIKE BIRDS

Plump, ground-dwelling birds. Several are important game birds in the Midwest. Bobwhites are in the New World quail family (**Odontophoridae**), while the others below are in the pheasant family (**Phasianidae**).

### NORTHERN BOBWHITE  *Colinus virginianus*

The familiar little quail of farms and brushy fields. Formerly common, now declining. Those seen in the north may be game farm releases. ▶ Reddish brown body, very short tail. *Pale eyebrow and throat,* white on male, buff on female. **Voice:** whistled *bob-whoit?* or *er-bob-whoit?* Covey call, whistled *quoy-kee.*

### GRAY PARTRIDGE  *Perdix perdix*

Introduced from Europe, locally common in prairie and farming regions. Often out of sight among tall grass. ▶ Gray and brown, with *orange face, dark belly patch.* **Voice:** metallic grating call.

### RUFFED GROUSE  *Bonasa umbellus*

Fairly common in mixed and deciduous woods. Usually seen on ground, also perches in trees. In spring courtship, male struts on log with neck ruffs puffed out, tail spread; rapidly drums the air with his wings, producing a deep thumping. ▶ Fan-shaped tail *reddish or gray,* with black band near tip. *Black bars* on sides.

### SPRUCE GROUSE  *Falcipennis canadensis*

A northern forest grouse, so tame it's easy to overlook: may sit motionless as you walk past. ▶ Male gray, with *black throat,* red above eye. Female shorter-tailed than Ruffed Grouse, *lacks* black bars on sides. **Voice:** clucks; deep hoots from displaying male.

### GREATER PRAIRIE-CHICKEN  *Tympanuchus cupido*

Formerly widespread, now in scattered colonies. Where they persist (mostly native prairies), males gather in spring on traditional "booming grounds," displaying to attract females. ▶ Brown with *heavy barring* below. In flight, shows *short black tail.*

### SHARP-TAILED GROUSE  *Tympanuchus phasianellus*

Favors a mix of prairie and woods; in winter, often feeds on buds in trees. Males display in spring to attract females. ▶ Like prairie-chicken but more *spotted* below, not barred. *Pointed tail.*

### RING-NECKED PHEASANT  *Phasianus colchicus*

Native to Asia, introduced here as a game bird. Common in woods, farmland, marshes. ▶ Flashy male unmistakable. Female mottled brown with *long, pointed tail.* **Voice:** harsh crowing.

### WILD TURKEY  *Meleagris gallopavo*

The native turkey was almost wiped out at one time, but has made a good comeback and is still increasing. Found in woods, farmland, even edges of towns. ▶ *Huge,* with naked head, long wide tail. Looks trimmer and stronger than domestic turkey, with darker rusty tail tip. **Voice:** loud gobbling.

# CHICKENLIKE BIRDS

(not all shown at same scale)

male

female

**Northern Bobwhite** 10"

**Gray Partridge** 12½"

**Ruffed Grouse** 17½"

female

male

**Spruce Grouse** 16"

males in courtship displays

**Sharp-tailed Grouse** 17"

**Greater Prairie-Chicken** 17½"

female

male

**Ring-necked Pheasant** 21" (female), 33" (male)

female

male

**Wild Turkey** 37" (female), 46" (male)

233

# LARGE WADING BIRDS

Cranes (family **Gruidae**) are sometimes confused with herons and egrets (family **Ardeidae**), but are completely unrelated. Cranes have shorter bills, big tuft of feathers over tail; they fly with neck outstretched. Herons (including egrets and bitterns) mostly wade in shallow water to prey on aquatic life; they fly with neck hunched back onto shoulders.

### WHOOPING CRANE    *Grus americana*

One of North America's rarest birds, almost extinct in 1940s, still making a slow comeback. A current project is to establish a new migratory flock nesting in Wisconsin and wintering in Florida; migrants are seen else-where in the Midwest. ▶ Huge, white, with red and black on head. Black wing pattern shows in flight. Juvenile has brown head. **Voice**: rich bugling.

### SANDHILL CRANE    *Grus canadensis*

Increasing in numbers in the Midwest, as both a nesting bird and a migrant, with a few now staying through the winter. Flocks feed on waste grain in fields, roost in marshes. ▶ Adult all-gray with red patch on head, sometimes brown staining on body feathers. Juvenile has brownish head. Great Blue Heron has very different shape. **Voice**: guttural crowing rattle, often given in flight.

### GREAT BLUE HERON    *Ardea herodias*

Our most widespread and familiar heron (although often called "crane"), throughout the Midwest in summer, more localized in winter. May be seen miles from water, flying with slow flaps, neck hunched back onto shoulders. Nests in colonies of stick nests in tall trees. ▶ Huge, gray, with *black crown stripe* on whitish head. Bill varies from dark to bright yellow. **Voice**: harsh squawks.

### GREAT EGRET    *Ardea alba*

Locally common in the Midwest, around marshes, lakes, rivers. Wanders widely in late summer. Often seen standing very still in the shallows. ▶ Tall and statuesque, long-necked, long-legged. All-white with *yellow bill, black legs*.

### SNOWY EGRET    *Egretta thula*

Very local as a nesting bird, but wanders widely, mainly in late summer. Often moves about actively in shallows. ▶ Much smaller than Great Egret. Slender build, *black bill* with yellow in front of eye, black legs with *contrasting yellow feet* ("golden slippers").

### CATTLE EGRET    *Bubulcus ibis*

Unlike its relatives, usually forages out in dry fields, catching insects scared up by grazing cattle and other animals. ▶ Stocky, with short yellow bill. Legs vary from yellow to blackish.

### LITTLE BLUE HERON    *Egretta caerulea*

Very local as a nesting bird, but wanders widely. ▶ Adult dark slaty all over. Young bird all-white at first, with greenish legs, pale bill base. Patchy "calico" phase follows as dark feathers molt in.

# CRANES AND HERONS

Whooping
Crane
52"

Sandhill
Crane
44"

Great Blue
Heron
47"

Great
Egret
39"

## SMALLER HERONS AND EGRETS
### (not at same scale as above)

Snowy
Egret
24"

Cattle Egret
19"

Little
Blue
Heron
24"

# SMALL HERONS AND MARSH BIRDS

The first four are in the heron family (see p. 234). Rails (family **Rallidae**) are shy marsh birds, heard more often than seen, while the snipe and woodcock are odd members of the sandpiper family (see p. 240).

### BLACK-CROWNED NIGHT-HERON    *Nycticorax nycticorax*

This bulky heron may spend the day roosting in dense cover near water, flying out at dusk to begin hunting. Waits along shorelines to spear fish at night. Uncommon in summer, very local in winter. ▶ Adult has clean pattern: *black cap* and back, gray wings. Juvenile brown with stripes, pale spots. **Voice:** low, hollow *wok!*

### YELLOW-CROWNED NIGHT-HERON    *Nyctanassa violacea*

A scarce southern heron, sometimes wandering north. ▶ Adult *gray* with *black and white face,* pale crown. Juvenile grayer than young Black-crowned, with longer legs. **Voice:** hollow *wak!*

### AMERICAN BITTERN    *Botaurus lentiginosus*

Bitterns are solitary herons that hide in marshes. If disturbed, they "freeze" with bills pointed up. ▶ Warm brown, broadly *striped* below, with *dark neck mark.* Compare to young night-herons. **Voice:** deep *ooom-ka-choom,* with sharp middle note.

### LEAST BITTERN    *Ixobrychus exilis*

A scarce, tiny bittern, most likely to be seen flying low over the marsh. ▶ Buff, with cap and back brown (female) or black (male). *Buff wing patch* obvious in flight. **Voice:** fast cooing gobble.

### GREEN HERON    *Butorides virescens*

A solitary little heron of wooded ponds, streams. ▶ Dark back glossed blue or green; *neck red-brown.* Black crown sometimes raised in bushy crest. *Legs yellow-orange.* **Voice:** sharp *skyowk!*

### VIRGINIA RAIL    *Rallus limicola*

Fairly common in marshes, but usually hard to see. ▶ Reddish brown with gray cheeks, long reddish bill, barred flanks. **Voice:** metallic *kik kidik kidik;* nasal, descending *wenk-wenk-wenk.*

### SORA    *Porzana carolina*

A small rail, sometimes seen out in the open. ▶ *Short yellow bill, black face* contrasting with gray chest. Young are duller. **Voice:** a rising whistle, *surr-reee!* Also descending whinny, sharp *keek!*

### WILSON'S SNIPE    *Gallinago delicata*

Mostly a migrant, local at other seasons. Usually solitary, lurking in marshes. ▶ *Long* bill. *Striped head* and back, barred sides. **Voice:** in nesting season, hooting trill in flight display.

### AMERICAN WOODCOCK    *Scolopax minor*

This odd "timberdoodle" hides in woods by day, probes for worms in wet fields at night. Males make musical courtship flights on spring nights. ▶ Long bill, orange-buff below, crosswise bars on head. **Voice:** nasal *pzeent;* twittering in flight display.

# SMALL HERONS, MARSH BIRDS

juvenile

**Black-crowned
Night-Heron
25″**

adult

**Yellow-crowned
Night-Heron
25″**

**American
Bittern
26″**

## SMALL MARSH BIRDS (not to same scale)

**Least Bittern
13″**

**Green
Heron
19″**

**Virginia
Rail
9½″**

**Sora
9″**

**Wilson's
Snipe
10½″**

**American Woodcock
11″**

237

# PLOVERS AND OTHER SHOREBIRDS

"Shorebirds" are not always on the shore. Plovers (family **Charadriidae**) have short bills and fairly short legs, avocets (family **Recurvirostridae**) are just the opposite, while sandpipers (see p. 240) vary in shape.

### KILLDEER  *Charadrius vociferus*

A noisy plover, common in fields, pond edges. Lays its eggs in scrape on bare ground; may fake a broken wing to lure intruders away from eggs or young. ▶ Has *2 black neck rings, orange* at base of tail. **Voice:** loud, clear *kil-deeah* and *dee-dee-dee . . .*

### SEMIPALMATED PLOVER  *Charadrius semipalmatus*

Nests on Arctic tundra, migrates through Midwest in spring and fall, stopping at mudflats, ponds. ▶ *Single* black chest band, short bill, *dark brown* back, *yellow-orange legs.* **Voice:** clear *chuweep.*

### PIPING PLOVER  *Charadrius melodus*

Endangered, a few nesting and migrating along Great Lakes. ▶ *Very pale* with *dark neck band, orange legs, stubby bill.* **Voice:** piping *peep-lo.*

### AMERICAN GOLDEN-PLOVER  *Pluvialis dominica*

A migrant, mainly on prairies and around Great Lakes. ▶ Spring adults with striking pattern, gold-spangled back. Fall birds (and some in spring) warm brown; note *shape.* **Voice:** rich whistle.

### BLACK-BELLIED PLOVER  *Pluvialis squatarola*

Common migrant around Great Lakes, fewer elsewhere. Often in open fields. ▶ Similar to Golden-Plover but *stouter,* larger-billed, grayer at all seasons. **Voice:** mournful whistle, *wheeyou-wee.*

### RUDDY TURNSTONE  *Arenaria interpres*

This sandpiper flips small rocks as it forages. Common migrant around Great Lakes, rare elsewhere. ▶ *Wedge-shaped bill, short orange legs.* Unmistakable pattern in spring; brown in fall, with dark chest pattern.

### UPLAND SANDPIPER  *Bartramia longicauda*

A bird of tall-grass prairies and meadows, now declining in many areas. Where it persists, often seen standing on fenceposts along roads in summer. ▶ Habitat and shape are best clues. Note thin neck, short bill, round dovelike head, relatively *long tail.* **Voice:** breathy whistle, *wrrreee wheeeyeeww.* Flight call, a rippling trill.

### WILSON'S PHALAROPE  *Phalaropus tricolor*

An odd sandpiper that swims and spins on water. Mainly western part of our region. ▶ Thin bill. Spring female has pale crown, *black and chestnut neck stripes.* Male and fall birds duller.

### AMERICAN AVOCET  *Recurvirostra americana*

A western shorebird, nesting at edge of our area, but widespread in migration. Wades in shallow water of ponds, marshes. ▶ Long thin legs, thin *upcurved* bill, black and white stripes on back. Head pale cinnamon or gray. **Voice:** shrill *kleeap.*

# PLOVERS AND OTHER SHOREBIRDS

downy young
Killdeer

Killdeer
10½"

fall
juvenile

spring
adult

Semipalmated Plover
7¼"

Piping Plover
7¼"

spring
adult

spring
adult

spring
adult

Black-bellied Plover
11½"

fall and
winter

American
Golden-Plover
10¼"

fall
juvenile

spring

fall

Ruddy
Turnstone
9½"

Upland
Sandpiper
12"

(not shown
to scale)

American
Avocet
18"

Wilson's
Phalarope
9½"

spring
female

# SANDPIPERS

(family **Scolopacidae**) are mostly migrants through the Midwest, with only a few staying to nest. Flocks pause in passage to feed at water's edge. "Fall" migration for some starts very early, by the first of July.

### SPOTTED SANDPIPER *Actitis macularius*

Common migrant at water's edge, also staying through summer to nest near ponds, creeks. Teeters unsteadily while standing; flies with stiff shallow wingbeats. ▶ *Round black spots* below in breeding plumage. Plainer at other seasons; note the *teetering action,* white shoulder mark. **Voice:** abrupt *peet-weet!*

### SOLITARY SANDPIPER *Tringa solitaria*

Mostly a migrant, at ponds, creeks, marsh edges. ▶ Suggests fall Spotted (and bobs head when excited) but slimmer, *darker,* with *white eye-ring.* **Voice:** shrill *pit-weet!,* higher than Spotted's.

### LESSER YELLOWLEGS *Tringa flavipes*

Common spring and fall migrant throughout region, in marshes, flooded fields, pond edges. Wades in shallows, often in small flocks. ▶ Slender shape, delicate actions, long *yellow legs.* **Voice:** flat *tu* or *tu-tu.*

### GREATER YELLOWLEGS *Tringa melanoleuca*

Another common migrant in wetlands of the region, in singles and small flocks. Wades actively in shallows. ▶ Like Lesser Yellowlegs but slightly larger. Distinctly longer bill, thicker at base, with hint of upcurve. In spring, more heavily marked belly. **Voice:** loud, ringing *whee whee whew!*

### DOWITCHERS *Limnodromus* sp.

These dumpy sandpipers wade slowly in shallow water, probing straight down with long bills, heads often submerged. Two very similar species, Long-billed Dowitcher and Short-billed Dowitcher, migrate through the Midwest. ▶ In breeding plumage, brownish orange on chest. Winter plumage much duller, grayer. Fall juvenile Short-billed very bright. **Voice:** Long-billed, sharp *keek* or *keekeekeek;* Short-billed, mellow *tututu.*

### LEAST SANDPIPER *Calidris minutilla*

Common in spring and fall on mudflats, marsh edges. ▶ Sparrow-sized with thin bill. Very brown, with dull yellow legs. **Voice:** thin *crreeeep.*

### SEMIPALMATED SANDPIPER *Calidris pusilla*

Another tiny migrant, sometimes in flocks on mudflats. ▶ A little grayer than Least Sandpiper, with paler chest, dark legs. **Voice:** low *chrk.*

### PECTORAL SANDPIPER *Calidris melanotos*

Fairly common migrant in marshes, grasslands, flooded fields. ▶ Sharp *contrast* between streaked brown chest, white belly. Legs dull yellow.

### DUNLIN *Calidris alpina*

Common migrant near Great Lakes, less common elsewhere, on mudflats, beaches. ▶ Long bill, *drooped* at tip. Winter plumage (most of year) very gray on back and chest. In spring, reddish on back, *black belly patch.*

SANDPIPERS

spring

fall

Solitary
Sandpiper
8½"

Spotted Sandpiper
7½"

spring

fall
juvenile

spring

Lesser
Yellowlegs
10½"

Greater
Yellowlegs
14"

juvenile
Short-billed
Dowitcher

fall

spring

dowitcher sp.
11"

fall

spring

fall
juvenile

spring

Least Sandpiper
6"

Semipalmated
Sandpiper
6¼"

Pectoral
Sandpiper
8½"

spring

Dunlin
8½"

fall

241

# MEDIUM-SIZED LAND BIRDS

These nine birds represent four different and unrelated families.

### MOURNING DOVE   *Zenaida macroura*

Pigeons and doves (family Columbidae) have small round heads and short bills. This native dove is very common in towns, farmland, all open habitats; more local in winter. ▶ Mostly plain. Black spots on wings. *Long, pointed tail* has white spots on edge. Scaly pattern on juveniles. **Voice:** mournful *coowah cooo, coo, cooo.*

### EURASIAN COLLARED-DOVE   *Streptopelia decaocto*

Introduced and spreading through the Midwest. ▶ *Pale* brown with *black neck ring,* white patches in tail. **Voice:** harsh cooing, hoarse shriek.

### ROCK PIGEON   *Columba livia*

This is the familiar city pigeon, native to the Old World, now common in towns and farms throughout the Midwest. ▶ Original wild type was gray with white rump, 2 black bars on wings. Domesticated forms vary from white to reddish to black, and flocks may contain all types.

### YELLOW-BILLED CUCKOO   *Coccyzus americanus*

Our 2 cuckoo species (family Cuculidae) are both slim birds that lurk in dense foliage, often feeding on hairy caterpillars. ▶ Bill *partly yellow,* underside of tail with *big white spots.* Wings show *reddish* in flight. **Voice:** hollow clatter, slowing toward end.

### BLACK-BILLED CUCKOO   *Coccyzus erythropthalmus*

Another summer lurker in woods and swamps. ▶ Like Yellow-billed but bill *all black,* thin red eye-ring, *narrow* white spots on tail, no reddish in wing. **Voice:** hollow *cucucu, cucucucu . . .*

### COMMON NIGHTHAWK   *Chordeiles minor*

Not a hawk, but a member of the nightjar family (Caprimulgidae) like the next 2 species. Pursues insects in high erratic flight, often near dusk. Nests on bare ground, or on flat gravel rooftops in towns. ▶ Long angular wings, crossed by *white band.* Heavily *barred* below. **Voice:** buzzy *pzeent.* In display dive, hollow *voom.*

### EASTERN WHIP-POOR-WILL   *Antrostomus vociferus*

Often heard at night in rich woods in summer. Hides by day, on ground or horizontal branch, relying on camouflage. ▶ Mottled gray and brown, with big head. In flight, tail corners white (male) or buff (female). **Voice:** rolling chant, *WHIP-prrr-WEEL.*

### CHUCK-WILL'S-WIDOW   *Antrostomus carolinensis*

Another voice in the night, summering in the south, rarely wandering north. ▶ Larger than Whip-poor-will, more buffy brown, less white in tail. **Voice:** rolling chant, *chuk weeyo WEEdow.*

### MONK PARAKEET   *Myiopsitta monachus*

Native to South America. Escaped cagebirds (Chicago and elsewhere) live in noisy colonies, build stick nests. ▶ Long-tailed, green with gray front.

adult

**Mourning
Dove
12"**

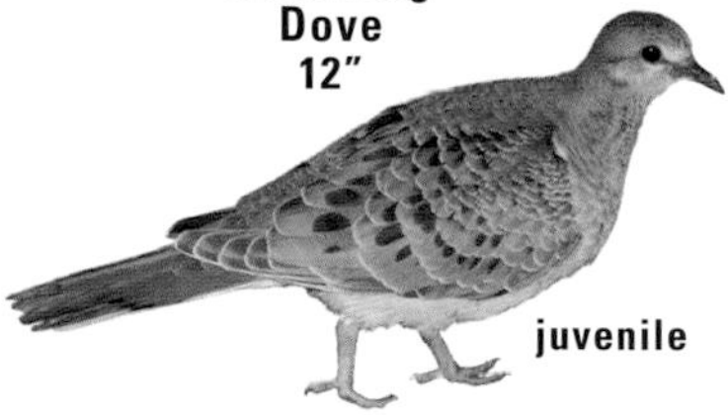

**Eurasian
Collared-Dove
12½"**

juvenile

**Black-billed
Cuckoo
11¾"**

**Rock Pigeon
13"**

**Yellow-billed
Cuckoo
12"**

**Eastern
Whip-poor-will
10"**

**Common Nighthawk
9½"**

**Chuck-will's-widow
12"**

**Monk Parakeet
12"**

# WOODPECKERS AND KINGFISHER

Woodpeckers (family **Picidae**) climb trees, clutching with strong feet, using chisel-like bills to drill for insects and to excavate nest holes. Kingfishers (family **Alcedinidae**) perch or hover above water, plunge for fish.

### DOWNY WOODPECKER   *Picoides pubescens*

Common in woods, towns, often visiting feeders for suet or seeds. In winter, often joins mixed flocks with chickadees and other birds. ▶ Small, with *stubby bill*. Patterned black and white, with big spots on wings, barred outer tail feathers. Male has red nape spot. **Voice:** flat *pik;* chattering, descending whinny.

### HAIRY WOODPECKER   *Picoides villosus*

Less common than Downy Woodpecker, usually in forests. ▶ Like Downy but slightly larger with distinctly *longer bill.* White outer tail feathers lack dark bars. **Voice:** sharp *peek!* and shrill rattle.

### RED-BELLIED WOODPECKER   *Melanerpes carolinus*

A southern bird gradually spreading north in this region, found in forests, towns. ▶ Zebra-backed pattern, red stripe running up nape (female) or all the way to forehead (male). Red on belly is hard to see. **Voice:** noisy. Loud *chiff, chiff* and rolling *churrrr.*

### RED-HEADED WOODPECKER   *Melanerpes erythrocephalus*

Formerly common, now uncommon in most areas. Found mainly in open oak savanna, swamps, other open country with scattered groves. ▶ *Completely red head,* black back, big *white wing patches.* Young are brown-headed. **Voice:** raspy *kreeyer!*

### YELLOW-BELLIED SAPSUCKER   *Sphyrapicus varius*

Its name sounds like a joke, but this is a real bird that drills neat rows of holes in bark, returning to drink the sap. ▶ Striped face, mottled back, *long white stripe* on wing. **Voice:** catlike *meeyah.*

### NORTHERN FLICKER   *Colaptes auratus*

This big brown woodpecker sometimes forages on the ground, eating ants. Common in forests, prairie groves, towns. ▶ Brown with black bars and spots, *black chest patch,* red on nape. Male has black moustache. In flight shows white rump, *yellow in wings and tail.* **Voice:** low ringing *kleeyah!* and *wik-wik-wik . . .*

### PILEATED WOODPECKER   *Dryocopus pileatus*

Our largest woodpecker. Declined with clearing of forest, now coming back in many areas. ▶ Crow-sized, black, with red crest. White wing-linings flash in flight. **Voice:** loud, ringing notes.

### BELTED KINGFISHER   *Megaceryle alcyon*

A solitary bird of the water's edge. Plunges headfirst to catch small fish in bill. Nests in burrows in dirt banks. ▶ Shaggy head, big bill, short neck, small feet. Blue Jay (p. 252) is also blue-gray and crested, but *very* different in shape. Female has rusty band across chest. **Voice:** loud rattle, often given in flight.

# WOODPECKERS AND KINGFISHER

**Hairy Woodpecker**
9"
*male*

**Downy Woodpecker**
6½"
*male*
*female*

**Red-bellied Woodpecker**
9½"

**Red-headed Woodpecker**
9¼"

## LARGER WOODPECKERS
(not shown to same scale)

**Northern Flicker**
13"
*male*
*female*

**Yellow-bellied Sapsucker**
8½"
*male*

**Pileated Woodpecker**
17"
*male*

**Belted Kingfisher**
13"
*male*

# HUMMINGBIRDS, SWIFTS, SWALLOWS

Hummingbirds (family **Trochilidae**) are only distantly related to swifts (**Apodidae**) and not at all to swallows (**Hirundinidae**), but all make their living on the wing: hummingbirds hovering at flowers for nectar, swifts and swallows catching insects in midair during graceful flight.

### RUBY-THROATED HUMMINGBIRD    *Archilochus colubris*

Common but easily overlooked. Hovers at flowers or sugar-water feeders; males perch high. ▶More likely to be mistaken for an insect than another bird; see hawkmoths (p. 342). Iridescent green above, whitish below. Male's *red throat* often just looks black. Female has white tail spots. **Rufous Hummingbird** (*Selasphorus rufus*), very rare fall visitor, strongly tinged reddish brown.

### CHIMNEY SWIFT    *Chaetura pelagica*

Our most aerial bird. Incapable of perching, can only cling to vertical surfaces; nests inside chimneys. Winters in the Amazon Basin. ▶ Very *short tail*, blunt head, long curved wings. Flies with rapid wingbeats and long glides. **Voice:** metallic chippering.

### PURPLE MARTIN    *Progne subis*

Our biggest swallow. Locally common, nesting in multiroomed houses put up for it. ▶ Male all-black (with purple sheen); compare to starlings (p. 266). Female and young grayer below, with white belly. **Voice:** musical, burry *dzeeb-dzurr*, other notes.

### TREE SWALLOW    *Tachycineta bicolor*

Common in summer. Nests in holes in trees and in houses put up for bluebirds. Eats insects like other swallows; also berries, so may arrive earlier in spring and stay later in fall. ▶ *Clean white* below, blue-black above; young browner. **Voice:** clear *tdeet*.

### BARN SWALLOW    *Hirundo rustica*

Very common in summer, building its mud nest inside barns, on porches, under bridges. ▶ Long, *forked tail* with white spots; chestnut throat and forehead. **Voice:** musical twittering.

### CLIFF SWALLOW    *Petrochelidon pyrrhonota*

Most nesting colonies today are on buildings or under bridges, not on cliffs. Gathers mud to make jug-shaped nest with entrance on side. ▶ Short, square-tipped tail, *buffy rump patch*, dark throat, white forehead. **Voice:** *churr* and creaks.

### BANK SWALLOW    *Riparia riparia*

Locally common. Nests in holes in dirt banks (riverbanks, quarries); many pairs often nest close together in colony. ▶ Brown back, sharp *brown band* below *white throat*. **Voice:** dry buzzes.

### N. ROUGH-WINGED SWALLOW    *Stelgidopteryx serripennis*

Like Bank Swallows, Northern Rough-wings nest in holes in dirt banks, but as isolated pairs, not in colonies. ▶ Bigger than Bank Swallow, throat and chest *entirely dusky*. **Voice:** buzzy *fzzzt*.

female

male

**Ruby-throated Hummingbird**
3¾"

**Chimney Swift**
5"

male

**Purple Martin**
8"

female

**Tree Swallow**
5¾"

at nest

**Barn Swallow**
7"

mud nest

**Cliff Swallow**
5½"

**Bank Swallow**
4¾"

**Northern Rough-winged Swallow**
5½"

# FLYCATCHERS

(family **Tyrannidae**) usually watch from a perch and then fly out to catch insects in midair. Most of our species spend the winter in the tropics.

### EASTERN KINGBIRD    *Tyrannus tyrannus*

During the warmer months, in farmland, woodland borders, and edges of ponds, this spunky bird draws attention with its bold behavior. It often drives away crows, hawks, and other large birds that come too close to its nest. ► Blackish above, white below, with broad *white band* at tip of tail. **Voice:** high *bzzeent!*

### WESTERN KINGBIRD    *Tyrannus verticalis*

Regular in summer on edge of region, often wandering farther east. Favors very open terrain. ► Pale gray above and on chest, yellow on belly. *Black tail* with *narrow white outer edge*. **Voice:** sharp *kep* and staccato "bickering" cries.

### EASTERN PHOEBE    *Sayornis phoebe*

Pronounced "fee-bee," and named after its song. Arrives early in spring along streams, forest edge, often placing its nest on porches or under bridges. ► Gray above, whitish below. Known by gentle *tail-wagging action*, dark face. **Voice:** burry *fee-bee;* sharp *pip*.

### GREAT CRESTED FLYCATCHER    *Myiarchus crinitus*

This colorful flycatcher is often hidden in forest foliage, and may be heard more than seen. Nests in holes in trees. ► *Yellow belly* contrasts with gray chest, bright *reddish brown* in tail and wings. **Voice:** whistled *wheeap!* and rough, rolling *berrg, berrg.*

### EASTERN WOOD-PEWEE    *Contopus virens*

A voice in the forests of summer. ► Gray, rather plain. Compact shape with long wingtips. Has *pale wing bars* but *no eye-ring*. **Voice:** clear, plaintive *peeyeeer* and *peey-ya-weee.*

### OLIVE-SIDED FLYCATCHER    *Contopus cooperi*

Uncommon and solitary. Summers in northern forest, migrates throughout the region. Often seen perched on a dead branch at the very top of a tree. ► Big-headed, short-tailed. *Dark sides* contrast with white center of belly (like *unbuttoned vest*). **Voice:** whistled *quick-three-beers!;* sharp *pip-pip.*

### EMPIDONAX FLYCATCHERS    *Empidonax* sp.
Five small flycatchers in the genus *Empidonax* occur commonly in the Midwest. All look so similar that even experts often just let them go as "empids." ► Small, olive or gray above and pale below, with contrasting wing bars and (usually) eye-rings. See Ruby-crowned Kinglet (p. 256). **Voice:** short, distinctive songs. **Least Flycatcher** *(E. minimus),* of woodland edges: snappy *che-bek!* **Willow Flycatcher** *(E. traillii),* of thickets: buzzy *FITZ-bew.* **Alder Flycatcher** *(E. alnorum),* of thickets: buzzy *frree-BEEyer.* **Yellow-bellied Flycatcher** *(E. flaviventris),* of northern bogs: soft *chebunk.* **Acadian Flycatcher** *(E. virescens),* of southern swamps: explosive *PEET-ssah.*

# FLYCATCHERS

**Eastern Kingbird**
8½"

**Western Kingbird**
8"

**Great Crested Flycatcher**
8½"

**Eastern Phoebe**
7"

**Eastern Wood-Pewee**
6½"

**Olive-sided Flycatcher**
7½"

**Empidonax flycatchers (2 examples)**
5½"

# THRUSHES AND THRASHERS

Robins, bluebirds, and other thrushes (family **Turdidae**) include many fine singers. Thrashers, catbirds, and mockingbirds (family **Mimidae**) take it to the next level, with many imitations worked into their varied songs.

### AMERICAN ROBIN    *Turdus migratorius*

Familiar almost everywhere from wilderness to city parks, hunting earthworms on lawns, building its nest on windowsills. In winter, flocks wander in search of berries, wild fruits. ▶ Brick red chest, gray back, streaked chin. Juvenile is heavily spotted at first. **Voice:** rich caroling, often starting well before dawn.

### EASTERN BLUEBIRD    *Sialia sialis*

One of America's favorite birds. Fairly common in open country. Often uses manmade nest boxes. ▶ *Blue back, rusty chest,* white belly. Female duller. **Voice:** soft warbling song; *true-lee* call.

### HERMIT THRUSH    *Catharus guttatus*

Common migrant, early spring and late fall; more localized in summer and winter. Like the other brown thrushes, a shy forest bird. ▶ *Reddish brown tail,* strong *eye-ring.* **Voice:** long clear note followed by soft quick warble; repeated on different pitch.

### SWAINSON'S THRUSH    *Catharus ustulatus*

A local summer resident of northern forest, and very common as a migrant throughout, mostly in May and September. ▶ Dull brown above with *bold buff eye-ring,* buff at sides of chest. **Gray-cheeked Thrush** (*C. minimus*), a migrant, much grayer with no obvious eye-ring. **Voice:** song starts with short clear note, then short phrases ending on higher pitch. Callnote, liquid *hwoit.*

### WOOD THRUSH    *Hylocichla mustelina*

Declining, but still fairly common in forest in summer. ▶ Rich *reddish brown* back and head, bold *eye-ring, round black spots* on white chest. **Voice:** fluting *eeyoh-lay* and snappy *pep-pep-pep.*

### VEERY    *Catharus fuscescens*

Locally common in summer in damp leafy woods. ▶ *Warm tawny brown above,* with plain, pale face, faint darker spots on chest. **Voice:** breezy, spiraling whistles, *veeyurr, veeyur, veeer, veer.*

### BROWN THRASHER    *Toxostoma rufum*

Lurks in thickets, thrashing fallen leaves on the ground. ▶ Bigger, longer-tailed than Wood Thrush, *striped* (not spotted) below, with *yellow eyes.* **Voice:** short rich phrases, usually doubled.

### GRAY CATBIRD    *Dumetella carolinensis*

Common in summer in forests, suburban gardens. Lurks in bushes but also can be boldly curious. Rare in winter. ▶ Slim, gray, with long tail, black cap, *rusty* under tail. **Voice:** catlike *mey-eww;* disjointed song of whistles, squeaks, whines.

fledgling

adult
male

**American Robin**
**10″**

female

**Eastern**
**Bluebird**
**7″**

male
at nest

**Hermit**
**Thrush**
**7″**

**Swainson's**
**Thrush**
**7″**

**Wood Thrush**
**7¾″**

**Veery**
**7″**

**Brown Thrasher**
**11½″**

**Gray**
**Catbird**
**8½″**

251

# MOCKINGBIRD, SHRIKES, AND CORVIDS

Mockingbird is related to thrashers on p. 250. Shrikes (family **Laniidae**) are predatory songbirds that may impale their prey on a thorn or barbed wire. Jays, crows, ravens, and magpies (family **Corvidae**, or corvids for short) are omnivores, thought to be among the most intelligent birds.

### NORTHERN MOCKINGBIRD  *Mimus polyglottos*

Most common toward south; wanders north. May sing all night on moonlit nights. Eats many berries in winter. ▶ Slim, long-tailed. *White in wings and tail* obvious in flight. **Voice:** varied phrases (including imitations), each repeated over and over.

### LOGGERHEAD SHRIKE  *Lanius ludovicianus*

Once common, now declining, in open country with scattered shrubs. Eats large insects, rodents, small birds. ▶ Gray with black wings, *thick black mask*. **Voice:** varied musical and harsh notes.

### NORTHERN SHRIKE  *Lanius excubitor*

A scarce, solitary winter visitor of open country. Catches rodents and small birds. ▶ Larger than Loggerhead Shrike, with thinner mask, *faint barring* below. Often best recognized by season.

### GRAY JAY  *Perisoreus canadensis*

In the north woods, this jay may be oddly tame, entering camp-sites for scraps. ▶ Gray with whitish head, black nape patch. Juvenile *sooty* with pale whisker mark. **Voice:** whistles, low notes.

### BLUE JAY  *Cyanocitta cristata*

A familiar, noisy bird of forests, parks, yards, often coming to bird feeders. Present all year in Midwest, but migrating flocks pass through in spring and fall. ▶ Our only *crested blue bird*. *Black necklace*, long tail with *white corners*, strongly patterned wings. **Voice:** screaming *jaayy!*, musical *beadle-beadle*, other notes.

### AMERICAN CROW  *Corvus brachyrhynchos*

Common in open country, increasingly in cities also. In winter, large flocks may gather in night roosts. ▶ All black, and *much* larger than blackbirds or starlings (p. 266). **Voice:** familiar harsh *caw! caw!* and other notes. **Fish Crow** (*C. ossifragus*), not shown, reaches edge of region; smaller with nasal voice, *annh-annh*.

### COMMON RAVEN  *Corvus corax*

Classified as a songbird, but big as a hawk. Most common in northern wilderness, but expanding its range. ▶ Much larger than crows, with very heavy bill, *shaggy throat feathers, wedge-shaped tail*. **Voice:** deep echoing croak, plus screams, gurgles, etc.

### BLACK-BILLED MAGPIE  *Pica hudsonia*
A flashy westerner, local in w. Minnesota, rare in Iowa, mostly in open country with scattered groves. ▶ Blue and green gloss on wings and *long black tail*. *White wing patches* flash in flight. **Voice:** varied harsh notes.

# MOCKINGBIRD, SHRIKES, CORVIDS

Northern Mockingbird 10½"

Loggerhead Shrike 9"

Northern Shrike 10"

Gray Jay 11½"

Blue Jay 11"

## LARGE CORVIDS
(not at same scale as above)

American Crow 19"

Common Raven 25"

Black-billed Magpie 19"

# CHICKADEES, NUTHATCHES, AND CREEPERS

These are all small birds that seek insects hidden in trees. Chickadees and titmice (family **Paridae**) mostly forage in the outer twigs, while the nuthatches **(Sittidae)** and creepers **(Certhiidae)** usually focus on trunks and main branches. In winter, mixed flocks of these birds travel together through the woods, often joined by Downy Woodpeckers and others.

### BLACK-CAPPED CHICKADEE    *Poecile atricapillus*

Active, confiding, and seemingly cheerful even on harsh winter days, chickadees are popular residents of woods, parks, and yards, often visiting bird feeders for suet or seeds. ▶ Black cap and bib, white cheeks. In southern Midwest, see next species. **Voice**: song a whistled *fee-bee-ee,* the first note higher. Chattering *chick-a-dee-dee-dee* and many other callnotes.

### CAROLINA CHICKADEE    *Poecile carolinensis*

Replaces Black-capped Chickadee in southern Midwest. Where they overlap, they may interbreed, so not safely identifiable in that zone. ▶ Slightly smaller than Black-capped, with less white in wings. **Voice**: song 4-noted, *see-bee-see-bay,* first and third notes very high. Also rapid chattering and other callnotes.

### BOREAL CHICKADEE    *Poecile hudsonicus*

An elusive chickadee of northern forest, rarely wandering farther south in winter. ▶ Like other chickadees but with a dusty or dingy look. *Brown cap,* brown sides, dingy cheeks. Wings *lack* pale edgings. **Voice**: hoarse *schick-ah-zzay-zzay,* other notes.

### TUFTED TITMOUSE    *Baeolophus bicolor*

A southern bird, gradually expanding northward. Common in woods, parks, often visiting feeders, usually in pairs or small groups. ▶ Gray above with short *crest,* pale face, wash of *orange* on sides. **Voice**: whistled *peeto-peeto-peeto;* scolding calls.

### WHITE-BREASTED NUTHATCH    *Sitta carolinensis*

Nuthatches walk down tree trunks headfirst, as well as climbing up and around them. This species is common all year in deciduous and mixed woods. ▶ Known by its behavior, short-tailed shape, *white face,* narrow black cap. **Voice**: nasal *yaank, yaank.*

### RED-BREASTED NUTHATCH    *Sitta canadensis*

A tame little acrobat of evergreen forest. Numbers moving south in fall and winter vary from year to year. ▶ Nuthatch shape and actions, orange chest, *black eye-stripe.* **Voice**: soft *henk, henk.*

### BROWN CREEPER    *Certhia americana*

Like a bit of bark come to life, creeping up the trunk and major limbs of one tree, then flying down to base of next tree. Often common, but easily overlooked. ▶ Streaked brown back, pale eyebrow, rusty base of tail. Best known by shape and behavior. **Voice**: high, reedy *tsseeee.* Song, short series of high notes.

# CHICKADEES AND OTHERS

**Black-capped Chickadee**
5"

**Carolina Chickadee**
4¾"

The overlap zone between Black-capped Chickadee (to the north) and Carolina Chickadee (to the south) in Illinois, Indiana, and Ohio

**Boreal Chickadee**
5¼"

**Tufted Titmouse**
6½"

**Red-breasted Nuthatch**
4½"

**White-breasted Nuthatch**
5½"

**Brown Creeper**
5"

# WRENS, KINGLETS, AND GNATCATCHERS

Small, active, insect-eating birds, these represent three families: wrens (**Troglodytidae**), kinglets (**Regulidae**), and gnatcatchers (**Polioptilidae**).

### HOUSE WREN  *Troglodytes aedon*

Common in summer in forests, parks, gardens, fussing about in brush piles, often holding tail up. Nests in birdhouses, sheds, tree holes. ▶ Rather plain brown, with thin bill, *faint eyebrow and eye-ring*. Bars on wings and tail. **Voice:** an explosive but musical song, jumbled and bubbling. Harsh, nasal, scolding callnotes.

### WINTER WREN  *Troglodytes hiemalis*

A stub-tailed gnome, hard to see as it scoots about fallen logs, forest thickets. ▶ Shorter-tailed, darker than House Wren. Voice differs. **Voice:** long, varied, tinkling trill; squeaky *kimp-kimp*.

### CAROLINA WREN  *Thryothorus ludovicianus*

More common toward the south. Usually in pairs, in thickets, woods, gardens, nesting in birdhouses or sometimes in buildings. ▶ Richly colored, *chestnut and buff,* with *white eyebrow.* **Voice:** a rollicking *liberty-liberty-liberty-whew.* Varied metallic calls.

### MARSH WREN  *Cistothorus palustris*

Common in cattail marshes in summer but usually hard to see. Nest is a spherical mass in stems above water. ▶ Dark, rich brown. Bold *white eyebrow;* white stripes on dark back. **Voice:** varied, sputtering, bubbling song. Callnote *chuk-chuk.*

### SEDGE WREN  *Cistothorus platensis*

Another wren of wet places, mostly in short grass or sedge meadows. Usually very secretive. ▶ *Buffy* overall with *narrow streaks on crown,* short bill, plainer face than Marsh Wren. **Voice:** dry staccato chatter speeding up to thin trill. Callnote *chyip* or *dzzt.*

### RUBY-CROWNED KINGLET  *Regulus calendula*

Kinglets constantly flick their wings partly open, especially when alarmed. The Ruby-crowned is a very common migrant, more local in summer and winter. ▶ Tiny, short-tailed, hyperactive, with bold *white eye-ring,* white and black wing bars. Ruby "crown" of male usually hidden. **Voice:** *chi-dit* call; loud bubbling song.

### GOLDEN-CROWNED KINGLET  *Regulus satrapa*

This kinglet favors evergreens at all seasons, is fairly widespread in winter. ▶ Tiny, hyperactive. Wing pattern and wing-flicking action like Ruby-crowned, but has *striped face* (with no eye-ring), yellow or orange crown. **Voice:** very high, thin *see-see-see.*

### BLUE-GRAY GNATCATCHER  *Polioptila caerulea*

A long-tailed sprite of the treetops, found in summer in leafy woods. ▶ Blue-gray above, whitish below, with *white eye-ring,* no wing bars. Long black tail has *white outer feathers.* **Voice:** thin, whining *shpeew* call. Song is a thin squeaky warble.

**Winter Wren**
4″

**House Wren**
4¾″

**Carolina Wren**
5¾″

**Marsh Wren**
5″

**Sedge Wren**
4½″

**Ruby-crowned Kinglet**
4″

**Blue-gray Gnatcatcher**
4½″

**Golden-crowned Kinglet**
3¾″

# WAXWINGS, VIREOS, AND CHATS

Waxwings (family **Bombycillidae**) are named for waxy red tips on some wing feathers. Vireos (family **Vireonidae**) are heard more than seen as they search among foliage for insects. They are mostly larger and thicker-billed than warblers (p. 260). Yellow-breasted Chat, formerly considered a large warbler, is an odd bird of uncertain relations.

### CEDAR WAXWING    *Bombycilla cedrorum*

Elegant, sociable nomads, Cedar Waxwings wander through our region at all seasons. Flocks of dozens may descend on fruiting trees to feed on small berries. ▶ *Yellow band* on tail tip, narrow *black mask,* short crest, pale yellow belly. Juvenile has blurry streaks below. **Voice:** thin, high-pitched *sseee.*

### BOHEMIAN WAXWING    *Bombycilla garrulus*

A few flocks of Bohemians visit our northern counties in winter, sometimes coming farther south. ▶ Larger and grayer than Cedar Waxwing, with *chestnut undertail coverts,* wing pattern of yellow and white. **Voice:** rough trill, lower than Cedar Waxwing's call.

### RED-EYED VIREO    *Vireo olivaceus*

A very common singer of summer forests, heard constantly as it forages high in trees. ▶ Strong head pattern, with black stripes setting off gray crown. Red eyes (brown on young birds) inconspicuous. **Voice:** short whistled phrases separated by pauses.

### WARBLING VIREO    *Vireo gilvus*

Another very persistent woodland singer, even on hot summer days. ▶ Confusingly plain, gray above, whitish below, with pale eyebrow. **Voice:** fast musical warble, rising at middle and end.

### WHITE-EYED VIREO    *Vireo griseus*

A vireo of low growth, usually hiding in thickets, woodland edge. ▶ *Yellow spectacles* around *white eyes.* Mostly grayish, with 2 wing bars. **Voice:** quick snappy jumble, *pick-up-a-real-chick!*

### BLUE-HEADED VIREO    *Vireo solitarius*

Nests in forest of hemlock or pine mixed with oak in northern Midwest. ▶ Blue-gray hood contrasting with *white "spectacles."* Two white wing bars. **Voice:** short, whistled phrases.

### YELLOW-THROATED VIREO    *Vireo flavifrons*

Widespread in oak woods in summer, more common toward the south. ▶ *Yellow throat, yellow "spectacles," white wing bars.* See Pine Warbler (p. 262). **Voice:** short phrases with hoarse sound.

### YELLOW-BREASTED CHAT    *Icteria virens*

The chat lurks in dense bushes, overlooked if not for its odd song. Male sometimes sings while fluttering above thickets with legs dangling. ▶ Yellow throat and breast, *white spectacles,* olive back. Compare Common Yellowthroat (p. 260). **Voice:** a disjointed series of gurgles, hoots, clucks, whistles, and short chatters.

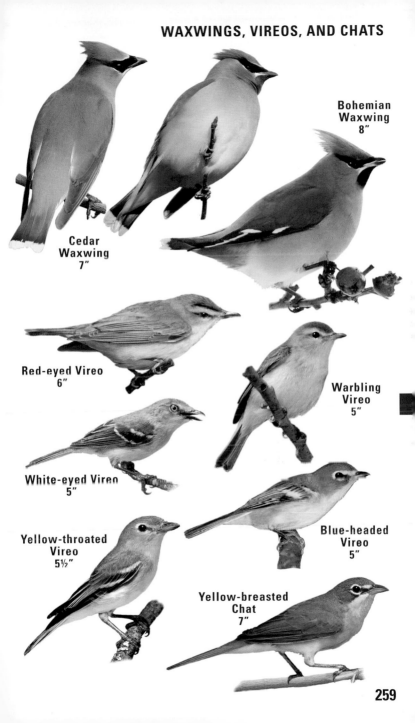

Bohemian
Waxwing
8"

Cedar
Waxwing
7"

Red-eyed Vireo
6"

Warbling
Vireo
5"

White-eyed Vireo
5"

Yellow-throated
Vireo
5½"

Blue-headed
Vireo
5"

Yellow-breasted
Chat
7"

259

# WARBLERS

(family **Parulidae**), favorites of many birders, are small, active, colorful insect-eaters. Almost 40 species occur in the Midwest, and it's possible to find 20 or more species in a day at the peak of spring migration. They can be harder to identify in fall, when some wear duller plumages.

### YELLOW WARBLER  *Setophaga petechia*

Very common in summer in woodland edges, willow thickets near ponds, streams. ▶ Yellow all over, adult male with *red stripes* on chest. Female and young duller yellow. Goldfinches (p. 272) have *thicker* bills. **Voice:** song, fast *sweet sweet weetaweet.*

### PROTHONOTARY WARBLER  *Protonotaria citrea*

Summers in wooded swamps, nesting in tree cavities, sometimes nest boxes. ▶ *Golden yellow* head and chest, *blue-gray* back and wings. Female duller. **Voice:** emphatic *weat weat weat weat.*

### WILSON'S WARBLER  *Cardellina pusilla*

A common migrant through the Midwest, mainly in late spring and early fall. ▶ Yellow-green all over, no pattern on wings, tail, or face. *Round black cap* of male diagnostic. **Voice:** rising chatter.

### COMMON YELLOWTHROAT  *Geothlypis trichas*

Our only warbler nesting in marshes. Also seen in thickets, woods, especially in migration. Rare in winter. ▶ Male's *bandit mask* is set off by *yellow throat,* white upper outline. Female duller, with yellow throat, plain face. **Voice:** fast *wichity-wichity-wichity.*

### HOODED WARBLER  *Setophaga citrina*

Mostly a southern warbler, living in the understory of moist, leafy woods. ▶ *Black hood* (faint on female) around *yellow face.* Often flashes *white tail edges.* **Voice:** *tawee tawee taweeTEEoh.*

### AMERICAN REDSTART  *Setophaga ruticilla*

Common in summer in open woods. Flits about, spreading wings and tail. ▶ Male black with *orange patches.* Female gray with *yellow patches* in wings and tail. **Voice:** varied thin, sweet phrases.

### BLACK-THROATED BLUE WARBLER  *Setophaga caerulescens*

Understory of mixed woods in eastern part of region. ▶ Male mostly dark blue and black, with *white wing spot.* Female plain and dull, but usually has wing spot. **Voice:** lazy, buzzy song.

### CERULEAN WARBLER  *Setophaga cerulea*

This beautiful treetop warbler is still widespread, but declining in numbers. ▶ Male *blue above,* white below, with thin *black necklace.* Female duller, with pale eyebrow. **Voice:** buzzy rising song.

### CANADA WARBLER  *Cardellina canadensis*

Mostly stays low in thickets of leafy woods. ▶ *Necklace of black streaks* on yellow breast, most obvious on adult male. Bold *eyering,* blue-gray back. **Voice:** fast, jumbled song.

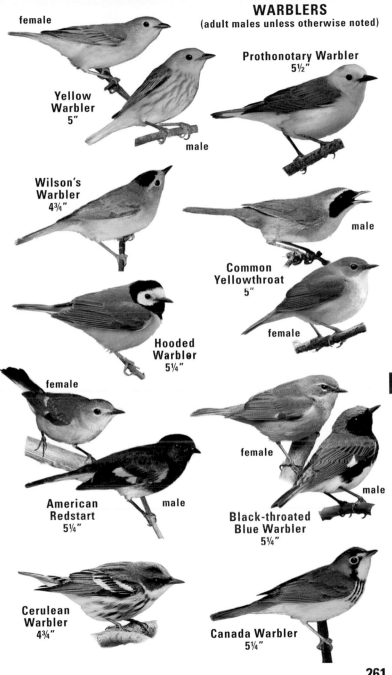

# WARBLERS
(adult males unless otherwise noted)

female

**Yellow Warbler**
5″

male

**Prothonotary Warbler**
5½″

**Wilson's Warbler**
4¾″

male

**Common Yellowthroat**
5″

female

**Hooded Warbler**
5¼″

female

**American Redstart**
5¼″

male

female

male

**Black-throated Blue Warbler**
5¼″

**Cerulean Warbler**
4¾″

**Canada Warbler**
5¼″

# WARBLERS

### YELLOW-RUMPED WARBLER    *Setophaga coronata*

Also called Myrtle Warbler. The most numerous migrant warbler in early spring and late fall, and the only one likely to be seen in winter, surviving by feeding on berries. ▶ *Yellow rump patch* (obvious in flight), white tail spots (shared by many warblers). Overall color varies from crisp gray of spring males to pale brown of fall birds. **Voice:** rambling, warbling song. Call, loud *check.*

### CAPE MAY WARBLER    *Setophaga tigrina*

Migrates through east of region, nests in spruce forest. ▶ Adult male has *chestnut ear patch, black stripes* on yellow chest. Female and young duller, well striped below. **Voice:** high thin song.

### MAGNOLIA WARBLER    *Setophaga magnolia*

A very common migrant, nesting in north. ▶ Yellow below, with *stripes* along sides. *Square-edged white tail band.* Adult male black above, female grayer. **Voice:** sweet *wayta wayta wayteeh.*

### BLACK-AND-WHITE WARBLER    *Mniotilta varia*

A warbler that acts like a nuthatch (p. 254), often creeping along trunks and limbs. Nests on ground. ▶ Striped pattern, including white central crown stripe. **Voice:** thin *weesee weesee weesee.*

### BLACKPOLL WARBLER    *Setophaga striata*

A champion migrant, wintering south to Brazil. ▶ Spring male has streaks, *black cap, white cheeks.* Female and fall birds greenish with wing bars, often yellow legs. **Voice:** thin *zi-zi-zi-zi-zi-zi.*

### BAY-BREASTED WARBLER    *Setophaga castanea*

A common migrant, nesting in northern forest. ▶ Spring male marked with *chestnut;* female duller. Fall birds greenish with white wing bars, hint of chestnut. **Voice:** high thin song.

### PINE WARBLER    *Setophaga pinus*

Usually seen in pines. Mostly uncommon, rare in winter. ▶ Adult male olive above, yellow below; female duller. Young female very drab, with hint of face pattern. **Voice:** slow musical trill.

### NASHVILLE WARBLER    *Oreothlypis ruficapilla*

Fairly common in summer in northern woodland edges. Migrant throughout. ▶ Gray head contrasts with *white eye-ring, yellow throat,* olive back. **Voice:** double notes followed by trill.

### BLUE-WINGED WARBLER    *Vermivora cyanoptera*

Common in summer in old fields, thickets. Interbreeds with next species, producing hybrids. ▶ Yellow with *black line through eye;* blue-gray wings with white wing bars. **Voice:** *bzzeee-buzzzz.*

### GOLDEN-WINGED WARBLER    *Vermivora chrysoptera*
A vanishing species, summering in northern wet woods, thickets. ▶ Black mask and bib, yellow cap and wing bars. **Voice:** *bzee-bz-bz-bz.*

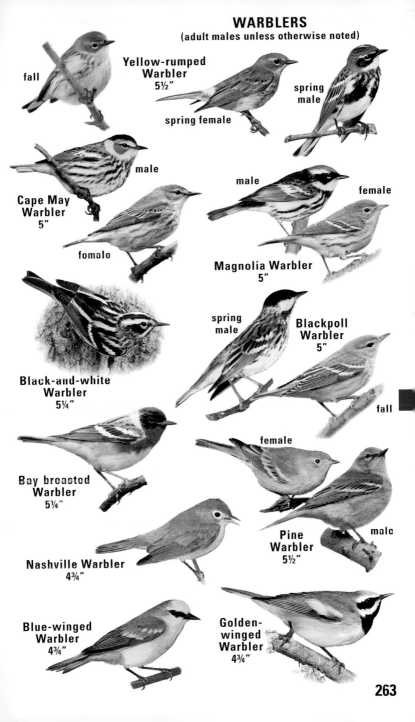

# WARBLERS
**(adult males unless otherwise noted)**

fall

**Yellow-rumped Warbler**
5½"

spring female

spring male

**Cape May Warbler**
5"

male

female

male

**Magnolia Warbler**
5"

female

**Black-and-white Warbler**
5¼"

spring male

**Blackpoll Warbler**
5"

fall

**Bay-breasted Warbler**
5¼"

female

**Pine Warbler**
5½"

male

**Nashville Warbler**
4¾"

**Blue-winged Warbler**
4¾"

**Golden-winged Warbler**
4¾"

263

### BLACK-THROATED GREEN WARBLER    *Setophaga virens*

Common in summer in evergreen and mixed forest; migrates throughout. ▶ *Bright yellow face,* green back, white wing bars. Adult male has black throat. **Voice:** buzzy *zoo zee zoozoo zee.*

### CHESTNUT-SIDED WARBLER    *Setophaga pensylvanica*

Fairly common in leafy second-growth woods. ▶ *Yellow cap,* small face mask, *chestnut* on sides. Fall birds plainer, lime green on back. **Voice:** song, *sweet sweet sweet seesaWEET chew.*

### BLACKBURNIAN WARBLER    *Setophaga fusca*

Like a glowing flame in dark spruces in summer. ▶ Spring male orange and black, with white back stripes. Female and young duller. **Voice:** thin wiry song like a mouse with a toothache.

### YELLOW-THROATED WARBLER    *Setophaga dominica*

A southern warbler, mostly in tall sycamores along rivers. ▶ Black and white face pattern, bright *yellow throat,* gray back, black stripes along sides. **Voice:** series of thin clear notes.

### NORTHERN PARULA    *Setophaga americana*

A tiny warbler, nesting in northern spruce forest and along southern rivers. ▶ *Blue-gray above,* white wing bars, yellow on chest. Male has *rusty* chest band. **Voice:** song, *zz-zz-zzzeee-wup.*

### PALM WARBLER    *Setophaga palmarum*

Migrates early in spring and late in fall, often seen low in open areas. Nests in northern bogs. ▶ *Bobs tail up and down constantly.* Rusty cap, pale eyebrow, *yellow under tail.* **Voice:** rough trill.

### PRAIRIE WARBLER    *Setophaga discolor*
Uncommon in summer in brushy overgrown fields. ▶ *Bobs tail up and down.* Strong pattern on yellow face. **Voice:** wiry rising *zee zee zee zee . . .*

### KIRTLAND'S WARBLER    *Setophaga kirtlandii*
An endangered species, nesting in young Jack Pines in northern part of Michigan's Lower Peninsula. A few pairs in Wisconsin and elsewhere. Winters in Bahamas. ▶ *Large* for a warbler, blue-gray above, yellow below. Dark streaks on sides, pale arcs around eye. *Bobs tail* like 2 preceding species. **Voice:** choppy quick jumble of notes, rising toward the end.

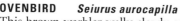

### OVENBIRD    *Seiurus aurocapilla*

This brown warbler walks slowly on the ground, tail often held up. Builds domed nest like old-fashioned oven. ▶ White eye-ring, *orange* crown stripe. **Voice:** ringing *chertea chertea chertea . . .*

### NORTHERN WATERTHRUSH    *Parkesia noveboracensis*

Another brown ground warbler, bobbing tail as it walks along streams, swamps. ▶ Strong *pale eyebrow,* streaks on yellow or whitish breast. **Louisiana Waterthrush** (*P. motacilla*) similar but whiter below, wider eyebrow; nests in southern Midwest.

# WARBLERS
### (adult males unless otherwise noted)

**Black-throated Green Warbler**
5″

female

male

**Chestnut-sided Warbler**
5″

male

female

**Blackburnian Warbler**
5″

**Yellow-throated Warbler**
5½″

**Northern Parula**
4½″

**Palm Warbler**
5″

**Prairie Warbler**
5″

**Kirtland's Warbler**
6″

**Ovenbird**
6″

**Northern Waterthrush**
6″

265

# STARLINGS AND BLACKBIRDS

The starling is our only member of an Old World family (**Sturnidae**). The blackbirds make up a varied family (**Icteridae**): some are omnivores that travel in large flocks, but orioles eat mainly insects and are less social.

### EUROPEAN STARLING — *Sturnus vulgaris*

Introduced from Europe, now abundant here. May travel and roost in huge flocks. Nests in holes, sometimes displacing native birds. ▶ Stocky, *short-tailed*. Black, with *pale spots* in winter. Bill dark in winter, *yellow* in spring. **Voice:** chatters, imitations.

### RED-WINGED BLACKBIRD — *Agelaius phoeniceus*

At every wet field and marsh in summer; more local in winter. In fall and winter, may gather in huge flocks, often feeding in open fields. ▶ Red on male can be obvious or mostly hidden. Female brown with heavy streaks. **Voice:** nasal *awnk-ah-rrhee*.

### YELLOW-HEADED BLACKBIRD — *Xanthocephalus xanthocephalus*

A bird of western marshes, wandering widely through other open habitats. ▶ Name describes male; also note white wing patch. Female brown, with yellow face. **Voice:** horrible, grating "song."

### COMMON GRACKLE — *Quiscalus quiscula*

Abundant in summer in open country, woods, towns. Flocks wander in winter. ▶ Pale eyes, *long* creased tail. Blue-black head contrasts with *bronzy body*. **Voice:** gurgling creaks, hard *chack*.

### BROWN-HEADED COWBIRD — *Molothrus ater*

A brood parasite, laying its eggs in the nests of other birds. Flocks forage in open fields, often around cattle or other farm animals. ▶ Male glossy black with *brown head*. Female confusingly plain; note size, bill shape. **Voice:** varied gurgles, whistles.

### RUSTY BLACKBIRD — *Euphagus carolinus*

Mostly a migrant, in swamps, wet woods. Scarce, declining. ▶ At most seasons, dull black or slaty with *yellow eyes*. In fall, *rusty feather edges, buff eyebrow*. **Voice:** high, creaking *kssh-dlleee*.

### BREWER'S BLACKBIRD — *Euphagus cyanocephalus*

Uncommon, mostly in open areas. ▶ Shaped like Rusty Blackbird. Male *glossy black* with white eyes. Female gray-brown with dark eyes, like female cowbird but larger, with longer bill.

### BALTIMORE ORIOLE — *Icterus galbula*

Common in summer in woods, towns, building a hanging nest in shade trees. ▶ Male unmistakable. Female dull orange below, white wing bars; note *bill shape*. **Voice:** rich whistles, chatters.

### ORCHARD ORIOLE — *Icterus spurius*

Uncommon summer resident of woodland edges, towns. ▶ Adult male *chestnut and black*. Female greenish yellow, young male similar but with *black throat*. **Voice:** fast jumbled song.

# STARLINGS, BLACKBIRDS

spring

**European
Starling**
8½"

young

winter

female

**Red-winged Blackbird**
9"

male

male

female

**Yellow-headed Blackbird**
10"

**Common Grackle**
12½"

female

male

**Brown-headed Cowbird**
1¾"

spring
male

fall

**Rusty
Blackbird**
9"

female

**Baltimore
Oriole**
8"

male

**Brewer's
Blackbird**
9"

female

**Orchard
Oriole**
7"

male

267

# BIRDS OF OPEN FIELDS

These birds belong to several different families, but all are usually seen on or near the ground in open fields. The first three species belong to the blackbird family, introduced on p. 266. The Dickcissel is in the family **Cardinalidae,** larks are in **Alaudidae,** pipits in **Motacillidae.** Longspurs and Snow Buntings are now placed in a distinct family, **Calcariidae**.

### EASTERN MEADOWLARK  *Sturnella magna*

Declining, but still locally common in farm country, prairies. Walks on ground, sings from fenceposts. ▶ Chunky, short-tailed. *White outer tail feathers* show in flight. Striped head, *black V on yellow chest.* **Voice:** clear whistles, *te-seeyeer seeeyaayy.*

### WESTERN MEADOWLARK  *Sturnella neglecta*

Less common than the preceding, except at western edge of our region. ▶ Almost identical to Eastern Meadowlark, best recognized by voice. **Voice:** rapid bubbling jumble of rich whistles.

### BOBOLINK  *Dolichonyx oryzivorus*

Locally common in meadows, where male's *bubbling flight song* is a delight of summer. Winters in South America. In hayfields, nests often destroyed by mowing. ▶ Summer male unmistakable. Female and fall male sparrowlike, buff, streaked.

### DICKCISSEL  *Spiza americana*

Can be abundant in summer on prairies, farms; numbers vary. Winters in South America. ▶ Male has *black bib* on *yellow* chest, rusty shoulder. Female like House Sparrow (p. 272) but with hint of male's colors. **Voice:** suggests name, *djjk, dkk, sizzs-sizzs-sizzs.*

### AMERICAN PIPIT  *Anthus rubescens*

Mostly a migrant. *Bobs tail* as it walks (sometimes in small flocks) on bare fields, shores. ▶ Pale gray-brown with *thin bill,* streaked chest, pale eyebrow. **Voice:** sharp *jeejeet,* often in flight.

### HORNED LARK  *Eremophila alpestris*

A bird of open ground: plowed fields, overgrazed pastures, airports. Absent from forested regions. Forms flocks in winter, sometimes with next 2 species. Starts nesting very early in spring in bare fields. ▶ *Black marks* on *chest* and *face;* tiny "horns" hard to see. **Voice:** tinkling, twittering song, often in flight.

### SNOW BUNTING  *Plectrophenax nivalis*

In winter, flocks of these pale birds walk on the ground in open country, flashing large *white wing patches* when they fly. ▶ In winter, pale brown and white, with black in wingtips and tail, pale buff collar. **Voice:** dry rattle and clear whistles.

### LAPLAND LONGSPUR  *Calcarius lapponicus*

A winter visitor from the far north, flocking in bare open fields, shores. ▶ Brown above, white below, with dark mottling on chest, *red-brown on nape and wings.* **Voice:** dry rattle, clear whistle.

# BIRDS OF OPEN FIELDS

**Eastern Meadowlark**
**Western Meadowlark**
9½"

fcmalo

**Bobolink**
7"

male

**Dickcissel**
6¼"

**American Pipit**
6½"

**Horned Lark**
7½"

**Snow Bunting**
7"

winter plumage

winter plumage

**Lapland Longspur**
6¼"

269

# SPARROWS

The most familiar "sparrow" in the Midwest, House Sparrow (p. 272), is an Old World introduction. Native sparrows (family **Emberizidae**) are more varied. At least 20 species of native sparrows occur in the Midwest; we show only a few of the most common or distinctive.

### CHIPPING SPARROW    *Spizella passerina*

Very common in summer in towns, parks, open woods. Rare in winter. ▶ Small with plain chest, *rusty cap,* white eyebrow, *black line* through eye. Fall birds duller. **Voice:** rapid, dry trill.

### AMERICAN TREE SPARROW    *Spizella arborea*

A common winter visitor; sometimes flocks with juncos. Favors weedy fields, not trees. ▶ Like Chipping Sparrow but with chest spot, rusty eyeline, *bicolored bill.* **Voice:** musical *twiddle-eat.*

### FIELD SPARROW    *Spizella pusilla*

This baby-faced sparrow lives in brushy, overgrown old fields, thickets. More scarce and local in winter. ▶ Rusty cap, *plain face, pink bill.* **Voice:** short plaintive whistles speeding up to a trill.

### SONG SPARROW    *Melospiza melodia*

Common in brushy woods, marshes, towns, usually close to the ground except when singing. Can become fairly tame in parks, yards. ▶ Strong face pattern, streaked below, chest often with dark central blotch. **Voice:** short notes followed by musical trill.

### FOX SPARROW    *Passerella iliaca*

Mostly an uncommon migrant, scarce in winter. Scratches with its feet in leaf-litter under thickets. ▶ Big, beautiful, mostly *foxy* red, brightest on tail. **Voice:** musical song with rich whistles.

### WHITE-THROATED SPARROW    *Zonotrichia albicollis*

Seasonally very common in forest thickets, parks, yards. ▶ *White* throat, *contrasting* head stripes (can be either white or tan). **Voice:** whistled *oh, sweet, Kimberly-Kimberly-Kimberly.*

### WHITE-CROWNED SPARROW    *Zonotrichia leucophrys*

Mostly a migrant, less common in winter, in thickets, brushy woods. ▶ *Striped head* (black and white on adults, tan on young birds), *pink bill,* gray chest. **Voice:** song of whistles and trills.

### LARK SPARROW    *Chondestes grammacus*

Mostly a western sparrow, favoring open areas, bare ground near thickets. ▶ *Strong face pattern,* dark chest spot, *white edges and corners* on fairly long tail. **Voice:** long series of varied notes.

### DARK-EYED JUNCO    *Junco hyemalis*

This "snowbird" is very common in winter, with small flocks in woods, fields, yards. Summers in northern forest. ▶ Slaty gray with pale bill, white belly, *white outer tail feathers.* Females are browner. **Voice:** musical trilling song; *tic* callnote.

# SPARROWS

**Chipping Sparrow** 5½"

**American Tree Sparrow** 6¼"

**Field Sparrow** 5¾"

**Song Sparrow** 5½"

**Fox Sparrow** 7"

**White-throated Sparrow** 6¾"

two variations

**White-crowned Sparrow** 6¾"

male

female

**Lark Sparrow** 6½"

**Dark-eyed Junco** 6"

# FINCHES AND OLD WORLD SPARROWS

Unrelated to American sparrows, House Sparrow is from an Old World family (**Passeridae**). All the others below are finches (family **Fringillidae**), sociable birds that feed on seeds and other plant matter at all seasons.

### HOUSE SPARROW    *Passer domesticus*

Introduced from Europe. Common in cities, towns, farms; rare in most natural habitats. ▶ Male has *black bib,* pale cheeks. Female has buff eyebrow, striped back. **Eurasian Tree Sparrow** (*P. montanus*), local in w. Illinois and se. Iowa, like male House Sparrow but with *brown crown, black ear spot.* **Voice:** chirps.

### HOUSE FINCH    *Haemorhous mexicanus*

Widespread and locally common around cities, farms, backyards. ▶ Male has variably red chest and eyebrow, striped flanks. Female striped below, plain on face. **Voice:** rich warbling, chirps.

### PURPLE FINCH    *Haemorhous purpureus*

A migrant in most areas, less common than House Finch. ▶ Like House Finch but heavier, shorter-tailed. Male *lacks* streaks on flanks, female has *stronger face pattern.* **Voice:** rich warbling.

### RED CROSSBILL    *Loxia curvirostra*

Odd bill shape allows crossbills to open cones of conifers. They wander in flocks, seeking good cone crops. ▶ Adult male *brick red,* female dull yellow, with darker wings. **Voice:** hard *kep-kep.*

### WHITE-WINGED CROSSBILL    *Loxia leucoptera*

This crossbill prefers spruces and hemlocks. Nomadic flocks arrive when cone crops are good. ▶ Adult male *rose red,* female dull yellow, with big *white wing bars.* **Voice:** slow rattle.

### COMMON REDPOLL    *Acanthis flammea*

This tiny Arctic finch is an irregular winter visitor, more common toward the north, at feeders, weedy fields. ▶ *Red cap, black chin,* streaks. Male has pink chest. **Voice:** rattles, soft notes.

### AMERICAN GOLDFINCH    *Spinus tristis*

Common all year, wandering in flocks through weedy fields, coming to feeders for thistle seed. ▶ Summer male gold with *black forehead,* wings, tail. Summer female dull greenish. In winter, *buff* with *black wings.* **Voice:** in flight, cheery *po-ta-to-chip.*

### PINE SISKIN    *Spinus pinus*

Often among goldfinch flocks, like a goldfinch in camouflage. Irregular migrant, sometimes common in winter. ▶ *Heavily striped, plain face, yellow in wings.* **Voice:** musical and harsh notes.

### EVENING GROSBEAK    *Coccothraustes vespertinus*

Uncommon, unpredictable. Flocks wander in winter, visiting feeders to eat sunflower seeds. ▶ Gray and gold, with big *white patch* on black wing, big pale bill. **Voice:** ringing *peeyr.*

# FINCHES AND OLD WORLD SPARROWS

female

**House Sparrow**
6"

male

female

male

**House Finch**
5¾"

female

male

**Purple Finch**
6"

**Red Crossbill**
6½"

male

male

**White-winged Crossbill**
6½"

male

**Common Redpoll**
5"

wintor

summer male

**American Goldfinch**
5"

**Evening Grosbeak**
8"

male

**Pine Siskin**
5"

female

# CARDINALS, TANAGERS, GROSBEAKS, ETC.

Despite their different names and different looks, the first six species below are all in the cardinal family (**Cardinalidae**). The towhee is related to the American sparrows, introduced on p. 270.

### NORTHERN CARDINAL  *Cardinalis cardinalis*

One of our most popular birds (the official state bird of Illinois, Indiana, and Ohio), common from forests to backyards. Visits bird feeders for sunflower seeds, and brightens winter days with its whistled song. ▶ Male is our only *crested red bird*. Female duller but shares *crest, massive pinkish orange bill*. **Voice:** varied song, *what-cheer, what-cheer,* etc. Callnote, *tchip*.

### SCARLET TANAGER  *Piranga olivacea*

Fairly common in summer in forest, especially among oaks, but can be surprisingly hard to see among treetop foliage. ▶ Summer male unmistakable. Female and fall male greenish with darker wings and tail. **Voice:** song of whistled phrases with hoarse sound (like robin with sore throat). Callnote, *chip-brrr*.

### SUMMER TANAGER  *Piranga rubra*

A summer bird of treetops in oak and pine forest, more common toward the south. ▶ Adult male all rose-red; young male yellow with red patches. Female rich yellow. *Large, pale bill.* **Voice:** song of robinlike whistled phrases. Callnote, crackling *pickituck*.

### INDIGO BUNTING  *Passerina cyanea*

Very common in summer in brushy places, where males sing from high perches. Shy brown females are seen less often. ▶ Male *dark blue* all over (often looks black at a distance). Female warm brown, with *faint streaks* on chest. **Voice:** bright, quick song, the notes often in pairs: *weet weet tsew tsew jif jif,* etc.

### BLUE GROSBEAK  *Passerina caerulea*

A southern species, uncommon in summer in brushy fields, woodland edges. ▶ Chunky, with *very thick bill,* wide *buff or cinnamon wing bars.* Male blue, female warm brown. Compare to Indigo Bunting. **Voice:** fast, low, husky warble.

### ROSE-BREASTED GROSBEAK  *Pheucticus ludovicianus*

A striking summer bird of leafy woods, often hard to see among foliage. May come to feeders for sunflower seeds, especially in spring migration. ▶ Adult male black and white with *rose patch* on chest. Female more sparrowlike, but note heavy bill, strong face pattern. **Voice:** fast caroling song, like a nervous robin.

### EASTERN TOWHEE  *Pipilo erythrophthalmus*

In the understory of brushy woods, this big sparrow scratches among leaf-litter on the ground with both feet. ▶ Dark hood and *rusty sides* contrast with *white* stripe down center of belly. Eyes *red*. **Voice:** ringing *drink-your-teeeeeee*. Callnote, *chwink*.

**Northern Cardinal**
9"
male
female

**Scarlet Tanager**
7"
male
female

**Summer Tanager**
7¾"
female
male

**Blue Grosbeak**
7"
female
male

**Indigo Bunting**
5"
female
male

**Rose-breasted Grosbeak**
8"
female
male

**Eastern Towhee**
8"
female
male

275

represent separate classes of animals, with reptiles thought to have branched off from amphibians more than 300 million years ago. Still, the science of Herpetology addresses both amphibians and reptiles, and collectively these creatures are often known as herptiles (or "herps").

**Reptiles (class Reptilia)** are represented in the Midwest by turtles, snakes, and lizards. Their skin is relatively dry and usually at least partly covered with scales. Those with feet usually have claws on their toes. Young reptiles are shaped like smaller versions of adults. **Amphibians (class Amphibia)** are represented here by salamanders, toads, and frogs. These have relatively moist skin without scales, and have no claws on their toes. Young amphibians are often aquatic and may be shaped very differently from adults (compare tadpoles to adult frogs, for example).

**Conservation of reptiles and amphibians** offers many challenges. While some species remain common and widespread, others have shown serious declines in population. Loss of habitat affects these creatures as much as any other animals, and they face additional threats as well. Amphibians, with their highly permeable skin, may be very sensitive to certain kinds of pollution. Snakes suffer unreasonable persecution by humans — many uninformed people still have a reflex to kill any snake they see. Even people who like reptiles and amphibians may deplete populations by catching them to keep in captivity. We recommend enjoying these animals in the wild, and speaking up for the protection of them and their habitats.

## REPTILES

**Turtles (order Testudines)** are famously slow-moving but can be very long-lived. In other parts of the world, giant tortoises may live over 150 years, and even the humble box turtle may live more than half a century. Most of our turtles are highly aquatic, spending most of their time in the water and hibernating underwater during the winter. The box turtles, by contrast, spend the summer wandering through woods and fields, and hibernate underground in winter. All female turtles, even the most aquatic ones, come out on land to dig holes in which to lay their eggs.

The shells of turtles are made of numerous bony plates, usually fused together; the upper shell (carapace) and lower shell (plastron) are joined by a bridge of bone or cartilage. The bony plates of the carapace and plastron are usually covered by large scales, called scutes.

**Snakes (order Squamata, in part)** are feared by some, but they are fascinating creatures with important roles to play in natural habitats. All snakes lack legs, eyelids, and external ear openings. But their lack of limbs does not prevent some species from moving very fast — some are even excellent climbers — and many have sharp eyesight. They use their long, forked tongues to pick up chemical clues from their surroundings and deliver them to a specialized organ in the roof of the mouth, called Jacobson's organ, which operates like a sophisticated sense of smell. Some snakes lay eggs (like most other reptiles), while others bear live young.

Snakes are most diverse in the tropics. They cannot tolerate subfreezing temperatures, so those in the Midwest hibernate in winter in sheltered sites, usually underground or in caves. These sites (called hibernacula) may be shared by many individuals and more than one species.

Venomous snakes are represented in the Midwest by the Copperhead, Massasauga, Timber Rattlesnake, Cottonmouth, and a very few Prairie Rattlesnakes, all treated on p. 288. These are all uncommon in the region. Some other snakes can deliver nasty bites if cornered or handled. The vast majority of snakebite cases occur when people are trying to catch snakes. It is usually more rewarding to observe snakes from a distance in the wild.

**Lizards (order Squamata, in part)** are most common and diverse in hot climates; the Midwest can boast only a handful of species. Most lizards are alert, fast-moving animals, with keen senses of eyesight, hearing, and smell. Many have tails that detach easily if the animal is attacked: if grabbed by a predator, the tail breaks off and continues to wiggle and thrash while the lizard itself escapes; the lizard usually can grow a new tail to replace it.

## AMPHIBIANS

**Salamanders (order Caudata)** look superficially like lizards but are totally unrelated. They have moist skin without scales, their toes lack claws, and most have a larval stage that lives in water. While lizards can survive in very arid climates, salamanders must remain in moist or wet environments to avoid drying out, and some are aquatic throughout their lives.

Female salamanders lay their eggs in the water or in damp places, and they often guard or brood the eggs until they hatch. Most species have an aquatic larval stage, living underwater and breathing with gills, before transforming to the terrestrial adult stage. Hellbenders and mudpuppies spend their whole lives in the water. All salamanders are predatory, feeding mostly on insects, worms, and other small invertebrates, although the largest aquatic species may take small fish or other creatures in the water.

**Frogs and toads (order Anura)** are familiar creatures, often seen and heard; voices of these animals are typical sounds of spring and summer.

Female frogs and toads lay their eggs in the water, and the eggs hatch out into small, legless, swimming creatures called tadpoles. Tadpoles are mostly vegetarians, feeding on algae and other submerged plant matter for a period of a few weeks to many months, until they go through metamorphosis and emerge as small froglets or toadlets. These tiny versions of the adults (often with partial tails at first) may be abundant near water for brief periods, and it may take up to three years for these young ones to grow to full size. The adults are carnivorous, mostly preying on insects and other invertebrates.

As we might expect of such vocal creatures, many of the frogs and toads have excellent hearing. Many have a conspicuous eardrum, or tympanum, on the side of the head, and its size or pattern may be a field mark.

These represent four different families. Snapping turtles are in the family **Chelydridae**; softshells make up the family **Trionychidae**; Blanding's and Spotted are in the **Emydidae**; Musk Turtle is in the **Kinosternidae**.

### SNAPPING TURTLE  *Chelydra serpentina*

A big, bad-tempered turtle, very common around most wetland habitats in the region. Can be dangerous if cornered on land, lunging with impressive speed and biting with powerful jaws, but usually harmless if encountered in the water. In early summer, females come out on land to dig holes for laying eggs. ▶ Shell can be more than a foot long. Big ugly head, small eyes, long tail with *saw-toothed upper ridge.* Baby Snappers are small and long-tailed, with a row of *pale spots* along edge of rough shell.

### ALLIGATOR SNAPPING TURTLE  *Macrochelys temminckii*

This huge turtle, local in Mississippi R. drainage, spends much of its time under water. ▶ Even larger than Snapping Turtle. *Massive head* with *hooked jaws;* tail *lacks* saw-toothed upper ridge. Shell has a series of raised, bumpy ridges.

### SPINY SOFTSHELL  *Apalone spinifera*

Softshells have round, flat, leathery shells, lacking hard scales. They spend most of their time in water, or basking at its edge, and can bite or scratch hard when caught. This species is widespread in rivers and lakes. ▶ Recognized by shape except where it overlaps with next species. Females average larger than males.

### SMOOTH SOFTSHELL  *Apalone mutica* (not shown)

Not as widespread as preceding species, mainly found in rivers and streams. ▶ Similar to Spiny Softshell but has smooth shell, *lacking* roughened bumps and spines. Also lacks stripes on feet.

### BLANDING'S TURTLE  *Emydoidea blandingii*

Widespread in the Midwest but mostly uncommon, in marshes, lakes, streams. Often basks on logs above water, and sometimes wanders on land. ▶ Shell dark with yellow dots and streaks (may be obvious on some, but often obscure). Relatively long neck with *bright yellow chin and throat.*

### SPOTTED TURTLE  *Clemmys guttata*

A small, beautiful turtle of marshes, wet meadows, vernal pools, other damp places. Basks in the open mainly in spring. Declining, now endangered or threatened in many areas. ▶ Dark shell with *small round spots.* Orange or yellow spots on head.

### EASTERN MUSK TURTLE  *Sternotherus odoratus*

Also called "Stinkpot," and exudes a smelly liquid when handled. Spends much time crawling on bottom of ponds. Can bite hard, so use caution if you catch one on your fishing line. ▶ Small, with rounded shell, two *thin pale stripes on head.*

# TURTLES

(size given is average shell length of adults)

**Snapping Turtle**
11"

**Alligator Snapping Turtle**
20"

**Spiny Softshell**
12" (female)

**Blanding's Turtle**
6"

SMALL TURTLES
(not shown at same scale)

**Spotted Turtle**
4"

**Eastern Musk Turtle**
4"

279

# TURTLES

These all belong to the diverse family **Emydidae.**

### PAINTED TURTLE  *Chrysemys picta*

Very common in shallow lakes, ponds, marshes, often basking in the sun on logs or rocks. ► Yellow stripes and spots on head, yellow and red stripes on legs. Shell mostly dark with paler edges of large scutes and with *red markings* along edges. In western half of our region, shell often paler with fine yellow lines, and red along edges of shell may be reduced.

### POND SLIDER (RED-EARED SLIDER)  *Trachemys scripta*

Native to the Mississippi drainage and elsewhere in the southern Midwest, this species might be seen anywhere north to the dashed line on the map, or even beyond, because so many people have released pet turtles into the wild. It has become a troublesome invasive in some areas. Thrives in marshy ponds and slow-moving streams, often basking on logs. ► Patterned shell, yellow head stripes, *red "ear" stripe* (less obvious on adult males).

### NORTHERN MAP TURTLE  *Graptemys geographica*

Common in rivers, lakes, other large bodies of water, sometimes basking in the open but quickly retreating into water if approached. ► Shell may have small bumps along midline. When young, strong pattern of pale lines on shell, suggesting a map. Big *yellow spot* behind eye. **False Map Turtle** *(G. pseudogeographica),* common in Mississippi R. drainage, similar but has *pronounced raised knobs* along midline of shell.

### EASTERN BOX TURTLE  *Terrapene carolina*

Fairly common in woods, often found plodding along far from water, especially on warm spring days or after summer rains. In hot weather, burrows under logs or rests in ponds. ► *High, domed shell,* variably patterned yellow or orange. Lower shell (plastron) is hinged and can close up tight when turtle is threatened.

### ORNATE BOX TURTLE  *Terrapene ornata*

An uncommon turtle of grassland and other open areas, often in regions of sandy soil. ► Similar to Eastern Box Turtle, but shell more flattened on top. Shell has very *strong pattern* of light lines on dark background, including on underside (plastron).

### WOOD TURTLE  *Glyptemys insculpta*

This is another "land turtle" often seen far away from wetlands, wandering in woods and fields. However, it also takes to water readily, and hibernates underwater. Formerly a locally common species, it has declined in most parts of this region. ► Adults have at least some *orange* on neck and legs. *Very rough shell,* each large scute with raised center surrounded by ridges.

## TURTLES
(size given is average
shell length of adults)

**Painted Turtle**
5¼″

**Pond Slider**
6″

**Northern
Map Turtle**
8¾″ (female)
5″ (male)

**Eastern Box Turtle**
5¼″

**Ornate Box Turtle**
4½″

**Wood Turtle**
6½″

281

are most diverse in warm, dry regions. In the Midwest we have relatively few species. Only skinks (family **Scincidae**) are well represented here; the other three species on this page belong to three distinct families.

### EASTERN FENCE LIZARD    *Sceloporus undulatus*

Common in woodland edges and semi-open country in the southern part of our region. Often seen on the ground, but when alarmed, likely to dash up the nearest tree trunk, stump, or rail fence. (Family Phrynosomatidae) ▶ Rough, pointed scales. Male pale brown with *bluish areas* at *sides of belly and throat.* Female grayer, with wavy dark bars on back.

### SIX-LINED RACERUNNER    *Aspidoscelis sexlineata*

A well-named, fast-running lizard of open ground: prairies, sandy areas, riverbanks. When alarmed, likely to seek shelter under rocks or other cover. (Family Teiidae) ▶ Six or 7 narrow light stripes, separated by thicker stripes of brown or green (often brighter green toward head). Male pale blue on belly. Different head shape, duller scales than skinks.

### COMMON FIVE-LINED SKINK    *Plestiodon fasciatus*

The most widespread lizard in our region, locally common in wet woods. Mostly seen on the ground or fallen logs, but also climbs trees. ▶ Skinks have shiny scales and small legs. Color varies; young has strong stripes and *blue tail,* female usually has dark stripes, adult male often plainer with red-orange on head.

### PRAIRIE SKINK    *Plestiodon septentrionalis* (not shown)

Fairly common in sandy prairies, loose soil of streambanks, and other open areas. May bask in the sun on spring days, but often out of sight in its burrows or under rocks. ▶ Similar to preceding species, mostly easily separated by range and habitat.

### BROAD-HEADED SKINK    *Plestiodon laticeps*

A large skink of wooded areas, usually seen up in trees. ▶ Varies in color pattern by age and sex; females and young are very similar to Common Five-lined Skink. Adult male known by large size, *wide head,* and olive-brown color; head orange in spring.

### LITTLE BROWN SKINK (GROUND SKINK)    *Scincella lateralis*

A small brown lizard of the forest floor, rarely seen climbing. When alarmed, wriggles away and hides in leaf-litter. ▶ Brown overall, with dark back stripe but *no pale stripes*.

### SLENDER GLASS LIZARD    *Ophisaurus attenuatus*

This legless but active and fast-moving lizard is found mainly in open woods and grasslands. (Family Anguidae) ▶ Easily mistaken for a snake, but has ear openings, movable eyelids, and stiff, thick-necked appearance. Variable pattern, but usually has dark stripes, especially when young.

# LIZARDS

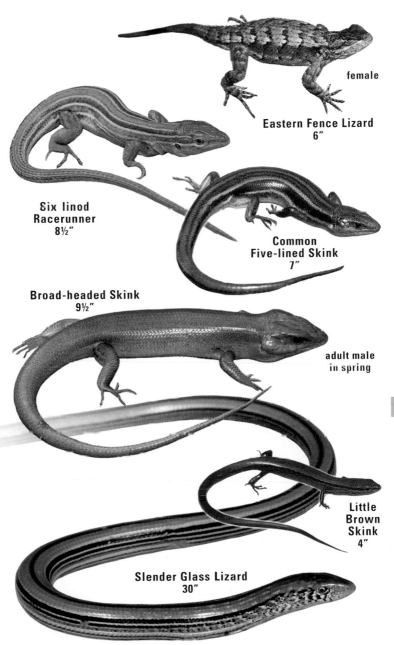

female

**Eastern Fence Lizard**
6″

**Six lined Racerunner**
8½″

**Common Five-lined Skink**
7″

**Broad-headed Skink**
9½″

adult male in spring

**Little Brown Skink**
4″

**Slender Glass Lizard**
30″

283

All of these, and all on p. 286, are in the family **Colubridae**.

### COMMON GARTERSNAKE    *Thamnophis sirtalis*

An abundant snake of fields, woods, wetlands, even found in some suburbs and city parks. ▶ *Highly variable.* Usually has 3 pale stripes (center of back and low on each side). Sides often reddish along western edge of region; often with black crossbars in Chicago area; may be all-black, especially in n. Ohio.

### PLAINS GARTERSNAKE    *Thamnophis radix* (not shown)

Very common in western part of region, in open areas, grassland. ▶ Like preceding species but pale stripe *higher* on sides (third and fourth rows of scales up from belly), *black bars* on lips.

### EASTERN RIBBONSNAKE    *Thamnophis sauritus*

Mainly in woods near water. Active and fast, harder to catch than a gartersnake. ▶ Patterned like some Common Gartersnakes, with 3 pale stripes, but incredibly long and slender. Replaced by **Western Ribbonsnake** (*T. proximus*) west of area shown on map.

### RING-NECKED SNAKE    *Diadophis punctatus*

Locally common in woods, but often hides under logs or other objects. ▶ Smooth dark gray or brown above with *yellow neck ring.* Belly bright yellow (with black spots in western areas).

### DEKAY'S BROWNSNAKE    *Storeria dekayi*

A small, gentle snake, easily overlooked, often hiding under objects in woods, swamps. ▶ Brown with vertical line or spot on face. *Rows of dark spots* on back may be joined by crossbars. Young ones have yellow neck ring; compare to preceding species.

### RED-BELLIED SNAKE    *Storeria occipitomaculata*

Sometimes common, but small and secretive, hiding under objects in woods and bogs. ▶ Brown or gray above (vaguely striped) with *plain reddish belly,* 3 *pale spots* on nape.

### KIRTLAND'S SNAKE    *Clonophis kirtlandii*

A Midwestern specialty, now seriously declining. Hides under debris or in crayfish burrows in wet meadows. If disturbed, flattens body and becomes rigid. ▶ Reddish belly with *row of bold round spots* along each side. Brown above with 4 rows of dark spots.

### ROUGH GREENSNAKE    *Opheodrys aestivus*

This well-camouflaged snake of the southern Midwest is an expert climber among shrubs and vines. Feeds mainly on insects and spiders. ▶ Slender body *bright green* above, very pale below. Each scale on upperparts has a *ridge* or "keel" down the center.

### SMOOTH GREENSNAKE    *Opheodrys vernalis*

Unlike the preceding species, mostly stays on the ground. This is another insect-eater; overuse of pesticides may be causing declines. ▶ Smaller than Rough Greensnake, with *smooth scales.*

# SMALL TO MEDIUM-SIZED SNAKES

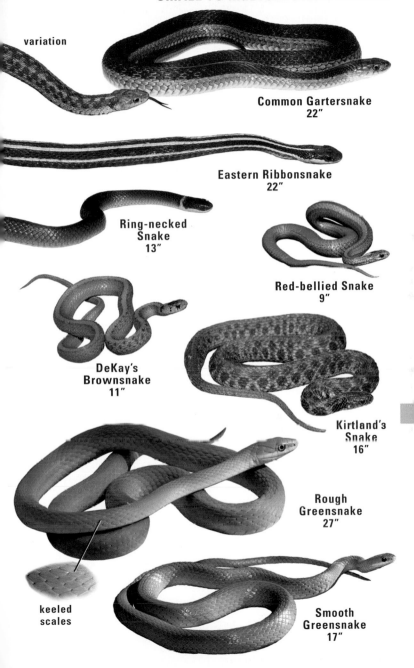

variation

**Common Gartersnake**
**22″**

**Eastern Ribbonsnake**
**22″**

**Ring-necked Snake**
**13″**

**Red-bellied Snake**
**9″**

**DeKay's Brownsnake**
**11″**

**Kirtland's Snake**
**16″**

**Rough Greensnake**
**27″**

keeled scales

**Smooth Greensnake**
**17″**

### GRAY (MIDLAND) RATSNAKE  *Pantherophis spiloides*
### WESTERN RATSNAKE  *Pantherophis obsoletus*

Ratsnakes are common in a variety of open or wooded habitats, sometimes climbing high in trees. ▶ Adults mostly blackish above, white on chin and throat, with some checkered pattern on whitish belly. Young (and some adults) gray with darker blotches. Formerly considered one species, now **Gray** east of Mississippi R. (green on map), **Western** farther west (purple on map).

### EASTERN FOXSNAKE  *Pantherophis vulpinus*
### WESTERN FOXSNAKE  *Pantherophis ramspotti*

Mainly in marshy habitat in eastern part of range; more widespread in fields and woods farther west. ▶ Yellowish to tan with bold dark blotches; head varies from *brown to orange.* (Compare to Copperhead, p. 288.) Now regarded as 2 species, with Mississippi R. as dividing line between Eastern and Western.

### NORTH AMERICAN RACER  *Coluber constrictor*

This alert, fast-moving snake hunts by day, chasing down rodents, toads, insects, lizards, and smaller snakes. When alarmed, it may dive into a burrow or climb up into branches. ▶ Long, slender. Color varies, mostly black or dull blue, to olive with yellow belly in western part of our region. Chin and throat usually white.

### GOPHERSNAKE (BULLSNAKE)  *Pituophis catenifer*

A big snake of grasslands and sandy prairies. Eats many rodents. May hiss loudly when alarmed. ▶ Large, mostly yellowish. Dark blotches on back (reddish brown to blackish) tend to be darkest near head and on tail, paler toward center of body.

### MILKSNAKE  *Lampropeltis triangulum*

The odd name is based on an old myth that it milks cows. Milksnakes do enter barns — to hunt rats and mice. Widespread in open woods, fields. ▶ Pale tan with large brown blotches on back and sides, *Y-shaped pale mark* on top of head. In sw. part of our region, much more reddish, back of neck with pale collar.

### EASTERN BLACK KINGSNAKE  *Lampropeltis nigra*

Kingsnakes are bold reptiles that eat other snakes, including venomous ones. They also eat rats, mice, other small animals. This species is widespread in forest edges and fields. ▶ Glossy black with pale scales hinting at pattern, sometimes heavily speckled. A similar snake in s. Iowa is **Speckled Kingsnake** (*L. holbrooki*).

### YELLOW-BELLIED KINGSNAKE  *Lampropeltis calligaster*

Also called Prairie Kingsnake. Fairly common in grassland, pastures, woodland edges. Active by day in spring and fall, at night in hot weather. ▶ Tan to brown with large, dark blotches. Yellowish belly has square dark spots. Compare to foxsnakes (above).

**SNAKES**
(size given is average
length of adults)

ratsnake sp.
50"

Eastern Foxsnake
45"

North American
Racer
45"

Gophersnake
(Bullsnake)
55"

Milksnake
30"

Eastern Black
Kingsnake
40"

Yellow-bellied
Kingsnake
36"

287

The first four below, like most North American snakes, are in the family **Colubridae**. The last four belong to the **Viperidae**. These venomous snakes are potentially dangerous, but they play valuable roles in natural ecosystems and their populations are worthy of protection.

### COMMON WATERSNAKE    *Nerodia sipedon*

Widespread and common in lakes, marshes, and slow-flowing rivers. Avoids people in the water, but may bite if cornered on land. ▶ Stout-bodied and dingy, with highly variable pattern of wide brown blotches and crossbands. A form on L. Erie islands, "Lake Erie Watersnake," is relatively pale and plain.

### DIAMOND-BACKED WATERSNAKE    *Nerodia rhombifer*

Locally common in swamps and quiet rivers. Often basks on branches above water. ▶ Dark brown chainlink pattern (roughly diamond-shaped in places) on paler brown back.

### QUEENSNAKE    *Regina septemvittata*

Another aquatic snake, usually seen swimming, sometimes basking above water. Feeds mostly on crayfish. ▶ Brown above with faint darker lines; *broad yellow stripe* low on side, yellow belly.

### EASTERN HOG-NOSED SNAKE    *Heterodon platirhinos*

This harmless snake may defend itself by puffing up and hissing, or by rolling over to play dead. Mainly in sandy woods, feeding on toads. ▶ *Upturned snout,* blotchy pattern, behavior. **Plains Hog-nosed Snake** (*H. nasicus*) occurs locally east to Illinois.

### COPPERHEAD    *Agkistrodon contortrix*

Uncommon, most likely to be found on rocky, wooded hillsides. **Venomous and should be avoided.** ▶ Copper-colored overall with *dark brown crossbands* in *hourglass shape,* usually narrowest at center of back. Wedge-shaped head, vertical pupils.

### MASSASAUGA    *Sistrurus catenatus*

This small rattlesnake is now threatened or endangered in most areas. It lives mainly in swampy areas or wet prairies. **Venomous, to be avoided.** ▶ Grayish with rounded, very dark spots down back, smaller spots on sides. Belly and rattle mostly blackish.

### TIMBER RATTLESNAKE    *Crotalus horridus*

Now rare and local in hilly forest and wooded river valleys. **Venomous. Most snakebites occur when people try to catch snakes.** ▶ Variable, with dark crossbands, *dark tail*, rattles on tail tip. The similar **Prairie Rattlesnake** (*C. viridis*) is rare in nw. Iowa only.

### COTTONMOUTH    *Agkistrodon piscivorus* (not shown)

Local in swamps and rivers of extreme s. Illinois, rare in s. Indiana. **Venomous and dangerous.** ▶ Stout-bodied and very dark, with only a trace of crossbands. When threatened, may hold its mouth wide open, revealing the *cottony white interior.*

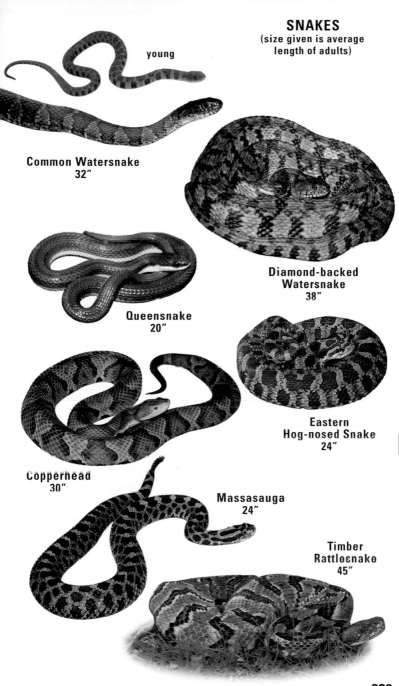

**SNAKES**
(size given is average
length of adults)

young

**Common Watersnake**
**32"**

**Diamond-backed**
**Watersnake**
**38"**

**Queensnake**
**20"**

**Eastern**
**Hog-nosed Snake**
**24"**

**Copperhead**
**30"**

**Massasauga**
**24"**

**Timber**
**Rattlesnake**
**45"**

can be common along streams and in wet woods, although they often go unnoticed. They are most diverse in the Appalachian region; more than 25 species have been found in the Midwest, but some of these barely spill across from adjacent states. The first six species below are in the family **Ambystomatidae,** while the newt belongs to the **Salamandridae.**

### EASTERN TIGER SALAMANDER    *Ambystoma tigrinum*

A wider range of habitats than most salamanders, including woods, marshes, farm ponds. ▶ Large, stout. Variable pattern, *yellowish blotches* surrounded by *network* of black or brown.

### SPOTTED SALAMANDER    *Ambystoma maculatum*

Like some other salamanders, may make a mass migration to vernal pools on the first warm, rainy night of late winter or early spring. ▶ Black with numerous *round, yellow to orange spots.*

### MARBLED SALAMANDER    *Ambystoma opacum*

Uncommon in forested areas, most often seen in early fall. Female lays eggs in dried-up pond, stays with them until the pond is flooded by autumn rains. ▶ *Strongly* but variably *patterned* with bands of white (male) or gray (female) on glossy black.

### SMALL-MOUTHED SALAMANDER    *Ambystoma texana*

Fairly common in forest and prairie areas, breeding in late winter in ponds, ditches. May hide by day in crayfish burrows. ▶ Stout, with *small head, short snout, short toes.* May interbreed with Blue-spotted, Jefferson, or Eastern Tiger Salamanders, so some individuals or whole populations may be impossible to identify.

### BLUE-SPOTTED SALAMANDER    *Ambystoma laterale*

Widespread in northern forests and meadows, migrating to its breeding ponds on rainy nights in very early spring. Interbreeds with Jefferson Salamander over a wide area, so many individuals will appear intermediate between the 2 species. ▶ Glossy black, very heavily marked with *blue or bluish white spots.*

### JEFFERSON SALAMANDER    *Ambystoma jeffersonianum*

The southern replacement for Blue-spotted Salamander. In between the areas mapped for these species, whole populations of salamanders may be found that are intermediate between the 2, and difficult to classify or to identify. ▶ Typically larger than Blue-spotted, with *longer snout* and longer toes. *Plain* overall, grayish to brownish, usually with fine blue speckles on sides.

### EASTERN NEWT    *Notophthalmus viridescens*

Has an odd life history. Aquatic as a larva and as an adult, but in between there is usually a stage, the Red Eft, that wanders on land for up to 3 years or even longer. Foul secretions from its skin protect the eft from predators. ▶ Adults olive with red spots. Red Eft is rough-skinned, orange to dull red, with red spots.

# SALAMANDERS

Eastern Tiger
Salamander
7½"

Spotted
Salamander
6½"

Small mouthed Salamander
4¾"

Marbled Salamander
4"

Blue-spotted
Salamander
4½"

Jefferson Salamander
5½"

Eastern Newt
3½"
(3 variations)

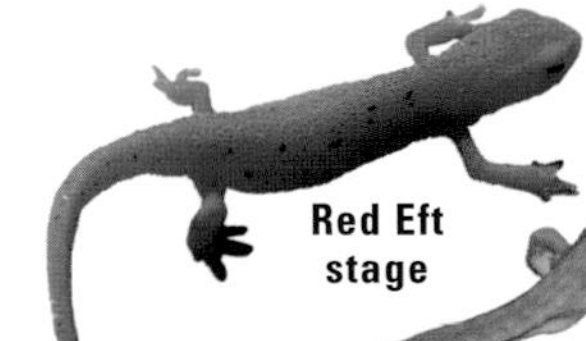

Red Eft
stage

**291**

# SALAMANDERS

The first six below are in the family **Plethodontidae,** salamanders that lack lungs altogether, breathing through their mouth lining and skin.

### EASTERN RED-BACKED SALAMANDER    *Plethodon cinereus*

Common in damp woods, often found under rocks or logs near streams. Unlike most salamanders, this and the next species *lack* an aquatic larval stage, hatching out of the egg with legs already formed. ► Small, slender, with tiny legs. May have a *broad red stripe* down back, or may be all dark. Belly *mottled black.*

### FOUR-TOED SALAMANDER    *Hemidactylium scutatum*

Locally common, mainly in areas of sphagnum and other mosses in bogs, woods. ► Yellowish brown with obscure marks above; belly *white* with *bold black specks.* Four toes on each foot (most salamanders have 5 toes on hind feet). Base of tail constricted.

### SOUTHERN TWO-LINED SALAMANDER    *Eurycea cirrigera*
### NORTHERN TWO-LINED SALAMANDER    *Eurycea bislineata*

Common, often found hiding under stones or logs near streams, swamps. ► Yellowish, with 2 *irregular dark lines,* running from each eye to tail. **Southern** found from Illinois to s. Ohio (green on map), **Northern** in ne. Ohio (purple on map).

### LONG-TAILED SALAMANDER    *Eurycea longicauda*

Fairly common under rocks or rotting logs near streams. ► Very long tail. Yellow to orange overall, with black markings on sides, developing into *vertical black bars* on sides of tail.

### NORTHERN DUSKY SALAMANDER    *Desmognathus fuscus*

Often found hiding under rocks, logs, or debris near flowing streams, springs. ► Tail *laterally compressed.* Gray or brown with darker spots. Usually a *pale line* from eye to corner of mouth.

### NORTHERN SLIMY SALAMANDER    *Plethodon glutinosus*

Fairly common on rocky hillsides in woods, active in hot, humid weather. The whitish slime from this salamander's skin glands can be very hard to wash off after it dries. ► Mostly glossy black with many small, sharply defined white spots.

### MUDPUPPY    *Necturus maculosus*
Active mostly at night, and totally aquatic, in rivers, lakes, large ponds. Sometimes caught on fishing lines; harmless, despite its startling appearance. Still widespread, but declining. (Family Proteidae) ► Large, stout, with laterally flattened tail. Gray-brown, with reddish brown gills.

### HELLBENDER    *Cryptobranchus alleganiensis*
Its nickname, "snot otter," fits this big aquatic salamander. Once widespread in rivers from Ohio to s. Illinois, has vanished from some areas, probably because of pollution. (Family Cryptobranchidae) ► Huge size, broad flat head, scattered dark marks, no external gills.

# SALAMANDERS

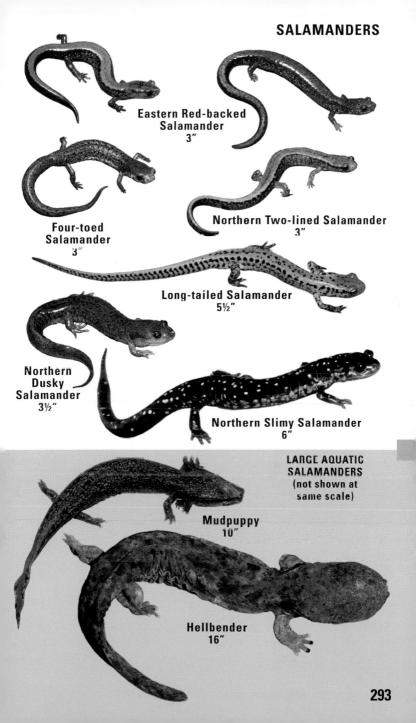

Eastern Red-backed Salamander
3″

Four-toed Salamander
3″

Northern Two-lined Salamander
3″

Long-tailed Salamander
5½″

Northern Dusky Salamander
3½″

Northern Slimy Salamander
6″

LARGE AQUATIC SALAMANDERS
(not shown at same scale)

Mudpuppy
10″

Hellbender
16″

293

These represent three distinct families: toads (**Bufonidae**), spadefoots (**Pelobatidae**), and treefrogs and related species (**Hylidae**).

### AMERICAN TOAD    *Anaxyrus americanus*

Common in most habitats, including gardens. ▶ Toads differ from frogs in shorter hind legs, bumpy skin. On this species, large dark spots on back have only 1 or 2 "warts" each, and chest usually has dark spots. In s. Indiana and Illinois ("Dwarf American Toad"), smaller and more lightly marked, with a higher-pitched voice. **Voice:** a long, mellow trill, lasting up to half a minute.

### FOWLER'S TOAD    *Anaxyrus fowleri*

Fairly common in open, sandy habitats. ▶ Similar to American Toad, but largest dark spots on back usually have *3 or more* raised warts, chest usually *lacks* dark spots. Replaced in w. Iowa by the similar **Woodhouse's Toad** (*A. woodhousii*). **Voice:** a short, nasal *wrraaah,* lasting up to 4 seconds.

### GREAT PLAINS TOAD    *Anaxyrus cognatus*

Common in open country along western edge of region. ▶ Back with *very large* dark blotches, each containing many small raised warts. When male is calling, inflated throat is sausage-shaped. **Voice:** sharp, metallic trill, lasting 20 seconds or more.

### EASTERN SPADEFOOT    *Scaphiopus holbrookii*

Rare and mysterious. Usually underground, coming out to breed on warm, rainy nights. ▶ Stout, big-eyed, with *pair of pale lines* on back. Black "spade" on hind foot. **Voice:** sharp, bleating grunt.

### GRAY TREEFROG    *Hyla versicolor* and *H. chrysoscelis*

Usually up in trees and shrubs, coming down to water's edge in spring breeding season. ▶ Variable color, from green to gray or brown. *Pale spot* below each eye. **Voice:** a loud, rough trill.

### SPRING PEEPER    *Pseudacris crucifer*

Common in most of region, calling at night from ponds, marshes, starting very early in spring. After breeding, wanders to woods, thickets. ▶ Very small and plain, but with *rough × pattern* on back. **Voice:** sharp, high-pitched *peep* every 1 or 2 seconds.

### CHORUS FROG    *Pseudacris triseriata* and *P. maculata*

Small frogs of shallow marshes, heard often in early spring. Now recognized as 2 species, with **Western Chorus Frog** (*P. triseriata*) in *eastern* 3 states of region, **Boreal Chorus Frog** (*P. maculata*) farther west. ▶ Dark stripe through eye and along side, 3 dark stripes down back. **Voice:** short, rising trill, *crrrrrrik!*

### BLANCHARD'S CRICKET FROG    *Acris blanchardi*

Formerly common, now declining, possibly harmed by runoff of farm chemicals. ▶ Small but stout, fairly plain, with dark triangle between eyes. **Voice:** ongoing series, metallic *tik tik tik tik . . .*

# TOADS AND FROGS

**American Toad**
2¾"

**Fowler's Toad**
2½"

**Great Plains Toad**
2¾"

**Eastern Spadefoot**
2"

**Gray Treefrog**
1¾"

(examples of
2 colors)

**SMALLER FROGS**
(not at same scale)

**Spring Peeper**
1"

**chorus frog sp.**
1¼"

**Blanchard's Cricket Frog**
1¼"

(family **Ranidae)** have relatively smooth skin and long legs, compared to most species on p. 294. Some of these are very common and widespread.

## AMERICAN BULLFROG *Lithobates catesbeianus*

Our largest frog, widespread and common at ponds, marshes, lakes, rivers. ► Large size, relatively unpatterned look. Lacks ridges on back shown by Green Frog. Male has yellowish throat. **Voice**: deep, rolling bass, *jug-a-rrumm.*

## GREEN FROG *Lithobates clamitans*

Common around marshes, ponds, and other fresh water in most of our area. ► Despite name, color varies; may be mostly green or brown (or rarely blue). Unlike Bullfrog, has *raised ridges* down back. **Voice**: a sudden, twangy *glunk,* sometimes repeated.

## WOOD FROG *Lithobates sylvaticus*

Found in moist forest, often far from water. Very cold-hardy, gathering at shallow ponds in late winter or early spring, then dispersing into surrounding habitat. ► Varies in color from brown to tan to pinkish, with a *distinct dark mask* behind the eye. **Voice**: a hoarse, fairly weak quacking sound.

## MINK FROG *Lithobates septentrionalis*

A frog of cold northern lakes and streams. ► Greenish, heavily spotted above. Green Frog can be very similar, but has dark crossbands on hind legs (Mink Frog has blotches there instead). **Voice**: throaty *tuk-tuk-tuk-tuk-tuk.*

## NORTHERN LEOPARD FROG *Lithobates pipiens*

Common around marshes and ponds in spring, wandering through open habitats in summer. Two similar species occur in Midwest: **Southern Leopard Frog** (*L. sphenocephalus)* mostly in s. Illinois and Indiana, **Plains Leopard Frog** (*L. blairi)* from Iowa east to Indiana. ► Green to brown with big, rounded dark spots, often pale-edged. **Voice**: a guttural, knocking trill, 1–3 seconds long, often with some croaking notes. **Southern L.F.:** short, slow trill. **Plains L.F.:** short, chuckling burst of 2–4 notes.

## PICKEREL FROG *Lithobates palustris*

Common around bogs, streams, and swamps, wandering into more open habitats in summer. ► *Squarish spots* arranged in *parallel rows* down the back. Yellow inner surface of hind legs sometimes visible. **Voice**: rough snoring, lasting up to 2 seconds.

## CRAWFISH FROG *Lithobates areolatus* (not shown)

Uncommon in southern grasslands and marshes, formerly also in se. Iowa. Hides underground by day, including in crayfish holes. Active at night, especially after heavy rains in spring. ► Stubby shape; irregular, rounded dark spots with *pale borders.* Overall color is variable. **Voice**: loud, vibrating, snoring sound.

FROGS

American Bullfrog
4½"

Green Frog
3"

Wood Frog
2¼"

Mink Frog
2½"

Northern Leopard Frog
2¾"

Pickerel Frog
2½"

297

# FISHES

Studying fish can open a whole new world of underwater life to the naturalist, or expand the knowledge and success of the angler. Once we realize that fish with tropical colors are darting just under the surface of a riffle, or that living fossils inhabit the waters of a swamp, many of us can't wait to learn more.

*Fishes section contributed by T. Travis Brown*

Throughout the Midwest, anglers pursue bass, catfishes, walleye, and various panfish on our lakes and rivers. Many anglers travel to the Great Lakes region to pursue specialties like Muskellunge, Northern Pike, and Lake Trout. Some clear, cold streams even support populations of trout. A growing number of naturalists and aquarium enthusiasts are heading to our creeks with a dip net or snorkel to check out Rainbow Darters and Brook Sticklebacks. This section will give you the tools to identify some of our most common fishes, and, we hope, some inspiration to seek out some of those lesser known species.

**Fish ID: habitat and behavior.** When you observe or capture a fish, its geographic location, habitat, position in the water column, and behavior can all give you clues to the fish's identity. For instance, a fish that prefers to live on the bottom of a river in the fast current of a riffle will probably not be seen swimming at the water's surface in a swamp.

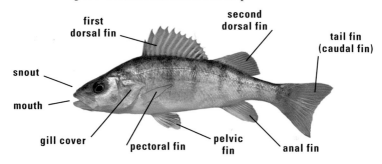

**Fish ID: shape and structure.** The general shapes of fishes (yes, it's correct to say fishes when you are talking about multiple species) are important for distinguishing them into basic groups. The direction that the mouth is pointed (upward, forward, downward) can tell you a lot about where the fish feeds and what it might be related to. It is also important to note the number and position of fins in relation to each other, and whether they are supported by sharp spines or soft rays. On a more detailed level, some fishes can be positively identified only by counting the number of spines in the fins, the number of scales in the lateral line, and other nearly microscopic characteristics. We have avoided these more complicated methods as much as possible, but it is still important to know some of the terminology associated with fish anatomy.

**Fish ID: coloration.** Coloration can be valuable in identifying fish, but it is important to note that many fish change color because of spawning season, water quality, stress levels, aggression, or other factors. In studying fish, we rely on many structural characteristics because color can be variable. In some species, coloration stays consistent year-round, but sometimes a pale brown fish turns into a blue and red beauty in springtime.

**Observing fish.** It is possible in some clear waters to observe fish underwater with a mask and snorkel. If you move slowly through the water, many fish will lose the fear they had when you were above the surface and will approach to within inches of your face. Water clarity is generally best when it has not rained for a while and where lakes and streams don't receive a lot of silt or nutrient loading from adjacent lands.

In many midwestern waters, you will have to capture the fish if you want to see them. Of course, larger fish can be captured with a hook and line, and smaller ones are best pursued with a dip net, seine, or cast net. In most cases, this will require that you purchase a fishing license and become highly familiar with the regulations in your state.

In some states it is legal to bring small fish home to live in an aquarium. This can be an ideal way to learn more about the fascinating behavior of fish and introduce them to others, provided that you do this with an appropriate species and do lots of research ahead of time on how to create habitable conditions. If it is not legal to keep them, you can at least bring along a small aquarium or clear plastic container to check out what your fish look like underwater.

**Conservation.** The greatest problem facing most of our midwestern fish is habitat degradation (past and current). Diverse and thriving fish communities cannot live in water that is clogged with silt, laced with chemicals, and devoid of oxygen. We often think about keeping large streams clean, and there are many important efforts focused on preserving beautiful sections of rivers. However, a river is the sum of its tributaries, so efforts focused on smaller streams in the watersheds are also important.

One simple way to improve water quality is to leave a thick buffer of lush vegetation next to streams, ditches, wetlands, and lakes. This helps to keep sediment from eroding into our waters and filters out many harmful substances. We can also help fish by reducing use of lawn chemicals, excess fertilizers, and other products not produced in a responsible manner.

In many areas, invasive exotic species introductions are also playing havoc with native fish ecology. For instance, the introduction of Sea Lamprey through our canals helped to destroy lake trout populations in the Great Lakes. More recently, introduced Asiatic carp species are multiplying in mind-blowing numbers in our waters, reducing the amount of food available for native species. Even moving a few fish, some snails, or a little bit of algae from one water body to another can have an ill effect, so it is important to never dump leftover bait from one water body into another and always clean your gear well.

The first five species below are in the Salmon family (**Salmonidae**). The sixth species also has an adipose fin and similar body form.

## LAKE TROUT    *Salvelinus namaycush*

This species is found in the clear, deep waters of lakes with rocky substrates. It is the largest native trout in the Great Lakes. There are multiple forms of this species, including the fatter "siscowet" found in Lake Superior and hybrids with Brook Trout called "splake." ▶ As in other members of the family, there is a small adipose fin between the dorsal and tail fins. Lake Trout have a large mouth that extends backward beyond the eye, a deeply forked tail fin, and a darker upper back and dorsal fin with light-colored spots and vermiculations.

## BROOK TROUT    *Salvelinus fontinalis*

Found in the cold, well-oxygenated waters of streams and northern lakes. ▶ Bright, light-colored *leading edges* on lower fins almost glow. Rear edge of tail fin is not forked. Light-colored, wormlike, wavy lines on dorsal fin and upper back. *Blue halos* around pink/red spots on sides.

## RAINBOW TROUT    *Oncorhynchus mykiss*

This species is native to the western U.S.; however, both Rainbow Trout and **Brown Trout** (*Salmo trutta,* an Old World species) are widely introduced in clear, cold streams and lakes of the Midwest. ▶ Rainbow Trout usually have a pink wash or stripe along their sides, and black spots on the back, upper fins, and tail. Brown Trout have red and black spots on the back, black spots on the gill cover, and generally lack spots in the tail. The rear edge of the tail fin in both species is *straight* (not forked).

## LAKE WHITEFISH    *Coregonus clupeaformis*

This was the most important food fish in the Great Lakes for centuries, but its numbers are now greatly reduced. Found in lakes and large rivers, where it swims in schools within a few feet of the bottom. ▶ Has an adipose fin, small mouth, and deeply forked tail similar to those of other ciscoes and whitefishes (*Coregonus* sp.); however, the Lake Whitefish has a concavity in front of the nape that creates a humpbacked appearance.

## CISCO    *Coregonus artedi*

This is one of about 8 very similar fishes in the Great Lakes and surrounding waters. This group of fishes once supported a "chub" fishing industry in the Great Lakes that has since collapsed. At least one species from this group is now extinct, and several others are seriously reduced in numbers. ▶ Like other ciscoes and whitefishes, has an adipose fin, small mouth, and deeply forked tail. It is nearly round in cross-section, and quite slender.

## TROUT-PERCH    *Percopsis omiscomaycus*

Found in lakes and sandy pools of streams, often coming into the shallows of lakes at night to feed. This is the only member of the trout-perch family (Percopsidae) found in the Midwest. ▶ Small, straw-colored fish with brown spots along the sides. The only fish in our region, besides catfishes, to have an adipose fin and sharp spines in most of the fins.

# SALMONLIKE FISHES
(Sizes given are average lengths of adults.
Some can be smaller or much larger.)

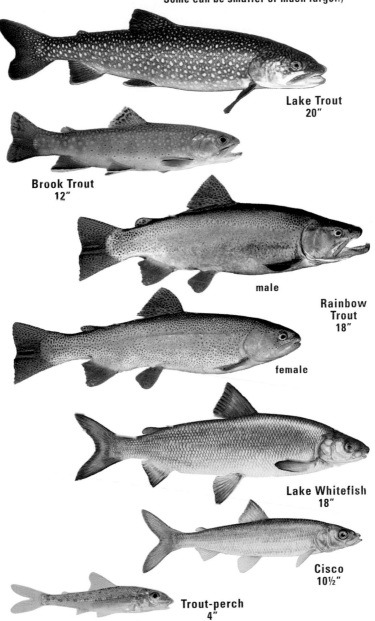

**Lake Trout**
**20″**

**Brook Trout**
**12″**

male

**Rainbow
Trout
18″**

female

**Lake Whitefish**
**18″**

**Cisco**
**10½″**

**Trout-perch**
**4″**

While they actually belong to two different families, the first five species on this page are commonly referred to as bass.

## WHITE BASS  *Morone chrysops*

Found in lakes, ponds, and pools of streams. Temperate bass family (Moronidae). ► This is a silvery white fish with 4–7 fine grayish lines (often interrupted) along the sides. The 3 spines in the anal fin *increase in length from front to back.* This species often hybridizes (both naturally and through human manipulation) with the **Striped Bass** *(Morone saxatilis),* a larger, more slender fish with more robust regular stripes.

## YELLOW BASS  *Morone mississippiensis*

Found in lakes, ponds, pools, and backwaters of lowland streams. Temperate bass family. ► Silvery yellowish fish with 5–7 *prominent* black stripes. Stripes are broken and offset along the lower flanks. The second 2 spines in the anal fin are roughly the *same length.*

## LARGEMOUTH BASS  *Micropterus salmoides*

The Largemouth inhabits ponds, lakes, sloughs, and quiet water of streams, often favoring vegetated areas with a sandy or muddy bottom. Sunfish family (Centrarchidae). ► Elongate silver-green fish with darker mottling and a relatively continuous stripe of darker coloration along the sides of the body. This species has a huge mouth, the rear edge of which extends backward *well past the eye.* The 2 dorsal fins (the front, spiny one and the rear soft one) are *nearly separate.*

## SMALLMOUTH BASS  *Micropterus dolomieu*

More associated with gravel-bottomed streams and rocky lakes than the Largemouth Bass. Sunfish family. ► A silvery tan fish, with 6–16 darker brown bars along the side. The mouth is "small" only in comparison to that of the Largemouth, extending backward to just under the eye. The 2 dorsal fins (the front, spiny one and the rear soft one) are *joined.* **Spotted Bass** *(Micropterus punctatus),* found in the southern Midwest, is very similar except with rows of spots along the lower sides, and a rough tooth patch in the center of the tongue that can be felt with a finger.

## ROCK BASS  *Ambloplites rupestris*

Found in vegetation, brush, and rocky crevices of clear streams and lakes — usually with rocky bottoms. Sunfish family. ► A slab-sided sunfish with tight rows of brownish spots running down the sides. It has a prominent *red eye,* 11–13 dorsal spines, and 6 anal spines (members of the genus *Lepomis,* p. 304, have only 3 anal spines).

## BLACK CRAPPIE  *Pomoxis nigromaculatus*

A popular game fish, found in lakes, ponds, and slow water of streams, often near vegetation and soft substrates. Sunfish family. ► A deep-bodied sunfish, with a gently sloping nape. Covered in dark spots and blotches, and the dorsal fin is blackish with lighter spots. It has 7–8 dorsal spines. The **White Crappie** *(P. annularis)* is lighter overall, has a light dorsal fin with darker spots, and has 6 dorsal spines. Both have 6 anal spines.

# BASSLIKE FISHES

White Bass
11"

Yellow Bass
10"

Largemouth
Bass
16"

Smallmouth Bass
12"

Rock Bass
7"

Black Crappie
13"

303

# PANFISHES

The popular term for these fishes refers to the fact that they generally don't get too large to fit in a frying pan whole. The first four on this page are members of the sunfish family, and of the genus *Lepomis.* They are among our most popular game fish because of their abundance and their willingness to bite on a variety of baits. They share a deep-bodied outline and have three anal spines. The fifth species below, the Yellow Perch, is another panfish popular with many anglers.

## WARMOUTH    *Lepomis gulosus*

This species is most commonly found in vegetated lakes, ponds, and sluggish parts of lowland streams with a muddy bottom. ▶ The Warmouth is a thick panfish with a large mouth, the rear edge of which extends backward to under the eye. Unlike the superficially similar Rock Bass (p. 302), this species has only 3 spines in the anal fin. The Warmouth has brownish, wavy lines on the cheek that radiate from the back of its red eye. It also has a toothy tongue.

## GREEN SUNFISH    *Lepomis cyanellus*

This species is found in ponds, lakes, and streams in quiet water, often near vegetation. The Green Sunfish is quite tolerant of conditions that would kill most other fish, and can be found in the tiniest pools of drying creeks. ▶ A small, slab-sided panfish with a large mouth, green vermiculations on the cheek, and a *dark spot* in the rear dorsal fin (as an adult). It also has *yellowish* rear edges on the dorsal, caudal, and anal fins.

## BLUEGILL    *Lepomis macrochirus*

The Bluegill is one of our most popular panfish species. It is found in lakes, ponds, and streams of virtually any size, especially around vegetation and brush. ▶ This is a very deep-bodied panfish with a *black spot* in the rear dorsal fin (as an adult). The mouth is small and pectoral fins are very *long* and pointed (extending past the eye when bent forward). There are usually *vertical bars* on the sides, except on those living in turbid water. In young specimens, these bars are typically thin and paired.

## PUMPKINSEED    *Lepomis gibbosus*

Pumpkinseeds are found in ponds, lakes, and sluggish parts of creeks and small rivers. ▶ This is a deep-bodied panfish with a *red spot* on its black ear flap. The mouth is small and the pectoral fins are very *long* and pointed (extending past the eye when bent forward). Unlike several similar sunfishes, there are wavy lines and/or orange spots in the *second dorsal fin.*

## YELLOW PERCH    *Perca flavescens*

The yellow perch is usually found in clear ponds, lakes, and stream pools around vegetation. It feeds primarily on invertebrates, but larger individuals will take fish. Perch family (Percidae). ▶ This is a yellowish fish with 7–9 elongate *dark saddles or bands* extending down the sides and a dark blotch at the rear edge of the front (spiny) dorsal fin. The two dorsal fins are separate.

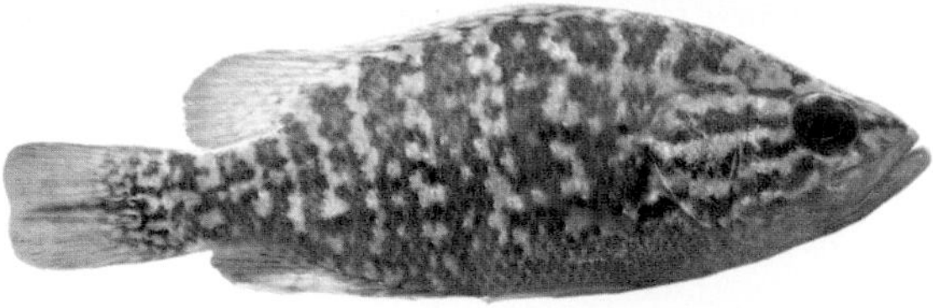

**Warmouth**
6½"

**Green Sunfish**
6"

**Bluegill**
7"

**Pumpkinseed**
7"

**Yellow Perch**
11"

The species on this page belong to two different families, but they are all popular game fish with prominent teeth.

### GRASS PICKEREL    *Esox americanus*

This species is found in swamps, lakes, and stream backwaters, usually among vegetation where it feeds on smaller fishes. Pike and mudminnow family (Esocidae). ▶ A relatively small pike species, with the typical cylindrical body, toothy duck-billed mouth, and dorsal fin located far back on the body. Grass Pickerel have a substantial *teardrop stripe* under the eye that slants noticeably toward the back of the body. Also, their gill cover is completely scaled.

### NORTHERN PIKE    *Esox lucius*

This species is found in clear, vegetated northern lakes and quiet waters of streams. As an adult it feeds primarily on other fish. Pike and mudminnow family. ▶ One of our large pike species, with the typical cylindrical body, toothy duck-billed mouth, and dorsal fin located far back on the body. Northern Pike have virtually *no* teardrop marking, and the bottom half of their gill cover is unscaled. They have a pattern of *light spots and lines* on a *darker* green background.

### MUSKELLUNGE    *Esox masquinongy*

The "musky" is found in clear, vegetated lakes, rivers, and quiet waters of streams. It feeds primarily on other fish, but will also take small mammals and birds. Musky, and hatchery-produced hybrids with Northern Pike (called "tiger musky"), are highly sought after as sport fish in many areas. The musky can reach almost 70 pounds! Indeed, the fish used as bait for musky would be "keepers" to many anglers. Pike and mudminnow family. ▶ A large pike species, with the typical cylindrical body, toothy duck-billed mouth, and dorsal fin located far back on the body. Musky have virtually *no* teardrop marking, and the bottom half of their gill cover is unscaled. They have a pattern of *darker bars and spots* on a *light* background.

### WALLEYE    *Sander vitreus*

Walleye are found in lakes and medium to large rivers, often near brush. This is a popular sport fish because of the fight it provides. The Walleye is named for its opaque, blind-looking eyes, a condition caused by an abundance of an eye tissue (tapetum lucidum) that allows them to see better at night. The "blue pike" was a color morph or subspecies formerly found in Lake Erie, but now considered extinct. Perch family (Percidae). ▶ The *strange eyes,* slender body, *black blotch* in the rear of the first dorsal fin, and large teeth easily identify this fish.

### SAUGER    *Sander canadensis*

Sauger are found primarily in runs, pools, and backwaters of rivers over sand and gravel, but also occur in some lakes and impoundments. Like Walleye, they are a popular sport fish. Perch family. ▶ The strange eyes, slender body, large teeth, and *rows of half-moon-shaped spots* in the front dorsal fin easily identify this fish.

# TOOTHY GAME FISHES
### (Not all shown at same scale.
### Sizes given are average lengths of adults.)

**Grass Pickerel**
**10"**

juvenile

**Northern Pike**
**28"**

**Muskellunge**
**35"**

**Walleye**
**20"**

**Sauger**
**17"**

307

# LARGE, UNIQUE FISHES

The species on this page attain reasonably large size, and they are from a variety of unique and/or ancient families.

### LAKE STURGEON    *Acipenser fulvescens*

A huge, ancient fish that inhabits large lakes and rivers, the Lake Sturgeon can reach 300 pounds and over 150 years of age! Sturgeon family (Acipenseridae). ▶ Sturgeon have asymmetrical tails resembling those of sharks, and their bony scutes make them appear as though their skeleton is on the outside; however, their internal skeleton is actually made entirely of cartilage. In other midwestern sturgeon species, the portion of the body directly in front of the tail fin (the caudal peduncle) is much more slender.

### PADDLEFISH    *Polydon spathula*

Like the sturgeon, this ancient fish also has a cartilaginous skeleton. It is found in large rivers, lakes, and impoundments where it filter-feeds on zooplankton and other small animals. There is a substantial market for paddlefish meat and caviar, and commercial farming operations have developed in the Midwest. Paddlefish family (Polydontidae). ▶ The paddlefish's *huge rostrum* has earned it the nickname "spoonbill." This rostrum, filled with electroreceptors that help it to detect concentrations of food, makes this fish virtually impossible to misidentify.

### LONGNOSE GAR    *Lepisosteus osseus*

This species is found in lakes, swamps, and still waters of creeks and rivers. As an adult it feeds mostly on fish. A member of an ancient group of fishes, it is capable of surviving in low-oxygen waters by gulping air at the surface. Gar family (Lepisosteidae). ▶ Gar are very long, cylindrical fish with a mouth full of teeth. The thick scales do not overlap like those of many other fishes. This species has the most slender, elongate jaws of the 3 gar species typically found in the Midwest.

### BOWFIN    *Amia calva*

The Bowfin is found in swamps, sloughs, lakes, sluggish streams, and rivers. It is the only surviving member of an ancient family, and has a lung-like swim bladder that allows it to live in very low-oxygen water by gulping air from the surface. Bowfin family (Amiidae). ▶ The Bowfin has a nearly cylindrical body with a dorsal fin extending along most of the length of the back. The serpentine motion of the dorsal fin suggests an eel's movements. It also has a large head and sharp teeth. A *black spot* surrounded by a *yellow halo* at the upper base of the tail fin on young, less obvious on adults.

### BURBOT    *Lota lota*

The Burbot is found in the deepest waters of our lakes and rivers. It digs a small trench where it waits to ambush prey. In late winter it emerges from the depths to breed in shallower water under the ice. The other 22 species in this family are marine. Cuskfish family (Lotidae). ▶ The Burbot is a flat-headed fish with dorsal and anal fins that extend along the length of much of the body. This species has a single, slender barbel in the center of the chin.

# LARGE, UNIQUE FISHES
(Not all shown at same scale.
Sizes given are average lengths of adults.)

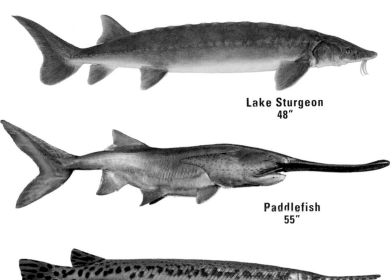

**Lake Sturgeon**
48"

**Paddlefish**
55"

**Longnose Gar**
34"

**Bowfin**
20"

**Burbot**
21"

### COMMON CARP     *Cyprinus carpio*

A native of Eurasia, the Common Carp now can be found anywhere there is plenty of mud and detritus for it to root through. Minnow family (Cyprinidae). ▶ This species is usually orange-brown with a long dorsal fin and a downward pointing mouth having 2 large barbels on each side.

### BIGHEAD CARP     *Hypophthalmichthys nobilis*

This species is native to eastern Asia, but is now established in many lakes, rivers, and backwaters. Minnow family. ▶ The eye is located below the center of the head. The rear half of the belly (from the pelvic fins back to the anus) has a sharp keel. On the very similar **Silver Carp** (*Hypophthalmichthys molitrix),* another invasive species, the belly is fully keeled up to the base of the gills.

### QUILLBACK     *Carpiodes cyprinus*

The Quillback is found in lakes and streams, where it inhabits pools, runs, and backwater areas. Sucker family (Catostomidae). ▶ It has a down-turned mouth with fleshy lips, typical of the sucker family. Unlike some similar suckers, it *lacks* a nipple-like protrusion on the lower lip. It is named for the elongated first ray of its dorsal fin, which trails backward.

### WHITE SUCKER     *Catostomus commersonii*

This species is usually found in small clear streams and rivers, but also in some lakes. Sucker family. ▶ Whitish with some faint mottling, and the male develops a *rosy stripe* along each side in breeding season. This species has a down-turned, fleshy mouth typical of the sucker family. The scales in front of the dorsal fin are very small and crowded compared to those farther back.

### NORTHERN HOGSUCKER     *Hypentelium nigricans*

Most commonly found in the riffles, runs, and pools of clear, rocky streams. Sucker family. ▶ The hogsucker's head has a *triangular* cross-section, with down-turned fleshy lips. The camouflaged body can blend so well with stream gravel and cobble that the fish is virtually invisible.

### GOLDEN REDHORSE     *Moxostoma erythrurum*

Found in lakes and many types of streams, in still areas and in currents. Sucker family. ▶ Like other members of the family, the Golden Redhorse has down-turned fleshy lips. It is silver to gold in color with red fins. The Midwest has a bewildering array of about 6 redhorse species (*Moxostoma* sp.), but this one is the most common and widespread.

### FRESHWATER DRUM     *Aplodinotus grunniens*

Found on the bottom of rivers and lakes, this drum is the only freshwater member of its family native to the U.S. Drum and croaker family (Sciaenidae). ▶ A silver fish with a *strongly arched* back. Its mouth is located on the bottom of the body, and it has a short first dorsal fin attached to a very long second dorsal fin.

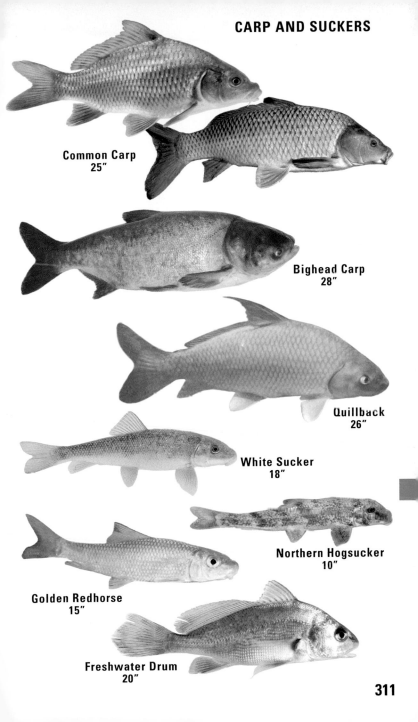

# CARP AND SUCKERS

**Common Carp**
25″

**Bighead Carp**
28″

**Quillback**
26″

**White Sucker**
18″

**Northern Hogsucker**
10″

**Golden Redhorse**
15″

**Freshwater Drum**
20″

**311**

These are all members of the catfish family (**Ictaluridae**). All have four pairs of barbels around the mouth, no scales, and an adipose fin between the dorsal and tail fins. Catfishes have spines in several of their fins. In the smaller species (bullheads and madtoms), these spines are accompanied by venom-producing tissue that can give a painful sting.

### CHANNEL CATFISH    *Ictalurus punctatus*

This species lives on the bottom of creeks, rivers, and lakes. It is widely sought after by anglers — especially at night — as a food fish, and is farmed in commercial ponds in many parts of the Midwest. ▶ The Channel Catfish reaches relatively large size. It is bluish gray with scattered dark spots on the back and sides. The anal fin margin of this species is rounded, while that of the similar **Blue Catfish** (*I. furcatus*) has a straight edge.

### FLATHEAD CATFISH    *Pylodictis olivaris*

As adults, these fish are usually found in sluggish rivers or impoundments with logs and debris on the bottom, but the young often inhabit rocky riffles of streams. This species is highly sought after by those who want to land a large fish, as their weight can reach over 120 pounds! ▶ This catfish has a wide, flat head with the lower jaw *projecting* beyond the upper. The upper tip of the tail fin is *white* until the fish becomes quite large.

### YELLOW BULLHEAD    *Ameiurus natalis*

The Yellow Bullhead is a common, medium-sized catfish found in ponds, sloughs, and sluggish streams with muddy substrate. ▶ Mainly *yellow,* and the lower barbels around the mouth are *whitish.* Unlike madtoms (see below), the rear edge of the adipose fin is free from the body.

### STONECAT    *Noturus flavus*

This species is found in rocky riffles and runs of creeks and rivers, and also inhabits the gravel shoals of some lakes. It spends most of the day hiding under a rock or in a log, coming out to forage at night. ▶ Among our catfishes, madtoms (genus *Noturus*) are easy to recognize because the rear edge of the adipose fin is attached to the body. The Stonecat is the largest of our madtoms, but still reaches only about 12" in length. It has light spots in front of and behind the dorsal fin and in the upper edge of the tail fin.

### TADPOLE MADTOM    *Noturus gyrinus*

This species is found in lakes, swamps, and pools of lowland creeks and rivers. ▶ Madtoms (genus *Noturus*) are distinct from other catfishes because the rear edge of the adipose fin is attached to the body. This species is quite chubby, loosely resembling a tadpole. It is a uniform tan/gray above and lighter below. The jaws are of *equal length,* and the rear edge of the pectoral spine lacks the "teeth" present on some other madtoms.

## CATFISHES
(Not all shown at same scale.
Sizes given are average lengths of adults.)

**Channel Catfish**
19"

**Flathead Catfish**
25"

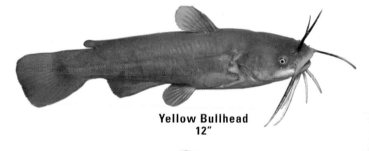

**Yellow Bullhead**
12"

**Stonecat**
7"

**Tadpole Madtom**
3"

313

# MINNOWS

**(family Cyprinidae)** make up our largest family of fishes, with over 260 species in the U.S. They have one dorsal fin, pectoral fins located under the belly, and fins with soft rays (usually no spines).

### CREEK CHUB    *Semotilus atromaculatus*

This may be the most common species found in small to medium-sized eastern streams. ▶ Silver to gray overall with a black spot at the front base of the dorsal fin and at the base of the tail fin. Mature males develop *rosy coloration* during early spring. Relatively large mouth. The scales in front of the dorsal fin are small and crowded.

### HORNYHEAD CHUB    *Nocomis biguttatus*

Found in rocky pools and runs of creeks and small rivers, this chub builds a nest of piled gravel that several species will spawn over. ▶ Most readily recognized by the red (male) or brassy (female) *spot behind the eye.* The breeding male develops warty tubercles on the head.

### CENTRAL STONEROLLER    *Campostoma anomalum*

Found mostly in rocky streams, where it spends most of its time scraping algae from rocks. ▶ Breeding males, with their *orange and black fins* and breeding tubercle-covered heads, are easily recognized. At other times of year a close look at the downward-facing mouth reveals a distinctive cartilaginous ridge on the lower lip.

### BLACKNOSE DACE    *Rhinichthys atratulus*

Found in small to medium-sized streams in rocky pools and runs. ▶ This is a small silver-gray minnow with tiny scales and many black speckles. The breeding male develops a wash of red. The mouth is downward-pointing, and the nose barely overhangs it. The nose is connected directly to the upper lip (no groove between).

### GOLDEN SHINER    *Notemigonus crysoleucas*

Found in vegetated ponds, lakes, swamps, and streams, Golden Shiners tolerate low oxygen well, and are popular as baitfish. ▶ This species has a very thin, tall body with a lateral line that curves strongly *downward*. It has a slightly upturned mouth and a scaleless keel along the belly between the pelvic and anal fins.

### SPOTFIN SHINER    *Cyprinella spiloptera*

Found in runs and pools of streams ranging from small creeks to large rivers. ▶ The Spotfin Shiner has shiny, silver scales that are taller than wide. It has a *blotch of black* in the *rear* portion of its dorsal fin, but no black pigment on the membranes of the front half of the dorsal fin.

### FATHEAD MINNOW    *Pimephales promelas*

Found in many habitats, including areas where water quality is distinctly inhospitable. ▶ It has very small, crowded scales in front of the dorsal fin, and a short, blunt head that is *flat* on top. There is usually a *herringbone pattern* on the upper front sides. The breeding male develops a black head with warty tubercles.

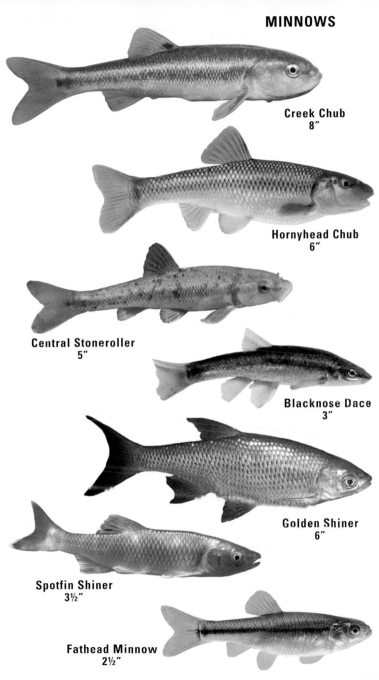

# MINNOWS

**Creek Chub**
8"

**Hornyhead Chub**
6"

**Central Stoneroller**
5"

**Blacknose Dace**
3"

**Golden Shiner**
6"

**Spotfin Shiner**
3½"

**Fathead Minnow**
2½"

# MINNOWS AND OTHER SMALL FISHES

The first three below are members of the minnow family, introduced on p. 314. The others are small minnowlike fishes of other families.

### COMMON SHINER    *Luxilus cornutus*
This species is found in rocky pools near riffles of small to medium-sized streams and in northern lakes. ▶ This is a whitish minnow with scales that are taller than wide. Adults have numerous *small dark crescents* along the sides of the body.

### REDFIN SHINER    *Lythrurus umbratilis*
Found in pools of small to medium-sized streams. ▶ The Redfin Shiner is deep-bodied with small, crowded scales on the nape, and its dorsal fin origin is behind the pelvic fin origin. There is a dark spot at the front base of the dorsal fin. The color ranges from olive to steel blue, and the breeding male develops red fins and blue head and body.

### EMERALD SHINER    *Notropis atherinoides*
This shiner is usually found in clear water over sand or gravel in lakes and medium to large rivers. ▶ This is one member of a genus *(Notropis)* that contains many very similar silvery, streamlined minnows. As shiners go, this species has a large mouth, with the rear edge extending backward to the eye. The origin of the dorsal fin is behind that of the pelvic fin.

### BROOK SILVERSIDE    *Labidesthes sicculus*
Despite its name, the Brook Silverside is most often found near the surface of open water in lakes and large streams. New World silverside family (Atherinopsidae). ▶ This is a very slender, silvery, and translucent fish. It has 2 dorsal fins (first one very small) and a long, beaklike snout about 1½ times longer than the eye diameter.

### CENTRAL MUDMINNOW    *Umbra limi*
This species is found in swamps, marshes, sloughs, and sluggish streams, often among mud and detritus. Pike family (Esocidae). ▶ The body form of this species is similar to that of a topminnow (see below) except that the mouth points forward (not upward) and the dorsal fin origin is far in front of the anal fin. There is a *black bar* at the base of the tail fin.

### BANDED KILLIFISH    *Fundulus diaphanus*
This species is found along the vegetated margins of lakes, ponds, and some streams. It feeds near the surface with its upturned mouth. Topminnow family (Fundulidae). ▶ The flattened head, upturned mouth, and dorsal fin located far back on the body give topminnows a distinctive shape. This species has 10–20 *brown bars* intermingled with *green-blue iridescence* on its sides.

### BLACKSTRIPE TOPMINNOW    *Fundulus notatus*
This is one of the more conspicuous fish usually seen near the surface of stream pools, lakes, and ponds. Topminnow family. ▶ Typical topminnow shape with flattened head, upturned mouth, and dorsal fin located far back on the body. This species has a *black stripe* on the sides, extending around the face and across the snout.

**Common Shiner**
3½"

**Redfin Shiner**
3½"

**Emerald Shiner**
3½"

**Brook Silverside**
3"

**Central Mudminnow**
2½"

**Banded Killifish**
4"

**Blackstripe Topminnow**
2½"

# DARTERS AND SCULPINS

These are small fish, generally living closer to the bottom than to the surface. The first six below are darters in the perch family (**Percidae**). There are roughly 200 species of darters in the U.S., and only a few can be included here. They have two dorsal fins, a spinous first dorsal and a second dorsal with soft rays.

### LOGPERCH    *Percina caprodes*
This is one of the largest darter species. It is often found on the bottom of pools in rocky streams, but can also inhabit vegetated lakes and impoundments. ▶ The Logperch has a protruding snout and a pattern of alternating *long and short vertical brown bars* on its tan sides.

### JOHNNY DARTER    *Etheostoma nigrum*
This darter is often found in pools of small- to medium-sized streams and along the shores of sandy lakes. ▶ This is a small, light-colored darter with a pattern of thin-lined *X and W markings* along its sides.

### BANDED DARTER    *Etheostoma zonale*
This darter is found in rock riffles in streams ranging from small creeks to medium-sized rivers. ▶ The Banded Darter has a pattern of 9–13 *vertical green bars* along its sides. Some of these extend under the caudal peduncle (just in front of the tail fin) to join the band on the other side.

### RAINBOW DARTER    *Etheostoma caeruleum*
This colorful species is found in riffles of small- to medium-sized rocky streams. ▶ This is a deep-bodied darter. The male is brilliant in the early spring breeding season. He has dark blue vertical bars along the sides with red between. The *red anal fin* has a *blue edge*. This latter character is present even in the relatively drab females and nonbreeding males.

### FANTAIL DARTER    *Etheostoma flabellare*
This species is found in streams ranging from tiny creeks to huge rivers. The dark-headed male, guarding eggs that are attached to the underside of flat rocks (and other surfaces), often can be found by lifting rocks in spring. ▶ This species has a protruding lower jaw and amber egglike decorations in the first dorsal fin of the male (especially prominent in spring).

### IOWA DARTER    *Etheostoma exile*
This species occurs farther north and west than any other darter, and is widespread in the northern two-thirds of our region. It can be a common fish in vegetated lakes and small- to medium-sized streams. ▶ This is a slender darter with a black teardrop. The breeding male has an alternating pattern of *blue and red bars* on the sides, and its front dorsal has a red band sandwiched between 2 blue bands. Clear anal fin.

### MOTTLED SCULPIN    *Cottus bairdii*
This species is found in tiny streams to medium-sized rivers and along rocky lake shores. Sculpin family (Cottidae). ▶ Sculpins have huge heads, large mouths, and no scales. The Mottled Sculpin's 2 dorsal fins are separate to the base, but not widely spaced.

# DARTERS AND SCULPINS

Logperch
6"

Johnny
Darter
2"

Banded Darter
2¼"

Rainbow
Darter
2¼"

Fantail Darter
2"

Iowa
Darter
2¼"

Mottled Sculpin
3½"

319

### AMERICAN BROOK LAMPREY  *Lethenteron appendix*

This lamprey lives in the sand and gravel of swift, clear stream riffles and runs. It is a nonparasitic species that feeds on detritus as a larval form for several years before transforming into an adult. Lamprey family (Petromyzontidae). ▶ The dorsal fin of this species is divided into 2 parts connected at the base. It has several groups of well-developed teeth, and the oral disk is *narrower* than the head.

### SILVER LAMPREY  *Ichthyomyzon unicuspis* (not shown)

This lamprey lives in lakes, large rivers, and impoundments as an adult, but migrates into smaller streams to spawn in spring. Larvae eat detritus, but adults are parasitic on other fishes. Lamprey family. ▶ The dorsal fin of this species has only a shallow notch and is not divided into 2 parts. The oral disc is at least as wide as the head, and teeth on either side of the throat opening are single-pointed. The **Sea Lamprey** *(Petromyzon marinus),* an invasive species to the Great Lakes that is partially responsible for lake trout declines, has prominent black mottling and a dorsal fin widely divided into 2 parts.

### MOONEYE  *Hiodon tergisus*

This species is found in large rivers, lakes, and impoundments, where it feeds on invertebrates. Mooneye family (Hiodontidae). ▶ A silvery fish similar to shad, but with an untoothed keel on the belly and a lateral line. The **Goldeye** *(H. alosoides),* the only other member of this family, is similar but has the anal fin even with the dorsal fin, not farther back.

### ALEWIFE  *Alosa pseudoharengus*

This species is found in the open water of large lakes. It is native to coastal waters and Lake Ontario, but was introduced to the other Great Lakes through Welland Canal. It upsets native food chains, and is infamous for the smelly die-offs that sometimes wash ashore when populations plummet. Shad family (Clupeidae). ▶ Members of the shad family have a sharp, sawtooth keel on the belly. This species *lacks* a thin filament attached to the dorsal fin and has a dark spot directly behind the upper gill cover.

### GIZZARD SHAD  *Dorosoma cepedianum*

This species is most common in large rivers, lakes, and impoundments. Shad family. ▶ Members of the shad family have a sharp, sawtooth keel on the belly. The Gizzard Shad has a thin filament extending backward from the dorsal fin, a downward-pointing mouth, a very blunt snout, and a deep notch in the center of the upper jaw.

### BROOK STICKLEBACK  *Culaea inconstans*

This species is found in lakes, ponds, creeks, and small rivers, usually in vegetated areas over a muddy bottom. Stickleback family (Gasterosteidae). ▶ Brook Sticklebacks have no scales, and the portion of the body in front of the tail fin (the caudal peduncle) is extremely narrow. The first dorsal fin consists of 4–6 short, isolated dorsal spines.

# SMALL AND SLENDER FISHES
### (sizes given are average lengths of adults)

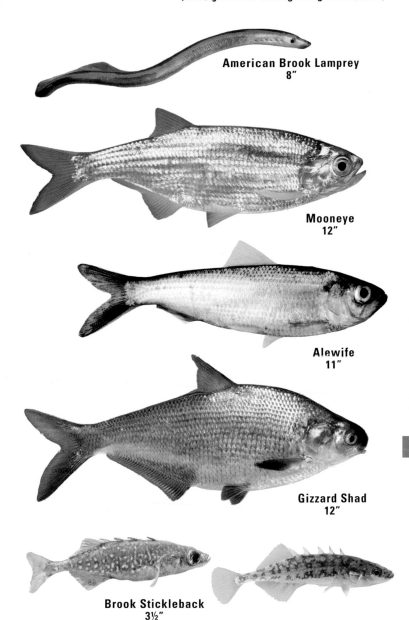

**American Brook Lamprey**
**8″**

**Mooneye**
**12″**

**Alewife**
**11″**

**Gizzard Shad**
**12″**

**Brook Stickleback**
**3½″**
**(2 examples)**

(order **Lepidoptera**) are undoubtedly the world's most popular insects (well, at least the butterflies are), and they are so conspicuous that we have placed them in their own section. For more information about the insects in general — most of which will apply equally well to butterflies and moths — please see the introduction to the next section.

**Life cycles** are similar for butterflies and moths. They all go through a complete metamorphosis, so their appearance and form change utterly during their lives. All begin life as an egg, which hatches into a caterpillar, also called a larva (plural, larvae). The larva has six legs like other insects but usually appears to have more, with several pairs of prolegs down the length of the body. The larva is an eating machine, munching away on a specific kind of food (usually a certain plant, or members of a certain group of plants) and growing. As the larva grows, it sheds its exoskeleton (or "skin") several times; the stages between these molts are called instars. After it is full grown, it pupates. The pupa of a butterfly is often called a chrysalis, while the pupa of a moth is often enclosed in a cocoon. Finally, the winged adult will emerge from the pupa, to begin the cycle again.

### LIFE CYCLE OF A BUTTERFLY (Black Swallowtail)

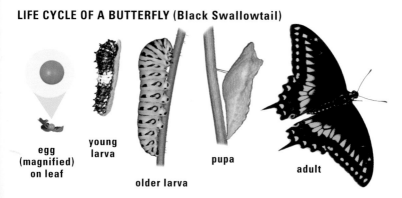

egg
(magnified)
on leaf

young
larva

older larva

pupa

adult

    In the rest of this section, when we mention butterflies or moths, we'll be talking about the adults unless specified otherwise.

**Butterflies vs. Moths:** These two groups may have very different reputations, but actual differences between them are minor. Butterflies are often considered to be more colorful, but there are many drab butterflies and many colorful moths. Butterflies in the Midwest are active only by day, while most moths are active mainly at night; however, a number of day-flying moths are common here. Butterflies usually rest with their wings spread out to the sides or raised straight above their backs, while moths often rest with their wings folded rooflike over their backs, but many moths are exceptions to this usual posture.

The two groups differ most visibly in their antennae. Butterflies have thickened "knobs" at the tip of each antenna, while the antennae of moths in North America are threadlike or fernlike, with no thickened tip.

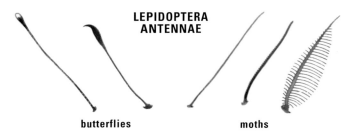

**LEPIDOPTERA ANTENNAE**

butterflies                    moths

A less-obvious distinction is in the diversity of each group. About 140 species of butterflies occur regularly in the Midwest. The number of moth species here is probably well over 3,500! Many are tiny "micro-moths," but that still leaves a rich variety for moth-watchers to enjoy.

**Finding butterflies** is a warm-season activity. Many butterflies are active only when the sun is shining, although a few will fly on cloudy days or in deep shade. Most will come to flowers for nectar, so gardens or fields of wildflowers are good places to look. There are a few kinds that rarely visit flowers but may come to rotten fruit, animal droppings, or even carrion. And some, especially blues and sulphurs, gather in "puddle parties" at the muddy margins of ponds, finding nutrients in the wet mud.

**Finding moths** is possible for much of the year in the Midwest; a few cold-tolerant species fly very late into the fall or very early in spring. Most nocturnal moths (but not all) are attracted to lights at night. Hanging a bright light up next to a white sheet or wall, close to a woodlot or other natural habitat, will attract a variety of moths. Some species come to "moth bait": our favorite recipe is a combination of rotten bananas, brown sugar, and stale (and cheap) beer, stirred up and painted on tree trunks. This is one of the best ways to attract underwing moths (p. 346).

**Rearing butterflies or moths** is a rewarding and educational experience. If you find the eggs or larvae in the wild, you can bring them indoors to raise and observe — just make sure you keep them supplied with fresh foliage from the same species of plant on which you found them. Cleaning out the container frequently will help to prevent mold and fungal infections. When the larvae stop eating and start crawling around inside the container, they are probably looking for a place to pupate. Most will either hang from an upright stem or burrow under dirt to pupate, so if you don't know what species you have, give them several options. Later, when the adult emerges from the pupa, you'll have a better chance of identifying it.

# SWALLOWTAILS

(family **Papilionidae**) include our largest butterflies. All species in our area have "tails" on the hindwings. Young caterpillars of many resemble bird droppings, but the older caterpillars have strong patterns.

### EASTERN TIGER SWALLOWTAIL    *Papilio glaucus*

Common and widespread in summer in woodland edges, open country, visiting flowers and puddles. ▶ Typical adults, yellow with black stripes, easy to recognize except where range meets that of Canadian Tiger Swallowtail. Some females are very dark with only a shadow of stripes; these are most common toward the south. **Larval foodplant:** cottonwood, Tuliptree, other trees.

### CANADIAN TIGER SWALLOWTAIL    *Papilio canadensis*

Common in northernmost parts of our region. ▶ Very similar to Eastern Tiger, but usually smaller and paler yellow. On underside of forewing, the pale stripe near the edge is *more continuous*, not broken into spots. The 2 species may interbreed where their ranges overlap. **Larval foodplant:** birch, aspen, other trees.

### ZEBRA SWALLOWTAIL    *Eurytides marcellus*

An elegant butterfly of spring and summer, usually seen in swift flight through moist forest and nearby clearings, but easy to approach at flowers. Rare northward; sometimes wanders north of mapped range. ▶ Pale greenish white with black stripes, *long* tails, *red* on hindwing. **Larval foodplant:** pawpaws.

### BLACK SWALLOWTAIL    *Papilio polyxenes*

Very common and widespread in open country, less numerous in heavily forested regions. ▶ Blackish above with 2 rows of yellow spots, more obvious on males. Blue sheen on hindwing, orange spots on underside of hindwing. Compare to next 2 species. **Larval foodplant:** parsley family: Queen Anne's Lace, dill, parsley, etc.

### SPICEBUSH SWALLOWTAIL    *Papilio troilus*

Most numerous toward the south, in forest clearings, meadows. ▶ Similar to Black Swallowtail (including double row of orange spots on underside of hindwing) but with pale green clouding on upperside. **Larval foodplant:** mainly spicebush and sassafras.

### PIPEVINE SWALLOWTAIL    *Battus philenor*

A southern swallowtail, sometimes common in the south of our region, scarcer northward. Some other dark butterflies may gain protection by "mimicking" this species, which carries distasteful compounds from its larval feeding. ▶ Black with *blue* sheen, *single* row of orange spots on hindwing below. See Red-spotted Purple (p. 336). **Larval foodplant:** pipevine.

### GIANT SWALLOWTAIL    *Papilio cresphontes*

Another southern butterfly that reaches our region. ▶ Very large. Wings dark above, with 2 pale bands that *cross* near wingtip. Wings pale yellow below. **Larval foodplant:** hoptree, rue, other members of citrus family.

# SWALLOWTAILS

**Eastern Tiger Swallowtail**

(gray outline = actual size)

larva

**Canadian Tiger Swallowtail**

**Zebra Swallowtail**

**Black Swallowtail**

larva

**Spicebush Swallowtail**

**Pipevine Swallowtail**

**Giant Swallowtail**

larva

# WHITES AND SULPHURS

(family **Pieridae**) are familiar fliers, common in open country. Most keep their wings folded above their backs when at rest, showing their bright uppersides mainly in flight. See three additional small species on p. 328.

### CABBAGE WHITE  *Pieris rapae*

Introduced from the Old World, now among our most abundant butterflies, flying from early spring to late fall. ▶ Forewing with 1 or 2 black central dots, dark tip. Hindwing below plain yellowish white. **Larval foodplant:** cabbage, others in mustard family.

### MUSTARD WHITE  *Pieris oleracea*

An uncommon white of northern forest, flying in late spring and early summer. ▶ Plain white above; below with dark scaling along veins, darker in spring. **Larval foodplant:** rock cress, other mustards.

### CHECKERED WHITE  *Pontia protodice*

Mainly a southern species, scarce toward northern edge of our region. ▶ Square dark spot on forewing, usually checkered edges, darker on female. **Larval foodplant:** many plants in mustard family.

### FALCATE ORANGETIP  *Anthocharis midea*

An early spring delight of woodland clearings. ▶ Tip of forewing *curved and pointed;* underside of hindwing marbled brown. Male has *orange* wingtips. **Larval foodplant:** rock cress, other mustards.

### OLYMPIA MARBLE  *Euchloe olympia*

Another spring flier, uncommon and local in dunes, savannah, cedar glades. ▶ Mostly white above, sparse yellow-green pattern on hindwing below. **Larval foodplant:** mainly rock cress.

### CLOUDED SULPHUR  *Colias philodice*

This and the next species are the common yellow butterflies of open country, towns. ▶ Lemon yellow, with black borders on upperside. Some females are mostly white. Compare to Orange Sulphur. **Larval foodplant:** alfalfa, clover, other plants in pea family.

### ORANGE SULPHUR  *Colias eurytheme*

Even more common than Clouded Sulphur in southern half of our region. Both species fly from early spring to late fall. ▶ Very much like Clouded Sulphur but has some orange above. The two sometimes interbreed, so some that look intermediate may not be identifiable. **Larval foodplant:** alfalfa, other plants in pea family.

### SOUTHERN DOGFACE  *Zerene cesonia*
A southern sulphur that wanders north to our region, sometimes in good numbers. ▶ Pattern on upperside, like a poodle's face, may show through from below. Note *pointed forewing.* **Larval foodplant:** plants in pea family.

### CLOUDLESS SULPHUR  *Phoebis sennae*
A subtropical species, wandering north every summer. ▶ *Twice the size* of our other sulphurs. Yellow to whitish above, varied brown marks below.

# WHITES AND SULPHURS

actual size

**Cabbage White**

**Mustard White**

**Checkered White**

male

**Falcate Orangetip**

**Olympia Marble**

**Clouded Sulphur**

**Orange Sulphur**

**Southern Dogface**

**Cloudless Sulphur**

327

# SMALL SULPHURS AND HAIRSTREAKS

Sulphurs were introduced on p. 326. Hairstreaks, of the gossamer-wing family (**Lycaenidae**), are small and subtle. Most have thin "tails" on the hindwings, and most perch with their wings folded above their backs.

### LITTLE YELLOW   *Pyrisitia lisa*

Common toward the south, flying low in open country. ▶ Small, with rounded wings. Male bright yellow, female yellow to whitish above, with *narrow* black borders. **Larval foodplant**: sennas.

### DAINTY SULPHUR   *Nathalis iole*

Flutters close to the ground in weedy places; wanders north in late summer. ▶ *Tiny and dingy*. Underside shows dull hindwing, black spots on forewing. **Larval foodplant**: various asters.

### SLEEPY ORANGE   *Abaeis nicippe*

Uncommon in southern areas, wandering farther north. ▶ Orange above with *wide* black borders. Mottled below. **Larval foodplant**: sennas.

### GRAY HAIRSTREAK   *Strymon melinus*

Widespread in many habitats, including gardens. ▶ Unlike most hairstreaks, may perch with wings open. *Very gray* above and below. Orange spot near "tail." **Larval foodplant**: flowers of many plants.

### BANDED HAIRSTREAK   *Satyrium calanus*

The most common of several brown hairstreaks of forest edge, meadows. ▶ Brown below with narrow white bands. Orange and blue spots near "tail." **Larval foodplant**: oaks and hickories.

### CORAL HAIRSTREAK   *Satyrium titus*

Common in brushy fields. Often attracted to orange flowers of Butterfly-weed. ▶ No "tails." Brownish gray, with *row of orange spots* on hindwing. **Larval foodplant**: wild cherry, wild plum.

### BROWN ELFIN   *Callophrys augustinus*

A spring butterfly of bogs, rocky woodlands, barrens. ▶ Warm brown below, usually darker at base of hindwing, more reddish toward margins. **Larval foodplant**: blueberries and other heaths.

### EASTERN PINE ELFIN   *Callophrys niphon*

Another spring flier, usually found perching on pines or on nearby flowers. ▶ *Striking pattern* below, with black and chestnut bands, whitish edges. **Larval foodplant**: Jack Pine and other pines.

### JUNIPER HAIRSTREAK   *Callophrys gryneus*

This little gem is uncommon and local around groves of Eastern Redcedar, and is easy to overlook when perched on the foliage. ▶ Greenish below with brown tinges and sharp white marks. **Larval foodplant**: Eastern Redcedar.

### WHITE-M HAIRSTREAK   *Parrhasius m-album*

Uncommon in southern part of our region. ▶ Large for a hairstreak. White band on hindwing makes an M (or W?) mark near tail. In flight, shows *brilliant blue upperside*. **Larval foodplant**: oaks.

# SMALL SULPHURS AND HAIRSTREAKS

**Little Yellow**

**Dainty Sulphur**

actual size

**Sleepy Orange**

**Gray Hairstreak**

**Banded Hairstreak**

actual size

**Coral Hairstreak**

**Brown Elfin**

**Eastern Pine Elfin**

**Juniper Hairstreak**

**White-M Hairstreak**

# BLUES, COPPERS, AND HARVESTER

make up three subfamilies of the gossamer-wing family, introduced on p. 328. These tiny butterflies are often common, but easy to overlook.

### EASTERN TAILED-BLUE    *Cupido comyntas*

Common in gardens and open country. ▶ Whitish below with *orange spot* on hindwing. Threadlike "tails" hard to see. Male blue above, female mostly gray. **Larval foodplant:** clover and others.

### SPRING AZURE/SUMMER AZURE    *Celastrina sp.*

Very common in spring and summer, probably comprising at least 2 species. ▶ Usually lightly marked below, especially in summer. Upperside of male bright pale blue; females vary from blue to white, with wide black borders. **Larval foodplant:** varied.

### SILVERY BLUE    *Glaucopsyche lygdamus*

An early spring blue, more common in the north. ▶ Rows of *round black spots* on both forewing and hindwing below. Male silvery blue above, female duller. **Larval foodplant:** vetches.

### REAKIRT'S BLUE    *Echinargus isola*

A southwestern blue, sometimes wandering throughout our region. ▶ Forewing below has row of *round, white-ringed black spots*. Hindwing more varied. **Larval foodplant:** flowers of legumes.

### "KARNER BLUE"    *Plebejus melissa samuelis*

An endangered race of the western Melissa Blue. Very local in oak savannah, meadows. ▶ *Row of orange spots* near edge of hindwing. A similar blue at far northern border of region would be **Northern Blue** (*Plebejus idas*). **Larval foodplant:** wild lupine.

### AMERICAN COPPER    *Lycaena phlaeas*

Common in roadsides, pastures, fields. Flies low, perching on ground or visiting flowers. ▶ Sharply two-toned. *Narrow* orange stripe on hindwing below. **Larval foodplant:** Sheep Sorrel.

### BRONZE COPPER    *Lycaena hyllus*

Widespread but usually uncommon, around marshes and wet meadows. ▶ Like American Copper but larger, with *broad* orange band near edge of hindwing. **Larval foodplant:** docks.

### GRAY COPPER    *Lycaena dione*

A large copper of prairies and damp meadows. ▶ *Mostly gray* above and below (including underside of forewing), with broad orange band on hindwing. **Larval foodplant:** docks.

### HARVESTER    *Feniseca tarquinius*

Uncommon and local, and rarely visits flowers, but may be seen basking on leaves near streams. ▶ Mostly red-brown below with *circular white marks*. Orange above with blotchy black border. **Larval foodplant:** not a plant! The carnivorous larvae feed on aphids, especially woolly aphids living on alders.

# BLUES, COPPERS, AND HARVESTER

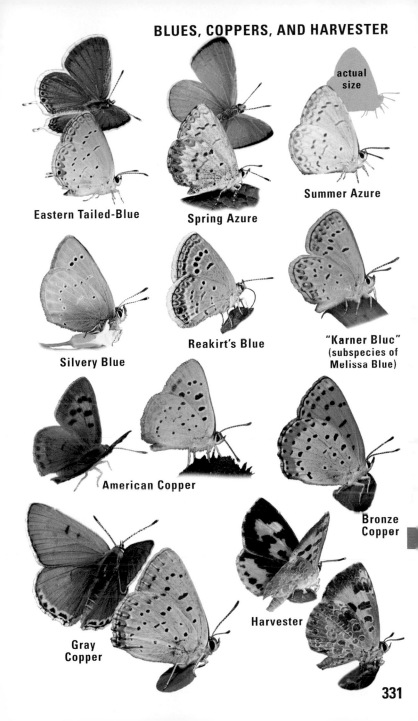

actual size

**Summer Azure**

**Eastern Tailed-Blue**

**Spring Azure**

**Silvery Blue**

**Reakirt's Blue**

**"Karner Blue"**
(subspecies of
Melissa Blue)

**American Copper**

**Bronze Copper**

**Gray Copper**

**Harvester**

# FRITILLARIES, CRESCENTS, CHECKERSPOTS

have intricate patterns above, more distinctive markings below. Almost 20 species occur in the Midwest; we show the most common. These are in the family **Nymphalidae,** brushfooted butterflies. They appear to have only four legs because the front two are reduced to brushy stubs.

## GREAT SPANGLED FRITILLARY    *Speyeria cybele*

Common and widespread, a splash of color in summer fields and gardens. ▶ Bright orange with fine black pattern. Hindwing below has silver spots, *broad pale band*. **Larval foodplant:** violets.

## APHRODITE FRITILLARY    *Speyeria aphrodite*

Usually less common than the preceding species. ▶ Like Great Spangled but a little smaller. On hindwing below, pale band paralleling outer edge looks *narrower*. **Larval foodplant:** violets.

## REGAL FRITILLARY    *Speyeria idalia*

A vanishing species. Formerly common in much of the Midwest, now gone from many areas. Still locally common in some tallgrass prairies. ▶ Large, with rounded wings. *Dark hindwings* (with *large white spots*), orange forewings. **Larval foodplant:** violets.

## MEADOW FRITILLARY    *Boloria bellona*

Several "lesser fritillaries" reach the Midwest; only this one is common, in open fields of all kinds. ▶ Smaller than the 3 preceding species, with forewings more *square-tipped*. Underside of hindwing has *muted* pattern. **Larval foodplant:** violets.

## VARIEGATED FRITILLARY    *Euptoieta claudia*

A southern species, moving north in summer, in open habitats. ▶ Orange-brown, with no silvery spots below. *Dark-rimmed pale spot* in center of forewing. **Larval foodplant:** passion vines, others.

## PEARL CRESCENT    *Phyciodes tharos*

Very common but easily overlooked, flitting close to the ground, visiting flowers in fields, roadsides, gardens. ▶ Very small, orange with intricate pattern above. Hindwing below usually pale yellow, lightly marked. In northern half of our region, overlaps with **Northern Crescent** (*P. cocyta),* almost identical but averaging a little larger. **Larval foodplant:** many kinds of asters.

## SILVERY CHECKERSPOT    *Chlosyne nycteis*

Widespread but often uncommon in streamsides, meadows, woodland edges. ▶ A little larger than Pearl Crescent, with wider black borders above, more varied pattern on underside of hindwing. **Larval foodplant:** Black-eyed Susan, wingstem, and others.

## BALTIMORE CHECKERSPOT    *Euphydryas phaeton*

A striking creature, living in local colonies around damp meadows, woodland edges. ▶ Unmistakable pattern of black, white, and orange-red. **Larval foodplant:** turtlehead, plantain, others.

# FRITILLARIES AND OTHERS

Great Spangled
Fritillary

actual
size

Aphrodite Fritillary

Regal Fritillary

Meadow Fritillary

Variegated
Fritillary

Pearl Crescent

Silvery Checkerspot

Baltimore
Checkerspot

## TYPICAL BRUSHFOOTS

This diverse family was introduced on p. 332. Most of these typically fly with several quick flaps followed by a flat-winged glide.

### EASTERN COMMA  *Polygonia comma*

In woods, usually at puddles or sap flows, not flowers. ▶ Angular wings; hindwing above may be black or orange. *Silver "comma"* in center of hindwing below. **Larval foodplant:** elms, nettles, hops.

### QUESTION MARK  *Polygonia interrogationis*

Hibernates as adult, may fly in winter thaws. ▶ Forewing with one more black spot than Eastern Comma. *Silver "question mark"* in center of hindwing below. **Larval foodplant:** elms, nettles, others.

### MILBERT'S TORTOISESHELL  *Aglais milberti*

Often common in north, visiting flowers in meadows, but numbers vary from year to year. ▶ Gray below; above wings dark at base, with orange-yellow outer band. **Larval foodplant:** nettles.

### COMPTON TORTOISESHELL  *Nymphalis l-album*

Uncommon in northern woods. Hibernates as adult. ▶ Angular wings, orange and black above, darker at base. *White spot* near leading edge of hindwing. **Larval foodplant:** aspens, birches, willows.

### MOURNING CLOAK  *Nymphalis antiopa*

Common, but usually seen singly. Hibernates as adult, may fly in early spring or during winter thaws. ▶ Rich brown above with *cream-yellow borders.* **Larval foodplant:** willows, birches, others.

### RED ADMIRAL  *Vanessa atalanta*

Common, sometimes abundant, invading northward in open country. ▶ Dark with *red-orange slashes* across wings. Cryptic, varied pattern below. **Larval foodplant:** nettles and related plants.

### AMERICAN LADY  *Vanessa virginiensis*

Fairly common in summer in open areas. ▶ On hindwing above, spots near trailing edge seem *smeared together.* Underside of hindwing has *2 large spots.* **Larval foodplant:** everlastings, others.

### PAINTED LADY  *Vanessa cardui*

An irregular migrant, varying from rare to common. ▶ Like American Lady but spots near hindwing edge *more separated,* both above and below. **Larval foodplant:** thistles, mallows, others.

### COMMON BUCKEYE  *Junonia coenia*

A regular invader from the south, often becoming very common in open country by late summer. ▶ Brown, with pattern of *bars and bold round spots* above. **Larval foodplant:** plantains and others.

### AMERICAN SNOUT  *Libytheana carinenta*

This odd butterfly is another that moves north through our area in late summer. ▶ Long, *snoutlike palpi.* Forewings square-tipped. Orange and white marks above. **Larval foodplant:** hackberries.

# TYPICAL BRUSHFOOTED BUTTERFLIES

**Eastern Comma**

actual size

**Question Mark larva**

**Question Mark**

**Milbert's Tortoiseshell**

**Compton Tortoiseshell**

**Mourning Cloak**

**Red Admiral**

larva

**American Lady**

**Painted Lady**

**Common Buckeye**

**American Snout**

335

### MONARCH  *Danaus plexippus*

Multiple generations move north in spring from wintering sites; final fall brood migrates from Midwest back to Mexico. ▶ *Large.* Orange with *black veins,* white dots on body. **Larval foodplant:** milkweeds; their chemicals make Monarchs distasteful to birds.

### VICEROY  *Limenitis archippus*

Common around streams, willows. ▶ Related to next species, but gains protection from predators because it looks like Monarch. Note *bar across hindwing.* **Larval foodplant:** willows, aspens, others.

### WHITE ADMIRAL  *Limenitis arthemis arthemis*

Common in northern forest edges. This and Red-spotted Purple are forms of the same species, and often interbreed. ▶ *Wide white band* across wings. **Larval foodplant:** leaves of many trees.

### RED-SPOTTED PURPLE  *Limenitis arthemis astyanax*

Common in southern Midwest. A mimic of Pipevine Swallowtail (p. 324). ▶ Blue iridescence, orange-red spots. Intermediates with White Admiral often seen. **Larval foodplant:** leaves of many trees.

### HACKBERRY EMPEROR  *Asterocampa celtis*

Fairly common at forest edge, mostly visiting sap or rotting fruit, not flowers. ▶ Dull orange with eyespot near edge of forewing, broken spots near leading edge. **Larval foodplant:** hackberries.

### TAWNY EMPEROR  *Asterocampa clyton*

As with Hackberry Emperor, seldom visits flowers. Often perches on tree trunks (or on people). ▶ Lacks eyespot on forewing; has 2 *unbroken* bars near leading edge. **Larval foodplant:** hackberries.

### LITTLE WOOD-SATYR  *Megisto cymela*

This and the next 3 are in the subfamily Satyrinae, formerly considered a separate family. This is a woodland butterfly with low, bouncy flight. ▶ Small *black wing spots* with yellow rings. Narrow reddish bands on underside of wings. **Larval foodplant:** grasses.

### COMMON WOOD-NYMPH  *Cercyonis pegala*

Common in meadows, woodland edges. ▶ Two *large eyespots* on forewing; fine wavy lines on underside. Some have large *yellow patch* surrounding the forewing spots. **Larval foodplant:** grasses.

### NORTHERN PEARLY-EYE  *Enodia anthedon*

Locally common in woods, clearings, coming to sap or rotting fruit, but not flowers. ▶ Relatively long wings; *bold pattern of large eyespots* on forewing and hindwing. **Larval foodplant:** grasses.

### COMMON RINGLET  *Coenonympha tullia*

A northern satyr, spreading south in Midwest, often in very open habitats. ▶ Gray and orange-brown, with small spot near tip of forewing, *pale line* on hindwing below. **Larval foodplant:** grasses.

# BRUSHFOOTED BUTTERFLIES

**Monarch larva on milkweed**

**Monarch**

actual size

**White Admiral**

**Viceroy**

**Red-spotted Purple**

**Hackberry Emperor**

**Tawny Emperor**

**Little Wood-Satyr**

**Common Wood-Nymph**

**Northern Pearly-eye**

**Common Ringlet**

# SKIPPERS

(family **Hesperiidae**) are mostly small, thick-bodied butterflies with hooked antenna tips. More than 60 species occur in the Midwest.

### SILVER-SPOTTED SKIPPER    *Epargyreus clarus*

Of the whole confusing skipper clan, this one is the simplest to identify, and one of the most common. A fast flier, but often easy to approach at flowers. ▶ A big skipper with gold bands on forewings, *silver spot* on hindwing below. **Larval foodplant:** legumes.

### NORTHERN CLOUDYWING    *Thorybes pylades*

Fairly common in clearings, open woods. ▶ Dark dusky brown with tiny white dots on forewing. Usually sits on flowers with wings only *half-opened.* **Larval foodplant:** various legumes.

### JUVENAL'S DUSKYWING    *Erynnis juvenalis*

Duskywings are dark, fast-flying skippers that sit with wings spread out flat. At least 8 similar species occur in the Midwest; this one is often most common in late spring. **Larval foodplant:** oaks.

### LEAST SKIPPER    *Ancyloxypha numitor*

In damp meadows and around marshes, this tiny skipper flutters weakly through the grass. ▶ Rounded wings look mostly dark on upperside, pale orange below. **Larval foodplant:** grasses.

### COMMON CHECKERED-SKIPPER    *Pyrgus communis*

A skipper of open fields, vacant lots, sometimes common in late summer. Sits with its wings held flat. ▶ Strongly *checkered white pattern* on dark gray wings. **Larval foodplant:** mallows.

### EUROPEAN SKIPPER    *Thymelicus lineola*

Introduced from Europe around 1910, still spreading westward, locally common in open country. ▶ Very small. Orange above, *veins blackened* inward from edges. Plain pale orange below. *Very short* antennae. **Larval foodplant:** timothy, other grasses.

### FIERY SKIPPER    *Hylephila phyleus*

A southern skipper, wandering north in late summer, sometimes common in fall in gardens, vacant lots. ▶ Wings yellow-orange below with small brown spots. Above, male's wings orange with black "toothed" margin, female darker. **Larval foodplant:** grasses.

### PECK'S SKIPPER    *Polites peckius*

Very common throughout the warmer seasons, in fields, gardens, roadsides. ▶ Underside rich brown with 2 *big yellow patches* on hindwing; a *central blotch* juts out from outer one. Orange and black above like many other skippers. **Larval foodplant:** grasses.

### HOBOMOK SKIPPER    *Poanes hobomok*

Common in woodland edges in early summer. ▶ Underside of hindwing brown with *broad yellow blotch* on outer half. Some females are mostly dark brown. **Larval foodplant:** grasses.

# SKIPPERS

Silver-spotted
Skipper

actual
size

Northern
Cloudywing

Juvenal's Duskywing

Least Skipper

Common
Checkered-Skipper

European Skipper

Fiery
Skipper

Peck's
Skipper

Hobomok
Skipper

# GIANT SILKMOTHS

(family **Saturniidae**) include some of our largest lepidoptera, but some are only medium-sized. They feed voraciously as larvae, but adults have only rudimentary mouthparts and do not feed at all. Adult females "call" to males by releasing a pheromone; males may follow this faint scent on the breeze for almost a mile in some cases.

### LUNA MOTH    *Actias luna*

Perhaps our most beautiful moth, and still fairly common in forested regions. It comes to lights at night from late spring through midsummer. ▶ Unmistakable. Large, pale green, with long "tails" on hindwings. **Larval foodplant:** Paper Birch, hickories, and others.

### IMPERIAL MOTH    *Eacles imperialis*

Mostly uncommon in wooded regions, flying mainly in midsummer. ▶ Note large size, wing shape. Patches of yellow and violet-brown. **Larval foodplant:** many, including oak, maple, pine.

### REGAL MOTH    *Citheronia regalis*

Uncommon in wooded regions. Best known for spectacular larva, "hickory horned devil." ▶ Adult orange-brown, wings marked with creamy spots and *red along veins*. Full-grown larva has curved "horns" on head. **Larval foodplant:** hickories and others.

### POLYPHEMUS MOTH    *Antheraea polyphemus*

Adults fly from late spring through midsummer. If disturbed, they flash startling eyespots on hindwings. ▶ Huge, pale brown, with *large spots* on wings. **Larval foodplant:** many trees and shrubs.

### CECROPIA MOTH    *Hyalophora cecropia*

Widespread and common, mainly in wooded areas, flying from late spring through midsummer. ▶ Huge and colorful. Gray-brown with big white spots and red bands on wings. **Larval foodplant:** many trees and shrubs including maple, wild cherry, birch.

### PROMETHEA MOTH    *Callosamia promethea*

Active mainly in early summer. Females fly day or night, males mostly by day. ▶ Females reddish brown, males (not shown) *mostly black*. **Larval foodplant:** many trees and shrubs.

### IO MOTH    *Automeris io*

Common and widespread, mainly in wooded areas, often seen at lights in summer. ▶ Looks like a dead leaf until it spreads its wings, revealing *stunning eyespots* and *red stripes* on hindwings. Female browner than male. **Larval foodplant:** many trees and shrubs.

### ROSY MAPLE MOTH    *Dryocampa rubicunda*

Often a common visitor to lights at night in summer, especially in eastern part of region. ▶ Variable. Usually *pink wings* crossed by *yellow stripe*, but can be mostly creamy yellow. Fuzzy body white to yellow. **Larval foodplant:** maple, sometimes oak.

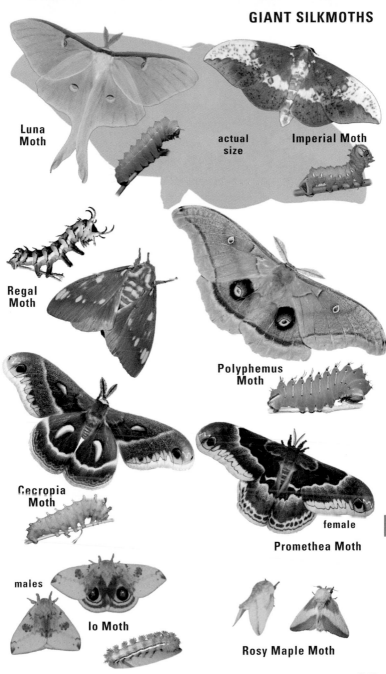

# GIANT SILKMOTHS

Luna Moth

actual size

Imperial Moth

Regal Moth

Polyphemus Moth

Cecropia Moth

female

Promethea Moth

males

Io Moth

Rosy Maple Moth

341

# SPHINX MOTHS

or hawkmoths (family **Sphingidae**) are strong, fast fliers that may hover at flowers in the manner of a hummingbird. They are generally among the larger moths. Their larvae are commonly called hornworms.

### WHITE-LINED SPHINX     *Hyles lineata*

Often active by day. Sometimes mistaken for a hummingbird as it hovers at garden flowers. ▶ Striped forewing, pink-barred hindwing. Larva variable. **Larval foodplant:** wide variety of plants.

### CAROLINA SPHINX     *Manduca sexta*

Most familiar for its larva, the common hornworm on tomatoes. ▶ Larva has reddish "horn." Adult has 6 pairs of yellow spots on abdomen. In **Five-spotted Sphinx** (*M. quinquemaculata*), adult has 5 pairs of spots. **Larval foodplant:** tomato and other nightshades.

### WAVED SPHINX     *Ceratomia undulosa*

Common, but may decline where ashes have been killed by Emerald Ash Borer. ▶ Brown forewing with dark *wavy lines,* dark-ringed white central spot. **Larval foodplant:** ash, also lilac, others.

### MODEST SPHINX     *Pachysphinx modesta*

Unlike many sphinx moths, adults of this species do not feed. They regularly come to lights. ▶ Heavy-bodied, gray, with darker band across forewing. **Larval foodplant:** poplar, cottonwood, aspen.

### HOG SPHINX     *Darapsa myron*

Also called Virginia Creeper Sphinx. Common in southern Midwest. ▶ Forewing marked *green* (duller when worn), hindwing washed *orange.* **Larval foodplant:** Virginia Creeper, grape, others.

### ONE-EYED SPHINX     *Smerinthus cerisyi*

Common, especially toward the north. In this and next 2 species, "eyes" in the names are eyespots on the hindwings. ▶ Grayish brown forewing. Blue eyespot (with one "pupil") in pink hindwing. **Larval foodplant:** poplar, willow, and others.

### SMALL-EYED SPHINX     *Paonias myops*

Common, often coming to lights at night. ▶ Dark brown. *Blue eyespot* on *yellow hindwing; orange stripe* on top of thorax. **Larval foodplant:** cherry, hawthorn, serviceberry, and others.

### BLINDED SPHINX     *Paonias excaecatus*

Common in forested areas. ▶ Warm brown. Blue eyespot (with no "pupil") in *pink hindwing. Black stripe* on top of thorax. **Larval foodplant:** various trees, including willow, basswood, birch.

### SNOWBERRY CLEARWING     *Hemaris diffinis*

This day-flying sphinx mimics a bumblebee. ▶ Longer antennae than bumblebee, and *hovers* in front of flowers (bees alight to feed). **Larval foodplant:** honeysuckle, snowberry, and others.

# SPHINX MOTHS

actual
size

**White-lined Sphinx**

**Carolina
Sphinx**

**Waved Sphinx**

**Modest Sphinx**

**Hog Sphinx**

**One-eyed Sphinx**

**Small-eyed
Sphinx**

**Blinded
Sphinx**

**Snowberry
Clearwing**

Our largest family of moths (**Noctuidae**), with hundreds of species here.

### GREAT OAK DAGGER    *Acronicta lobeliae*
A typical example of the more than 30 daggers in the Midwest. ▶ Pale gray with whitish lines, lengthwise black pattern. **Larval foodplant**: oaks.

### CORN EARWORM    *Helicoperva zea*
Moves north in late summer. Larva is a notable pest on corn. ▶ Forewing yellowish with darker band; hindwing gray. **Larval foodplant**: corn and others.

### DINGY CUTWORM    *Feltia jaculifera*
Common at lights in late summer and fall. Another moth named for its larva. ▶ Rich brown with black pattern. **Larval foodplant**: grasses, others.

### ARMYWORM MOTH    *Mythimna unipuncta*
Invades from the south, can be abundant by late summer. ▶ Tan with *white dot;* wingtip has dark line. **Larval foodplant**: feeds at night on many plants.

### IPSILON DART    *Agrotis ipsilon*
Another invader from the south, common in warmer months. ▶ Slim shape, *paler band* near wingtips. **Larval foodplant**: various low plants.

### HENRY'S MARSH MOTH    *Simyra insularis*
Fairly common around wetlands, open country. ▶ Whitish veins contrast with long brown streaks on wings. **Larval foodplant**: cattails, sedges, others.

### CELERY LOOPER    *Anagrapha falcifera*
Common; active day and night. ▶ Bumpy outline at rest. *Curved white line* surrounds *warm brown* inner area. **Larval foodplant**: many low plants.

### COMMON LOOPER    *Autographa precationis*
Common from spring to fall. ▶ Bumpy outline at rest. *Doubled silvery white spot* on forewing. **Larval foodplant**: many low plants.

### GREEN MARVEL    *Agripodes fallax*
Widespread but uncommon, flying in spring and summer. ▶ Pale green with thick, angular black markings. **Larval foodplant**: viburnum.

### LARGE YELLOW UNDERWING    *Noctua pronuba*
Introduced from Europe; unrelated to true underwings (p. 346). ▶ Forewing variable, hindwing yellow with black bar. **Larval foodplant**: grasses.

### BEAUTIFUL WOOD-NYMPH    *Eudryas grata*
By day, may rest on leaves, looking like a bird dropping. Also visits lights at night. ▶ Forewings white with *smooth-edged* brown border and edge markings; hindwings yellow. **Larval foodplant**: grape, Virginia Creeper.

### PEARLY WOOD-NYMPH    *Eudryas unio*
▶ Like preceding but with wavy border. **Larval foodplant**: many low plants.

### EIGHT-SPOTTED FORESTER    *Alypia octomaculata*
Visits flowers by day. ▶ Two *pale yellow* spots on each forewing, 2 white spots on each hindwing. **Larval foodplant**: grape, Virginia Creeper.

# NOCTUID MOTHS

**Great Oak Dagger**

**Corn Earworm**

actual size

**Dingy Cutworm**

**Armyworm Moth**

**Ipsilon Dart**

**Henry's Marsh Moth**

**Celery Looper**

**Common Looper**

**Green Marvel**

**Large Yellow Underwing**

**Eight-spotted Forester**

**Beautiful Wood-nymph**

**Pearly Wood-nymph**

These were formerly treated as members of the Noctuidae (see p. 344), but are now separated out in another large family, **Erebidae**.

### FORAGE LOOPER    *Caenurgina erechtea*
Very common, often flushed out of grassy fields during the day; also comes to lights at night. ▶ Pale brown to gray-brown with curved darker bars, spots near forewing tip. **Larval foodplant**: grasses, clover, other low plants.

### LUNATE ZALE    *Zale lunata*
Zales sit with their wings spread out to the sides, suggesting the posture of a geometer moth (p. 350). This is the most common of several species, often attracted to lights or to sugary bait. ▶ Wing edges finely scalloped; strong lines across wings, sometimes white patches. **Larval foodplant**: many.

### DARK-SPOTTED PALTHIS    *Palthis angulalis*
These odd little moths often come to lights. ▶ Distinctive *shape,* like a tiny fighter jet. Male has long palps ("snout"). **Larval foodplant**: various trees.

### GREEN CLOVERWORM    *Hypena scabra*
Often very common, especially in late summer. ▶ Long, *narrow,* triangular shape. Dark, plain; dark line at midwing. **Larval foodplant**: many low plants.

### HERALD MOTH    *Scoliopteryx libatrix*
Fairly common at lights, bait. Adults hibernate in winter. ▶ *Scalloped* wing edges; orange wash on gray wings. **Larval foodplant**: poplar and willow.

### DIMORPHIC BOMOLOCHA    *Hypena bijugalis*
Common around open woods, edges. ▶ Female (shown) has sharp-edged, rich brown patch on forewing. Other bomolochas are similar. Male is darker, with single white spot on forewing. **Larval foodplant**: dogwood.

### SWEETHEART UNDERWING    *Catocala amatrix*
Underwings have striking hindwing patterns, hidden by their cryptic fore-wings when at rest, good camouflage when on tree trunks. The Midwest has more than 45 species; this one is common. ▶ Pink stripes on hindwing; black patches on gray forewing. **Larval foodplant**: poplar and willow.

### DARLING UNDERWING    *Catocala cara*
Fairly common from midsummer to fall. ▶ Pink-striped hindwing; fore-wing dark with hints of green and purple. **Larval foodplant**: poplar, willow.

### OBSCURE UNDERWING    *Catocala obscura*
Common in forests in late summer. ▶ Hindwing black with whitish edge. Forewing gray, with obscure zigzag lines. **Larval foodplant**: hickory, walnut.

### YELLOW-BANDED UNDERWING    *Catocala cerogama*
Widespread, late summer to fall. ▶ *Even-edged* band of *ochre-yellow* on hindwing. Distinct pattern on gray forewing. **Larval foodplant**: basswood.

### WOODY UNDERWING    *Catocala grynea*
Common in summer. ▶ Small. Hindwing banded yellow-orange; rich brown on *inner edge* of forewing. **Larval foodplant**: apple, hawthorn, others.

# OWLET MOTHS

**Forage Looper**

**Lunate Zale**

actual size

**Dark-spotted Palthis**

**Green Cloverworm**

**Herald Moth**

**Dimorphic Bomolocha**

**Sweetheart Underwing**

**Darling Underwing**

**Obscure Underwing**

**Woody Underwing**

**Yellow-banded Underwing**

347

**(family Erebidae, subfamily Arctiinae)** mostly have very fuzzy larvae.

**ISABELLA TIGER MOTH** *Pyrrharctia isabella*
Best known for its larva, the "Woolly Bear" that crosses roads in fall and even in winter thaws. Adults visit lights in summer. ► Mustard yellow with brown dots, pinkish tinge. **Larval foodplant:** wide variety of plants.

**SALT MARSH MOTH** *Estigmene acrea*
Despite the name, common in many habitats. ► Dotted wings, *yellow* on abdomen. Smaller male has *yellow hindwings.* **Larval foodplant:** many.

**VIRGINIAN TIGER MOTH** *Spilosoma virginica*
Common from spring to fall, visiting lights. ► Adult white with black dots, some *yellow on body and legs.* Larva varies in color. **Larval foodplant:** many.

**GIANT LEOPARD MOTH** *Hypercompe scribonia*
Flies in summer, more common in southern areas. ► Large, white, with *blue-black spots and rings.* **Larval foodplant:** many trees and low plants.

**DELICATE CYCNIA** *Cycnia tenera*
Fairly common and widespread from spring to fall. ► Yellow head, *yellow leading edge* on silky white wings. **Larval foodplant:** Indian hemp, milkweed.

**HICKORY TUSSOCK MOTH** *Lophocampa caryae*
Common in early summer, often coming to lights. ► Network of pale or translucent spots, dark brown lines. **Larval foodplant:** hickory, other trees.

**HARNESSED TIGER MOTH** *Apantesis phalerata*
These tiger-striped moths are often common at lights. ► One of several similar species. Patterned forewing, colorful hindwing. **Larval foodplant:** many.

**LE CONTE'S HAPLOA** *Haploa lecontei*
Haploas fly by day or night, visiting flowers, lights. ► Creamy forewing with chocolate pattern. One of several similar species. **Larval foodplant:** asters.

**MILKWEED TUSSOCK MOTH** *Euchaetes egle*
Often found by people seeking Monarch larvae (p. 336). ► Tufts of rust, cream, and black. Adult gray, inconspicuous. **Larval foodplant:** milkweeds.

**VIRGINIA CTENUCHA** *Ctenucha virginica*
Visits lights at night, flowers by day. ► Suggests a wasp; note long antennae, *orange* head, *blue sheen* on body. **Larval foodplant:** grasses, sedges, others.

**YELLOW-COLLARED SCAPE MOTH** *Cisseps fulvicollis*
Another daytime flower visitor, often on goldenrod. ► Smaller than Virginia Ctenucha, duller, less blue. **Larval foodplant:** grasses, sedges, others.

**SCARLET-WINGED LICHEN MOTH** *Hypoprepia miniata*

**PAINTED LICHEN MOTH** *Hypoprepia fucosa*
These 2 colorful pixies are locally common in woods. ► **Scarlet-winged:** red thorax, wings striped red and gray. **Painted:** gray spot on thorax, more yellow mixed with red on wings. **Larval foodplant:** lichens growing on trees.

# TIGER MOTHS

**Isabella Tiger Moth**

larva
("Woolly Bear")

male

actual size

female

**Salt Marsh Moth**

larva

**Virginian Tiger Moth**

**Delicate Cycnia**

**Hickory Tussock Moth**

**Giant Leopard Moth**

**Le Conte's Haploa**

**Milkweed Tussock Moth**
larva

**Harnessed Tiger Moth**

**Scarlet-winged Lichen Moth**

**Virginia Ctenucha**

**Yellow-collared Scape Moth**

**Painted Lichen Moth**

(family **Geometridae**) make up another large family, with hundreds of species in the Midwest. Adults of many rest with wings spread out to the sides. Larvae are "inchworms" that loop along stems and leaves.

### FALSE CROCUS GEOMETER    *Xanthotype urticaria*
Common and widespread. ▶ Yellow with brown mottling. **Crocus Geometer** *(X. sospeta)* is usually more lightly marked. **Larval foodplant:** many.

### LARGE MAPLE SPANWORM    *Prochoerodes lineola*
Very common in late summer, often visiting lights at night. ▶ Shape and overall pattern are consistent, but color varies from pale tan to dark violet-brown. **Larval foodplant:** Wide variety of trees and low plants.

### TULIP-TREE BEAUTY    *Epimecis hortaria*
Common in forested southern and eastern parts of region. ▶ Notably *large* with scalloped edge of hindwing. *Complex pattern* of pale-edged darker lines creating scalloped design. **Larval foodplant:** leaves of various trees.

### CONFUSED EUSARCA    *Eusarca confusaria*
Common from spring to fall. ▶ Varies from tan to gray. Darker line cuts across angular wing to wingtip. **Larval foodplant:** asters and others.

### BENT-LINE CARPET    *Costaconvexa centrostrigaria*
Common from spring to fall. ▶ Parallel dark bands on wings, most prominent on forewings, outer one broken. **Larval foodplant:** various low weeds.

### CHICKWEED GEOMETER    *Haematopis grataria*
Very common in open grassy spots, active by day, also coming to lights at night. ▶ Yellow with *pink lines.* **Larval foodplant:** clover, other low weeds.

### LARGE LACE-BORDER    *Scopula limboundata*
Common in summer. ▶ Variable in pattern, but often has dark lacy marks near wing borders. **Larval foodplant:** twiglike larvae feed on many plants.

### PALE BEAUTY    *Campaea perlata*
Common at lights in summer. ▶ Silky whitish to very pale green. Wings with faint, *nearly straight lines.* **Larval foodplant:** many shrubs and trees.

### BEGGAR MOTH    *Eubaphe mendica*
Fairly common at lights from late spring to fall. ▶ Translucent *yellow* wings with *gray spots.* **Larval foodplant:** maples and violets.

### LESSER GRAPEVINE LOOPER    *Eulithis diversilineata*
When visiting lights, often holds abdomen curled up over back. ▶ Angular tan wings with narrow lines. **Larval foodplant:** grape and Virginia creeper.

### COMMON SPRING MOTH    *Heliomata cycladata*
Common in most of region, late spring to early summer, often flying by day. ▶ Black and cream pattern. **Larval foodplant:** locusts.

### WAVY-LINED EMERALD    *Synchlora aerata*
Common in summer. ▶ Very small, pale green, with wavy white lines. One of several similar geometers. **Larval foodplant:** asters and others.

# GEOMETER MOTHS

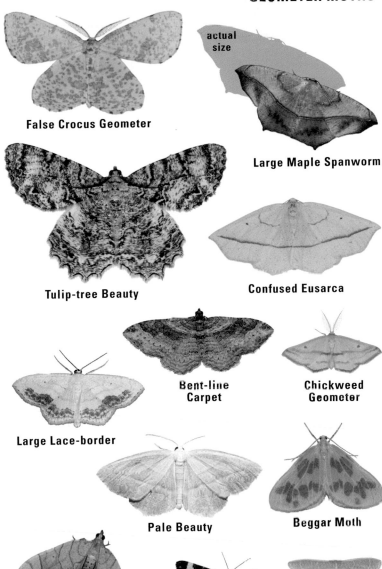

**False Crocus Geometer**

actual
size

**Large Maple Spanworm**

**Tulip-tree Beauty**

**Confused Eusarca**

**Bent-line
Carpet**

**Chickweed
Geometer**

**Large Lace-border**

**Pale Beauty**

**Beggar Moth**

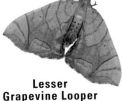

**Lesser
Grapevine Looper**

**Common
Spring Moth**

**Wavy-lined
Emerald**

The first three below are in the Prominent family (**Notodontidae**), while the final eight represent seven different families. The Midwest has many hundreds of species of tiny moths, not covered in detail in this book.

### DATANA PROMINENT    *Datana* sp.
Half a dozen similar species of *Datana* are common in the Midwest. ▶ Tan wings with darker lines, rich brown furry thorax. **Larval foodplant**: varied.

### DOUBLE-TOOTHED PROMINENT    *Nerice bidentata*
Fairly common in open woods, clearings. Like other prominents, often comes to lights, but then usually sluggish and slow to leave. ▶ Brown outer part of forewing has 2 "teeth" pointing inward. **Larval foodplant**: elms.

### WHITE FURCULA    *Furcula borealis*
Common in forests in spring and summer. ▶ White with broad gray median band and many small black dots. **Larval foodplant**: wild cherry.

### GYPSY MOTH    *Lymantria dispar*
Introduced from Europe, now abundant in New England and spreading through Midwest. Larvae can be major forest pests, but efforts to control them can cause damage of other kinds. (Family Erebidae, subfamily Lymantriinae) ▶ Female much larger and paler than male; both with similar pattern of lines and dots. **Larval foodplant**: especially oaks, also 500+ others.

### SKIFF MOTH    *Prolimacodes badia*
This and the next are slug moths (family Limacodidae), small moths that visit lights. ▶ Brown half-circle on each forewing. **Larval foodplant**: many.

### SMALLER PARASA    *Parasa chloris*
▶ Brown with irregular pale green crossband. **Larval foodplant**: various trees.

### MAPLE CALLUS BORER    *Synanthedon acerni*
Clearwing borers (family Sesiidae) look like wasps; larvae bore into stems and roots of plants. ▶ *Orange tuft* at tip of abdomen. **Larval foodplant**: maple.

### EASTERN GRASS-VENEER    *Crambus laqueatellus*
This and the next are in the Crambidae, a large family of mostly very small moths. ▶ Small and narrow; intricate pattern. **Larval foodplant**: grasses.

### GRAPE LEAF-FOLDER    *Desmia funeralis*
Common, widespread; active day and night. ▶ White spots on narrow black wings. **Larval foodplant**: larvae fold and feed on edges of grape leaves.

### PLUME MOTHS    family Pterophoridae
Common and widespread, often attracted to lights. ▶ Recognized by their resting posture, wings held out to the side, like tiny airplanes. Several species occur, some patterned, some plain. **Larval foodplant**: various.

### AILANTHUS WEBWORM MOTH    *Atteva aurea*
Common, often seen visiting lights at night, flowers by day. (Family Yponomeutidae) ▶ Pale orange with beadlike network of *black-ringed white spots*. **Larval foodplant**: ailanthus and other trees.

# PROMINENTS AND OTHER MOTHS

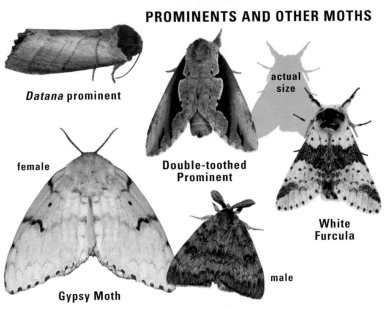

*Datana* prominent

Double-toothed Prominent

actual size

White Furcula

female

Gypsy Moth

male

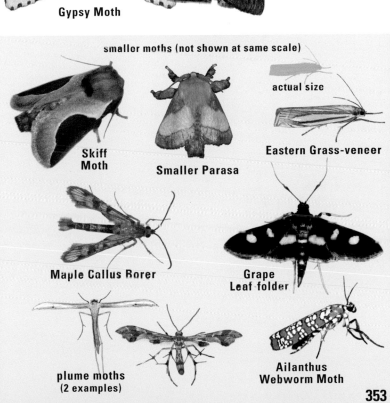

smaller moths (not shown at same scale)

actual size

Skiff Moth

Smaller Parasa

Eastern Grass-veneer

Maple Callus Borer

Grape Leaf-folder

plume moths (2 examples)

Ailanthus Webworm Moth

Butterflies and moths, because they are so popular, are treated in their own separate section (starting on p. 322). The present section covers everything else: all the other insect orders besides the Lepidoptera.

*Sections on insects and other invertebrates contributed by Eric R. Eaton*

**Insects are animals,** even though it is tempting to believe they are aliens, or at least belong to a kingdom other than Animalia. Truth is, we share over 20 percent of our DNA with *Drosophila* flies. (Do you like bananas?) Fortunately, the overwhelming majority of insects do us no harm, and most are, in fact, critical to the proper functioning of ecosystems, be they natural (prairies, forests, and wetlands) or artificial (agricultural lands, urban and suburban landscapes). Insects pollinate our crops, dispose of manure and carcasses, figure in the development of new medicines, and advance our technologies.

Insects are invertebrates in the phylum Arthropoda, which means "joint-footed." Other types of arthropods include arachnids (spiders, scorpions, mites, and their kin), myriapods (centipedes and millipedes), and crustaceans (crabs, lobsters, shrimp). All arthropods have an exoskeleton, in contrast to the internal skeleton of vertebrates.

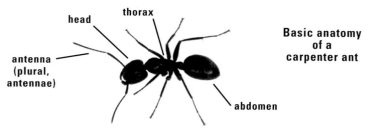

**Basic anatomy of a carpenter ant**

head
thorax
antenna (plural, antennae)
abdomen

**The insect body** is composed of three major regions: head, thorax, and abdomen. The head features compound eyes, antennae, and mouthparts. The thorax is locomotion central, as all six legs and two pairs of wings (one pair in flies and some other insects) arise from there. Bringing up the rear, the abdomen contains organs that function in digestion, excretion, and reproduction. Antennae are often thought of as "feelers," but while they do have a tactile function, their main purpose is to pick up scents and other chemical cues. Compound eyes detect motion far better than our own eyes, and can see in the ultraviolet end of the light spectrum. Mouthparts can taste morsels before the insect ever takes a bite. Most insects do not hear airborne frequencies, but they readily detect vibrations. Legs may be modified for running, jumping, swimming, or digging, allowing insects to collectively exploit almost every conceivable niche in the environment. Wings permit adult insects to disperse over vast distances.

**The life cycle of insects** revolves around metamorphosis. Once hatched from an egg, the nymphs of grasshoppers, cockroaches, and true bugs simply grow incrementally larger, eventually accruing reproductive organs and often wings. This is termed "simple," "gradual," or "incomplete" metamorphosis. More advanced insects like flies, beetles, bees, butterflies, and moths undergo "complete metamorphosis," passing through an egg, larva, and pupa stage before becoming an adult. Growth in all instances is achieved by shedding the exoskeleton (molting). The animal gets bigger in the brief interval before the new cuticle hardens. "Albino" insects are soft, freshly molted individuals in which pigments have not yet been expressed. Periods between molts are "instars." Larval insects of most species pass through 4–6 instars prior to pupating. The pupa may appear lifeless on the outside, but inside genes are being turned on and off, and the cellular structure is being reorganized. Adult insects do not molt and therefore cannot increase in size. A "baby beetle" is thus a smaller species or individual. The true "baby" would be a larva.

**Exotic and endangered species.** Some insects in the Midwest don't belong here. They have been introduced, intentionally or accidentally, from elsewhere. With few natural enemies, they become pests of farms or forests. Recently, the Emerald Ash Borer and Asian Longhorned Beetle have made headlines, but Japanese Beetle and European Corn Borer have been with us seemingly forever. Our policies of free trade have had their price, and this is one example.

At the opposite end of the spectrum are native species that are endangered. Certain aquatic insects, cave insects, and those species living in unique habitats are especially vulnerable. The Hine's Emerald dragonfly, Karner Blue and Mitchell's Satyr butterflies, and American Burying Beetle are federally endangered species found in the upper Midwest, but there are insects on state threatened and endangered lists, too.

**Finding insects** is easy. They are everywhere! Identifying them is much more difficult. Insects don't usually sit still for close examination of the subtle characters needed to distinguish them from similar species. Even individuals that appear identical may be different species based on DNA that the average person can't analyze. Don't despair. Simply taking notice and spending time observing is more than most people do. Take a picture. Take several pictures from different angles. Compare your images to those in guides like the *Kaufman Field Guide to Insects of North America* to narrow the insect to an order, family, genus, or even species. Supplement field guides with online resources like Bugguide.net for even better results.

Try planting a butterfly garden, building a bee box for solitary bees, or even installing a dragonfly pond if you are really ambitious. Participate in National Moth Week, or another event to meet experts and citizen scientists. Join Ohio Coleopterists if you like beetles. The opportunities for involvement are endless.

# SOME PRIMITIVE INSECTS

These are among the most primitive insects, in the evolutionary sense. Springtails are even classified as "non-insect hexapods." All undergo simple metamorphosis, the young resembling small versions of adults.

**Earwigs (order Dermaptera)** do not infest ears or wigs. The name may be a corruption of "ear wing," describing the appearance of the folded wings. The **European Earwig** *(Forficula auricularia)* is a common, nonnative species. Yes, it can fly. At rest the wings are so intricately folded as to make origami look like child's play. European Earwigs are mostly scavengers, but occasional pests of roses and other garden plants. Females faithfully guard their eggs and young.

**Termites and Cockroaches (order Blattodea)** are both despised pests and valuable decomposers. Termites, formerly in the order Isoptera, are "social cockroaches" that turn decaying wood back into soil with the help of symbiotic microbes in their tiny termite tummies. **Eastern Subterranean Termite** *(Reticulitermes flavipes)* is abundant and problematic. Soil tubes across your home's foundation indicate termites are venturing from underground nests to feed on wood. Swarms of winged males and females are liberated in the spring. These are future "kings" and "queens" that, once coupled, will shed their wings and establish new colonies.

Cockroaches include outdoor natives like the **wood cockroaches** (genus *Parcoblatta*). Males may fly to lights at night. Females have short, nonfunctional wings. By day they hide under bark and in rotting stumps. Immigrant species that probably originated in Africa are household pests. The large **American Cockroach** *(Periplaneta americana)* is often encountered inside furniture. The **German Cockroach** *(Blattella germanica)* is an insidious kitchen pest. Roaches are suspected in the mechanical transmission of bacteria, but their molts (shed exoskeletons), body parts, and feces are proven allergens that can aggravate asthma.

**Silverfish** and their allies **(order Zygentoma)** have an appetite for starchy materials such as paste used in bookbinding. The **Firebrat** *(Thermobia domestica)* likes warm, dry areas such as near furnaces and insulation around water heaters. **Four-lined Silverfish** *(Ctenolepisma lineata)* is common under shingles, in garden mulch, and in garages, attics, and voids in walls.

**Jumping bristletails (order Microcoryphia** or **Archaeognatha)** are bizarre but common nocturnal forest insects. Look for them under stones, bark, and in leaf-litter by day, or on stone walls at night. They feed on algae, lichens, mosses, and decaying vegetation.

**Springtails (class Collembola)** are named for a hinged organ ("furcula" or "furca") at the rear of the abdomen that the organism uses to launch itself. Tiny but abundant, especially in moist soil, leaf-litter, compost heaps, and on the surface of water and snow, not all species "spring." Indoors, they thrive in potting soil of houseplants, and around drains of bathtubs, showers, and basins. They eat decaying organic matter, and/or spores of molds and mildews. **"Snow fleas,"** genus *Hypogastrura*, can cover the snow in unimaginable numbers. *Lepidocyrtus* is a typical genus of slender springtails, family **Entomobryidae,** found in damp situations.

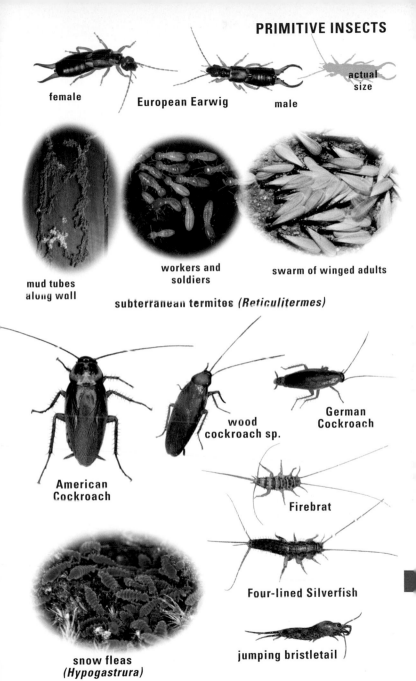

# PRIMITIVE INSECTS

female

**European Earwig**

male

actual size

mud tubes along wall

workers and soldiers

swarm of winged adults

**subterranean termites** *(Reticulitermes)*

**American Cockroach**

wood cockroach sp.

**German Cockroach**

**Firebrat**

**Four-lined Silverfish**

snow fleas *(Hypogastrura)*

jumping bristletail

357

are growing in popularity as "watchable wildlife." Large, colorful, and fairly abundant, they belong in the order Odonata along with damselflies. They are predatory in all life stages, and aquatic as nymphs ("naiads"). Nymphs have a hinged lower lip that shoots out and grabs prey. They leave a ghostly exoskeleton above the water line when they molt to adulthood. The aerial prowess of the adult insect is legendary. They actually create turbulence to generate lift, flapping front and back wings alternately. A few species are migratory, so watch for swarms flying south in late summer and fall, especially around the Great Lakes.

**Darners (family Aeshnidae)** are large, slender-bodied, and typically brown with a mosaic pattern of green and/or blue. They may congregate in mixed-species swarms over fields, especially in late afternoon, the airborne equivalent of a shark "feeding frenzy." The all-green thorax of the **Common Green Darner** *(Anax junius)* makes it readily identifiable. Mature males have a mostly blue abdomen, females brown or greenish. The **Shadow Darner** *(Aeshna umbrosa)* is especially common in late summer and fall, around slow-moving streams, ponds, bogs, and lakes.

**Clubtails (Gomphidae)** have their eyes widely separated, and usually have a club-shaped abdomen. They are associated with flowing waters. The **Cobra Clubtail** *(Gomphus vastus)* usually favors large rivers where the males patrol a long, linear path near shore, perching periodically on overhanging foliage or rocks. The **Black-shouldered Spinyleg** *(Dromogomphus spinosus)* has a slender "club" compared to most gomphids. Look for them perching along forest edges, or the shady periphery of sunny open spots.

**Spiketails (Cordulegastridae)** are named for the knife-like ovipositor of the female. The **Arrowhead Spiketail** *(Cordulegaster obliqua)* breeds in spring-fed rivulets in forest habitats. Males patrol and perch along these narrow watercourses. When frightened, they fly straight up, over the tops of trees. **Cruisers (Macromiidae)** are similar to spiketails. Male **Illinois River Cruisers** *(Macromia illinoiensis)* fly unwavering straight-line paths along river shores or roads. One "beat" may be 50 yards long. Look for them perched vertically on the tips of twigs between flights.

The family **Corduliidae** includes green-eyed "emeralds" that are almost exclusively boreal (found in the extreme northern U.S. and Canada). Most are confined to bogs, seeps, fens, and similar wetlands. **Hine's Emerald** *(Somatochlora hinei)*, not shown, is a federally endangered species with localized populations mostly in marshy fens or seeps along the western shore of Lake Michigan. "Baskettails" get their name from the female's habit of holding an egg ball at the tip of her abdomen. She dips her abdomen briefly in the water and the ball springs into a rope of eggs about 6" long. The **Common Baskettail** *(Epitheca cynosura)* often swarms over meadows or open water in late afternoon. **Prince Baskettails** *(Epitheca princeps)* resemble darners with spotted wings, but they land even less often than darners! Watch them flying over ponds for what seems like hours on end. Twelve-spotted Skimmer and female Common Whitetail (see p. 360) are similar, but perch frequently.

# DRAGONFLIES

actual size

Common Green Darner

Shadow Darner

Cobra Clubtail

Arrowhead Spiketail

Black-shouldered Spinyleg

Illinois River Cruiser

Prince Baskettail

Common Baskettail

359

# SKIMMERS

Members of the family **Libellulidae**, collectively known as skimmers, are among the most conspicuous dragonflies around ponds, lakes, and slow-moving rivers, and they are often seen in open habitats far from water. Most perch frequently on reeds, cattails, and emergent objects.

The **Blue Dasher** *(Pachydiplax longipennis)* lives up to its name. Mature males are powder blue, and dash out from perches to defend territories. Females and immature males are largely black with yellow spots and stripes. The **Eastern Pondhawk** *(Erythemis simplicicollis)* occasionally eats other dragonflies. Mature males resemble the Blue Dasher, but are slightly larger. Females and immature males are bright green and black.

Many skimmers have bold wing markings. Male **Common Whitetails** *(Plathemis lydia)* have wide black bands across both wings. Females have 12 black spots. This species is often found away from water, perching on logs or the ground. The **Twelve-spotted Skimmer** *(Libellula pulchella)* has longer wings than the Common Whitetail, and males have the black wing spots separated by white spots. The **Halloween Pennant** *(Celithemis eponina)* and **Calico Pennant** *(Celithemis elisa)* (not shown, similar but wings not tinged orange) tend to alight on tall stalks near shore or in pastures, perching horizontally like pennants blowing in the breeze.

"Meadowhawks" are the bright red dragonflies you see around ponds and in open fields. Only the mature males are so colorful, females and immature being mostly dull yellow. These members of the genus *Sympetrum* are the equal of gulls on the degree of difficulty scale of identification. Five species are fairly common in the region covered by this guide. The **Yellow-legged Meadowhawk** or **Autumn Meadowhawk** *(Sympetrum vicinum)* is a late-season species, persisting after similar ones have vanished.

Look for the **Dot-tailed Whiteface** *(Leucorrhinia intacta)* from May through July around ponds, bogs, and slow-moving watercourses. The dark body and bright white face are characteristic of the genus. The ivory spot on the abdomen confirms the species. The genus is largely boreal, and four other species occur in the states covered by this guide.

Some dragonflies glide effortlessly and seemingly endlessly over fields and meadows. The broad hind wings of the **Black Saddlebags** *(Tramea lacerata)* allow it to soar with minimal wingbeats — a useful ability for this long-distance migrant. The dark "saddlebag" marking on the hindwings are distinctive. The **Wandering Glider** *(Pantala flavescens)* often joins saddlebag dragonflies in feeding swarms over fields. This species occurs everywhere but Europe and Antarctica and is a well-known migrant. Look for roosting specimens hanging vertically from sumac and other trees that form thickets in otherwise open areas. It breeds almost anywhere, even in fountains. Females may try to lay eggs on cars or other reflective objects they mistake for water.

The **Eastern Amberwing** *(Perithemis tenera)* is among our smallest dragonflies, sometimes mistaken for a wasp as it lilts over tall grasses in fields and along the edges of ponds. Males have amber wings; females have clear wings with dark spots of varying intensity.

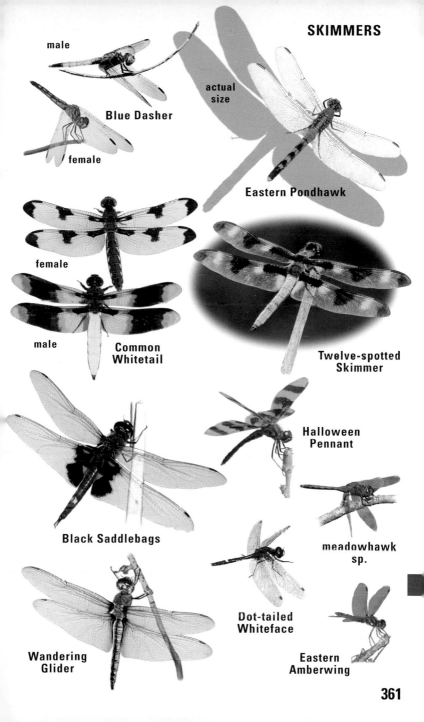

# SKIMMERS

male

Blue Dasher

female

actual size

Eastern Pondhawk

female

male

Common Whitetail

Twelve-spotted Skimmer

Black Saddlebags

Halloween Pennant

meadowhawk sp.

Wandering Glider

Dot-tailed Whiteface

Eastern Amberwing

All of these insects live underwater in their youth (as naiads, or larvae).

Damselflies are smaller, more slender relatives of dragonflies. **Broad-winged damselflies (family Calopterygidae)** are large and frequent streams and rivers. The **Ebony Jewelwing** (*Calopteryx maculata*) can be seen along forest edges and on overhanging streamside vegetation. Females have a white "stigma" on each wing; males have all-black wings. **Spread-winged damselflies (Lestidae)** perch with wings splayed. The **Slender Spreadwing** (*Lestes rectangularis*) favors shallow, partially shaded standing water and slow-moving streams. **Narrow-winged damselflies (Coenagrionidae)** are abundant. "Dancers" hold their wings above the abdomen at rest, and are most common around rivers and streams. **Blue-fronted Dancer** (*Argia apicalis*) often perches on the ground. "Bluets" usually fold their wings against the abdomen when perched. The **Familiar Bluet** (*Enallagma civile*) prefers the still waters of ponds, like most members of the genus.

**Mayflies (order Ephemeroptera)** are unique in that they molt once as adults. The "subimago" ("dun" in angler-speak) emerges from the aquatic immature stage, followed shortly by the imago, or "spinner." Adults live perhaps a day, long enough to procreate. Females of **small minnow mayflies (family Baetidae)** have a darkened leading edge on the forewing. Males have split eyes, the upper half mushroomlike. **Common burrowing mayflies (Ephemeridae)** dig in the sediments of rivers and lakes as naiads. Adults are large with three streaming "tails" (caudal filaments). *Hexagenia* is the common genus. Hatches in certain locations along the Great Lakes and Mississippi River can be so prolific that the dead adult mayflies must be plowed from roads and docks.

**Stoneflies (order Plecoptera)** live in flowing waters. Most have two caudal filaments at the rear of the abdomen. Naiads of **common stoneflies (family Perlidae)** are predatory on other underwater organisms. Adults emerge in summer and are sometimes attracted to lights at night. *Perlesta* and *Acroneuria* are common genera. **Perlodid stoneflies (Perlodidae)** are diurnal as adults. Species of *Isoperla* are yellow or green. Look for them on foliage near water in spring or summer. **Small winter stoneflies** (aka "snowflies," **family Capniidae**) can be seen in late winter and early spring on snow or bridges, and eat blue-green algae. Males of some species have rudimentary wings. The naiads feed on aquatic plants.

**Caddisflies (order Trichoptera)** resemble moths. Their aquatic larvae build "mobile homes" of sand, pebbles, or plant material, or spin silken tubes or nets. The **netspinning caddisflies (Hydropsychidae)** live in fast-flowing streams and spin silk mesh to snare food: algae, debris, and small animals. "Little Sister Sedges" in the genus *Cheumatopsyche* are among those hydropsychids in the upper Midwest. The **Zebra Caddisfly** (*Macrostemum zabratum*) may come to lights. **Northern caddisflies (Limnephilidae)** larvae make cases of plant or mineral matter depending on the species. They live in still or slow-moving waters. Adults are large and may fly to lights at night. **Longhorned caddisflies (Leptoceridae)** are small, with very long antennae. Life histories vary with the different groups.

# INSECTS WITH AQUATIC LARVAE

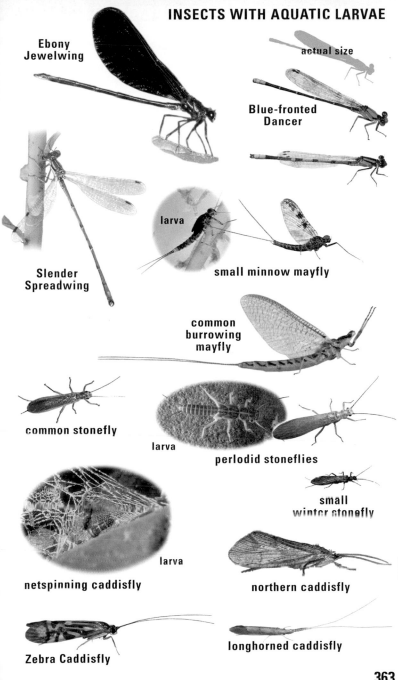

Ebony Jewelwing

actual size

Blue-fronted Dancer

Slender Spreadwing

larva

small minnow mayfly

common burrowing mayfly

common stonefly

larva

perlodid stoneflies

small winter stonefly

larva

netspinning caddisfly

northern caddisfly

Zebra Caddisfly

longhorned caddisfly

# GRASSHOPPERS, KATYDIDS, AND CRICKETS

Grasshoppers and their allies (order **Orthoptera**) are insect musicians. They have hind legs modified for jumping, and many can fly well, too. All go through gradual metamorphosis. Few are pests in agricultural fields, and in fact most are omnivores that may scavenge dead insects or actively prey on healthy ones. Many are incredibly cryptic.

**Short-horned grasshoppers (family Acrididae)** are named for their short antennae. They are diurnal and most conspicuous in summer and fall. The **Carolina Grasshopper** (*Dissosteira carolina*) is well camouflaged at rest but displays black hindwings margined in pale yellow when it takes flight. The **Northern Green-striped Grasshopper** (*Chortophaga viridifasciata*) overwinters as a nymph and is one of the first adult grasshoppers of spring. Females are usually green, males brown. **Kiowa Rangeland Grasshopper** (*Trachyrhachys kiowa*) inhabits barren or sandy areas. Like other band-winged grasshoppers it can make crackling sounds in flight by rapidly rubbing front and hind wings together. The big, slow **Differential Grasshopper** (*Melanoplus differentialis*) is common even in gardens. Herringbone pattern on the hind femur (thigh) is distinctive. **Short-winged Green Grasshopper** (*Dichromorpha viridis*) is common in moist grassy areas like the edges of ponds. Males of the **Handsome Grasshopper** (*Syrbula admirabilis*) call females by stroking the inside of the hind femur ("thigh") across special veins on the front wing. Look for them in summer in dry grassland. Females are larger and have a different color pattern.

**Katydids (Tettigoniidae)** have ultra-long antennae. Most are nocturnal, and males sing by rubbing a "scraper" on one front wing against a "file" on the other. The **Common True Katydid** (*Pterophylla camellifolia*) sings *katy-did, katy-didn't* from the very tops of trees. The raspy chorus sounds more like a frog call. The **Greater Anglewing** (*Microcentrum rhombifolium*) is more readily seen, even flying to lights at night. Its calls include a loud, brief *lisp* and a series of softer *tic* notes. Round-headed katydids, genus *Amblycorypha* (not shown), usually haunt understory vegetation in deciduous forests. The male **Sword-bearing Conehead** (*Neoconocephalus ensiger*) produces a loud continuous buzz from amid tangled shrubs and grasses in moist fields and along roadsides. The **Black-legged Meadow Katydid** (*Orchelimum nigripes*) perches high in tall grasses around wetlands. The male's song is a repeated *tic-tic-tic-buzzzzzzz*.

**Crickets (Gryllidae)** include husky **field crickets** (genus *Gryllus*) that chirp from the mouth of burrows, or from under stones, boards, and logs. Look on foliage for the slender **tree crickets** (*Oecanthus* spp. and *Neoxabea bipunctata*). Male tree crickets can be confused with green lacewings as their front wings are highly modified for sound production. Crickets sing in the same manner as katydids, and can be heard in the daytime, too.

**Camel crickets (Rhaphidophoridae)** are wingless and lanky. They like cool, damp places like cellars, basements, old wells, and caves. Some are burrowers found only in sand dunes. Members of the genus *Ceuthophilus* are most abundant. The blade-like "stinger" on katydids and camel crickets is the female's egg-laying organ (ovipositor) and is harmless.

# GRASSHOPPERS, KATYDIDS, AND CRICKETS

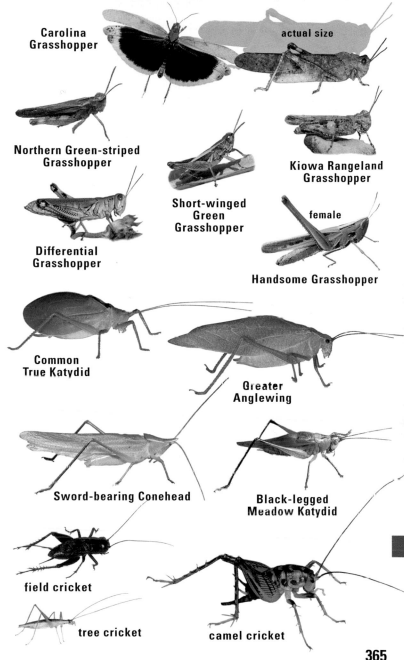

Carolina Grasshopper

actual size

Northern Green-striped Grasshopper

Kiowa Rangeland Grasshopper

Short-winged Green Grasshopper

Differential Grasshopper

female

Handsome Grasshopper

Common True Katydid

Greater Anglewing

Sword-bearing Conehead

Black-legged Meadow Katydid

field cricket

tree cricket

camel cricket

# DISTINCTIVE LARGE INSECTS

You can't miss these behemoths, representing three different orders of insects. Some are well camouflaged, but they may visit lights at night or otherwise make themselves obvious.

**Mantids (order Mantodea)** are large insects that use their raptorial front legs to seize prey in a vise-like grip. They ambush or actively stalk potential victims. The female deposits eggs in a mass called an ootheca, covered with a foamy substance that hardens to protect them from desiccation. The nymphs emerge en masse, seemingly flowing out of the egg case. They disperse quickly lest they fall prey to brothers and sisters. They undergo simple metamorphosis. The **Chinese Mantis** (*Tenodera sinensis*) can be 3–4" (77–103 mm) long as an adult. Typically brown with green stripes along the front wings, they can also be entirely green. They are indiscriminate hunters that kill beneficial insects, and even hummingbirds, as well as pests. This species was introduced from Asia around 1896. Another introduced species, **European Mantis** (*Mantis religiosa*), is known by the black "bull's-eye" spot on the inside of the front thigh. The **Carolina Mantis** (*Stagmomantis carolina*) is native. Adult females are large, flightless, and green or mottled gray. Males are smaller, slender, and fly well. Look for this species south of Michigan and Minnesota in the Great Lakes region.

**Stick insects (order Phasmida** or **Phasmatodea)** are the vegetarian equivalents of mantids. **Northern Walkingsticks** (*Diapheromera femorata*) are common, even abundant in some years, but they live high in the forest canopy, feeding on leaves of oak, hazelnut, and other deciduous trees. Occasionally they are glimpsed climbing in a halting gait up a tree trunk or wall. Adult males are slender with modified middle legs, and claspers at the tip of the abdomen. Females are more . . . robust. Eggs are dropped one at a time onto the forest floor. Fecal pellets and eggs can sound like rain when populations of these insects are extreme.

**Cicadas (order Hemiptera, family Cicadidae)** are more often heard than seen. Males of most produce earsplitting "songs" with paired organs called tymbals in each side of the abdomen. A muscle is rapidly vibrated, the sound resonating in a chamber and then broadcast through a covered opening. Nymphs live underground feeding on sap in the roots of plants. They spend years there, but some "annual" cicadas (genus ***Tibicen***) emerge aboveground as adults each year in midsummer. They have piercing and sucking mouthparts to extract sap. **Periodical cicadas** (*Magicicada* spp.) are the famed "17-year locusts" that emerge synchronously in overwhelming numbers every 17 years (or every 13 years for some forms) in late spring. Check your local listings for a Roman numeral "brood" near you.

**Giant water bugs (order Hemiptera, family Belostomatidae)** are aquatic predators that also fly to lights at night. "Electric light bugs," genus ***Lethocerus,*** are frequently mistaken for cockroaches, crayfish, or beetles when found "stranded" in the morning after a night on the town. More at home in ponds and sloughs, they kill and eat other aquatic insects, tadpoles, frogs, even small snakes. They can be pests in fish hatcheries. Beware: the short, beaklike mouthparts can inflict a painful bite in self-defense.

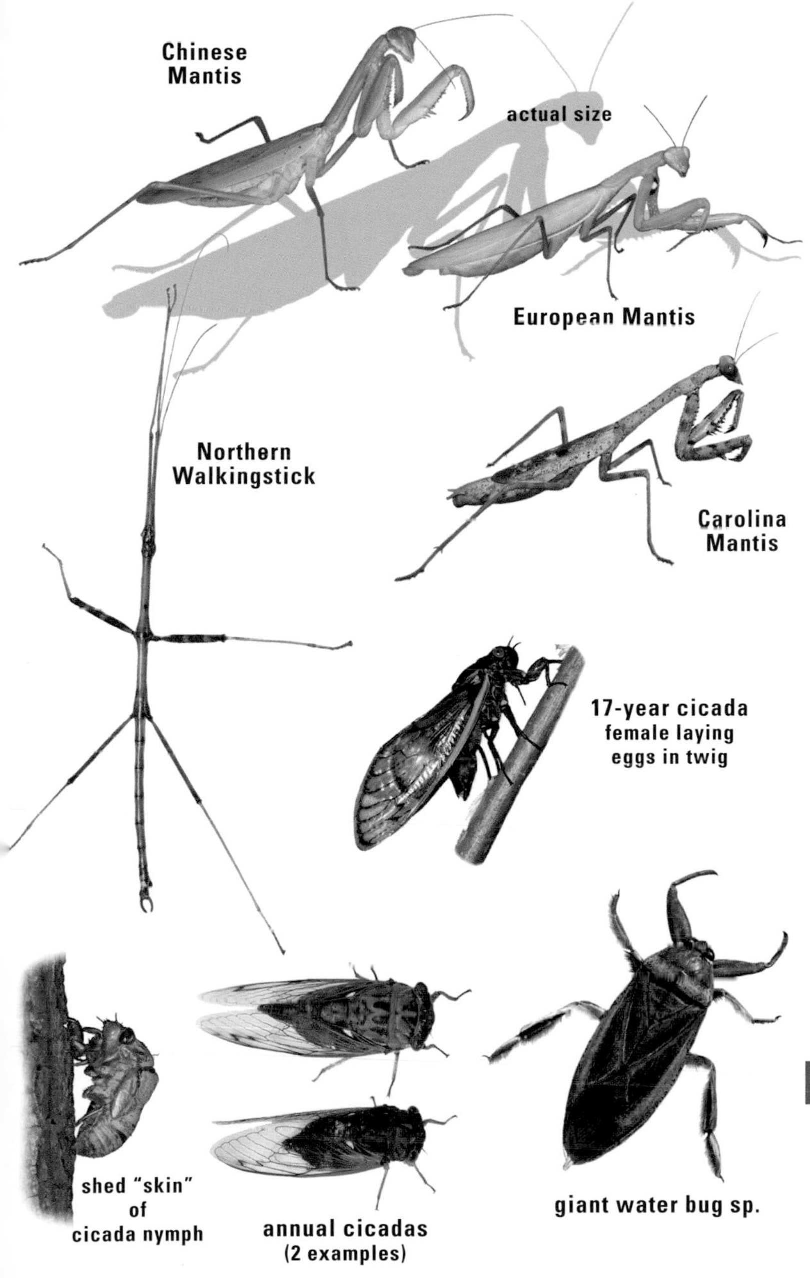

# DISTINCTIVE LARGE INSECTS

Chinese Mantis

actual size

European Mantis

Northern Walkingstick

Carolina Mantis

17-year cicada
female laying
eggs in twig

shed "skin"
of
cicada nymph

annual cicadas
(2 examples)

giant water bug sp.

# LEAFHOPPERS, APHIDS, AND OTHERS

True Bugs (order **Hemiptera**) have piercing-sucking mouthparts. The ones shown here were formerly classified in the order Homoptera. Cicadas (p. 366), whiteflies, jumping plant lice (psyllids), and adelgids fall into this order, too. Many are sap-sucking pests of farm, orchard, and garden. Their life cycle is gradual metamorphosis. Ants protect many aphids, scales, and treehoppers as a source of "honeydew," a sweet liquid waste produced by the bugs that ants crave.

Nymphs of **spittlebugs (family Cercopidae)** blow air and liquid waste from their anus to create a foam shelter that protects them from dehydration and predators. The **Meadow Spittlebug** *(Philaenus spumarius)* comes in a wide array of color patterns, and feeds on over 400 plant species. **Dogwood Spittlebug** *(Clastoptera proteus)* is found mostly on hardwoods.

    **Leafhoppers and sharpshooters (Cicadellidae)** are quick to dodge, jump, and fly when approached. The **Red-banded** (or "Candy-striped") **Leafhopper** *(Graphocephala coccinea)* feeds on ferns, rhododendron, forsythia, and cranberries among other host plants. *Coelidia olitoria* is common in fields. The nymph has an upturned abdomen. The **Speckled Sharpshooter** *(Paraulacizes irrorata)* is huge for a leafhopper, at about half an inch. Look for it on grasses and plants in the aster family. Members of the genus *Draeculacephala* have pointy "noses." They feed on grasses and sedges.

    **Planthoppers** of several families occur in the upper Midwest. Among the more common are **Cixiidae, Flatidae, Acanaloniidae,** and **Derbidae**. Many occur on shrubs and vines; a few will come to lights at night. The **Citrus Planthopper** *(Metcalfa pruinosa)* is a common flatid.

    **Treehoppers (Membracidae)** are often disguised as thorns or buds. The top of the thorax is modified into crests, spikes, or other shapes extending over the abdomen. *Publilia concava* is common on goldenrod and giant ragweed, and often tended by ants. Treehoppers in the genus *Ceresa* resemble little green buffalo. They are abundant but alert, quick to fly when approached. *Smilia camelus* is a crested species found on oak trees.

    **Aphids (Aphididae)** are tiny but prolific. They secrete copious amounts of "honeydew," a liquid waste that coats your parked car, grows sooty molds, and attracts ants, flies, wasps, and bees. Female aphids can lay eggs or give "live birth" to nymphs. Many species switch host plants over a year, creating a winged generation to fly to the alternate host. Woolly aphids resemble flying lint or fairies, depending on your inclination. Elm, alder, birch, and beech are frequent hosts of woolly aphids.

    **Scale insects** are immobile and resemble lumps, bumps, and limpets more than insects. There are several families and their life cycles and biology are beyond the scope of this book.

    **Galls** are abnormal growths stimulated by bacteria, viruses, fungi, mites, nematode worms, and insects like gall wasps, flies, aphids, adelgids, and psyllids. Insect galls are formed by the female as a protective capsule and a vast reservoir of nutritious food for her offspring. Oaks, and rose family plants, are often hosts. Galls rarely cause more than cosmetic damage.

# LEAFHOPPERS AND OTHERS

Pine
Spittlebug

Meadow
Spittlebug

actual
size

Dogwood
Spittlebug

*Coelidia olitoria*
nymph and adult

Red-banded
Leafhopper

Speckled Sharpshooter

leafhopper
(*Draeculaecephala*)

planthopper
(*Acanalonia*)

Citrus
Planthopper

aphid

*Publilia
concava*

*Ceresa*

treehoppers
(4 examples)

Oak
Apple
Galls

*Smilia
camelus*

*Campylenchia*

369

# TRUE BUGS

Traditional true bugs **(order Hemiptera, suborder Heteroptera)** are often mistaken for beetles, but they have piercing-sucking mouthparts, and gradual metamorphosis.

**Water striders (family Gerridae)** skate over the surface of ponds, lakes, and slow-moving rivers using their long middle and hind legs. They seize prey with shorter, vise-like front legs. *Aquarius* is one common genus. **Backswimmers (Notonectidae)** row themselves upside down underwater with oarlike hind legs. They eat other aquatic insects like mosquito larvae. Look for them even in swimming pools; or crashing onto car hoods as they mistake the reflective surface for water. Genus *Notonecta* is most common.

**Plant bugs (Miridae)** are diverse, small, and often brightly colored. The **Four-lined Plant Bug** *(Poecilocapsus lineatus)*, at least ¼" long, is large compared to most mirids. The **Tarnished Plant Bug** *(Lygus lineolaris)* is widespread and often very common. *Phytocoris* is a highly diverse genus. Note the long hind legs. Many species prey on aphids or other small insects instead of feeding on plant sap.

**Damsel bugs (Nabidae)** are not meek, being efficient predators of other small insects. Look for *Nabis* and other genera on foliage, and at lights at night. **Assassin bugs (Reduviidae)** prey on other insects. *Zelus luridus* is a lanky species that prowls over leaves of trees. Males of the **Black Corsair** *(Melanolestes picipes)* may fly to lights at night. Females are usually wingless, living under stones or logs. In the southern Midwest, the **Wheel Bug** *(Arilus cristatus)* is uncommon, but sure to make an impression when found. **Ambush bugs,** genus *Phymata,* lie in wait on goldenrod and other flowers. They kill bees and other insects many times their size.

**Seed bugs (Lygaeidae)** include **Small Milkweed Bug** *(Lygaeus kalmii),* which has a broader taste in plants and won't pass up an injured insect as food. The **Large Milkweed Bug** *(Oncopeltus fasciatus)* feeds on the pods of plants in the milkweed family. The **Long-necked Seed Bug** *(Myodocha serripes)* **(family Rhyparochromidae)** often flies to lights at night.

**Leaf-footed bugs** and squash bugs comprise the family **Coreidae.** When molested, they emit a strong odor from glands in the thorax. They feed on seeds. The **Western Conifer Seed Bug** *(Leptoglossus occidentalis)* is still spreading and increasing in the Midwest. **Squash bugs** (genus *Anasa*) may sometimes plague the gourds in your garden.

The **Eastern Boxelder Bug** *(Boisea trivittata)* is one of the **scentless plant bugs (Rhopalidae).** It invades homes in fall in large numbers. At least they don't smell; and they disperse quickly come spring.

Glands in the thorax of stink bugs **(Pentatomidae)** produce a pungent aroma if the insect is molested. Most feed on plants, but the **Spined Soldier Bug** *(Podisus maculiventris)* preys on many pest insects. **Rough stink bugs,** genus *Brochymena,* mimic the bark of trees and overwinter as adults. Accidentally introduced in the late 1990s, the **Brown Marmorated Stink Bug** *(Halyomorpha halys)* has now been found in all states of our region and has become a major nuisance in some, invading houses and attacking various crops.

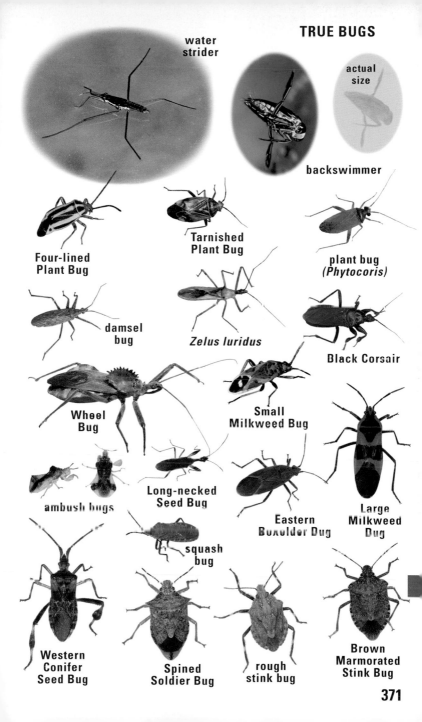

TRUE BUGS

water strider

actual size

backswimmer

Four-lined Plant Bug

Tarnished Plant Bug

plant bug (*Phytocoris*)

damsel bug

*Zelus luridus*

Black Corsair

Wheel Bug

Small Milkweed Bug

ambush bugs

Long-necked Seed Bug

Eastern Boxelder Bug

Large Milkweed Bug

squash bug

Western Conifer Seed Bug

Spined Soldier Bug

rough stink bug

Brown Marmorated Stink Bug

371

# BEETLES

Beetles (order **Coleoptera**) include favorites like "ladybugs" and fireflies, and pests like Japanese Beetles. Most are neither friend nor foe, but vital to healthy ecosystems. The most diverse of all organisms, beetles account for one of every five species. Look for them everywhere, even inside your home (carpet beetles, granary weevils, etc.). Beetles have chewing mouthparts, and complete metamorphosis. Their front wings are modified into armored plates called elytra, which are not used in flight.

**Tiger beetles and ground beetles (family Carabidae)** are agile predators. The **Six-spotted Tiger Beetle** *(Cicindela sexguttata)* sprints, stops, and flies short distances along woodland paths in daylight. The **Festive Tiger Beetle** *(Cicindela scutellaris)* and most other species prefer sandy beaches, dunes, and blowouts. Ground beetles are usually shiny black or brown, nocturnal, and abundant. *Chlaenius tricolor* is colorful but stinky. Look for it at lights at night.

**Whirligig beetles (Gyrinidae)** gyrate across the surface of ponds, lakes, and rivers. Their divided eyes let them see above the surface and underwater simultaneously. Adults and larvae are predatory.

Male **stag beetles (Lucanidae)** often have enormous jaws they use to battle each other over females. They feed in decaying wood as larvae. The **Pinching Beetle** *(Lucanus capreolus)* is common at lights at night.

The **Bess Beetle** *(Odontotaenius disjunctus)* **(Passalidae)** is a large, shiny insect found in colonies in rotten logs. Adults and larvae communicate by stridulating (making sounds by rubbing one body part against another). They are most common in the southern part of our region.

**Scarabs (Scarabaeidae)** include **May Beetles,** genus *Phyllophaga,* attracted in large numbers to lights at night. Larvae are "white grubs" that feed on roots. The **Japanese Beetle** *(Popillia japonica)* is a pest of foreign origin, now abundant here. The **Bumble Flower Beetle** *(Euphoria inda)* mimics bees by flying with wing covers closed. It eats sap, pollen, nectar, and overripe fruit. Dung beetles like *Copris fricator* are also scarabs.

**Metallic woodborers (Buprestidae)** bore beneath bark as larvae ("flathead borers"). The **Emerald Ash Borer** *(Agrilus planipennis)* is native to Asia but wreaking havoc here. Its arrival has prompted the removal of many trees in urban areas. *Dicerca* species are native and not pests.

**Click beetles (Elateridae)** are common at lights at night. They snap a spine into a groove in their "chest," making an audible "click" and propelling themselves several inches into the air. The big **Eyed Elater** *(Alaus oculatus)* is surprisingly well camouflaged on tree trunks during the day.

**Fireflies (Lampyridae)** glow as larvae, and as adults in many species. The genus *Photinus* is common, blinking in meadows and fields in the evening. Female *Photuris* fireflies have broken the code of *Photinus,* and lure the males to eat them.

**Soldier beetles (Cantharidae),** also called leatherwings, have softer wing covers than most beetles. Larvae eat other insects, as do the adults, though many feed on nectar and pollen. The **Goldenrod Soldier Beetle** *(Chauliognathus pensylvanicus)* is abundant in late summer.

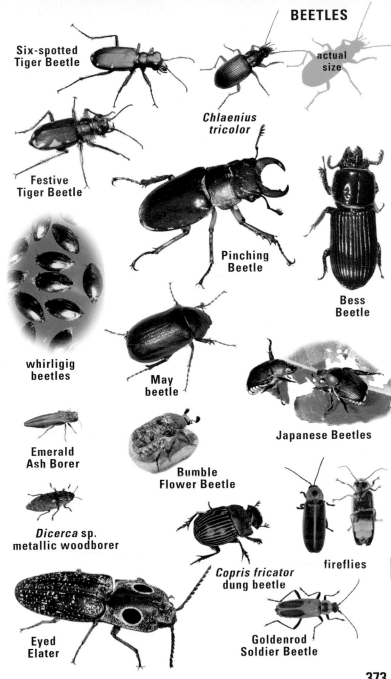

# BEETLES

Six-spotted Tiger Beetle

actual size

*Chlaenius tricolor*

Festive Tiger Beetle

Pinching Beetle

Bess Beetle

whirligig beetles

May beetle

Japanese Beetles

Emerald Ash Borer

Bumble Flower Beetle

*Dicerca* sp. metallic woodborer

*Copris fricator* dung beetle

fireflies

Eyed Elater

Goldenrod Soldier Beetle

373

**Lady beetles (Coccinellidae)** endear themselves to us because of their appetite for aphids and other pests. The adult beetles are not always red with black spots: The **Multicolored Asian Lady Beetle** *(Harmonia axyridis)* is an introduced species that may have no spots, or spots fused to the degree that it appears nearly black. "C-7" is the **Seven-spotted Lady Beetle** *(Coccinella septempunctata)*, native to Europe and implicated in the decline of native lady beetles. The **Spotted Lady Beetle** *(Coleomegilla maculata)* is frequently seen on flowers because it eats pollen.

**Darkling beetles (Tenebrionidae)** are so diverse in shape, size, and color as to be confused with other kinds of beetles. *Alobates pennsylvanica* is the **False Mealworm Beetle.** The slow-moving adults live under bark on logs and stumps in deciduous woodlands. Males of the **Forked Fungus Beetle** *(Bolitotherus cornutus)* have paired horns on the thorax. They are incredibly cryptic and found only on (and inside) woody *Ganoderma* fungi, usually on dead, standing trees.

**Blister beetles (Meloidae)** are named for their toxic nature. When molested they secrete a liquid chemical, cantharidin, from their joints. Cantharidin can raise blisters, and can be fatal if swallowed. Even horses can die from ingesting blister beetles accidentally baled in hay. The **Black Blister Beetle** *(Epicauta pennsylvanica)* is common on goldenrod in late summer.

**Longhorned beetles (Cerambycidae)** are called roundheaded borers in the larval stage. Nearly all species bore in wood as larvae, but few are pests. The large **Brown Prionid** *(Orthosoma brunneum)* sometimes flies to lights at night. The **Banded Longhorn** *(Typocerus velutinus)* can be common on flowers in June and July. The **Elm Borer** *(Saperda tridentata)* visits lights at night. Larvae bore under bark of weakened elms. The **Red Milkweed Beetle** *(Tetraopes tetrophthalmus)* is common on milkweeds.

**Leaf beetles (Chrysomelidae)** resemble lady beetles at first glance, but they feed on plants, not other insects. Most are host-specific, feeding on plants in one particular family or genus. The **Mottled Tortoise Beetle** *(Deloya guttata)* feeds on morning glory, bindweed, and related plants. Adults are seen mostly in June. Larvae hide under a dried umbrella of their own poop, held in place by filaments on their rear end. The **Milkweed Leaf Beetle** *(Labidomera clivicollis)* occurs on milkweed. Look for adults and larvae in July and August. The **Dogbane Beetle** *(Chrysochus auratus)* is brilliantly metallic. It can be locally common on dogbane. The menu of the **Spotted Cucumber Beetle** *(Diabrotica undecimpunctata)* extends to many crops and garden plants.

**Weevils (Curculionidae)** are perhaps the most diverse family of all insects. Nut and acorn weevils in the genus *Curculio* have long snouts with their jaws at the end. The female uses hers to bite a hole in a nut so she can lay an egg inside. Larvae of the **Cocklebur Weevil** *(Rhodobaenus quinquepunctatus)* bore in the stems of cocklebur, ragweed, and other composites. Weevils in the genus *Lixus* are cigar-shaped and covered in a powdery bloom that rubs off easily. They are associated with plants in the Compositae and Polygonaceae.

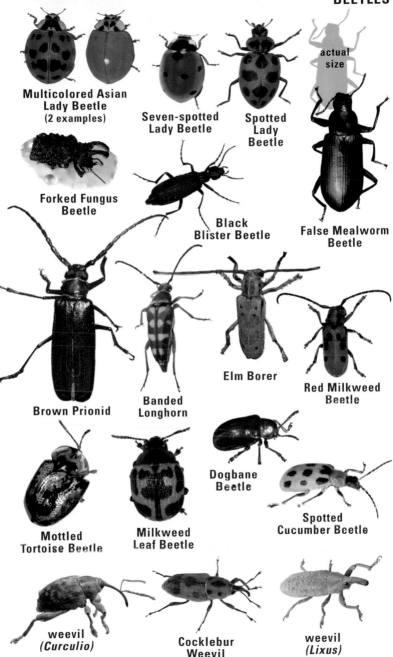

Multicolored Asian
Lady Beetle
(2 examples)

Seven-spotted
Lady Beetle

Spotted
Lady
Beetle

actual
size

Forked Fungus
Beetle

Black
Blister Beetle

False Mealworm
Beetle

Brown Prionid

Banded
Longhorn

Elm Borer

Red Milkweed
Beetle

Mottled
Tortoise Beetle

Milkweed
Leaf Beetle

Dogbane
Beetle

Spotted
Cucumber Beetle

weevil
*(Curculio)*

Cocklebur
Weevil

weevil
*(Lixus)*

# LACEWINGS AND OTHERS

The order **Neuroptera** is known as the "nerve-winged insects" for the dendritic pattern of wing venation in most of the adult insects. Included here are mostly predatory insects that go through complete metamorphosis. Some are aquatic in the larval stage. At the bottom of this page, scorpionflies and hangingflies are in a distinct order, **Mecoptera**.

**Dobsonflies, fishflies, and their allies (family Corydalidae)** are sometimes put in the order Megaloptera. They are indeed huge. Males of the **Eastern Dobsonfly** (*Corydalus cornutus*) have jaws like ice tongs. Females have "normal" mouths, but can bite hard. Both sexes fly to lights at night. Larvae are the predatory "hellgrammites" of fast-flowing rivers and streams. The **Spring Fishfly** (*Chauliodes rasticornis*) and **Summer Fishfly** (*C. pectinicornis*) are nearly identical. Larvae of both are omnivores that prefer quiet flowing water. Look for **dark fishflies**, genus *Nigronia,* from April to July on vegetation near streams.

    **Green lacewings (Chrysopidae)** are delicate insects common around lights at night. Known as "aphidlions" in their larval stage, they kill and eat many soft-bodied insect pests. Some larvae pile debris, lichens, and/or dead victims on their backs, such that they resemble animated garbage. Adult females lay eggs in small groups, each one atop a hairlike filament. This helps keep the first hatchling from eating its siblings.

    **Antlions (Mymeleontidae)** might be mistaken for damselflies but have thick, clubbed antennae. Larvae of the genus *Myrmeleon* are the "doodlebugs" that make funnel-like pits in fine, dry soil at the base of trees, under bridges, and other sheltered situations. They eat ants and other insects that fall into the trap. Larvae of other genera bury themselves in the soil and attack passing insects.

    **Owlflies (Ascalaphidae)** are fast-flying predators most active at dusk. They occasionally fly to lights at night. By day they rest on stems and twigs with the abdomen held at a 45° angle. The antennae are long and clubbed. Members of the genus *Ululodes* have the compound eyes divided. Larvae look and behave much like antlion larvae, but do not dig pits.

    **Mantispids** or "mantidflies" **(Mantispidae)** look like the offspring of a mantis crossed with a lacewing. They use their raptorial (vise-like) front legs to grab smaller creatures that they eat alive. Larvae of many species feed on spider eggs, infiltrating the egg sac when the female spider creates it. *Climaciella brunnea* is a day-active species that mimics paper wasps. *Dicromantispa sayi* often comes to lights at night.

    **Scorpionflies** are in the order **Mecoptera**. The name comes from the enlarged, upturned claspers on males of most species. Scorpionflies undergo complete metamorphosis. **Common scorpionflies (Panorpidae)** are scavengers that often steal prey from spider webs. Look for them along forest edges and in the understory. **Hangingflies (Bittacidae)** resemble crane flies, hanging from vegetation in the forest understory and manipulating prey with the hind legs. The **Forcepfly** (*Merope tuber*), family **Meropeidae,** is rarely seen. Its larva is unknown, and the nocturnal adult insects are pretty much a mystery as well. Males have long, caliper-like claspers at the tip of the abdomen.

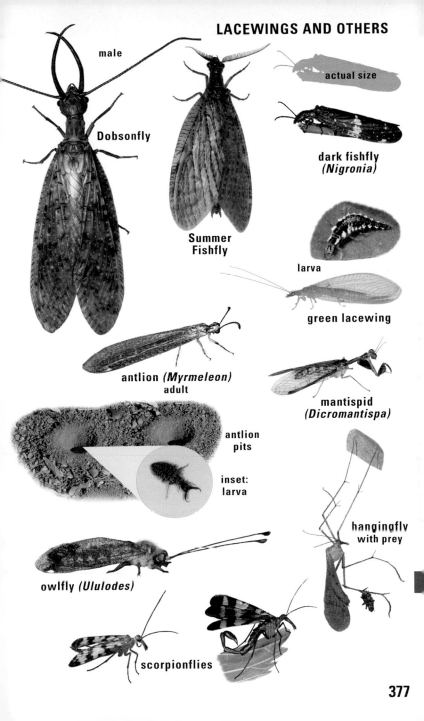

# LACEWINGS AND OTHERS

male

Dobsonfly

**Summer Fishfly**

actual size

**dark fishfly (Nigronia)**

larva

**green lacewing**

**antlion (Myrmeleon) adult**

**mantispid (Dicromantispa)**

antlion pits

inset: larva

**hangingfly with prey**

**owlfly (Ululodes)**

**scorpionflies**

377

(order **Diptera**) include the house fly, mosquitoes, gnats, punkies, blue-bottles and greenbottles, among other pesky insects, but most species are beneficial, or of no economic or health consequence. Flies have sponging or piercing-sucking mouthparts as adults. They go through complete metamorphosis, from egg to maggot to pupa to adult. Here is a small selection of the many families of flies in the region.

**Crane flies** (**Tipulidae, Limoniidae,** and 2 other families) are mostly large, lanky flies that resemble huge mosquitoes. They do not bite and are rather fragile. Larval habits vary dramatically, some being aquatic. Adult crane flies can be abundant, especially in spring and early summer.

**Mosquitoes (Culicidae)** are bloodthirsty pests, but most species feed preferentially on birds, or mammals other than us. They can carry a number of diseases such as West Nile virus and Eastern equine encephalitis, so apply repellents with DEET as the active ingredient. Larvae ("wrigglers") and pupae ("tumblers") are aquatic. Drain standing water and dump rainwater from containers to control mosquitoes.

**Midges (Chironomidae)** look much like mosquitoes, but do not bite. Note long front legs held off the substrate at rest. Males often form dense swarms over lakes or tall objects to attract females. Larvae are aquatic, living mostly in silken tubes in bottom sediments. Midges are more common at lights than mosquitoes.

**Horse flies and deer flies (Tabanidae)** often have eyes banded or spotted in bright, colorful patterns. The adult female insect slices open a victim and then sponges up the blood. Larvae live mostly in water or mud where they are predatory on other small animals.

**Robber flies (Asilidae)** are predators that include bumblebee mimics (genus *Laphria*). Most are slim and medium-sized. *Promachus hinei* is very large. These insects usually perch on foliage, twigs, or the ground and dart out to intercept other insects. They then return to their perch to eat. Habits of the larval stages are mostly a mystery.

**Bee flies (Bombyliidae)** are mostly fuzzy. Many can hover perfectly in midair. *Bombylius major* and other species use their long beak to sip nectar. Larvae of various species are parasitic or predatory on other insects. The **Tiger Bee Fly** (*Xenox tigrinus*) is parasitic on carpenter bees.

**Long-legged flies (Dolichopodidae)** are the bright metallic flies that run around on leaves seeking small prey. Other species skate across the surface of water. Larvae of most are predators in decaying organic matter.

**Flower flies (Syrphidae)** are astonishing mimics of wasps and bees. Abundant in yards, gardens, fields, and forests, they are fairly effective pollinators. The sluglike larvae of many species feed on aphids.

**Blow flies (Calliphoridae)** include "greenbottles" (*Lucilia* spp.) and "bluebottles" (*Calliphora* spp.). Larvae are major decomposers of carrion. These are abundant flies, more so than house flies in urban areas.

**Tachinid flies (Tachinidae)** are mostly robust, spiny flies that, as larvae, are internal parasites of other insects, especially caterpillars. Look for the adult flies on flowers and foliage.

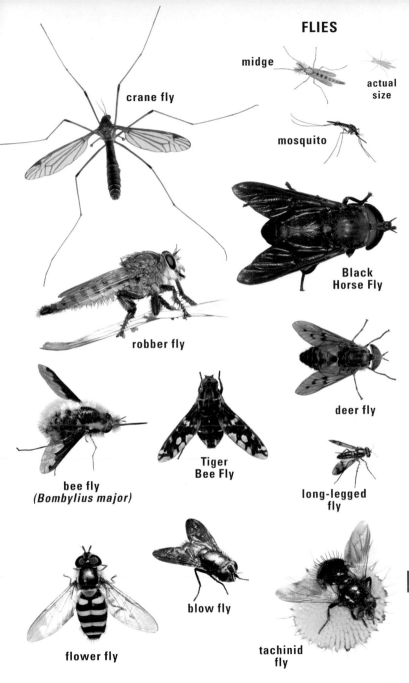

# FLIES

midge

actual size

crane fly

mosquito

Black Horse Fly

robber fly

deer fly

bee fly
*(Bombylius major)*

Tiger Bee Fly

long-legged fly

flower fly

blow fly

tachinid fly

The order Hymenoptera is often referred to collectively as "the social insects" because ants, bees, and wasps are classified here, but the great majority of species lead solitary lives. All undergo complete metamorphosis, have chewing mouthparts, and have two sets of wings (although some are wingless). Many kinds of wasps do not sting, and of those that do, it is only the females. Several families are omitted here because the species are tiny and seldom seen.

The **Poison Ivy Sawfly** (*Arge humeralis*) is a member of the family **Argidae.** The last antennal segment of argids is very long. Many species are red and black. Larvae resemble caterpillars and eat foliage. Sawfly larvae have 7 pairs of prolegs (the fleshy "stumps" on each abdominal segment). Butterfly and moth caterpillars have no more than 5 pairs of prolegs.

The **Elm Sawfly** (*Cimbex americana*) is large, with the short, clubbed antennae typical of the family **Cimbicidae**. The caterpillar-like larvae feed on foliage and coil up when disturbed. Sawflies do not sting.

**Common sawflies (Tenthredinidae)** are abundant, diverse, and feed on plants in the larval stage. The genus *Tenthredo* is typical. Adult *Tenthredo* prey on small insects, but also visit flowers. Larvae of **Willow Sawfly** (*Nematus ventralis*) are sometimes common on willows. Female sawflies have serrated, blade-like egg-laying organs used to insert eggs in plant tissue.

**Horntails (Siricidae)** are large, stingless wasps. The spearlike appendage on the abdomen is the female's egg-laying organ, called an ovipositor. Females of the **Pigeon Tremex** (*Tremex columba*) drill into dead or dying trees to lay their eggs. The larvae that hatch bore in the wood with the help of a fungus that the mother wasp deposits with each egg.

**Ichneumon wasps (Ichneumonidae)** include giant *Megarhyssa* species that parasitize horntails (Siricidae, above). The whiplike "tail" is actually the female's ovipositor, inserted into trees and logs to reach horntail grubs boring within. Most ichneumons are parasites of caterpillars, the adult wasp emerging from the chrysalis (pupa) stage. Some ichneumons sting, but the stinger is retracted and not visible until deployed.

**Braconids (Braconidae)** are small, stingless parasites of other insects, especially the caterpillars of moths and butterflies. Caterpillars covered in egglike cocoons are parasitized by braconids.

**Gall wasps (Cynipidae)** create odd growths on plants, especially oaks. The tiny female wasp lays an egg that stimulates abnormal growth, furnishing a protective refuge and food for her offspring. Galls are most obvious in winter. Flies, aphids, mites, fungi, and other organisms make them, too.

The **American Pelecinid** (*Pelecinus polyturator*) is the only North American member of the **Pelecinidae**. Females are large, long-bodied wasps. The shorter-bodied males are rare, so this species can probably reproduce without them. Larvae are parasites of scarab grubs.

**Cuckoo wasps (Chrysididae)** are small, active, and bright metallic green or blue, sometimes red or copper. Look for them on flowers, around aphid colonies, and the exterior of barns. They are stingless parasites of other wasps like mud daubers or sand wasps.

# WASPS AND SAWFLIES

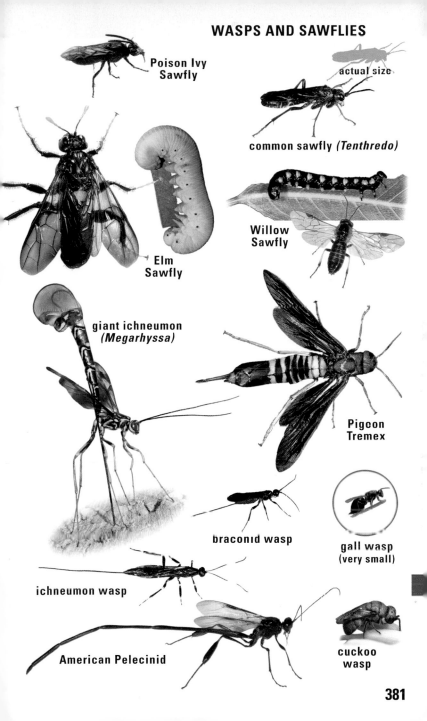

Poison Ivy
Sawfly

actual size

common sawfly *(Tenthredo)*

Willow
Sawfly

Elm
Sawfly

giant ichneumon
*(Megarhyssa)*

Pigeon
Tremex

braconid wasp

gall wasp
(very small)

ichneumon wasp

American Pelecinid

cuckoo
wasp

# WASPS, BEES, AND ANTS

continue the order Hymenoptera, introduced on p. 380.

**Sphecid wasps (Sphecidae)** are slender, with a long petiole linking the thorax and abdomen. They are solitary, and the females sting. The **Great Golden Digger** *(Sphex ichneumoneus)* stores paralyzed katydids in cells in an underground burrow. The grass-carrier wasps, genus *Isodontia,* may use window tracks as nesting space. They stock paralyzed tree crickets and small katydids as food for their offspring.

Wasps in the family **Crabronidae** were formerly part of Sphecidae. All are solitary, and females sting. Most dig burrows in the ground or nest in cavities in wood or hollow twigs. **Eastern Cicada Killers** *(Sphecius speciosus)* may nest near each other in sandy soil. The fly-killing sand wasps in the genus *Bembix* are much smaller. "Beewolves," genus *Philanthus,* are also common. They hunt bees and other small wasps.

**Sweat bees (Halictidae)** are named for their habit of landing on people and licking their perspiration. Also in this family are brilliant metallic bees like those in the genus *Agapostemon.* All nest in burrows in the soil and some are primitively social. **Megachilidae** includes solitary mason bees and leafcutter bees. Females collect pollen in a brush on the underside of the abdomen. Leafcutters, genus *Megachile,* snip pieces of leaves and shape them into barrel-like cells for their larval offspring. They stack the cells inside a linear, pre-existing cavity in wood, rock, or other material.

Female bees in the family **Apidae** collect pollen in "baskets" or scopae (dense brushes of hairs) on the hind legs. Settlers brought the **Honeybee** *(Apis mellifera)* to Jamestown in 1622. Bumblebees, genus *Bombus,* are native, and also social. The **Virginia Carpenter Bee** *(Xylocopa virginica)* nests in dead, solid wood, sometimes in exterior beams of homes.

**Scoliids (Scoliidae)** are large, hairy wasps. The solitary females dig up grubs of scarab beetles, sting them, and lay a single egg on each victim. The wasp larva will live as an external parasite, eventually dooming the grub.

**Velvet ants (Mutillidae)** are solitary wasps, females of which are wingless. They are parasitic in the nests of other wasps or bees. Look for them in sandy areas, but be careful of their potent sting. Both genders "squeak" by rubbing their abdominal segments together.

The social yellowjackets, European Hornet, and paper wasps are in the family **Vespidae** along with solitary potter and mason wasps. The **European Paper Wasp** *(Polistes dominulus),* a recent arrival in the region, is now widespread and numerous. Yellowjackets (including the **Bald-faced "Hornet,"** *Dolichovespula maculata*) are mostly fly-killers, but some scavenge at picnics and barbecues. Paper, mason, and potter wasps hunt caterpillars. All fold their wings lengthwise at rest.

**Ants (Formicidae)** are social, with at least one queen and usually hundreds or thousands of female "workers" in each nest. Ant colonies spawn a new generation of winged queens and males each year. Males die after mating, while queens shed their wings and set up housekeeping. Carpenter ants, genus *Camponotus,* do not eat wood, but simply tunnel in wood for nesting space. *Lasius* ants are abundant in fields and lawns. Some ants defend themselves by squirting formic acid, but others sting.

# WASPS, BEES, AND ANTS

Great Golden Digger

grass-carrier wasp

actual size

sand wasp
*(Bembix)*

beewolf
*(Philanthus)*

Eastern
Cicada
Killer

*Agapostemon*

bumblebee

leafcutter
bee

Honeybee

Virginia
Carpenter Bee

scoliid
wasp

velvet ant

European
Paper Wasp

Bald-faced
Hornet

carpenter ant

*Lasius* ant

383

Spiders are arachnids, not insects. They lack wings and antennae, and have only two main body parts: the cephalothorax and the abdomen. Like all arachnids, spiders possess eight legs. They spin silk from spinnerets on the end of the abdomen. Most spiders have eight eyes, but only hunters like wolf and jumping spiders have good vision. Spiders are often feared because they are venomous, but few are dangerous to healthy people or pets. Most spiders have different color patterns on the top and bottom. Those on the facing page are shown from the top or side.

The **Long-bodied Cellar Spider** (*Pholcus phalangioides*) is frequently confused with "daddy-longlegs," another kind of arachnid (p. 388). This member of the family **Pholcidae** spins a broad, tangled web in basements, cellars, crawlspaces, and similar locations. When disturbed, it is likely to shake violently in its web.

**Orb weavers (family Araneidae)** build beautiful circular webs that are most conspicuous in late summer and fall. Adult females of **Hentz's Orb-weaver** (*Neoscona crucifera*) sit in the hub (center) of their webs at night, hiding by day in foliage at the perimeter of the snare. This is a common species along forest edges and in parks and gardens. Females of the **Banded Garden Spider** (*Argiope trifasciata*) are large but cryptic. Males are much smaller and seen less often. They build their webs mostly amid tall grasses and weeds. The snares usually include a zigzag band of silk called a stabilimentum. The **Spined Micrathena** (*Micrathena gracilis*) spins a tight orb web in the understory of deciduous forests, often across trails where hikers blunder into them face-first. The **Orchard Spider** (*Leucauge venusta*) is a member of the long-jawed orb weaver family **Tetragnathidae**. It makes a horizontal orb web, usually close to the forest floor. The spider hangs upside down, and the red mark on its belly is suggestive of a black widow. Note the green legs and silvery top side of the abdomen.

**Sheetweb weavers (family Linyphiidae)** make flat, concave, or convex webs. The **Bowl-and-doily Spider** (*Frontinella communis*) can be abundant in yards, gardens, fields, and forest edges where it spins a bowl-shaped web with a flat sheet beneath it. Look for the webs in trees and shrubs. The **Filmy Dome Spider** (*Neriene radiata*) makes a domelike web usually a couple of feet off the ground.

**Cobweb weavers** in the family **Theridiidae** include the potentially dangerous **Northern Black Widow** (*Latrodectus variolus*). The adult female is black with a broken red hourglass marking on the underside of the abdomen, as well as stripes and/or spots on top. They are secretive, sitting in their tangled webs only at night. The **Common House Spider** (*Parasteatoda tepidariorum*) is abundant around buildings and homes.

**Jumping spiders (family Salticidae)** are agile hunters that have the keenest vision of any land invertebrate. Two of their eight eyes are large and forward-facing. Their alert and curious nature is often misinterpreted as aggression. The **Zebra Jumper** (*Salticus scenicus*) is small but common, often seen prowling the outside walls of buildings. The larger **Bold Jumper** (*Phidippus audax*) hunts amid the foliage of shrubs and trees.

# SPIDERS

Hentz's Orbweaver

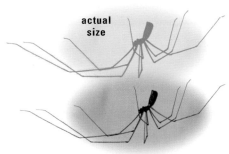

actual size

Long-bodied Cellar Spider

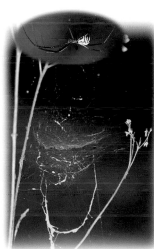

Banded Garden Spider

Spined Micrathena

Orchard Spider

hanging in web

Northern Black Widow

Filmy Dome Spider

Common House Spider

Bowl-and-doily Spider
(with web)

Zebra Jumper

Bold Jumper

**Crab spiders (family Thomisidae)** have long front legs, short hind legs. Most wait motionless for insects to blunder within striking range. The female **Red-banded Crab Spider** *(Misumenoides formosipes)* can change color from white to yellow, or vice versa, over a period of days in order to match the flowers she chooses to sit on.

The **Brown Recluse** *(Loxosceles reclusa),* family **Sicariidae,** is truly dangerous, but thankfully found only in isolated populations in the region covered here. Note the 6 eyes, arranged in 3 pairs. This is the *only* character that can be used to reliably identify them. Take care in moving contents in long-neglected storage areas to avoid being bitten.

Members of the family **Gnaphosidae** are fleet-footed hunters. **Eastern Parson Spider** *(Herpyllus ecclesiasticus)* sometimes enters homes, but prefers living outdoors under rocks, boards, and other debris in woodlands.

**Funnelweb weavers (Agelenidae)** spin thick, sheetlike webs attached to a funnel-shaped retreat where the spider lives. Flying insects are intercepted by overhead foundation threads and fall to the non-sticky sheet below. The spider dashes out and bites its victim, dragging it back into its lair to eat. The **Barn Funnel Weaver** *(Tegenaria domestica)* is commonly found in old barns and other buildings, even indoors in cluttered garages, sheds, and windowsills.

Prowling spiders of the family **Miturgidae** include the **Yellow Sac Spider** *(Cheiracanthium mildei)*. Native to Eurasia and northern Africa, this pale, nomadic spider spins a "sleeping bag" where walls meet the ceiling inside homes. It rests there during the day and prowls at night, spinning a new shelter after each foray. It has been mistakenly considered as venomous to people. The species is now widespread in the U.S.

**Nursery web spiders (Pisauridae)** include the huge, sprawling **Dark Fishing Spider** *(Dolomedes tenebrosus)*. Look for it on fenceposts, tree trunks, and other vertical surfaces, especially at night. *Pisaurina mira* is variable in color pattern. It is common on foliage in hedgerows, along forest edges, and in the understory. Females in this family carry their egg sac in their jaws, eventually hanging it in a "nursery web" where the female stands guard over it.

**Lynx spiders (Oxyopidae)** like the **Striped Lynx** *(Oxyopes salticus)* are abundant in fields and meadows where they actively stalk prey or wait in ambush on foliage. They can pounce, too. Note the spiny legs.

**Wolf spiders** of the family **Lycosidae** are the muscle cars of the spider world. Powerful hunters, they are usually seen on the ground or rocks, logs, and other horizontal objects (in contrast to fishing spiders usually seen in the vertical plane). Female wolf spiders carry the egg sac from their spinnerets. Once the spiderlings hatch, they ride on mom's back until their next molt, after which they disperse. Like most wolf spiders, the **Striped Wolf Spider** *(Rabidosa rabida)* is mostly nocturnal. Try going out at night with a headlamp or flashlight. The eyes of wolf spiders sparkle with reflected light in the darkness. Thin-legged wolf spiders in the genus *Pardosa* are mostly diurnal, and especially common on stones in streambeds.

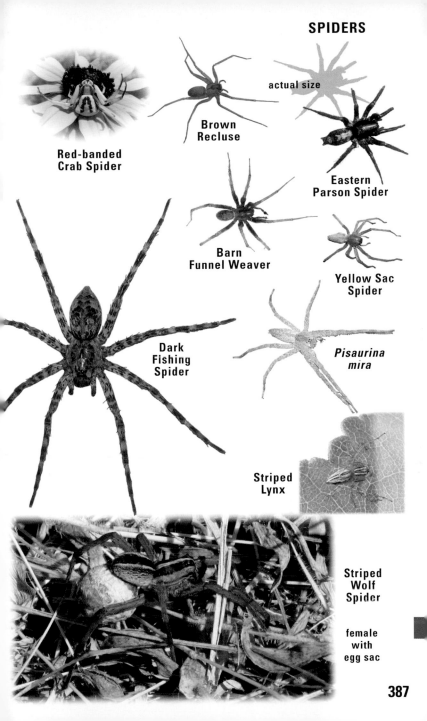

# SPIDERS

actual size

Red-banded
Crab Spider

Brown
Recluse

Eastern
Parson Spider

Barn
Funnel Weaver

Yellow Sac
Spider

Dark
Fishing
Spider

*Pisaurina
mira*

Striped
Lynx

Striped
Wolf
Spider

female
with
egg sac

387

# OTHER ARACHNIDS

Arachnid diversity extends beyond spiders. Even Striped Bark Scorpion *(Centruroides vittatus)* reaches sw. Illinois, though it is rare. Harvestmen, pseudoscorpions, and mites are abundant, but most are so tiny that one needs high magnification to recognize them even to the order level. It is more important to understand their ecological roles anyway.

**Harvestmen (order Opiliones),** also known as "daddy-longlegs," are not venomous, and are not spiders. Compare their single body section to the two that spiders have; and one pair of eyes elevated on a tubercle, as opposed to a spider's eight eyes. They mostly scavenge decaying organic matter, but also kill weak or injured invertebrates. Harvestmen shed a leg or two when attacked, a self-preservation tactic known as "autotomy." They secrete defensive chemicals from pores near the base of the second pair of legs. The **Eastern Harvestman** *(Leiobunum vittatum),* family **Sclerosomatidae,** is among the most common species. *Phalangium opilio* (family **Phalangiidae)** is the most-studied of all harvestmen. Native to Eurasia, it is most at home here in disturbed habitats.

Mites are ridiculously diverse and abundant, but most are microscopic and seldom seen. Order **Ixodida** is the ticks. **Family Ixodidae** includes our common species. The **American Dog Tick** *(Dermacentor variabilis)* might enter your home on the pooch, but inspect yourself and other family members, too, after hiking in open woodlands and along forest edges. Ticks lurk on foliage and the tips of weeds, "questing" for hosts with outstretched legs. The dog tick can transmit Rocky Mountain spotted fever, tularemia, and "tick paralysis." **Black-legged Tick** *(Ixodes scapularis)* is the "deer tick" that vectors Lyme disease. The larval stages in the 2-year life cycle feed mostly on deermice. The second-year nymphs peak in summer when we are outdoors ourselves. Smaller than adults, they are difficult to detect before they latch on. The **Lone Star Tick** *(Amblyomma americanum),* once regarded as a southern species, is increasingly common here. It is a vector of ehrlichiosis, which affects both people and dogs.

Many mites can be observed on the bodies of insects. Among the most conspicuous are those in the genus *Poecilochirus,* which ride on carrion beetles **(family Silphidae).** They disembark when the beetle arrives at a carcass. There, they feed on fly eggs, eliminating the beetles' chief competition for the corpse. Some mites are aquatic, living in freshwater habitats. A few of those have a parasitic stage, and the larvae of the genus *Arrenurus* are frequently seen on adult damselflies and dragonflies.

"Velvet mites" in the genus *Leptus* are commonly seen scrambling over foliage. Larvae are parasitic on other arthropods, especially harvestmen. They go through an inactive stage before emerging as predatory adults.

**Pseudoscorpions (order Pseudoscorpiones)** get attention because of their resemblance to tiny, tail-less scorpions. They are not dangerous, but at least some species have venom glands in their pincers. Pseudoscorpions are tick-sized predators normally found in soil, leaf-litter, under bark, and in caves. They hitch rides on flying insects by clamping onto a leg or hiding under the wing covers of longhorn beetles.

# OTHER ARACHNIDS

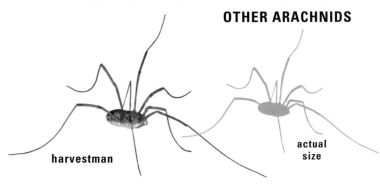

harvestman

actual size

---

All of the creatures below are truly tiny in real life, and they are shown here *much* larger than their actual sizes.

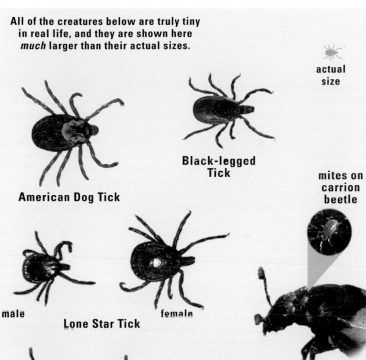

actual size

**American Dog Tick**

**Black-legged Tick**

mites on carrion beetle

male

**Lone Star Tick**

female

velvet mite
*(Leptus)*

red velvet mite

pseudoscorpion

# LAND INVERTEBRATES

Often casually dismissed as mere "bugs," these deserve a closer look.

**Pillbugs and Sowbugs** are terrestrial crustaceans in the order **Isopoda**. Both the **Woodlouse** *(Armadillidium vulgare)*, family **Armadillidiidae**, and the **European Sowbug** *(Oniscus asellus)*, family **Oniscidae**, are native to Europe. Sowbugs are more flattened, and cannot roll up like the Woodlouse can. They are valuable decomposers of organic material.

**Centipedes (class Chilopoda)** are fast-moving, serpentine predators. They have one pair of legs per body segment, the first pair modified into venomous fangs. The order **Scutigeromorpha** includes the **House Centipede** *(Scutigera coleoptrata)*, a startling but harmless visitor in many homes. *Scolopocryptops sexspinosus* **(order Scolopendromorpha)** occurs in moist leaf-litter, or under rocks or logs from Ohio to Iowa. It has 23 pairs of legs, and mature specimens sometimes exceed 50 millimeters. **Stone Centipedes (order Lithobiomorpha)** are common under rocks and boards, and in rotting logs. Adults have 15 pairs of legs. **Soil Centipedes (Geophilomorpha)** are small, skinny, and usually yellowish or whitish. They are blind, and adults have 27–191 pairs of legs.

**Millipedes (class Diplopoda)** are slow-moving, mostly nocturnal scavengers and vegetarians with 2 pairs of legs per body segment. **Flat-backed millipedes (order Polydesmida)** include the **Greenhouse Millipede** *(Oxidus gracilis)*, an Asian import now found in all states. *Semionellus placidus,* native to North America, glows under ultraviolet light. **Order Spirobolida** includes our largest (up to 10 cm) millipedes. The *Narceus americanus-annularis* complex occurs throughout our region. Crested millipedes in the genus *Abacion* (order **Callipodida**) are recognized by their corrugated texture.

**Earthworms (phylum Annelida, class or subclass Oligochaeta)** found here are not indigenous. Native earthworms were eradicated from the Great Lakes region by glaciers in the last ice age. European and Asian species that arrived in ships' ballast, or in root balls of imported plants, now dominate our soil fauna. A study by the University of Minnesota demonstrated that invasive earthworms dramatically change the soil, and understory flora, where they have infiltrated forests. Different earthworms live at different depths. Anecic earthworms occupy deep vertical burrows but visit the soil surface. These big "night crawlers" can tunnel 6 feet deep. Epigeic earthworms live and feed in leaf-litter. The **"Red Wriggler"** *(Eisenia foetida)*, sold for home composting, is an epigeic species. Endogeic worms are small and lack pigment. They make extensive horizontal burrows in topsoil.

Many **snails** and most **slugs (phylum Mollusca, class Gastropoda)** are also aliens from overseas. They eat mostly vegetation, scraping the surface with a toothed, tongue-like organ called a radula. Their eyes are situated on tentacle-like stalks they retract quickly in the face of danger. Each individual is both male and female, but they still must fertilize each other. The **Leopard Slug** *(Limax maximus)*, family **Limacidae**, is native to Europe but locally common in the Midwest. The **Whitelip Snail** *(Neohelix albolabris)*, family **Polygyridae**, is common in second-growth forest.

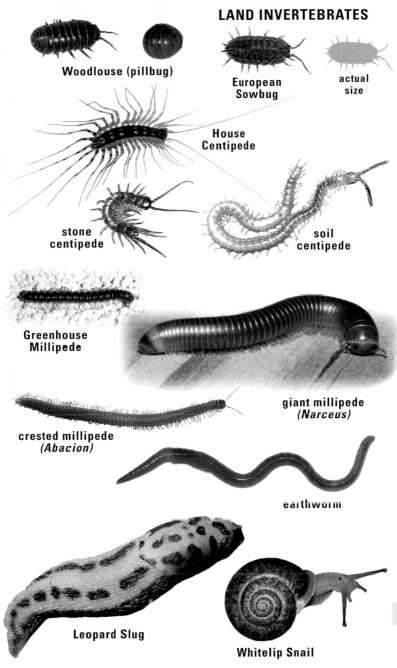

# LAND INVERTEBRATES

Woodlouse (pillbug)

European Sowbug

actual size

House Centipede

stone centipede

soil centipede

Greenhouse Millipede

giant millipede
*(Narceus)*

crested millipede
*(Abacion)*

earthworm

Leopard Slug

Whitelip Snail

Our natural resources play a vital role in the quality of life in the Midwest. Even people not actively interested in nature can still appreciate the sight of spring flowers or the sounds of bird song. But the value of our natural heritage goes far beyond its undeniable aesthetic appeal. For example, outdoor and nature-related tourism plays a major role in the region's economy. Many other commercial activities also depend on native wildlife and plants. Beyond that, there is the more basic fact that everything in nature is interconnected and interdependent. Conservation of natural resources should be of importance to everyone.

## SUSTAINABILITY

When the first European settlers came to this region, they found extraordinary natural riches. From forests of magnificent trees to broad, sweeping prairies; from lakes teeming with fish to marshes alive with wild ducks; from elk and bison and deer to the vast flocks of wild pigeons overhead; from sparkling rivers to deep, rich soil — it seemed that nature's bounty in this land would be inexhaustible.

Unfortunately, it proved all too exhaustible. Native American tribes had lived in a balance with their surroundings here for thousands of years, but the European settlers depleted the natural resources at an alarming rate. Most of the primeval forests were cut, most of the elk and other large animals were shot, and some of the most abundant fish began to disappear. Rivers were fouled with pollution and with excessive runoff from cleared land, and soil in some regions was depleted and degraded. It was becoming obvious that resources were being used at a level that could not be sustained for the long term.

What the pioneers were learning, the hard way, was a series of lessons about sustainability.

The movement toward sustainability is not just a matter of environmental issues — it has economic and social aspects as well — but in this section we are concerned with how it relates to the use of natural resources. The basic idea is that future generations should have access to the same resources that we enjoy today, or to even higher levels of these resources.

Of course, some resources are finite. Fossil fuels such as oil and coal will eventually run out. Besides, burning of these fuels leads to an increase in the carbon dioxide in the atmosphere, which may be implicated in changing the overall climate of the planet. Ultimately we will have to switch to energy sources that are fully renewable, such as solar power or wind power, but these have potential negative effects on the environment as well. Creating true sustainability for future centuries will take a concerted effort, collective wisdom, and good science.

## BIODIVERSITY

They say variety is the spice of life. As naturalists, we certainly agree. A meadow filled with white asters might be attractive, but we prefer a meadow with dozens of different kinds of flowers. A morning chorus of robins may sound beautiful, but we prefer to hear the songs of many kinds of birds. But beyond these aesthetic issues, variety is important for scientific reasons.

For the natural world, variety is more than just spice; it's an essential main ingredient. In nature, variety is often referred to as biodiversity. A simplified definition for this term would be "the variety of all life forms within a given habitat, ecosystem, or region, or an entire planet." The Midwest is blessed with rich biodiversity, and many thousands of distinct species of living things find their niches here.

A healthy habitat, or ecosystem, has many, many species interacting in countless ways. A single oak tree may be assailed by hundreds of species of insects that eat its leaves, acorns, wood, or roots, but those insects are kept in check by scores of other insects and dozens of birds, not to mention bats, toads, lizards, and other creatures. Some of the insects that attack the oak in some life stages may be pollinating its flowers in other stages of their lives. The acorns produced by the oak may be eaten by squirrels, jays, turkeys, or other creatures, but some of those animals will carry acorns away and bury them, thus unintentionally planting the next generation. When the oak dies, its fallen trunk will be broken down by many kinds of fungi, creating soil that will sustain future oaks and other plants. And so on. Every living thing is involved in this web of connections, all adding up to an intricate balance of nature.

**Swamp White Oak**

Although every species has its own niche, a large amount of overlap is built into the system. Take away one species and it may not make a big difference: something else will pollinate that flower, bury that acorn, or eat that insect. But as we begin to take away more species, serious and unexpected consequences can result.

Imagine that you are building the wooden frame for a house. For it to be sturdy and durable, you'll probably use more nails than the absolute bare minimum necessary; and after it's built, you could probably pop out a nail here, a nail there, without it falling down. But how many nails can you remove before the frame becomes unstable? What happens if you remove one critical nail and the frame begins to collapse? A natural ecosystem is like that, on a much grander and more complicated scale: once we start removing species, we risk causing serious problems.

This is part of the reason why it's important to preserve biodiversity: not just so we can enjoy all that variety, but so the machinery of nature can continue to function. This is part of the reason why conservationists work to prevent extinction of species. Ironically, adding species to a habitat can cause as many problems as taking some away. In the next two sections we'll talk about two sides of this issue: endangered species and invasive species.

# ENDANGERED SPECIES

The extinction of species is a natural thing. But it isn't inevitable — at least, not on the time scales that we usually think about. Over long ages of time, some species may adapt and change radically as conditions change, while others may go extinct. But other kinds of living things may continue to exist, essentially unchanged, for millions of years, as long as their surroundings continue to satisfy their requirements for survival.

During the last few centuries the world has seen an unnatural wave of extinctions, most caused (directly or indirectly) by humans. Before wildlife management was understood and before laws were in place, some species found in the Midwest were hunted to extinction. Passenger Pigeons once darkened the skies of the Midwest in immense flocks, but their numbers in the wild dropped from billions to zero in the length of a few decades. The very last living Passenger Pigeon, a solitary female named Martha, died in the Cincinnati Zoo in September 1914. Other species that no longer occur in the Midwest but are still found elsewhere, such as Puma (Mountain Lion) and Grizzly Bear, are said to be extirpated from this region.

The slaughter of the American Bison, which took place mostly just to the west of our region, is a dark chapter in the history of North American wildlife. With no laws to protect them, the mighty herds were destroyed by market gunners. No one thought about a sustainable harvest; instead, it was every man for himself, competing to see who could kill the most. In the space of a few years, the vast herds were reduced to small, localized populations. Today, the term "buffalo hunt" is often applied to any senseless and unsustainable overuse of a resource.

**Endangered Species Act.** Concern over loss of species led to the passage in 1973 of a landmark piece of legislation, the U.S. Endangered Species Act (ESA). The stated purpose of the ESA was to protect and recover populations of imperiled species of animals and plants, and the ecosystems upon which they depend. Under the ESA, after careful scientific review, a species in trouble could be listed as either threatened or endangered, and a series of legal protections and other actions would come into effect. The ESA has had some successes: for example, Osprey, Bald Eagle, and Peregrine Falcon, all in serious trouble in the 1970s, have recovered extremely well.

**State designations.** In addition to the federal list, most states in the U.S. also maintain lists of species considered endangered or threatened within the state, sometimes adding other categories such as "Species of Special Concern." Species are often rare at the outer edges of their ranges, so animals or plants are likely to show up on the lists for states where they are peripheral. For example, Big-leaved Aster, American Water-willow, and Cinnamon Fern are all listed as endangered in Iowa, but occur more commonly farther east in our region. Of course conservationists are interested in maintaining diversity at the state and local level, but most effort goes into species in danger of extinction throughout their ranges.

Here are examples of species in need of protection everywhere.

**Kirtland's Warbler.** It was first discovered as a migrant near Cleveland, Ohio, in 1851, but the breeding grounds of Kirtland's Warbler were not found until 1903. We now know that most Kirtland's Warblers nest in a few counties in Michigan, with isolated small colonies in Wisconsin and Ontario. They nest only in stands of young Jack Pines: a habitat that grows up briefly after fires. Nest parasitism by Brown-headed Cowbirds has also played a role in the decline of this species. Controlled burning to create more habitat and control of cowbird numbers have helped populations rebound, and there is discussion of removing Kirtland's Warbler from the endangered species list. Citizen scientists have contributed greatly to the recent success of this species, volunteering thousands of hours monitoring nests and gathering valuable data used in the recovery program.

**Karner Blue.** A denizen of pine barren and black oak savanna and dependent on wild lupine, the only known larval food plant, the tiny Karner Blue butterfly packs a lot of beauty into a small package. Once fairly widespread in the upper Midwest and Northeast, it was driven to the brink of extinction by habitat loss. This led to the development of the Karner Blue Recovery Plan, which, in addition to many other action items, includes range-wide and regional management guidelines. Small, localized colonies can still be found in Illinois, Indiana, Michigan, Minnesota, Ohio, and Wisconsin, as well as New York and New Hampshire, but few of these sites have viable and self-sustaining populations. The Karner Blue is usually classified as a subspecies of the more widespread western Melissa Blue, but the Endangered Species Act applies to subspecies as well as full species.

**Karner Blue**

## INVASIVE SPECIES

Vast numbers of plant species have been transported around the world by humans. Some are unknowingly introduced when seeds cling to shoes and clothing. Once established, without the normal natural balance of insects and diseases that would keep them in check within their native range, many exotic invasives spread aggressively, disrupting habitats and food sources for native species.

Most exotic species cause only minor damage. Often they are mostly confined to sites where the soil has been disturbed numerous times. For example, a high percentage of the plants growing in vacant city lots and along roadsides will be exotic species. A more serious issue involves those exotic species that spread aggressively beyond the disturbed sites and into native habitats. These plants may compete with and crowd out native plants, while reducing the value of the habitat for native animals.

An example of an invasive with an obvious impact is Purple Loosestrife. A perennial with a strong, tough root system, this gaudy flower has taken over many wetland areas almost completely, turning marshes and wet meadows into solid stands of this species. Because marshes and other wetlands are scarce and valuable habitats that host many rare native species, a takeover by Purple Loosestrife leads to an overall loss of biodiversity.

It is important to learn what plant species are invasive in the areas where we live and where we travel, and to take precautions against inadvertently transporting them into other areas. The Midwest Native Plant Society is a good source of information on the issue. In this guide, look at the final pages of each plant chapter for more on invasives.

It is not only invasive plants that can wreak havoc on the natural balance. A number of invasive animals have had a significant impact in North America. First introduced in New York City in 1890, the European Starling eventually became one of North America's most widespread and abundant birds. Adaptable and aggressive, starlings compete with several species of native cavity-nesting birds, including Eastern Bluebirds, Purple Martins, and Red-headed Woodpeckers. In many areas, the starlings may have caused permanent reductions in the populations of these natives.

Asian carp now pose a serious threat to the Great Lakes. This term applies to at least five species of fish from Asia, but most of the concern is focused on Bighead Carp and Silver Carp. These were brought to the U.S. in the 1970s to help get rid of algae on catfish farms and water treatment plants. At some point, some of the fish escaped into the Mississippi River system, and began to expand their range. They have worked their way north, and experts fear the damage they could do if they invade all of the Great Lakes. Asian carp are filter-feeders, straining tiny plankton out of the water. They could provide serious competition to many native fish that rely on the same food source. A variety of state, provincial, and federal agencies are now working on action plans, both for how to keep Asian carp out of the Great Lakes and for how to deal with them if they do invade.

## GRASS-ROOTS CONSERVATION

Much of the work of conservation is done by dedicated professionals in state and federal agencies or in large environmental organizations. But that doesn't mean there's no role for the efforts of private citizens. In fact, most highly successful conservation efforts have begun with the efforts of individuals and small organizations, banding together to bring about major changes.

Consider the founding of the Izaak Walton League of America. Today it's a large and effective group with chapters all over the U.S., particularly in the Midwest. But it got its start in 1922 because a group of sportsmen saw a need to step up and protect the nation's waterways and wild areas. They formed an organization to combat water pollution and to protect woods and wildlife, and they took the name of Izaak Walton, the famed 17th-century English angler, conservationist, and writer.

Although it began as a group of a few dozen sportsmen, the Izaak Walton League grew to the point where it could have a positive impact on national policy. It has played an important role in passing the Clean Water Act, supported the expansion of refuges and wilderness areas, helped to focus public attention on the problems of acid rain, and taken part in many other vital conservation efforts.

Other groups with strong national and international impact have come from similarly small beginnings. But for some kinds of conservation efforts, smaller groups of citizens can be more effective. This is particularly true in dealing with issues requiring quick action and local knowledge. Some of the best work can be accomplished when a small group with local expertise collaborates with a larger organization with national clout. The authors of this guide have been involved in several such efforts. For example, Jeff Sayre and his colleagues discovered a rare patch of prairie fen habitat in Michigan, and they worked with The Nature Conservancy for three years to arrange for its protection. Kimberly Kaufman, in her role as director of the Black Swamp Bird Observatory, has worked with the American Bird Conservancy to protect vital stopover habitats for migratory birds in Ohio. Such partnerships are often more nimble and more powerful than either a local or a national organization could be by itself.

## WHAT CAN YOU DO FOR CONSERVATION?

Everyone can help with the conservation of our natural resources. The first step toward doing your part is to be well informed.

**Bird-friendly coffee.** Coffee grown in the traditional way in the American tropics, shaded by the canopy of native trees, provides rich habitat for migratory birds. Unfortunately, since the 1970s, vast areas have been converted from shade coffee to sun coffee. The area is bulldozed and doused with fertilizers, herbicides, and pesticides. Terrible for the soil, dangerous for people who tend the plants, and disastrous for migratory birds that need wintering habitat, the only payoff is higher yields in the short term.

With growing awareness of this issue, some companies cheat the system by planting a few nonnative trees and slapping a "shade-grown" label on their product. To ensure that the coffee you purchase actually comes from a farm that supports bird life, look for the Smithsonian Migratory Bird Center seal of Bird-Friendly coffee. This is the gold standard for coffee that is good for birds and good for people. It can still be a challenge to find; a good source is the company Birds & Beans. Learn more at www.birdsandbeans.com.

**Keep cats indoors.** Domestic cats can be wonderful companions. However, scientific studies have proven that when cats are allowed to roam outside, they have a devastating impact on birds and small mammals. In fact, studies estimate that roaming house cats and feral cats kill billions of birds each year. This is even more disturbing when you consider that some of our most threatened and endangered species, such as Piping Plover and Wood Thrush, are among those impacted. Learn more by consulting the American Bird Conservancy at www.abcbirds.org.

**The Three Rs: reduce, reuse, recycle.** This campaign urges all of us to reduce what we use, reuse items as much as possible, and recycle products once they can no longer be used. Seems simple enough, and yet there are still too few who follow the Three Rs philosophy. We have become a society overrun with our own refuse. Simple steps can make a difference. Live the Three Rs philosophy. Avoid purchasing water and other products in plastic bottles; reduce the amount of waste you produce by avoiding single-use products such as paper towels and napkins; and bring your own reusable grocery bags when you go shopping.

**Reduce your energy consumption.** There are many ways to reduce the amount of energy we use. Replacing regular light bulbs with compact fluorescent bulbs saves money in the long run. They use one-quarter the energy of ordinary bulbs and last 8 to 12 times longer. Slight adjustments to your thermostat — even by just two degrees — can make a big difference throughout the course of one year. So can turning your computer off every night, and hanging clothes up to dry rather than using the dryer. Put all of these things into practice, and the energy savings add up.

**Your carbon footprint.** Most forms of transportation burn fossil fuels. Riding a bike, walking when possible, carpooling, and using public transportation are ways to reduce your "carbon footprint" — that is, the amount of carbon dioxide you put into the atmosphere. When you travel long distances, try researching available programs that allow you to calculate and offset your carbon footprint through donations that support sustainable, responsible, renewable energy projects. Reforestation projects actually reduce the amount of carbon in the atmosphere by sequestering carbon dioxide emissions, providing health benefits for people and wildlife.

**Support federal and state conservation agencies.** This can be as easy as buying a stamp. The annual Federal Migratory Bird Hunting and Conservation Stamp, commonly known as the "Duck Stamp," is a vital tool for wetland conservation. About 98 cents out of every dollar generated by Duck Stamp sales goes to purchase or lease wetland habitat for the National Wildlife Refuge (NWR) System. In the Midwest, for example, more than 86 percent of the area of Ottawa National Wildlife Refuge in Ohio and more than

99 percent of Horicon National Wildlife Refuge in Wisconsin were purchased with Duck Stamp dollars. The refuges are fabulous places for birds and other wildlife; like many other birders and naturalists, we are proud to buy our Duck Stamps every year.

**Support conservation organizations.** One of the most effective ways to help with conservation is to add your support to organizations that are already doing good work. The Midwest is blessed with many conservation groups. Some operate at the national or international level, some do their work at the state or regional level, while some are strictly local. All have their place in the big picture. We recommend researching the many groups out there, learning about how they carry out their missions and about how they will make use of the support that you give them.

## BE A VOICE FOR CONSERVATION

*"We abuse land because we regard it as a commodity belonging to us. When we see land as a community to which we belong, we may begin to use it with love and respect."*
— Aldo Leopold

Born and raised in the Midwest, American author, scientist, and environmentalist Aldo Leopold is considered by many to be the father of wildlife management. His ethics of nature and wildlife preservation had a profound impact on the environmental movement, and continue to influence conservation today. His book *A Sand County Almanac*, published in 1949, is widely regarded as one of the most influential environmental books of the 20th century. The book introduced Leopold's concept of the land ethic. "In short, a land ethic changes the role of Homo sapiens from conqueror of the land community, to plain member and citizen of it," he wrote. "It implies respect for his fellow members, and also respect for the community as such."

But you don't have to write a masterpiece to make an impact. If you love the outdoors, one of the best things you can do to encourage proper stewardship of our natural resources is to talk about it. The crucial first step in building support for conservation is to help connect people with nature. If you're a bird watcher, consider inviting a nonbirding friend, family member, or colleague along on your next field trip. If you're a hiker, camper, or backpacker, invite a few new friends along on your next outing. You don't have to be an expert to foster an interest in nature. All it takes is a willingness to share the wonder and value of time spent outdoors.

# ACKNOWLEDGMENTS

**Kenn and Kimberly Kaufman write:** In a sense, all three of the authors have been working on this book all our lives. But for the two of us, it has occupied much of our attention since about 2007. During that time we have received help from many individuals and institutions. Compiling this guide truly was a team effort.

Our biggest debt of gratitude is owed to our superb coauthor, Jeff Sayre, who took on responsibility for the entire botanical section and contributed heavily to other parts of the book as well. Three other experts served as guest authors for sections of the guide. Eric R. Eaton, primary author of the *Kaufman Field Guide to Insects,* wrote almost all the text on insects and other invertebrates for this guide as well. His vast knowledge and clear writing style are evident on every page. T. Travis Brown, a field biologist with a remarkable breadth of expertise, wrote the section on fishes; Travis also went out of his way to obtain photos of specific plants, reptiles, and invertebrates for us. Thomas D. Bain, a leader in conservation work and an expert on earth sciences and birds, wrote the section on geology.

Illustrations play an essential role in any field guide. Most illustrations in this guide are digital images based on photos. More than 1,100 of the photos used here were taken by the Kaufmans or Sayres, but we received hundreds more images from the photographers listed on pp. 404–405. Some of these images had been used in previous books in the Kaufman Field Guides series, so we benefited once again from the photo research done by Nora Bowers and Rick Bowers for those earlier guides.

While researching this guide, we traveled throughout the seven states of the region. We cannot begin to list all the state parks, national forests, national wildlife refuges, and other preserves that we visited, but we regard all of these as vital places to be treasured and protected. Likewise, we can't begin to list all the individuals who have taught us things about natural history, but the following people gave us specific help in finding or identifying species for this guide: Tim Bollin, Laura Bonneau, Phil Chaon, Jim Davidson, Lee Garling, Cheryl Harner, David J. Horn, Ken Keffer, Jim McCormac, Lynne Schoenborn, and Mark Shieldcastle.

Some of our photos of elusive animals were taken at Back to the Wild, a wildlife rehabilitation center in Castalia, Ohio. Mona Rutger, an amazing individual who pours her heart and soul into running this facility, was generous in allowing us to observe and photograph some of the creatures in her care. We studied and photographed some reptiles and amphibians at the Toledo Zoo, thanks to the generosity of Kent Bekker, R. Andrew Odum, and Andi Norman.

Katie M. Andersen put in hundreds of hours of skillful photo editing work on images for this field guide. Julie A. Shieldcastle did much of the preliminary photo editing, and also compiled some text materials. Barb Myers also did preliminary photo editing for many images.

Working with the consummate professionals at Houghton Mifflin Harcourt is always an inspiration. Our editor, Lisa White, once again treated every aspect of the project with wisdom, patience, and attention to detail. Others who helped us in essential ways included Beth Fuller, Brian Moore, Laney Everson, Katrina Kruse, Taryn Roeder, and Jill Lazer.

Finally, thanks to our agent, Wendy Strothman, for her strong and un-failing support of our desire to teach the public about nature.

**Jeff Sayre writes:** In creating a field guide to nature, it is not sufficient for authors to rest on past experience nor rely on previous adventures. It is important to engage in intensive research by getting out into the field to experience the places likely to be visited by readers.

We visited numerous places throughout the Midwest, taking notes and photos, and simply reveling in the breathtaking species richness, unique geology, and stories of the many local, state, and national parks, as well as private preserves, in our region. We were honored to have met and been guided by a number of stewards who are true heroes in the fight to pre-serve and return nature to its former grandeur.

In particular, we would like to thank: Chris May, director of steward-ship, The Nature Conservancy of Michigan; Dan Ray, Sleeping Bear Dunes National Park; Ralph Hart, U.S. Forest Service; Stuart Goldman, resto-ration specialist, The Nature Conservancy of Illinois, Cody Considine, restoration ecologist, The Nature Conservancy of Illinois, who took us around the amazing 3,000+ acre Nachusa Grasslands project; and Bob Jacksy, naturalist at Oak Openings Preserve, Toledo Metroparks.

A fond thanks also goes out to the knowledgeable, friendly, and pro-fessional staff at Cardno JFNew, where Jeff served as director of its native plant nursery division, and one of its partners, for six years. In particular, we would like to thank Mark O'Brien, Bob Allison, Jason Fritz, Jenny Alli-son, John Richardson, and Clayton Wooldridge (you will be missed).

A special thanks to Travis McFarlane, a senior technical support techni-cian with Apple, Inc., who helped Jeff successfully navigate a system melt-down when he was one week out from finishing work on our field guide. An additional special thanks to Apple, Inc., for honoring their Apple Care warranty and fixing Jeff's computer at no cost even though the warranty had expired six weeks prior to the system meltdown.

A thanks to Dr. Robert Lücking and Dr. Sabine Huhndorf of Chica-go's Field Museum who helped recommend appropriate reviewers for the fungi and lichen section.

Finally, and with much appreciation and admiration, we would like to thank our botanical and mycological reviewers for their expert and critical eyes: Scott Namestnik, a partner with Orbis Environmental Consulting, and Brad Slaughter, lead botanist at Michigan Natural Features Inventory, for reviewing parts of the botanical sections; Dr. Andy Miller, herbarium director and mycologist at the Illinois Natural History Survey at the Uni-versity of Illinois Urbana–Champaign, for reviewing the fungi; and Dr. Alan Fryday, assistant curator–non-vascular cryptogams, Michigan State University Herbarium, for reviewing the lichens.

# PHOTOGRAPHER CREDITS

Most illustrations in this guide are digitally edited images based on photographs. Kenn and Kimberly Kaufman took more than 800 of these photos (not listed here, to save space), and Jeff and April Sayre took almost 300; for the rest, we relied on the fine photographers acknowledged below. Photos are listed by page number; images on each page are numbered from top to bottom and from left to right.

John C. Abbott: 359-1
John Acorn: 331-12
Dr. J. Scott Altenbach: 207-2, 6, 7, 8
Jennifer Anderson/USDA: 69-6
Ron Austing: 253-3; 265-9
Thomas D. Bain: 11-2, 3; 12-3, 4; 13-1, 2, 3, 4; 15-1; 17-1, 2
Roger W. Barbour: 203-7; 205-1
Troy Bartlett: 369-17; 383-10; 385-7, 8
Scott Bauer/USDA ARS: 369-11
Giff Beaton: 365-4
R. A. Behrstock: 359-5, 6
Nic Bishop: 381-3
Rick and Nora Bowers/
    BowersPhoto.com: 189-3; 191-1, 2, 3, 5, 6; 193-3, 4, 7; 195-1, 5, 7, 8; 197-2, 4; 199-3, 5, 6, 7; 201-9, 10, 12; 207-3, 5, 9, 10; 211-3, 4, 8, 9, 13; 213-1, 2, 3, 4, 6, 7, 9; 215-6, 10, 11, 16, 17; 217-3, 4, 5; 219-7; 221-3, 14; 223-1; 225-12,13; 227-5, 6, 10, 12; 229-11; 231-9; 233-1, 4, 5, 6, 11, 12; 235-2, 3, 4, 5, 11; 237-2, 5, 6, 7, 9; 239-5, 7, 9, 10, 13; 241-2, 9; 243-8, 9; 245-2, 4; 247-1, 7, 11, 15; 249-3; 253-1, 4, 5, 6, 7, 8; 255-3, 4; 259-6, 8, 9; 261-5; 265-6; 267-1, 6, 7, 15; 271-10; 273-3, 13; 275-3, 5, 8, 10; 281-1; 291-1; 295-3, 8; 325-1, 9, 10, 11; 327-3, 6, 13, 20, 22; 329-6, 8, 9; 331-1; 333-4, 5, 7, 12; 335-2, 5, 11, 13; 337-11, 12; 339-12; 361-10; 379-6
Jim P. Brock: 325-4; 327-1, 2, 7, 10, 11, 12, 14, 15, 16, 18, 19, 21; 329-1, 2, 3, 5, 7, 17, 19; 331-2, 7; 333-8, 11; 335-12; 339-8, 14
T. Travis Brown: 95-2; 107-5; 109-4; 117-9, 10; 121-10, 11; 123-6, 7; 127-4, 5, 7, 8; 155-3; 165-9; 281-3; 287-8; 291-6; 303-2, 5; 305-1, 2; 309-3, 4; 311-4, 6, 7; 313-3, 5; 315-1, 3, 4, 5, 6; 317-2, 4, 5, 7; 319-1, 2, 3, 4, 5, 6, 7; 321-5, 6; 393-3
William S. Clark: 225-6, 8, 9, 10; 229-9, 14
Tom Coates: 371-2
James Cokendolpher: 357-8; 365-14;

383-14
Will Cook: 121-6; 143-2; 149-1, 2
Jay Cossey: 341-8; 357-10
Rob Curtis: 357-4; 363-15; 367-5; 369-2, 4, 5, 9; 371-1, 4, 5, 7; 375-5, 7, 12; 377-3; 379-2, 8, 10, 12; 381-2, 9, 11; 383-1, 3, 7, 9, 12; 389-3; 391-5
Daderot Creative Commons: 393-5
Mike Danzenbaker: 213-16; 215-5; 221-9; 247-3, 4; 267-11
Dezidor Creative Commons: 311-3
Larry Ditto: 197-6
Eric R. Eaton: 357-12; 359-2, 3, 4; 363-2, 4, 8, 13; 365-5, 10; 367-3; 369-3, 7, 8, 10, 12, 13, 16; 371-6, 16; 373-1, 2, 3, 10, 11, 12, 16; 375-8, 9, 10, 16, 18; 377-1, 10, 11, 12; 381-1, 4, 6, 7, 10; 383-2, 4; 385-1, 4, 5, 6, 9; 387-1, 2, 3, 4, 5, 6, 7, 8, 9; 389-4, 5, 8; 391-6, 7, 8, 9
Ellen Edmonson/NY Biological Survey: 301-5, 6; 309-1, 5
Ross Ellet: 23-1
Randy Emmitt: 337-13
Estormiz Creative Commons: 259-3
Arthur V. Evans: 357-7; 373-5
William Ferguson: 357-5; 379-11
Evelyn Fitzgerald: 131-6; 143-1; 153-6
David H. Funk: 363-9, 10, 12, 14; 365-7, 11; 377-4; 379-9
Bob Gress: 189-4, 5; 193-6
D. E. Herman/USDA: 151-4
Charlie Hickey: 69-9; 101-4, 5, 8; 145-8; 147-6; 151-2; 165-7
John Himmelman: 345-1
Cathy and Gordon Illg: 201-5
IowaAgateMan CC: 14-1
Jean Iron: 217-1
Bill Johnson: 367-9; 383-11; 385-10
Jomegat Creative Commons: 57-9
Kevin T. Karlson: 215-15; 243-2, 6, 10; 249-5; 251-8; 255-7; 271-5; 275-9, 12, 14
Gary Kramer: 233-3
George O. Krizek: 339-13

Greg W. Lasley: 211-15; 233-7; 249-2; 359-8

Tom and Pat Leeson: 189-1, 6; 195 2, 4; 197-1, 3; 199-1, 4; 201-1, 2, 3, 4, 6, 7, 8

Richard Leung: 383-5

W. Liller, NASA: 39-1

Steve and Dave Maslowski: 197-9, 10

D. Mccabe Creative Commons: 393-4

Charles W. Melton: 215-4

Anthony Mercieca: 201-13

Jeffrey Miller: 341-2, 4; 353-4

Robert H. Mohlenbrock/USDA: 61-6, 7; 123-13; 127-6; 143-5; 149-4, 5; 151-3

Dan Mullen: 129-10; 147-4

Tom Murray: 357-3; 365-3; 391-12; 393-2

Scott Namestnik: 107-3; 169-4; 175-4

NASA: 8-1

Alan G. Nelson: 195-6

Blair Nikula: 361-7, 11; 363-3

John Roger Palmour: 131-1

James F. Parnell: 189-2; 197-8

Michael Patrikeev: 197 5; 205-5, 8

Jeffrey S. Pippen: 141-8

Betty Randall: 197-7

Bryan Reynolds: 383-6

D. Gordon E. Robertson CC: 157-1

Edward S. Ross: 373-6

Jane Ruffin: 329-13, 14, 18; 339-16

Andrée Reno Sanborn: 77-5; 93-6; 143-4; 157-7; 181-5; 281-6; 291-7, 8

Jeff and April Sayre: 5-1; 40-1; 51-1, 2, 3, 7; 53 1, 2, 3; 55-4, 5; 57-5, 6, 7, 8, 13; 59-1, 2, 3, 4, 7, 8, 9, 10, 11; 61-1, 2, 3, 8, 9, 10, 11; 63-3, 4, 5, 6, 7, 8, 9, 10; 65-2, 4, 5, 6, 7, 8, 9, 10, 11, 12; 67-1, 2, 3, 4, 5, 6, 7, 10; 69-5; 71-2, 3, 5, 6, 10, 11, 12; 73-5, 6, 7, 13; 75-2, 3, 4, 5, 6, 7, 8; 77-1, 6, 7; 79-3, 5, 6, 7; 81-1, 3, 4, 5, 6, 7, 8, 9; 83-1, 2, 3, 8, 9, 10; 85-1, 2, 3, 4, 5, 6, 7, 8; 87-1, 2, 3, 4, 5, 6, 7, 9; 89-2, 4, 6; 91-5, 6, 7, 8, 9, 10; 93-1, 2, 3, 4, 5, 8; 95-6; 97-3, 5, 6, 7, 99-8; 101-3; 105-1, 2, 3, 4, 5, 6, 7; 107-1, 2, 4; 109-1, 2, 3, 5, 6, 7; 111-3, 4, 5, 7, 8; 113-1, 2, 3; 119-9; 121-8, 9; 123-8; 125-7, 11, 12, 13; 127-12, 13; 129-5, 6, 7; 131-5, 7, 10, 11; 133-15, 17; 137-2, 3, 12; 139-4, 5, 9, 10, 12, 13, 14; 141-1; 143-3; 145-5, 9; 147-5; 151-5, 6, 7, 8; 153-1, 2, 3, 4, 5, 7, 8; 155-1, 4, 6, 8; 157-2, 4, 5, 6, 8, 9; 159-1, 2, 3, 4, 5, 6, 7, 8; 161-1, 3, 4, 5, 6, 7, 13; 163-1, 2, 5, 6, 9, 11; 165-2, 3, 4, 8; 169-1; 171-2, 6; 173-1, 3, 4; 175-1, 2, 3, 5, 6, 7; 179 1, 2, 3, 4, 5, 6, 7, 8, 9, 10, 11, 12; 181-1, 2, 3, 7, 8, 10, 11; 183-2, 3, 5, 6, 7, 8, 9; 185-3, 4, 5, 6; 341-6; 343-13; 371-20

Nick Scobel: 279-3, 5; 283-1, 2, 3; 285-8, 9, 10; 287-1, 2, 4, 7; 289-4, 5; 293-4, 8; 297-6

Lynn Scott: 353-5

John Shaw: 335-7; 337-14, 16; 339-6

Ann and Rob Simpson: 195-3; 357-3

Brian E. Small: 211-16; 213-5, 13, 14, 15; 215-1, 2, 8, 9, 14; 219-6, 8, 12; 221-11, 13, 15; 223-12; 225-17; 227-3; 229-8, 10; 231-6; 233-2, 8; 237-8; 239-6, 8, 14; 241-13, 15; 243-11; 245-1, 8, 10; 253-2; 255-2; 257-5, 7; 263-16; 267-12, 16, 17; 269-4; 275-4, 6, 7, 11

Eric H. Snyder: 11-4; 12-1, 2

John Sorensen: 229-12

Bill Stark: 363-11

William Tanneberger: 137-5; 139-1, 2

Nate Tessler: 301-3, 4; 303-1; 307-3, 4; 309-2; 311-2; 313-2; 321-1, 3

Uland Thomas: 303-3; 307-1, 5; 311-1, 8; 313-1, 4; 315-2, 7; 317-1, 3; 321-2, 4

Merlin D. Tuttle: 207-4

John and Gloria Tveten: 193-5; 203-1, 2, 3, 4, 6, 9; 205-2, 3, 4, 6, 7; 207-1; 325-3; 327-5, 8, 9; 329-16; 331-4, 6; 333 6; 337-4, 7; 339-4; 341-3, 5, 9, 10, 11; 343-2, 12; 353-11; 357-6; 369-1; 371-8, 19; 377-6, 13; 381-8; 385-12

Tom J. Ulrich: 203-5

U.S. Geological Survey: 393-6, 7, 8, 9

R. W. Van Devender: 203-8

Per Verdonk: 135-11; 149-3

Tom Vezo: 193-1, 2; 201-11; 221-6; 223-11; 229-7; 233-9; 241-1; 243-7; 247-8; 251-3, 4; 255-1; 265-8; 267-2; 269-3

Robyn Waayers: 365-1

Michael Wigle: 363-5, 6

Alex Wild: 381-13; 383 16

Kenneth Paul Wray III: 279-2; 281-5; 283-4, 5, 6; 285-5, 7; 287-5, 6; 289-3; 291-3, 6; 293-1, 2, 3, 6, 9; 295 2, 4, 5, 6, 9; 297-4

Jonathan Zander CC: 11-1

H. Zell Creative Commons: 101-9

Brian J. Zimmerman: 301-1, 2, 7; 303-6; 305-4; 307-2; 311-5

Dale and Marian Zimmerman: 225-14, 15; 229-4, 5, 15; 249-6; 273-7, 14

The quick index on p. 416 covers some of the most popular entries. This index includes all species in the guide. In seeking entries, look under group names. For example, to look up Pin Oak, start by looking under O for Oak, not under P for Pin. With few exceptions, we have not indexed scientific names, but we've included some alternate English names.